MANAGING THE CORPORATE INTRANET

MITRA MILLER

ANDREW J. ROEHR

BENJAMIN BERNARD

WILEY COMPUTER PUBLISHING

John Wiley & Sons, Inc.

New York ◆ Chichester ◆ Weinheim ◆ Brisbane ◆ Singapore ◆ Toronto

Publisher: Robert Ipsen
Editor: Robert M. Elliott
Managing Editor: Angela Murphy
Text Design & Composition: North Market Street Graphics

This book is printed on acid-free paper. ♾

Published by John Wiley & Sons, Inc.

Published simultaneously in Canada.

Library of Congress Cataloging-in-Publication Data:
Miller, Mitra.
Managing the corporate intranet / Mitra Miller, Andrew Roehr, Benjamin Bernard.
p. cm.
"Wiley Computer Publishing."
Includes index.
ISBN 0-471-19978-8 (pbk. : alk. paper)
1. Intranets (Computer networks) 2. Business enterprises—Computer networks. I. Roehr, Andrew, 1964– . II. Bernard, Benjamin, 1971– . III. Title.
HD30.385.M18 1998
658'.0546—dc21 97-41086

Printed in the United States of America.

10 9 8 7 6 5 4 3 2 1

This book is dedicated to:

Our fiancés,

Our families (who still don't have a clue what we do but provide encouragement anyway),

BSGers around the country, who make it a pleasure to come to work, and

Our clients, with whom we share the challenges and experiences that have allowed us to produce this book.

ACKNOWLEDGMENTS

The authoring of this book was simultaneously a labor of love and endurance. All three of us are lucky enough to enjoy our work, our clients, and the challenges presented to us. However, there is no doubt that the production of this work was above and beyond what we anticipated due to some interesting and intriguing events. Therefore, we wish to thank our family, friends, and coworkers who encouraged us through India, an engagement, a reorganization, another engagement, taxes, four weddings and a funeral, and 58 flights, 17 states, 3 continents, and 10 airlines.

What a team effort this has been! As with our previous book (*Building the Corporate Intranet,* Wiley, 1996), this work is an interesting mix of talents and backgrounds, bringing together a dream team of consulting talent. (The running joke is that if you combined the three of us you would have the ultimate IT consultant.)

Andy brings with him an incredible diversity of knowledge and experience from both corporate IS and consulting—most recently as one of the senior architects and systems strategist at Per-Se. He is proficient in a range of technology, spanning mainframe, many generations of client/server, and massively distributed Web systems. His breadth and depth of knowledge in networking, architecture, and enterprise systems integration was a crucial component of this book, and continues to impress even us, his closest co-workers, on a daily basis.

Ben is our chief application designer who lives in the trenches, working actively on multiple large-scale intranet implementations, including some of the most significant I-Net systems produced to date. He's the guy who always seems to know a vendor's toolsets better than their own staff—to the point where he finds ways to use and configure technology beyond what the designers had dreamed. One of those people gifted with both experience and instinct, Ben consistently produces solutions that dazzle.

Mitra is our proponent of organization of people, technology, and process for effective management, with special emphasis on the front end of intranets, tools, and techniques. She has broadly diversified experience on both the technical and business sides of the systems equation and, as such, is a frequent speaker and translator of the value proposition to constituencies. She is also the one who rode herd over this writing effort, managing to apply appropriate pressure to get the project to completion.

Beyond the three authors, however, there were many people who made this book possible. We extend a special note of thanks to Morgan Pierce and the entire New York office at Per-Se for encouraging us as we double-dutied through the writing of this book. Also, we thank Sue Spiner, who helped get this book off on the right track when it was only a gleam in our collective eye.

We thank Mark Sherman at corporate for sponsoring our efforts, and Eric Dirst for sharing his valuable project experiences. Thanks also to Sandy Mechael and James Fugitt for contributing cheerful research and editorial support when we needed it! Last, but of course not least, we thank Bob Elliott and Brian Calandra at Wiley Computer Publishing for sponsoring this effort and believing in our product.

If you wish to write to us about this book, please send comments via our Web site at www.per-se.com or this book's companion Web site at www.wiley.com/compbooks/miller. We look forward to your feedback and experiences!

CONTENTS

Foreword xiii

Introduction xvii

Chapter 1 The Call for Intranet Management 1

We're Just Trying To Keep Up! 3
What Is Intranet Management? 5
Examine the Planning and Implementation Phases of Your Intranet 7
People and Process 10
Roles and Responsibilities 10
Methodology: A Management Framework 24
Goals and Objectives 25
Policy and Procedures 26
Intranet Management: Using the 10-Layer Model 28
Using the Layered Model for Analysis 37
Summary 41

Chapter 2 Client Management 43

Technology Options 44
HTML 45
DHTML 45
Client-Side Scripting 46
ActiveX Controls 48
Netscape Plug-ins 50
Java 50
Software Distribution 51
Custom Installation Scripts 51

Systems Management Server 52
Browsers 52
Mail and News Readers 53
Adobe Acrobat 54
Conferencing Software 54
Specialized Viewers 54
Security 55
Configuration Management 60
Hardware 61
Operating System 62
DMI 62
SNMP 64
SMS 66
Summary 76

Chapter 3 Network Communications 77

Bandwidth Management 78
IP Traffic Management 83
Resource Reservation Protocol (RSVP) 87
Umbrella Managers 88
Best-of-Breed 89
Integrated 90
Performance Management 91
Fault Isolation 92
Capacity Planning 92
Naming Standards 93
Domain Naming Service (DNS) 95
How To Name 96
What To Name 96
DNS and System Redundancy 97
How DNS Works 98
Copyrights and Branding 99

IP ADDRESSING 101
Dynamic Addressing 107
Technology Alternatives 108
SUMMARY 111

Chapter 4 Hardware Evolution 113

SERVER PLATFORM 114
IBM: Proprietary But Effective 115
Hardware Architectures 116
WEB SERVER SOFTWARE 130
Application Type 131
NETWORK DESIGN 137
CONTINUITY OF BUSINESS STRATEGY 138
SUMMARY 141

Chapter 5 Server Software 143

WEB SERVER SOFTWARE 144
Netscape Enterprise Server 145
Microsoft Internet Information Server 148
RELATED SERVER SOFTWARE 150
FTP Servers 151
Proxy Servers 152
Mail Servers 153
News Servers 156
INTRANET APPLICATION SERVER SOFTWARE 161
CGI 161
NSAPI 162
ISAPI 163
ASP 164
LiveWire 164
Version Control 164
Distribution 167

MANAGING LOGS 167
SUMMARY 168

Chapter 6 Content 177

ORGANIZING CONTENT 177
- Site Maps 178
- Functional Maps 180
- Interface Design Documentation 183
- Editorial Calendar 185

STANDARDS 188
- Basic Development and Administration Standards 190
- Creating Templates 192
- Keeping Documentation and Records 194

VERSION MANAGEMENT 201
CONTENT APPROVAL PROCESSES 203
- Extending the Development and Approval Environment 209

LINK MANAGEMENT 211
USAGE ANALYSIS 212
USING PUSH TECHNOLOGY FOR CONTENT DISTRIBUTION 214
SEARCH ENGINES 218
SUMMARY 219

Chapter 7 The Application Connection 223

DAILY MANAGEMENT 225
EXPANSION 229
EXTENSION 230
TECHNOLOGY CHANGE 232
- Choosing an Initial Technology Set 233
- Planning for Change 234
- Setting Some Ground Rules 235
- Dealing with Change When It Hits You 236

When To Say No 236
SUMMARY 257

Chapter 8 Security 259

THE TIMES THEY ARE A-CHANGING 260
IN SEARCH OF SUFFICIENCY 261
THE NETWORK 264
SNOOPING 266
Spoofing 274
Encryption 285
RESOURCES FOR SECURITY INFORMATION 289
Computer Incident Advisory Capability Group (CIAC) 290
Computer Operations, Audit, and Security Technology (COAST) 290
U.S. Computer Emergency Response Team (CERT) 291
Emulating an Attack 297
Summary of Security Action Items (Checklist) 305
Some Existing Security Tools 309

Chapter 9 Legacy Systems Integration 311

ARCHITECTING FOR INTEGRATION 311
GETTING IT TOGETHER 314
PRESENTATION LAYER INTEGRATION 314
Using Stored Procedures 321
BUSINESS SERVICES LAYER INTEGRATION 324
Remote Procedure Calls (RPCs) 325
Messaging-Oriented Middleware (MOM) 336
Publish and Subscribe: A Message-Passing Integration Strategy 340
Object Request Brokers (ORBs) 341
DATA ACCESS LAYER INTEGRATION 352
Transaction Processing Monitors (TPMs) 353
SUMMARY 355

Appendix A Web Administrator's Checklist 357

Appendix B The 12 Steps to Building an Intranet 385

Appendix C Sample Policies and Procedures 401

Index 415

FOREWORD

With all the hype that surrounds I-Net technology these days, I find it amazing how little practical advice is available on how to actually *use* and *manage* it, especially on a very large scale. This is due partly to the relative newness of the Web, but also to a more fundamental lack of attention to the very serious business of running and troubleshooting large systems. This book has been put together by some of Per-Se's most talented systems strategists and managers to start addressing these crucial management issues.

The Web is certainly not the first technology to romance us down the primrose path without sufficient time or attention to long-term implementation and maintenance issues. Both mainframe and early PC solutions had their own problems as well. For instance, the short-term savings gained by omitting two bits within calculations has yielded long-term mega problems in the form of the Year 2000 "bugs."

Not so very long ago, client/server development experienced similar problems with particular difficulty developing around performance, version control, and distribution of business rules and logic. In fact, many companies with "legacy" client/server systems are still struggling to find reliable ways to assess the impact of changes made to their systems and then to deploy these changes to their users.

At Per-Se, our mission is to help companies build their business with leading-edge, enterprise-scale technology. For over ten years we have worked with various generations of client/server and I-Net technology, honing time-tested methods for planning, building, integrating, and sustaining world-class information systems. We do this by carefully balancing our attention to the people, process, and technology that are the building blocks for IT success.

Managing the Corporate Intranet is our seventh book; the others cover a range of topics from networking to designing multi-tiered applications to building intranets. We have built a strong reputation in the IT services industry as dedicated technologists who harness the power of best-of-breed tools. In writing this book about managing intranets, we are furthering our commitment to sharing the strategies and experiences that have helped us most.

A significant part of our success is due to our focused development of excellence in several well-defined areas. Intranets are only part of the technology landscape that we cover, although we are rapidly finding that our customers have a growing demand for *integrating* their intranet with their other systems. As a result, our ability to build and understand a wide range of systems has been one of our most valuable assets. Far beyond understanding the fundamentals of TCP/IP and Web browsers, Per-Se is a recognized expert at

- *Technical Architecture and Infrastructure Planning.* Our architects have developed a unique, values-based method to develop a scalable technical strategy built on the core values of your business.
- *Data Warehousing and Data Mining.* Giving companies versatile ways to understand their customer, target their markets, and share vital information across functional groups is the intent of data warehousing and data mining. Our experience has led us to develop a warehousing strategy based on three core principles—Quality of Data, Training, and Warehouse Administration—to deliver the functionality a business requires.
- *Call Center.* Implementing and customizing the software of premier call-center vendors such as Vantive, Clarify, and Quintus, our call center practice has the best track record in the business.
- *Traditional and Multi-Tier Client/Server.* We built our reputation by being one of the first to deploy large-scale client/server applications utilizing best-of-breed tools and techniques. This tradition continues with 3-tiered and N-tiered designs for "massively-distributed" applications.

- *In-Depth Industry Knowledge.* In addition to understanding the technical toolsets, our consultants have developed the industry knowledge that is required to build systems that truly serve business needs. We are best known for our work in Multi-Unit Retail (both restaurant and merchandising), Finance, Energy (electric, oil, and gas), and Telecommunications.

As your intranet grows in size and complexity, I'm sure you too will find it useful to have a breadth of talent to assist in the effort. There is much more to managing intranets than selecting a browser, developing web content, adding some "cool" security, and maintaining 100 percent up-time. Intranets are intricately integrated environments that extend client/server as we know it—whether they include fat or thin clients, client- or server-based applications, or Java or ActiveX. Therefore, do not hesitate to develop or otherwise acquire the talent you need to maintain this complex ecosystem of tools and technologies.

I hope that you enjoy *Managing the Corporate Intranet* and find it helpful in your own management efforts. Please be sure to visit our website at http://www.per-se.com and send us your questions and comments.

STEVEN G. PAPERMASTER
Chairman
Per-Se Technologies

Note: Per-Se Technologies is the company that was formed by the union of BSG Alliance/IT, Atwork Consort, and HDS in November of 1997. It is a wholly-owned subsidiary of Medaphis Corporation (http://www.medaphis.com).

INTRODUCTION

Although the intranet has been a buzzword for over two and a half years, we generally have found the industry to be sorely lacking advice about how to actually run a business on one. Consequently, companies that dutifully jumped on the intranet bandwagon lest they be left in the technical dust are now trying to manage a perplexing jumble of web servers, tools, and organic application growth without adequate support.

Managing the Corporate Intranet is our attempt to start filling the void. It is a practical, no-nonsense guide to addressing the most common organizational and technical issues that we encounter during our intranet projects. Somewhat surprisingly, the range of topics that intranet managers must tackle is really quite diverse. Consequently, this book will cover a variety of issues that stem from the three core systems components: *people, process,* and *technology.*

What You'll Find in This Book

Chapter 1 starts off the book by specifically addressing people and process issues, specifically how to arrange an intranet team. Instead of giving hard and fast "rules" for organization, we show you the flexible model that we use in our own projects you can scale for your needs. We also take a look at the function of policies to reinforce the operating processes of your intranet organization.

Chapter 2 starts off our technology discussions (which comprise the bulk of the book) with client management issues. There is a myth that intranets have "no maintenance" clients. Although this certainly can be the case (or nearly so), there are very significant tradeoffs between maintenance and performance of which you should be aware. The value of a no-maintenance user interface may not be so great if the application is excruciatingly slow. In this chapter, we show you some of the pro's and con's of thin- and thick-client applications so you can make the decision appropriate for your needs.

Chapter 3 takes a hard look at managing the network infrastructure that supports the intranet. Beyond the basic considerations of running your LAN/WAN, the intranet poses some interesting new challenges. Our discussions include performance monitoring in an intranet environment, fault isolation, design and capacity planning considerations, and IP addressing issues.

In Chapter 4 we start looking at server issues, first concentrating on the critical components of the hardware. We will take a look at various intranet hardware architectures, the issues of hardware scalability, and the coherency of distributed systems.

Chapter 5 revolves around the management of server software. Beyond applications themselves that run on servers, there is a very real issue of managing the underlying operating system and services that support them. Here we focus on software distribution, version control at the server level, server software integration and performance tuning.

Chapter 6 looks at mechanisms to manage content—the most simple of Web applications. Beyond just "posting pages" on your intranet, content management involves understanding the who, what, where, why, and when's of the process. Template control, link management, document version control and approval, and usage tracking are all necessary to help a Webmaster run an efficient and reliable application.

The Web-based application itself is the subject of Chapter 7. We look at the issues of daily management of the application as well as how to expand it over time. Our solutions look at two management scenarios: managing applications with Microsoft Interdev and how to migrate an application from CGI to ASP.

Chapter 8 looks at security from a management perspective; in other words, it is *not* a discussion about firewalls (there are other wonderful books on that subject). Instead, we look at the security risks that the intranet manager should be concerned about; tools that will help you find security weak spots in your environment, and other resources for information and support.

In Chapter 9 we look at the increasingly interesting subject of integrating an intranet to legacy systems. There are many options available to this, especially message-oriented middleware (MOM), remote procedure calls (RPCs), and object request brokers (ORBs). For each of these we explain what they are and where they are appropriate.

Finally, in the appendices to the book we provide some sample checklists and project plans that may help you in your own management activities, as well as some of our own sample policies and procedures for your reference. (Please remember to customize the policies for your own individual needs and then have your legal counsel review and bless them!)

Management: An Evolutionary Subject

Perhaps it is needless to say that good management practices will continue to evolve as more and more Web-based systems are built and as new companion tools are developed. As such, we have crafted the majority of our comments to be as timeless as possible by de-emphasizing the particular features of version A versus version B of software, and instead looking at the underlying principle. (Lest our words be outdated before they can reach a bookstore!)

The material that we present here is basically the same advice and methods that we incorporate into our own intranet management practices on our projects. As such, if you are a Per-Se Technologies customer (or a customer of BSG, the name by which we were previously known) some of the topics may be familiar to you. That is because at the bottom line, good management concepts can be applied to almost any IT organization, regardless of the business that it supports. These are the principles that have served us well on project after project. We hope that you will find them as useful as we have.

If you have comments or anecdotes that you would like to share, we can be reached at the following e-mail addresses. We look forward to hearing from you.

Mitra Miller (mitra@mci2000.com)
Andy Roehr (aroehr@msn.com)
Ben Bernard (benbernard@sprintmail.com)

CHAPTER ONE

The Call for Intranet Management

The phenomenon of the intranet is well established in corporate business systems. A year ago when we wrote *Building the Corporate Intranet* (Wiley, 1996) the term *intranet* was still being mistaken as a misspelling of *Internet.* Today, *I-Net* or *net-based* systems—systems that use the Internet Protocol (IP) and software that are the DNA of the Internet and the World Wide Web—have a presence in almost every major corporation on the planet. (Not to mention that those companies without them are seriously worried about how far behind they really are.)

During the past year intranets with varying degrees of sophistication have been springing up. From Sweden to Australia and Brazil to Japan, companies are realizing the importance of net-based information systems to staying competitive in a global economy and have started migrating application services to this platform. Recent surveys show that in 80 percent of U.S. corporations, intranet technology is a "significant portion" of the 1997–98 information technology (IT) budget and a major focus for new development.

But how far have intranets come, really? Studies show that as of early 1997, 60 percent of U.S. intranets were primarily used for static information retrieval—policies and procedures, marketing literature, and other online information—and a full 80 percent were not enterprise scale, being implemented primarily on a departmental scale. Although many have been supplemented with threaded discussion forums, electronic mail, and news services, there is an equally good chance these services are provided through nonintranet applications.

So why is there still such clamoring about intranets when so few mission-critical systems reside on them? Because revolutions—even blazing technology revolutions—can't happen overnight. What has transpired in the past year is truly only the beginning of net-based systems as they will be known. Corporations have taken their first, tentative steps into this technology sphere, but they are far from embracing it as yet. Like any other large-scale investment—and intranet systems are reputedly going to be one of the largest shifts in systems computing to date—it is naturally approached with caution.

Remember the buzz in 1995 about the Internet, the *Information Superhighway,* and how it was going to radically transform people's lives? Although true enough, it has taken a full two years for most people to get to the point where they truly understand the meaning of those statements. And even yet, there are millions of ordinary Americans who have never seen the Internet in spite of all the hype.

In 1996 the majority of corporate America got Internet access, Internet E-mail, World Wide Web sites galore, and the first *static content* Web servers at a departmental level. By late 1996 and early 1997, it was time to supplement and enhance the corporate intranet infrastructure so that departments could share more information across the organization. These changes all had to take place to reach the point technology is now at: the true dawn of a new age of computing. Throughout the *next* couple of years—basically until the turn of the century—usage of intranets will continue to evolve for more and more sophisticated applications, both packages and custom-built.

The major roadblock to this development, however, is corporate IT's ability to effectively manage an intranet system. Having overcome many of the other barriers to mature, efficient intranet systems—including young technologies, lack of standards and predictability, lack of infrastructure, lack of expertise, and large-scale proofs of concept—intranets are now positioned for expansive growth, with the exception of a predictable method for managing them.

This book is aimed to address that issue. Having helped plan and install intranets across the United States, we have become increasingly aware that the next "burning platform" (or critical need) is management. For organizations that were already overwhelmed with the technologies of the late 1980s and early 1990s (i.e., client/server), the management of an intranet is truly confusing. The myriad, complex issues threaten to overwhelm those that are ill prepared, and the stakes in this new, open environment are incredibly high.

We're Just Trying To Keep Up!

Intranets introduce all kinds of complexity to organizations. Not only is the technology new, but the way it is used is also very different from traditional systems environments. In most companies, intranets are still only a small portion of the full IT landscape, but their impact is being felt because of the speed of their evolution and the demand for their services by the lines of business. As such, mixtures of networks, protocols, applications, hardware, and software make distributed environments difficult to manage—and that's assuming that nontechnical departments aren't surreptitiously installing unknown hardware and software (a common affliction in corporate America).

TIP *Remember that intranets are* real *systems. Take an intranet (all I-Net) system as seriously as you would any mission-critical technology such as your mainframe or your high-end UNIX systems. Within the next one to three years, depending on the pace of your business, the intranet* will *be that mission critical. This means dedicating a portion of your time and resources to planning and supporting intranets as part of your core technology. Unfortunately, many companies have failed to do this, considering intranets to be nothing more than simple document repositories; to their chagrin, the technology has mushroomed and they are unprepared.*

Managing intranet systems is both similar to and different from managing other systems. It is similar in that it is still the art and craft of maintaining high-availability, enterprise-scale, mission-critical-quality systems. The needs of the organization and its demands upon IT systems are relatively similar to what they have always been: to have the information they need at their fingertips. The obvious difference is the set of technologies and tools with which that information is delivered. Additionally, the characteristics of these new tools bring new types of advantages and complexities to the IT environment.

This book has been written to answer questions raised by our clients and readers who used *Building the Corporate Intranet* to get their systems in place and who want to know, "Now what?" Consequently, this book assumes that the reader has some sort of intranet in place and is now trying to enlarge, enhance, modify, or simply manage that system. A basic understanding of the underlying principles and technologies of the intranet (TCP/IP protocols, services, and infrastructure components) is also assumed, although less common and very technical points will be explained in more detail. In general, anyone with a solid systems background will be able to follow the discussions, but this book is definitely not written for the casual reader. Primarily, it is directed to the IT director and the intranet owner (read on for a definition of an "owner" of an intranet)—those persons responsible for making sure that the intranet successfully serves the organization.

This first chapter will define intranet management and then discuss management structure and organization. This includes definitions of the major roles and responsibilities in typical intranet management configurations, as well as discussions of how those roles can work together to manage the intranet and the importance of policies and procedures as part of the management documentation. This is followed by a look at our 10-Layer Model for intranet systems and an explanation of the approach taken to understand the management issues of each layer as discussed in the remainder of this book.

What Is Intranet Management?

Ah, management. The word typically means the ability to tame, harness, and develop a resource. When used successfully, it is the art of conducting actors and events to accomplish a particular goal or task.

This book on intranet management has been written to address how to best use available resources to maintain and sustain a stable, efficient intranet. This is not an easy task, however, as the ever increasing speed of change makes the concept of managing an intranet tricky, if not just plain impossible. Even at a technical company like ours, in spite of our dedication to maintaining expertise in this area, we too find it challenging to keep abreast of the multitudinous tools and techniques that continue to appear. And the same is true for everyone in the business.

To help make sense of complex systems, our philosophy is to regard systems as a combination of people, process, and technology. All three of these issues are critical to the success of technology, and deficiencies in any one can cause major problems.

People refers to the brainpower and participation that go into systems from the executive level down to the most rudimentary user. Everyone who uses, designs, develops, sustains, pays for, or in any way touches a system has a real impact on its success. Thus, this book will examine the impact of various people upon the management of intranets, as well as the impact of the intranet upon people.

Process is the way that systems are implemented and used—most commonly a series of activities that produces a result. Processes may or may not be formalized (official or unofficial), but they always play a very real role in how systems are built and used. As such we will review the interaction of people in the process of creating and sustaining successful intranet applications.

Technology is the actual machinery, code, wiring, bits, and bytes that physically compose a system. As powerful, glitzy, and fascinating as it may be, technology really is meaningless on its own; it requires people to use it and processes to implement and support it in order to have value. However, in spite of the fact that technology is merely the "tool", it is none-the-less critical and deserves significant attention. We will spend a significant portion of this book reviewing this critical aspect.

TIP *Keep up with intranet news. All kinds of information is available* free *to intranet managers and developers, and more is coming every day. Periodically (perhaps once a month or once a quarter) we recommend spending an hour looking for new, useful information via your favorite search engine. Some of our favorite sites include:*

> *http://rs.internic.net has some of the most solid and non-vendor-biased information on the Web, as provided by the InterNIC. Beyond standards, policies, Requests for Comment (RFCs), and other tips from the Internet Engineering Task Force (IETF), you'll find information on everything from IP addressing to how to train your user community.*
>
> *The W3 Consortium at www.w3.org is an independent organization with members from all the major Internet and intranet vendors and representation around the world. This body seeks to set standards and guidelines for Web-based development with special emphasis on user interface (such as HTML standards and style sheets), technology and society (including security), and architecture.*
>
> *The* Intranet Design *Webzine (or electronic Web magazine) and the* Intranet Exchange *site at http://www.innergy.com/index.html provide chatty, informal ways to post questions, give opinions, and find links on new tools and techniques.*
>
> *The* Data Communications *magazine site at www.data.com, for down-and-dirty techie topics, is a favorite of architects.*

Given these definitions, it is clear that a comprehensive approach to intranet management should consider all three of these components. The effective execution of one without the other(s) will yield a lopsided strategy and a less-than-optimal result.

Examine the Planning and Implementation Phases of Your Intranet

Throughout this book you will find running commentary on how to address various aspects of intranet management. Although the planning and building of an intranet is not the topic of the discussion in this book, it is actually quite germane. In our experience we have found that many management problems really have their roots in insufficient planning or in the absence thereof.

Intranets suffer from a reputation of being "cheap and easy" to build. Consequently, many organizations started their intranets without considering the long-term ramifications of incubating a new system destined for tremendous growth. The result is often an intranet that cannot scale to the demands placed upon it. This problem will be greatly accentuated as intranets move toward more sophisticated E-Commerce applications that require a serious infrastructure and administration policy to support high-volume transactions. Throughout the industry, this need for reinforced intranet strategizing is being noted by analysts, consultants, and even vendors who are looking to sell products to customers who cannot scale their systems to use them.

TIP *If you do not already have a "real" strategy for your intranet, invest some time in creating one that will satisfy your business needs. A lot of solid advice that can help you in this process is available in trade journals, from newsgroups on the Internet, and in books. This will save you time and money in the long run.*

When a client talks to us about intranet management concerns, we invariably start the process by talking about how the system was planned and built. We ask the intranet managers to examine their implementation and its major components. We then compare this to the basic implementation components outlined in the 12-Step Program in our previous book. The 12 steps serve as the framework for our implementation methodology and break down an intranet into discrete, easy-to-discuss and -plan pieces (see Figure 1.1). We use this framework to understand a client's intranet, to identify and assess gaps, and to make recommendations. Completing this process provides the context necessary to analyze and discuss management concerns.

Because this comparison process has been so useful for many of our clients, we have included a high-level summary of the 12 steps from *Building the Corporate Intranet* in Appendix B of this book.

TIP *Look for gaps in your implementation: items that were deferred or omitted that may cause problems down the road. The most common culprits are:*

- Architectural planning. *This includes insufficient bandwidth, network congestion, lack of load balancing, and hardware that cannot scale.*
- Definition of application ownership and administration. *This especially applies to a clearly defined organization with appropriate tasks and responsibilities.*
- Change management. *This includes lack of communications, support and training strategy when migrating a new technology into the corporate environment.*
- Performance monitoring and tuning. *Including both the application and the underlying infrastructure.*
- Systems support. *This especially includes backup and recovery strategies.*

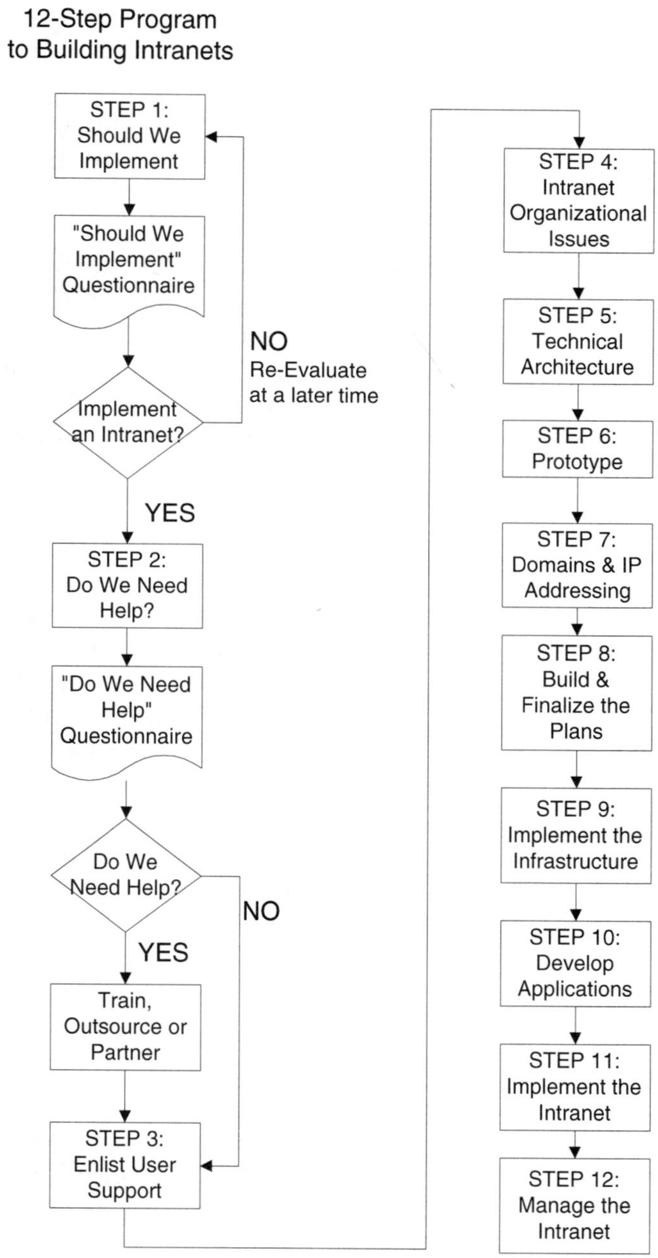

Figure 1.1 The basic 12 steps.

People and Process

Perhaps the most confusing question in intranet management is simply determining who controls what. Who rightly should be responsible for management? And what does that responsibility entail for an individual?

It seems like the issue of assigning responsibility would be fairly easy to resolve. Simply identify a manager and have that person figure out the details. But the combination of new, unknown technology and competing interests of the various stakeholders makes the issue really quite complex. Not only are IT and data services departments interested in the intranet, but so are corporate communications, marketing, sales, finance, and field operations departments. All of them can list myriad ways in which this technology can serve them, and each department believes it has the right to pursue its own path.

Indeed, intranet technology can be empowering. The availability and seeming simplicity of the toolsets dispel much of the mystery and complexity that typically surround systems, and these qualities encourage department staff to experiment and build their own intranet sites free of IT's supervision. No wonder they are often loathe to give away any control or authority!

However, as mentioned earlier, the bottom line is that intranets are most definitely business systems and, as such, they deserve serious attention. And the first step to managing the intranet as a system is to assign clear roles and responsibilities for it.

Roles and Responsibilities

In *Building the Corporate Intranet* we made a point of stating the importance of defining roles and responsibilities throughout the intranet planning, implementation, and support process. Little did we realize that this task would actually be very complex for many organizations. Competing interests and egos both inside and outside of the traditional IT organization suddenly came into play. In the past, IT was a service group for the organization, and no one else really took much interest in systems except to get basic desktop and file services or, on occasion, custom applications.

This is certainly no longer the case. The easy accessibility of I-Net technology has given rise to competing interests in this technology area. Now *any* department can quickly develop the resources required to put up a basic Web server and start developing HTML pages. In fact, this is already happening in almost every major company in America. Renegade user groups are developing "systems" without IT's knowledge or consent. This, of course, poses a huge dilemma for IT: With the technology already out there in the hands of the ordinary user, how can it be taken away? On the other hand, how can IT realistically take responsibility for these systems that it did not implement or plan for?

Obviously, an elaboration of the basic roles and responsibilities that are commonly used in intranet building and management is in order. Consequently, the next section outlines the core roles that we typically use and recommend. Although the roles are given titles such as owner and administrator for the discussion in this section, other organizations may choose to name them differently for cultural or logistical reasons. Don't let this be a source of confusion however, for it is the responsibilities assigned to each role that is most significant. These responsibilities are defined explicitly so that the various roles may have definite expectations of each other. As such, we intentionally have left the opening definitions of these roles somewhat open so that they may customized for the specific needs of an organization. The key is to use the roles and responsibilities consistently across the organization.

Figure 1.2 shows the basic intranet roles and the general way they relate to each other. Note that each role has certain responsibilities associated with it. Basic expectations for each role and its associated responsibilities are described as follows.

Owner. This is the individual who controls the application itself and logically is the coordinator of the effort. Most often the owner is the head of a department or a member of the department appointed by the head. As "spiritual" leader of the application, this individual is the source of design, ideas, content, and changes, and is specifically responsible for:

- Making sure other participants know and understand their role(s) in the process

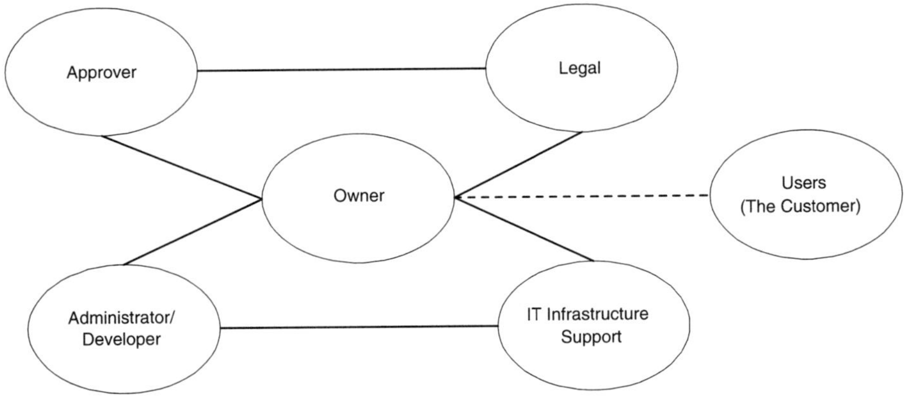

Figure 1.2 Roles and responsibilities.

- Watching budgets and schedules for the overall delivery and administration of the application
- Adding or removing resources to/from other roles in order to meet objectives
- Generating and collecting ideas for current and future applications
- Maintaining a calendar of application content and development
- Providing content to the administrator and/or developer
- Providing functional and business expertise
- Maintaining user/customer relationships
- Developing a change management/integration plan for the application to increase its acceptance and success

Administrator/developer. In a simple static-content site, this role is often filled by only one person, designated the *Webmaster.* However, as the application becomes more complex, the added responsibilities of the application developer and administrator may be distributed to several people. As such, the role of the administrator specifically includes:

- Making technical design recommendations
- Implementing basic content components such as HTML pages, downloadable files, and animated graphic interchange formats (GIFs)
- Managing daily operations and support of the application, including maintenance of the hardware, software, and database
- Installing the application and updates on the designated site, ensuring its operability once installed, and ensuring interoperability and linking with other applications
- Maintaining user lists and passwords and coordinating application security with the operations department
- Tracking usage of the application and maintaining log files and application records
- Providing user assistance unless a separate helpdesk has been designated
- Coordinating maintenance and performance functions with the operations department

The developer specifically is responsible for:

- Guiding and implementing the functional and technical design of the application
- Developing the application and any corresponding documentation
- Coordinating unit and integration testing with the owner
- Coordinating implementation of the application with the administrator and the operations department
- Making technical updates/changes to application

Content approver. Anything published on an externally visible site has the potential to adversely affect the company's public image. Anything published on an internal site has the potential to affect employees' morale and productivity. For both of these reasons, it is recommended that, where appropriate, department management and the marketing department have input or sign-off on I-Net applications.

Management within the department must ensure that the information provided is accurate and consistent with the intentions of the application. The marketing department or the public relations office must ensure that the application is consistent with the company's internal and external image if the application will be seen by customers or external partners or vendors (as required by intranet development policy). Specific individuals within the marketing department should be identified as the content approvers for each application that will have a public presence. This person or persons will coordinate primarily with the owner, but may also work with the legal approver to handle specific issues including:

- Ensuring that the message(s) communicated are consistent with company standards
- Reviewing the content for veracity and accuracy
- Advising the owner of necessary and suggested modifications

Legal approver. The content of net-based applications and sites, both externally and internally available, can create legal risks and responsibilities. Therefore, it is critical that the legal department approve applications, in some cases with the additional input of other departments affected by them. Specifically, the legal approver is responsible for:

- Setting guidelines for acceptable content based on general policies for security, conduct, and information usage
- Reviewing content for company policy conformity
- Assessing legal exposure and advising the owner of necessary modifications
- Creating legal waivers, disclaimers, or other statements that will be incorporated into the application

IT infrastructure support. The IT Infrastructure role is in charge of the infrastructure operations of the application. (This role could also be filled by department-level IT if appropriate.) It oversees:

- Security: Ensuring that the application security is consistent with the company security model and coordinating the integration of the application into the corporate structure. IT should coordinate with the legal department as well to ensure that the security model is meeting the legal needs of the company. If password security is used, IT's role is to ensure that the local security configuration meets company standards and is kept up to date. When certificate-based security is used, IT distributes and administers certificates.
- Backup and recovery: Establish backup policies for the system and perform those backup functions.
- System monitoring: An often neglected aspect of operations, monitoring is an important source of information for planning future net-based applications. Monitoring the utilization of a system can help determine whether it is serving its intended purpose. It can also point to systems that could be combined onto shared servers to decrease cost. Monitoring performance and reliability will help determine the need for expansion of hardware, software, or communications for this or other systems.
- Providing corporate network services and Internet access for the corporate environment.
- Providing technical consultation and assistance to departments implementing I-Net systems.

Users. It is important to consider the target audience of any system throughout the planning and development process. For this reason, users are included as an explicit role. It is often desirable to have a user representative involved in the design, testing, and deployment processes, specifically responsible for:

- Generating ideas
- Providing regular feedback

Beyond these core roles, there are two other hybrid roles that often are useful to develop:

Project/application manager. The individual responsible for ensuring that the overall project is planned and executed properly on a day-to-day basis on behalf of the actual owner if the owner chooses not to perform managerial functions. The manager identifies and resolves issues, ensures that team members have the resources they require, and communicates progress and status to the owner and sponsor.

Project/application sponsor. Although not an everyday member of the application team, this critical role should be filled by an individual with executive-level authority to promote and support the project. The sponsor provides necessary assistance to overcome hurdles in order to maintain project success.

TIP *There is a strong possibility that many of the people functioning in various roles critical to your application will not understand systems, how they are built, or the criticality of their responsibilities to other team members. Therefore, you, as the owner or designated project manager, should invest some time explaining how your team is organized and how it will operate. Telling a person that he or she is your "approver" without detailing what that will mean will only leave you disappointed and delayed when the person fails to execute.*

ASSIGNING ROLES AND RESPONSIBILITIES

Roles are designed so that they need not be a one-to-one relationship to individual people. In other words, a separate individual does not have to fill each role. On the other hand, a team of people may fill a given role within in an organization.

In a typical one-to-one relationship, a single person is given a particular role and its associated responsibilities. For example, the administrator for a human resources policies and procedures application would be a single person responsible for learning how to use an HTML editor and post the Web pages to the HR intranet site on a regular basis (see Figure 1.3).

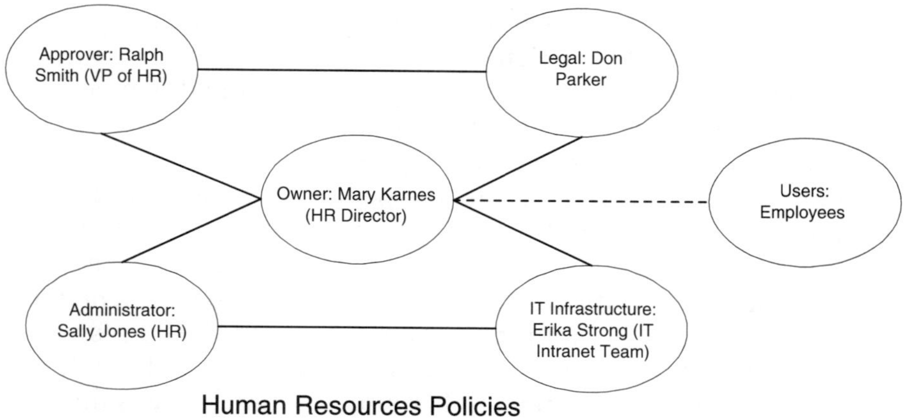

Figure 1.3 One-to-one role assignment.

In larger application efforts, however, a role may be filled by a team of people. That same administrator/developer role might be a team of five VisualBasic and Active Server Page developers who are creating an online customer account system (see Figure 1.4).

In very small projects, a single person may actually take on multiple roles. For instance, the internal communications writer

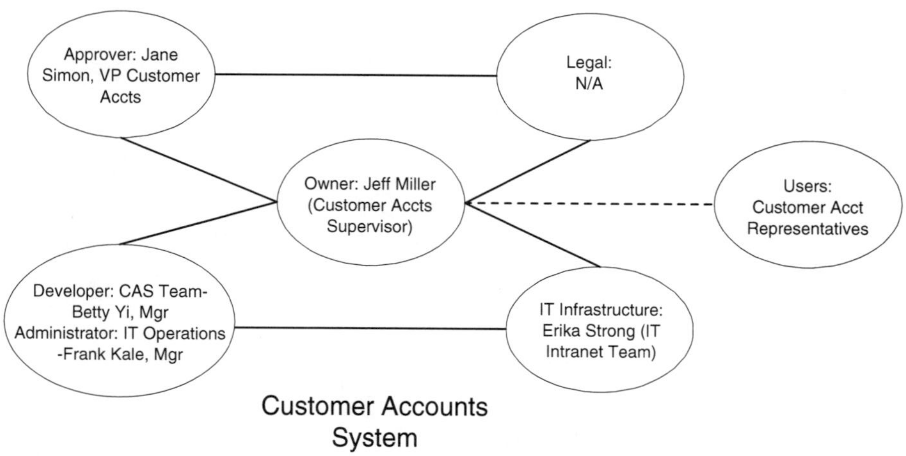

Figure 1.4 Team role assignment.

may be the owner, administrator, and approver for the Daily News page on the intranet (see Figure 1.5).

As you might imagine, the crucial part of making this model work is ensuring that all roles are consistently filled and there is accountability for the associated responsibilities.

In proper assignment of a role, the person or persons in that role must have the corresponding authority to perform those duties. If they do not have this authority, then they properly should not have the accountability. Instead, the role should be reassigned to those who actually do hold the authority to make the corresponding decisions. It may seem like this is more easily said than done, but properly assigned responsibility and accountability is the only way that members of a distributed organization can function in relation to each other.

ROLES WORKING TOGETHER

Figure 1.6 illustrates the interrelated nature of the primary roles in a simple development and administration scenario. This illustration technique is borrowed from the world of business process mapping, and illustrates the connection of roles and actions. Each role is represented in the way it relates to the others, based on a series of commitments. There is the "customer" of the agreement, the person for whom the action(s) are being performed. On the

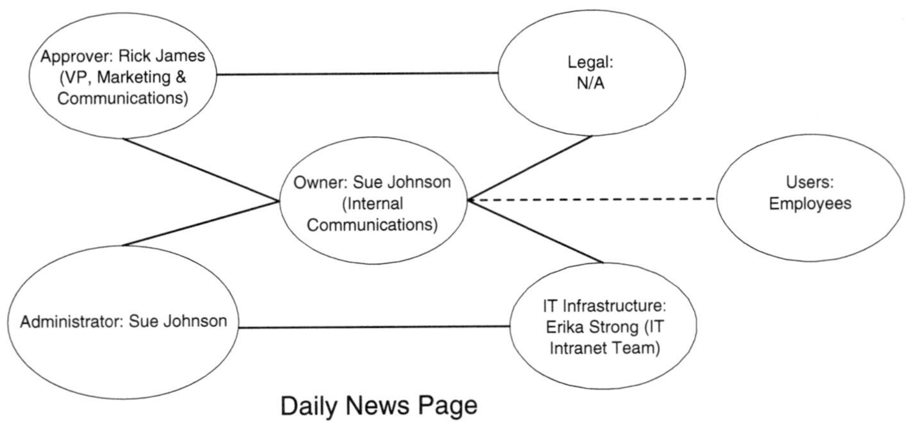

Figure 1.5 Multiple roles assigned to an individual.

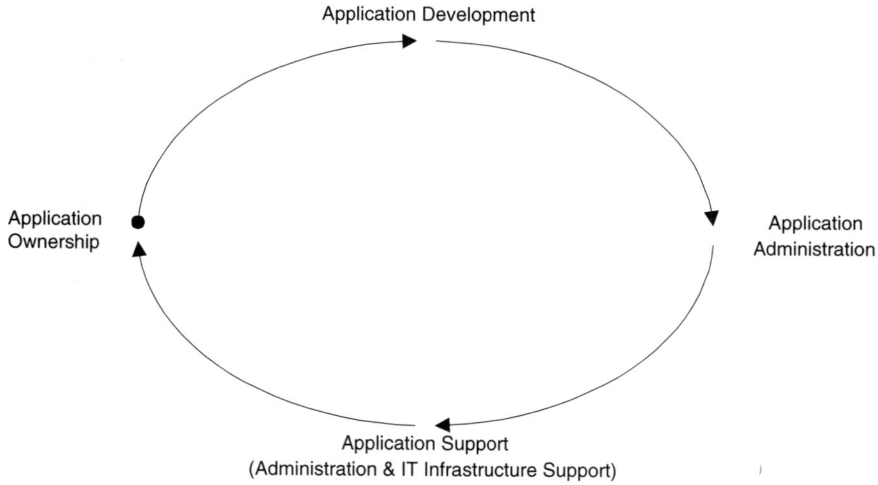

Figure 1.6 Roles in basic application development flow.

other side there is the performer of the action, the person who makes the commitment to perform or provide some service.

In intranet applications, the process always begins and ends with the application owner. The performer on the other end of the equation is the application administrator, who commits to performing the basic function of developing the application and delivers that commitment to the owner.

The process may be elaborated to expand upon the dependencies upon one another of the multiple roles, for example, as depicted in Figure 1.7. At the basic points in the application life cycle (ownership, development, implementation, and support), there are subprocesses that compose them. These subprocesses are other commitments for service that are made as part of the larger process, yet each has the same customer–to–service provider relationship that the larger process does. This basic understanding of these relationships will serve as the framework for communicating needs between departments and IT.

These subprocesses can be defined in greater and greater detail with dependencies to each other as well as to the central effort. For your own purposes, you may wish to define what these pro-

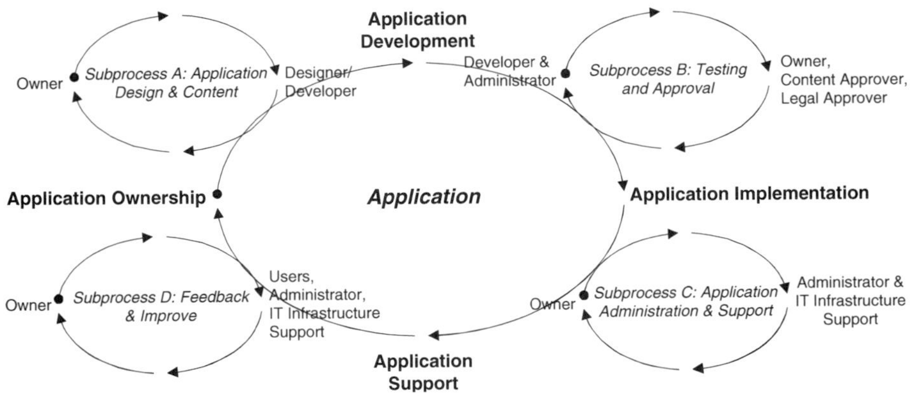

Figure 1.7 Roles in subprocesses of application development.

cess will be in order to help clarify the activities for your participants. This is probably necessary only if most of your team is new to systems development and needs to understand the criticality of activities that IT professionals take for granted—such as design, documentation, prototyping and feedback loops, writing of business cases and test plans (prior to development), testing, implementation, support, and performance monitoring.

USING ROLE RELATIONSHIPS IN INTRANET MANAGEMENT

Probably the biggest fundamental mistake made in intranet management stems from the belief that the intranet is a singular application. Nothing could be further from the truth! *Intranet* is almost as broad a term as *information systems* itself—and eventually the two will be almost synonymous. An intranet is composed of the network, infrastructure, hardware, software, servers, desktops, databases, and multiple applications that live within it. Managing an intranet, therefore, should be treated as the management of multiple applications; each with its own owner, administrator, and so forth.

Another important point is that there really are no fundamental differences between *intranet, Internet, extranet,* and *virtual private intranet* (VPI), or any such term. They are made of essentially the same technologies (browsers, Web servers, back-end services), simply serving different constituencies. We predict that as all of these nets continue to grow and evolve, the lines between them will blur and they will all become parts or extensions of intranets. As the discussion of intranet management continues, you will see this philosophy clearly in the organizational designs.

One problem that appears in many organizations with ad hoc intranets is a lack of clarity about who is responsible for making decisions at a global level. Typically, there are lots of owners of small applications around the organization, but no clear owner of the intranet itself. Consequently there is often a lack of consistency, standards, system administration, and technical support.

Typically, application developers (meaning the folks who are developing the HTML pages and Java applets) are at a loss when they need decisions on issues such as which browser features to develop for, how security will function in their application, and so on. Because there is a lack of clarity about these issues, they often make up their own rules and anarchy reigns, with each application developer making his or her own decisions. Although this mode of operation allows for great creativity, it does not ensure any sort of reliability or consistency as required by a serious business—a very scary thought for any IT manager responsible for delivering quality systems.

To help rectify this situation, we have developed a basic model for understanding the roles described earlier in this chapter, which can be layered to provide ownership for both small and large issues. In designing it, we wanted a model that would be both flexible and expandable, allowing for growth of the intranet and the various services within it. What we ended up with is something like the diagram in Figure 1.8, which we adjust or customize on a case-by-case basis.

The top, thin layer is the overall intranet ownership, which loosely governs the applications within it. This role is probably filled by an IT director or some other manager who is skilled at coordinating the multiple applications that live within the intranet. Within this framework are the components of the intranet: security; infrastructure; the intranet development team(s); the various application services such as E-mail, news, and collaboration; the Internet applications; and departmental

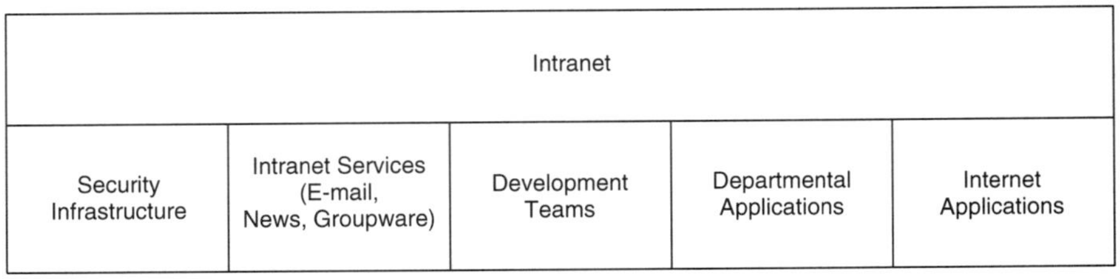

Figure 1.8 Simple intranet organization.

applications. Each of these applications must also have its own owner, administrator, and so forth. In relation to the corporate intranet, the owner of each application is providing the service of delivering that application (acting in the delivery capacity). Within his or her own application team, the owner serves in the traditional sense of driving the application development process (acting in the customer capacity).

At the next level of granularity, we end up with a relationship of applications, roles, and responsibilities that looks something like the diagram in Figure 1.9, which illustrates the interrelationship of the multiple levels of subcomponents in the intranet.

There are applications within larger application frameworks, each with its own owner. So the owner of the HR Policies and Procedures application is in charge of making sure the responsible people are involved in his or her application (whether they be from HR, the legal department, or IT). This owner has accountability to the owner of all HR, however, as this application is also a part of the larger HR presence. The HR owner, in turn, has accountability to the overall Intranet owner to ensure that his or her applications—including the Policies and Procedures—fit within the overall context.

We have used this organizational structure for intranet applications in several companies with great success. Naturally, modification can and should be made for specific needs, but in general this model helps all the players and stakeholders quickly understand both their own and other people's responsibilities. It provides the much needed organization that intranet systems typically lack.

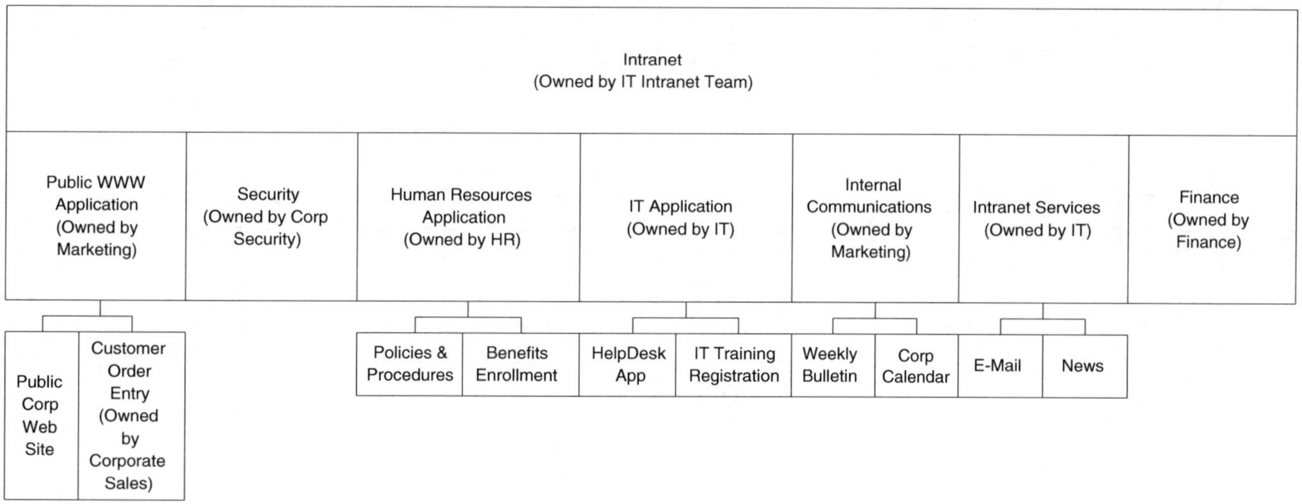

Figure 1.9 Expanded organizational relationship.

One of the interesting points that companies often question us about is the treatment of the Internet as an intranet application. They seem to feel that this relationship is backward—that the intranet is really only part of the larger Internet. In a sense, this is true on a global scale; on the Internet, the resources of various organizations are provided on hundreds of thousands of intranets across the world. However, this is not our focus inside the corporation. From our perspective, we are serving information to the company, its vendors, and end customers. Our focus is not on making sure our piece of the World Wide Web functions and provides value within the overall Internet; our context is one of providing value to the corporation itself. Consequently, the Internet is seen as a service to our organization and is treated as such.

Methodology: A Management Framework

For those who hate methodology, we have bad news: When managing an intranet (or any enterprise system, for that matter) having a set of methods for operating is invaluable. If your intranet and your management team are small, you probably can manage without much guidance. However, if your intranet is large—or if it is expected to grow—methodology will help.

Methodology provides a set of tools for communicating and assessing the completion of goals and expectations among team members. If all are expected to operate by the same basic methods, then there are common terminology and an understanding of duties. This is especially helpful as you assign certain responsibilities to roles (see the discussion below).

The good news is that you do not need a new, intranet-specific methodology to manage your resources. Most likely, your existing methods are more than adequate and can be adjusted to suit your needs. At the bottom line, managing technology requires some fundamental components, regardless of the flavor:

- *Common goals and objectives* that all team members know and can strive to achieve are needed. (They may be formal or informal depending on how the organization communicates.)

- *Common procedures* should be established for operation and administration of intranet sites and applications that can give consistency.
- *Common roles and responsibilities* should make accountability clear for all who are involved.
- *Common standards* should be set so that performance expectations are communicated and can then be assessed and managed (or corrected as necessary).
- *Tools and technology* are needed to facilitate and streamline the process.

Goals and Objectives

The foundation of a successful intranet is having a clear mission and purpose for its existence. If you have read intranet strategy and building books, you know this song. If you have not—and if you do not have a mission and expected return for your intranet investment—we urge you to develop one before continuing. By developing a common goal for your system and how it is expected to improve your company's business, administrators will know how their duties are expected to make that goal a reality.

To reinforce this, we suggest also setting a common set of criteria that communicate the level of quality expected for intranet applications. These criteria may vary depending on the sophistication of the "administrator" audience—experienced C and C++ programmers will operate under different guidelines from those of departmental administrators who create only static HTML pages. However, a common yardstick will help you manage your overall system quality. For example, some measures set at other companies include:

Satisfying user expectations. Solicit periodic user feedback to assess the effectiveness of a site or application. There should be an acceptable rating level and emphasis on improvement based on user input. It is amazing how departmental Webmasters often develop applications for their own entertainment instead of as information resources, in essence falling prey to the "technology as a toy" mentality for which IT used to be criticized.

Low number of errors. This includes everything from broken links to programming errors in applets to validation errors in forms.

Reliable method for migrating and implementing code. This includes page updates, versioning, backup, and recovery.

Good design. Layouts of sites and applications should be clear and easy to navigate for both the user and the support person or administrator.

Good documentation. This is needed for the reference of those who manage and support the applications, as well as for those who will be enhancing and growing these information assets in the future.

Policy and Procedures

So from here on we will assume that your mission is known both to you and to others. The next policy you will need is one that explains who owns the intranet and who sets standards. You may choose to have an advisory council or a standards-setting body that also plays a role in the governing of the intranet. That is fine, as long as the owner is clearly designated and is given the authority to do the job.

Next, it is important to establish all your intranet policies and procedures. Usage policies typically cover issues such as the ownership of corporate IT resources (such as E-mail), access to the Internet during office hours, and restriction from illicit Web sites. You should also design policies about standard software to be used (e.g., if Microsoft IE is your standard browser, there should be a policy against downloading copies of other browsers from the Web). Also a statement about licensing is strongly recommended, as there are often copyright laws applying to shareware that many unsuspecting users will fail to comply with—and it is your company that will pay the bill if the situation is discovered. Last, a virus-scanning policy, if you do not already have one, is vital.

We have included samples of some of these policies for your reference in Appendix C. Please be aware that you should have your own legal counsel create policies tailored for your needs—ours are provided only for illustration. The following list of typical IT intranet policies is suggested at a minimum.

Policies

- Implementation process
- Use policies—the basic who/what/where/when/why of intranet use such as:
  - Definition of appropriate and inappropriate sites on the Internet
  - Standard browser and other software (i.e., don't download unlicensed copies of Navigator)
  - Download policy—how much, how to treat it
  - Virus scanning
  - Licensing of hardware and software and documentation storage
  - Levels of disciplinary action
- Legal implications
- External site blocking
- Style guide

Procedures

- Needs definition
- Architecture definition
- Roles assignment
- Development (publishers, authors, Webmasters)
- Approvals
- Deployment
- Maintenance
- Backup and recovery
- Noncompliance with intranet policies
- Q/A and review

Of course, many other types of policies are needed in order to manage the technical side of the intranet (e.g., development procedures). In Chapter 6, we will talk more about these types of policies for creating and managing application content.

TIP *The best way to simultaneously inform and reinforce the usage of the intranet is by using it to communicate your intranet policies and procedures. A site dedicated to providing information, tools, templates, and guidelines for implementing and administering an intranet application should be accessible and built to expand and change over time as new needs arise.*

If you are using "push" technology, such as BackWeb, Pointcast, or Castanet, you should consider providing an intranet developers *channel.* This channel could be dedicated to announcing policy changes, new templates, brainstorming sessions, and general technology news relevant to Webmasters throughout the organization. The nice thing about using a mechanism like this is that (a) if you don't have "news," you are not encumbered to create some to fill a periodic news page; you distribute information only as you need to; and (b) you know that important information really will hit people's desktops and is not reliant on their periodically reading a site.

Intranet Management: Using the 10-Layer Model

Intranet management requires integration of the three core components of any system: people, process, and technology. The preceding section covered the first two topics, but this is not really a book about personnel management or process reengineering—it's about technology and how to effectively use and manage it in an intranet context, the topic to which the rest of this book is dedicated.

To effectively explain the management of intranet technology components, it is necessary first to have a clear understanding of

SOLUTION SCENARIO

Injecting Policies and Procedures into an Uncontrolled Intranet

Policies and procedures may sound like a small nuisance to some, but trust us that they are important. For example, a client of ours found that a lack of policy was causing them to address issues and answer questions about tools and technologies they didn't even know they were responsible for.

The client was a large, international research, manufacturing, and distribution company, with large offices in both the United States and Europe. Corporate IT was located in the United States, but senior management was split pretty evenly between the two continents. IT responsibility was split between the centralized, corporate IT group that maintained large corporate systems such as the mainframes and networks, and small, departmental IT support staff that reported directly to the department (corporate IT had little or no authority over those staff).

Several of the large, sophisticated departments were experimenting with Web-based applications, both on intranets and the Internet. The "official" corporate presence on the World Wide Web was owned by the marketing department, but otherwise there were no real rules. Therefore, lots of little intranet applications—primarily research documentation, search engines, and marketing literature—popped up all over the company.

For a while, everything worked fine. But in reality, each department was choosing its own server hardware, server software, and browser interface, not to mention setting its own development guidelines. As they began contemplating expanding to larger, more sophisticated application services,

(*continued*)

SOLUTION SCENARIO *Continued*

the departments looked at a wide range of development tools without knowing about the efforts of other groups. And as the applications they planned grew in size and scope, it was obvious that they were going to have a tremendous impact on the corporate IT environment.

Suddenly, it seemed, corporate IT needed to make some fast, smart decisions about how it would support corporate intranet applications. There was an impulse to make some general policy statements that would be a short-term answer to the questions that had arisen, but it was clear that the long-term implications could have serious repercussions. Consequently, IT decided to invest a few weeks to think through a long-term, scalable set of policies that could govern its efforts yet allow room for flexibility. IT assigned a small team to review standards that had been suggested by various departments and build a set of guidelines that could be used.

What seemed clear was that, first, the organization needed to weigh the benefits of allowing the departments to remain autonomous in their intranet development versus standardizing at the corporate level. The culture was such that complete centralized control was neither logical nor palatable to anyone, including corporate IT. Therefore, the desire was to produce some guidelines that would increase consistency without taking ultimate control from the departments. What was really needed was a way for everyone to peacefully coexist and collaborate.

So corporate IT took on the role of overall owner of the intranet, without truly taking responsibility for the applications that were in it. Knowing that there were many competing and conflicting interests in the intranet, IT made a decision to delegate certain responsibilities to those de-

(*continued*)

SOLUTION SCENARIO *Continued*

partments that wanted to take them. The most obvious and logical was giving the look and feel of the intranet to the marketing group. The marketing department led the charge to develop a common interface and design template for the intranet. It set a corporate banner, a footer, a color scheme, and a navigational metaphor that would give various intranet applications some consistency. Marketing worked with IT to create standard graphics and layouts that kept file sizes small enough to prevent the network from overloading. The policy, when complete, was merely referenced by the IT Intranet Guideline document and linked to that portion of the online manual.

The more technical aspects were addressed by the IT team assigned in conjunction with system architects, application developers, network administrators, and systems management, to produce a set of guidelines that could be realistically supported. The team did not succumb to pressure to address all needs immediately, leaving open such issues as chat software (IRC) and multiuser domains (MUDs) that were not urgently needed, with the plan of adding these policies at a later date.

Planning. The planning of the proposed effort took two days, at the end of which a list of areas that needed standardization and policy statements had been identified.

Time. Three weeks of research, planning, and writing were required to prepare this information (not including corporate review and approval, which was subsequent to the development effort). The reason for the short duration was that the need was urgent enough that

(*continued*)

SOLUTION SCENARIO *Continued*

answers were received without hesitation or delay. Under other, more bureaucratic, circumstances, you might expect this duration to double or triple depending on the need for approvals and so forth.

Effort. This required one lead analyst/developer, whose duties were to research configuration alternatives and write corresponding sections of the policy statement, and two managers, one part-time within corporate IT and one dedicated to the creation of the policy statement, whose duties were to identify issues and resolve them with the appropriate departments, research, write, and edit the final document.

Results. The final deliverable was an HTML document that was delivered to senior management for approval and then used as the corporate governing document. It resides on the corporate IT intranet site, with links to other relevant policies, procedures, FAQs, and advice provided by IT as a service to Webmasters and administrators in the organization. To give you an idea of what was included in this detailed, 100-page (single-spaced) document, the table of contents is shown in Figure 1.10.

Figure 1.10 Intranet guidelines sample table of contents.

Purpose of this Document
Internet and Intranet Usage Policy
Hardware and Software Architecture
  Client Configuration
    Hardware Platform
    Operating System
    Browser
    HTML Version Compliance
  Web Server
    Hardware and Software

(*continued*)

SOLUTION SCENARIO *Continued*

Figure 1.10 *Continued* Intranet guidelines sample table of contents.

Application Server
Web System Elements
Communications Infrastructure
Security
Net-Based Systems Security Goals
Security Issues
Designing a Security Strategy
Security Guidelines
Risk Assessment
Setting Policy
Standards
Guidelines
Developing a Workable Policy
Scanning for Viruses
Configuration
Reports
Firewalls
Background on Firewalls
Uses of Firewalls
Anatomy of a Firewall
Internal Firewalls
Building a Firewall
Planning Your Configuration
Assembling the Firewall
Setting up the Choke
Access-list command: Creating an Access List
Access-class Command: Protecting Virtual Terminals
IP access-group Command: Protecting IP Interfaces
Accounting access-violations Command: Using IP Accounting
Setting Up a Gate
Supported Services
Activity Logging
Auditing
Alarms
Responding to an Attack

(*continued*)

SOLUTION SCENARIO *Continued*

Figure 1.10 ***Continued*** Intranet guidelines sample table of contents.

Vendor Support
Day-to-Day Operations
Firewall Architecture
Routers, Gateways, and Hosts
Security Policy
Rule Base
Typical Configurations
Installing the Firewall
Configuring the Firewall
Disaster Recovery/Contingency Planning
Importance of Backups
Types of Backups
Security for Backups
Testing the System
Roles and Responsibilities
Publishing Process Guidelines
Systems Management Components
Core Systems Management Policies
Basic Systems Management Components
Knowing the Environment
Client Management
Infrastructure Management
Usage Tracking
Performance Monitoring
Monitoring Performance on NT
Monitoring Performance on UNIX
Performance Problems
Contingency
Development Methodology
The Net-Based Development Landscape
Application Architecture
Basic Architecture Designs
Managing the Development Effort
Broadcast Technology ("Push" and "Pull")
Multimedia
Audio Files
Video Files
Whom to Call

what those components are and how they work together. We will be using our 10-Layer Model (Figure 1.11) as the basis for discussion. If you have read *Building the Corporate Intranet,* this model will look very familiar.

The diagram in Figure 1.11 illustrates the multiple components involved in an application services configuration. This information is provided as a framework for understanding the nature and relationships of components in a multitiered architecture and will serve as the basis for the discussions through the rest of the book. The ten layers are as follows:

1. *Presentation.* This is the user interface (UI) layer that presents the artifacts that are physically seen and manipulated by the user, appearing as the "application" from the user's perspective.
2. *Client Browser.* This is essentially the rendering "container" for the presentation layer components, the interpreter of HTML, and the space where client-side components such as ActiveX and Java reside.
3. *Network Communications Services.* This layer contains all of the hardware, software, and underlying ser-

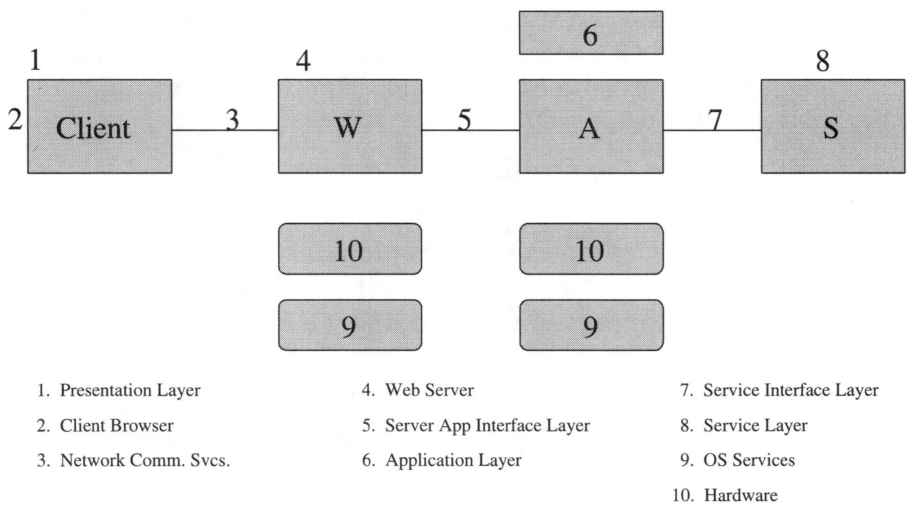

Figure 1.11 10-Layer Model.

vices that enable the browser to communicate with the Web server. This layer involves numerous alternatives, depending on client and server location, bandwidth requirements, cost constraints, and so on. The International Standards Organization (ISO) has a standard model called the Open Service Interconnect (OSI) for decomposing this layer into its constituent components.

4. *Web Server.* This is the software that supports HTTP for the exchange of information with a client (e.g., Netscape Suite Spot, Microsoft IIS, or the O'Reilly Web site). HTML pages, and possibly other server objects, are stored and served from this layer.
5. *Server Application Interface.* This layer provides the abstraction and actualization methods for the underlying business services. While your choice of application invocation mechanism at this layer is important, the level of abstraction that it supplies to the underlying application is even more important because abstraction provides the basis for system scalability and flexibility over time. The various mechanisms also differ in performance and development capabilities. There are three primary interface protocols for this layer:

    Common Gateway Interface (CGI). Although portable, CGI scripts are typically implemented in C or Perl and suffer from a lack of performance and scalability.

    Netscape Application Programming Interface (NSAPI). This is part of Netscape's ONE strategy.

    Microsoft's Internet Information Server Application Programming Interface (ISAPI). This is highly Object Linking and Embedding (OLE) ActiveX–centric

6. *Application.* This layer contains the application logic and business processing services, which automatically apply context to the raw data. The sophistication and modularity of this layer are critical to supporting rapidly

evolving business requirements. To a certain extent, this layer can be simplified by applying libraries.

7. *Service Interface.* This layer abstracts an underlying data repository, transaction system, or other service from the actual application. Abstraction at this level provides a basis for hiding the nature of the underlying system from the user. It also serves as a basis for continual technical evolution with minimal impact on the application. Because this layer wraps the native invocation mechanism of the service and manipulates returned data into a consistent, non-service-specific context, a programmer can use the business services layer without understanding the nature of the underlying service itself.
8. *Service.* This layer incorporates the underlying services (e.g., database management system [DBMS], document manager, imaging, engine, text engine, transaction program [TP] monitor, remote procedure call [RPC] messaging, E-mail, and 3270 streams) that provide the process and data manifest in the Web presentation layer. These services represent both new and legacy system components.
9. *Operating System Services.* This layer incorporates the file, print, and program execution services, and extends across all of the computers throughout the system.
10. *Hardware.* This layer incorporates all of the various client and server (and possibly services) components. Like the Operating System Services layer, it extends across all computers in the system.

Using the Layered Model for Analysis

The layered model takes the components of an intranet and breaks them down to their basic level; however, in practical application these components are often lumped together or omitted, as simple applications don't require some components. We have also found that ten layers are very difficult for some people to assimilate—it's just too many pieces.

So we have found a way to group the components into four major parts. First, there is the *client,* which involves the presentation and client browser. Second, there is *network communications,* which is a core part of the infrastructure of the entire model. Third is the *server;* this is an enormous topic that covers both hardware and software. Last is *content,* the applications and information themselves.

Although we will continue to use the 10-Layer Model to explain pieces of systems, the rest of this book concerns the management of these four topics, plus a section on security. For each topic we have included some Solution Scenarios derived from our own experiences, both at our own company and our clients'. Because we run into these management issues as a part of our regular work at dozens of companies, we have sought to capture the most valuable experiences from them and present them so that you may avoid such pitfalls and quickly resolve the inevitable problems.

Client Management. When we talk about client management in an intranet, one of the biggest issues is software distribution. This complex task has been a constant source of headaches for administrators in the client/server world. In intranets, software distribution takes on some interesting new characteristics. Depending on the design you choose—for example, helper applications or use of client-side objects and applets—you may have high- or low-maintenance clients. We'll explain the key considerations in deciding how much you want to reside on the desktop versus on a server, and the trade-offs for each.

We will also look at configuration management issues, how to set standards for your desktop and how to use the Desktop Management Interface (DMI) and Simple Network Management Protocol (SNMP).

Network Management. Managing the network infrastructure of the intranet is absolutely vital and is usually not given the attention it deserves at the planning and implementation stage. As a result, all sorts of management and maintenance headaches develop, which can bring the intranet to its knees. The management issues that we find most important in the intranet context involve bandwidth (users *love* to share those 5- to 15MB graphics files and Java applets!), IP traffic, and performance. We will share ideas on some of the best tools we have found to manage these issues, as well as some practical observations from the front lines when it comes to ideological wars over topics like static versus dynamic IP addressing and how to implement it.

Servers Management. In the early days of intranets everyone told stories of how great it would be to have a massively distributed environment with "servers, servers everywhere!" Well the reality in corporate IT is that every one of those many, many servers still must be maintained and supported. That is a very big job and such a complex topic that we have divided it into two major parts: hardware and software.

The management of the host is as critical to the intranet as it is to the mainframe. Therefore, we will take a hard look at the components of various types of servers and how to plan for, use, and maintain them. Performance monitoring is one critical aspect: understanding how to use the information to deliver efficient applications. Other complex issues such as multithreading and memory management play a key role in server management, and we will show you how these issues should be handled for different types of applications. Last, we will look at traditional maintenance issues such as redundancy, high availability and the ultimate upgrading and replacing of servers.

Managing server software is a whole other issue altogether. Depending on the type of box you have (and we will look at both Windows NT and UNIX platforms), there are different mechanisms for supporting your servers. Here we will look at issues such as software distribution to the server and version control. With the server playing such a key role in intranet applications, efficient and consistent management of these issues is critical.

There are also some unique issues surrounding the integration of Web, application, and database server software, whether the application is small and departmental or mission-critical and massively distributed. We will also look at how various server software packages such as mail, news, and conferencing fit into the picture, and how to manage each in the overall intranet context. Last, we will look at how to performance-tune the software—a decidedly different issue from tuning the server hardware.

Content Management. The management of content and applications themselves are covered in separate chapters. First we will look at more fundamental management for basic Web administrators, or Webmasters, including using good management techniques such as naming conventions, setting standards for design and development, and exercising version and source code control.

We will also spend some time exploring how to rein in out-of-control growth of the intranet. Many companies have a proliferation of content that they can no longer manage, even with Web crawlers and search engines to help! We will give you our plan for bringing this situation back under control and streamlining efforts, using some useful tools such as site maps, editorial calendars, storyboards, and basic publishing procedures.

For more technically sophisticated and complex applications, another level of management is warranted. We will spend a good bit of time going through utilization tracking of applications and tuning them appropriately. Beyond the basic integration of software packages discussed in Chapter 5, we will examine the finer point of optimizing application and database servers. Additionally, in providing the application services, there are some detailed issues of status and performance monitoring to consider.

Security Management. As always, security concerns are paramount to the intranet; therefore, this topic has its own chapter in this book. Many corporations are terrified of the unknown danger of the Internet and the havoc that could be wreaked in the IT environment. There is no doubt that there is justification for concern, yet the reality is that everyone lives with a certain amount of risk every day of their lives. Instead of letting fear keep you from doing your business and implementing the systems you need, you should analyze your risks and decide how much to invest to minimize the threats.

To manage security, we will show you, first, how to assess the risk potential and determine if the security you have is sufficient. Then we will review management techniques for watching for security breaches and other threats, and tell you how to troubleshoot and address issues as they arise.

We will look at each of the major security measures—authentication, encryption, firewalls—and show you how to detect problems, test for completeness, and upgrade or modify if necessary.

Summary

This chapter offered a general understanding of what is meant by *intranet management* and how various roles and responsibilities work together to accomplish it, as well as the importance of setting some fundamental usage policies for the user community.

The 10-Layer Model for intranet applications and systems will serve as the basis for the following chapters of this book: Client Management, Network Communications, Server Hardware, Server Software, Content, Application considerations, Security, and Legacy Integration.

CHAPTER TWO

Client Management

A significant cost of managing a typical client/server environment is managing the client workstation itself. Each new application has to be distributed to and installed on each workstation. If the new application requires new database or network drivers, or new operating system configuration settings, these changes have to be made. Conflicts between the new application and other software over common libraries must be resolved. User-specific settings may need to be preserved. If the new application is an update to an older version, the problems are compounded by the need to preserve and convert old data files and for the server side of the application to work with multiple versions of the client. All in all, a very problematic affair.

This is one of the problems which has been pushing the industry toward thin-client intranet solutions. (See Figure 2.1.) After all, an intranet application runs on the server, so there is no need to worry about the client workstation configuration, right? Well, almost. It is possible to implement an intranet application that is almost entirely browser-independent and that therefore requires virtually no client workstation management. This is often a strong business driver behind intranet applications. In doing so, however, you may incur other costs in terms of performance, usability, and implementation time.

Most intranet applications make some compromises, balancing the desire for simplified client management with the need for high-performance applications. In order to make these decisions, you need to understand the capabilities and costs of the various technologies available. The first part of this chapter will discuss the impact of different intranet client technologies on the task of client workstation management.

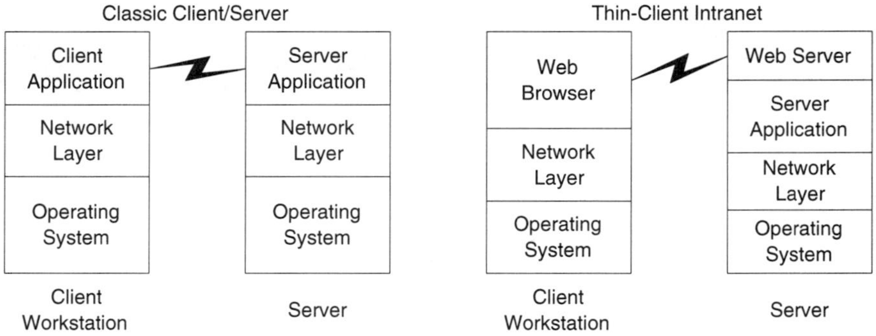

Figure 2.1 Architecture of a classic client/server application compared to a thin-client intranet application.

If we have been unable to entirely eliminate the task of client management, where does that leave us? We must be able to control the configuration of the workstation hardware, operating system, and support software; we must be able to manage the workstation's connectivity to the network; and we must be able to distribute the elements of the intranet applications themselves. These tasks are what is meant by intranet client workstation management, and they are the focus of the second part of this chapter. We will discuss tools and techniques for dealing with all three of these layers, but network connectivity will be addressed in more detail in Chapter 3.

This chapter presents a pair of solution scenarios dealing with client software installation. The first covers a small thin-client intranet scenario, in which client software installation will be handled through a custom installation script on a CD or network share. The second covers a large network or heavy-client scenario, in which Microsoft SMS will provide centralized software distribution. Both are common intranet scenarios, and these solutions help illustrate the trade-offs made between performance, usability, and ease of management.

Technology Options

The technologies that you choose to use on your intranet will have a strong impact on the tradeoffs just explained. Pure HTML imposes little management requirements on the client-side, but also results in less responsive and often less usable applications. At the other extreme, ActiveX controls can be created to implement business logic on the client and provide extremely responsive applications, but tend to require more client-side maintenance effort. This section explains how several technologies can be expected to affect your intranet.

HTML

The simplest of all intranet applications, from a client management perspective, is an application that runs entirely on the Web server, producing portable HTML, which is sent back to the client and displayed by the browser. Such an application could be implemented using any number of server-side technologies, which will be discussed in Chapters 5 and 7. This architecture would allow the client to connect to the server using any standard Web browser, running on any standard operating system.

In this scenario, the complexity of client management is close to nonexistent. To update the application, the administrator need only update the server(s) on which it is running. From a usability standpoint, though, this model is far from ideal. Implementing usable applications in standard HTML is notoriously difficult. Without any form of client-side scripting, it is necessary to perform all processing, including basic field-level validations, in the server-side application. This seriously limits the user responsiveness of the application. The sort of sophisticated controls used in traditional client/server applications (grids, treeviews, listviews, etc.) are completely unavailable in standard HTML, resulting in an inflexible, clumsy user interface.

DHTML

Microsoft's Dynamic HTML is one of the newest client-side technologies to enter the Internet/intranet fray. DHTML is a combination of client-side scripting and Microsoft's implementation of HTML. Essentially, it allows a Web page to change its appearance while displayed, without pulling new HTML from the server. Although at this writing DHTML is too new to assess thoroughly, it can be expected to have some of the benefits of pure HTML (fairly light transfers) and of VBScript (improved user-responsiveness) with some of the drawbacks of both (business logic mixed in with the user interface, excessively large pages). Microsoft has worked to reduce the impact of many of these issues by improving caching and processing speed in Internet Explorer 4.0, and the result will likely be a powerful new tool for intranet development. An important note about DHTML is that it is subject to the same version control cautions mentioned for client-side scripting and HTML style sheets: if you use DHTML, be sure that you have a way to see, from the browser, which versions of your DHTML files are used to produce any given display.

Client-Side Scripting

Improving the user interface will require some form of client-side programming. One simple addition would be client-side scripting to provide for local field-level validation. The user interface would look the same, but when the user submitted a form, the browser would run a script embedded in the HTML page. This script could ensure that the values entered by the user were of appropriate data types for the fields. Client-side scripting can also allow a more responsive user interface by reacting to user actions without communication with the Web server.

Scripting does introduce some compatibility concerns. Microsoft Internet Explorer understands two scripting languages: VBScript and JScript. Netscape Navigator understands the Javascript language. Most other browsers do not support scripting at all. JScript and Javascript are similar but are not fully compatible. This means that there is no one scripting language that is supported by all browsers. If you do plan to use client-side scripting, you will either have to provide Explorer-compatible and Navigator-compatible scripting (an expensive proposition) or limit your intranet to one or the other.

If you select Explorer, you limit your supported operating systems to the Microsoft Windows family, the Apple Macintosh, and certain flavors of UNIX. If you select Navigator, your choice of operating systems is considerably larger. Either way, imposing the selection of a browser requires that you ensure that the correct browser is available across the intranet and that users are accessing your application using the correct version of that browser.

An additional drawback of client-side scripting is that it is embedded in the HTML sent by the Web server. This means that the scripting code is transferred to the client when needed. If the page is static, the code may be cached for some time, but otherwise the code will be transferred on each use. Sophisticated applications will tend to use large client-side scripts, resulting in large HTML files and slow transfers. On an intranet based on a local area network (LAN), this may not be a serious concern, but on a slow wide area network (WAN) or modem link, this performance hit may be unacceptable. This is no different from the considerations involved with any distributed system design, in which network bandwidth, performance, and so on all need to be balanced. Like any system, a design that assumes a high-bandwidth, low-latency network design will not translate well to low-bandwidth, high-latency deployment. You must understand the likely target lowest common denominator for the deployment network and design for that in building these systems.

There are some tricks you can use to minimize the performance drawbacks of client-side scripting. The normal way of distributing scripting is indeed within HTML pages. When the HTML is sent over, the scripts are sent in comments. This assures that the script version matches the page version, but it means sending the script *every time* the page is loaded. If you have large scripts, this can make your application quite slow.

Another solution is to embed all of your scripts in a single HTML page. This page is then loaded into a hidden frame on the browser when the application starts up. Other pages refer to the scripts on the hidden page, making them significantly smaller and faster to load. There is no need to transfer the scripts again until the application is restarted. A further gain can be made by setting a long expiration time on the script page. It can then remain in cache between application sessions. Avoid excessively long expirations, though: If you need to update the scripts, you may find that, until all the existing pages have expired, clients continue to use their older cached versions.

A final solution is to distribute a page containing scripts as part of your application setup process. Like the previous solution, this makes use of a hidden frame to provide access to these standard scripts. This solution can be attractive if you have large scripts but your client workstations are accessing through a very, very small pipe. If you cannot afford to transfer scripts even once per session, consider prepackaging them and sending them out on disk. Be warned, though, that any updates to those standard scripts will require a new installation disk, and you are now stuck with the out-of-sync version problem again.

One caution with client-side scripting involves code management. When you embed verification logic or similar lightweight business rules in the presentation layer via scripting, you now have an element of the system's business processing model that needs to be tracked and maintained. Frequently, we run across intranet solutions that suffer from the same "lost logic" problem that plagues "classic" client/server systems. Part of this results from the poor tool support for managing distributed logic, but more so from an undisciplined development and deployment methodology. For more on version control, see Chapter 7.

ActiveX Controls

ActiveX controls are small user-interface controls, usually coded in Visual Basic, Visual C++, or Visual J++, which can be embedded in an HTML page within Microsoft Internet Explorer. Their compilation makes them processor-specific, unlike interpreted Java, which can be run on any processor.

The biggest advantage of ActiveX controls, from a software distribution perspective, is that they can be transferred to the client workstation automatically on first use and can be cached there for future use. They can also be automatically updated when a new version becomes available on the Web server. The control is implemented as executable code resident in a file with the extension "OCX." This file is made available to clients from the Web server, usually in a directory with other controls. The intranet application makes use of the control by referencing it from within HTML pages using the syntax:

```
<object classid="…" codebase="/Controls/MyControl.cab"…>…</object>
```

In this statement, the classid is the *universally unique identifier* (UUID) of the control. The codebase is a URL referencing the file containing the control's code. The first time a browser needs an OCX, it loads it from the server using the codebase. The control is then cached on the local hard drive for use on subsequent pages. If a page specifies a newer version of a control than the one in the cache, the browser checks the server to see if the newer version is available. If so, it is transferred and replaces the version in cache. If not, the page will not display correctly.

TIP *To see what ActiveX controls you have on your workstation, look in the directory c:\windows\occache.*

The biggest disadvantage of ActiveX controls is their nonportability. They can be used on Windows, Macintosh, and some UNIX machines. Native support for ActiveX controls is available only in Microsoft Internet Explorer, but there is a Netscape plug-in that provides support for ActiveX controls in the Netscape browsers. If the platform restriction is okay for your situation, using ActiveX controls can greatly simplify your software distribution.

Managing different versions of ActiveX controls can sometimes become complicated. A control's "identity" is defined by its public interface. As long as a control keeps the same public interface, it can keep the same UUID. However, once the public interface changes, it is, from an OLE point of view, a new control. It must have a new UUID. This means that, as your application evolves, you have two choices regarding controls: Either enhance their functionality without changing their interfaces (a difficult task—at most, you might be able to improve performance and to modify logic slightly) or you have to issue whole new controls, potentially cluttering workstations with multiple versions of a control and potentially causing big version synchronization problems. Neither option is attractive. The only real solution is to get the controls working well before they are released and to release very, very few updates.

Netscape Plug-ins

Netscape plug-ins provide much the same functionality as ActiveX controls. Plug-ins are typically installed by manually downloading an install program from the Web server, then running it on the local workstation. While this process is easily accomplished by either the system administrator or the application user, it is not automatic. In addition, there is no built-in mechanism for checking for new versions, so using Netscape plug-ins really buys you little from a software distribution standpoint.

So where would you want to use them? Anytime you need a sophisticated, robust content handler that will be very stable over time (few new versions) a Netscape plug-in can make sense. Note, though, that while plug-ins can be used in both Netscape Navigator and Microsoft Internet Explorer, you will need a different version for each operating system (OS) and microprocessor you plan to support.

Java

Java applets are machine-independent code that is stored in independent files on the Web server. Special tags in HTML pages reference these files, causing the browser to download the applets and interpret them on the workstation. Java applets can be used to perform user-interface tasks, complex business logic, or simple validation. Java can be used with client-side scripting or without. Unlike ActiveX controls, Java applets are not cached between browser sessions. This means that each Java applet in an intranet application must be downloaded fresh each time the browser is restarted.

If you have a large application implemented using Java, or some of your workstations have slow connections to your server, you may find that waiting for the Java classes to download to the workstations each time is impractical. In this case, you may want to preload parts of the applets onto each workstation as part of the installation process.

One trick is to divide your Java applets into commonly used but rarely changed code (standard libraries) and specialized and frequently changed code (the applets themselves). Your standard libraries can be copied onto the workstation during your install process, leaving the applets themselves to be transferred as needed. This should result in smaller applets and, thus, less transfer time. Of course, now you have an additional step in your installation process, and you must track the version numbers of your standard Java libraries installed on each workstation. You have bought performance with management complexity.

TIP *To see the Java classes and libraries that are installed on a workstation, look in the directory c:\windows\Java.*

Software Distribution

This section discusses different packages of software you might need to install on your intranet's client workstations, as well as specific mechanisms for doing so. Your software distribution mechanism will depend largely on the diversity of the workstations on your intranet. In a purely Windows-based network, you can use a number of tools designed to assist in this task. In mixed networks, you will probably have to custom-build installation scripts or implement more sophisticated distribution solutions from companies like Tivoli/IBM and Hewlett-Packard.

Custom Installation Scripts

Nearly any piece of software can be installed using a custom installation script. On Windows-based machines, most packages use a file called setup.inf to store initial configuration options. The setup program for the application reads settings from setup.inf and uses them to configure the application. You can create a custom .inf file for your installation, tell the setup program to use your file, and run the installation in batch mode. Copying the setup and custom .inf files for your entire workstation software suite onto a single CD or network share would allow you to install a standard set of software onto each workstation in a single batch operation.

Systems Management Server

This is essentially the process that Microsoft Systems Management Server (SMS) follows to perform automated software installations. You must tell SMS both the software packages to install and the settings to use in a set of configuration files. In SMS, this is done at an SMS site server. You can then schedule the installation, and SMS will copy the job onto other SMS servers and distribute the new software, complete with custom settings, at the specified time.

There is no magic in what SMS provides: It depends heavily on a carefully planned and executed network configuration. While SMS does help with the configuration (see the next section) it requires a serious and thorough planning stage in order to return any benefits at all. For more details on SMS, see the Solution Scenario at the end of this chapter.

Browsers

Maintaining a consistent version of your browser of choice on each workstation on your intranet may be a more difficult task than you would expect. Users are notorious for downloading and installing new versions of browsers the moment they become available, even to the point of installing beta releases replete with bugs and lacking support. As an intranet manager, you have a couple of ways to deal with this problem.

If your Internet connectivity is provided through a proxy server, you can block access to the download sites for Navigator and Explorer. Simply add the addresses of the download servers at Microsoft and Netscape to the proxy's list of blocked addresses.

Be sure to add an exception for yourself or someone on your staff: You may need to download new versions for testing to decide whether to roll them out across the intranet.

If your Internet connectivity is a direct connection through a gateway or you have a firewall, you can add a restriction to block traffic on ports 80 (HTTP) and 21 (FTP) to the browser download servers. Again, you will want to add an exception for some machines in your IT shop to allow the intranet administrator access to new versions.

If you allow your users to install their own Web browsers, you have little control of their local configuration options. If you install the browser, either using SMS or a custom-install process, you can ensure that each workstation has certain standard settings.

If you have a high degree of control over the environment, you can implement a periodic system image reload. In this scenario, the user's machine is periodically wiped out and a new, "clean" system image is downloaded. This wipes out all user-installed software and restores the machine to a "pristine" condition.

The most important of these is the proxy server setting. If you are using a proxy server to allow access to the Internet, each workstation's browser must be told the name or address of that proxy server. You may also wish to set standard security options, such as whether to run ActiveX controls. Last, you may wish to set the user's home page (the page displayed automatically when the browser loads) to be some site within your intranet.

Mail and News Readers

If you already have a corporate E-mail standard, the intranet has little impact on your installation concerns. Companies that rely on Lotus Notes, for example, are unlikely to change that standard as part of their conversion to an intranet.

If you do not yet have a corporate E-mail standard, however, consider adopting a software suite. While it is rare that all of the members of a software suite are best-of-breed, there are real advantages to an integrated suite. If you are using Microsoft Internet Explorer as your intranet browser, consider using Microsoft's Internet News Reader and Internet Mail Reader, even though there are significantly better ones available. The consistent user interface and feature set will reduce your support costs. Likewise, Netscape Navigator has sibling products that provide Mail and News access.

Adobe Acrobat

Another product to consider seriously is Adobe's Acrobat. Although the software to produce Acrobat's PDF file format is not free, the viewers are. Unlike HTML, PDF files are fully WYSIWYG. This means that a PDF file viewed in a browser will exactly match the same PDF printed on paper. This can be useful if you need to allow users to browse reports prior to printing or to view online archives of reports.

Conferencing Software

The real wild card right now is conferencing software. There are many flavors available now, but none are cross-platform compatible. The closest so far is from Netscape and should be available by the time you read this. A currently popular option is Microsoft's NetMeeting. This allows users to share not just text, but voice and applications as well. Its limitation: It works only on Microsoft's Windows 95 and Windows NT. If you need a truly cross-platform solution, consider one of the strictly text-based options from the UNIX world. IRC is a popular conferencing option, with clients available for Windows, Macintosh, and UNIX. Its biggest limitation: There is no commercially supported client or server.

Specialized Viewers

Although Adobe's PDF format is widely used to distribute WYSIWYG documents, it is by no means the only specialized format available. If you plan to use any other special file formats within your Intranet applications, you will need to provide special viewers for them.

For example, most current browsers have no built-in support for playing animation or video files. The most popular such file formats are .AVI and .MPEG, so if you plan to use video clips in your applications, you should choose one of these to support. You will then need a custom viewer that supports that particular file format. These viewers are available for most common platforms.

Security

Although the various components involved in security on the client side fit into the preceding categories, it is useful to address them together. Only the most basic security mechanism, username and password security, does not require special components on the workstation. Everything beyond that requires either special software or special data files, or both.

Both Netscape Navigator and Microsoft Internet Explorer provide for full certificate-based security. The certificates can be manually installed during workstation configuration, but can also be distributed automatically from a Web server. As always, there is a trade-off: Automatically distributing certificates may seem easier, but it is less secure. Manually installing certificates is a significant chore, but there is no substitute if your need for security is high.

Other security mechanisms may require special software as well as certificate files. For example, the implementation of Nortel Entrust security, one of the best in the industry, provided by Tradewave Corporation, uses a special client-side program that runs as a local proxy server. This piece will have to be installed onto each workstation manually.

In general, the stronger your security measures, the more difficult they will be to install, maintain, and administer. Security can also slow down your application: Software encryption is a notoriously slow process. Where possible, limit the amount of data encrypted. One of our intranet implementations actually used two different Web servers: one secured for transactions and confidential data, the other open for images, general text, and downloaded controls. This technique can enhance performance quite significantly.

SOLUTION SCENARIO

Preparing a Custom Software Installation Set

PLANNING:

1 *What software will be installed by this installation set?*
You may decide to create one large installation set that installs everything you need on each workstation, from operating system to browser, or you may choose to create a number of smaller installation sets, each of which handles a set of related tools. The monolithic approach works well for the initial installation of a large number of similar workstations, but falls apart when it comes to updating different software on different workstations or installing on workstations with a substantially different configuration.

2 *Can the installation of each piece of software be automated?*
Even though most software packages can be installed with a set of parameters stored in a setup file, not all can. If any of your programs require user intervention during setup, you may want to install those separately. Otherwise, if users run the installation, you will have no control over what they enter when prompted.

3 *Where will the software be installed?*
If the software is to be installed to run from a file server, distribution becomes much simpler. Only the file server needs to be updated. In most cases, however, at least one of your installation sets will be intended for workstations. You need to decide in advance whether the same installation set will apply to all workstations, or whether some are just too different to be handled generically. In addition, you need to decide where on each workstation the software will be installed. In

(*continued*)

SOLUTION SCENARIO *Continued*

the root? In c:\program files? On another hard drive altogether? In one client, the installation of the application software on the network server simplified management but caused response times on the application to more than double and the network traffic to increase over 50 percent. Reducing the network traffic required a memory upgrade for each desktop to improve local caching, which cost $500 each for 3000 desktops.

4 *What are the configuration settings?*
The easiest way to gather all of the configuration settings you will need is to perform the installation manually on one workstation. As you go, note the settings you choose. You can then be sure that the software is installed exactly the way you want it and you can tweak any last settings before you commit them to the installation set.

5 *Who will run the installation?*
Is this installation set going to be run automatically on each workstation? Is a trained IT staff member going to install it? Will a power user in each office handle it? Or does each user install it? Your target audience will affect the complexity and user-friendliness of your installation script. If your end users will be running the installation, you will need to test it very thoroughly prior to distribution.

6 *How will the installation be distributed?*
Many companies write their own CDs with standard installation suites on them. This allows easy distribution to widely dispersed offices and project sites. Others opt for the electronic approach: The installation set is loaded onto a network file server, and its location is broadcast in E-mail. Either

(*continued*)

SOLUTION SCENARIO *Continued*

approach works fine, but they impose different limitations on size and mutability.

7 *Will the installation save you anything?*
After answering all of the previous questions, ask yourself again if the batch installation approach is actually any simpler than just performing manual installations. If the answer is not yes, this is a good time to find out!

TIME:

The time required for planning and creating an installation set will vary dramatically depending on the size and complexity of the installation set and on the diversity of the workstations you intend to cover. A simple installation set for a perfectly homogeneous set of workstations could be planned, assembled, tested, and released in a matter of several days. For a full software suite covering an enterprise and encompassing heterogeneous applications and client types, expect a week for planning, a week for assembling, several days for testing, and at least a day for releasing—per configuration supported. This is by no means an upper limit: There are many factors that could push you well past the 2½-week time line.

EFFORT:

Once the planning decisions are made, the remaining steps are fairly straightforward:

1 *Gather the individual installation sets.*
You will need to create a directory on a hard drive to assemble the various components you are installing. Each component should be stored in its own subdirectory of the master installation directory. If there are sets of files you don't

(*continued*)

SOLUTION SCENARIO *Continued*

intend to install (books online, etc.), you can remove them from the master installation set at this point.

2 *Create the setup configuration files.*
For each product being installed, you need to record the settings you plan to use in the .inf file (or its equivalent). For most installations, this is as simple as listing the options in an ASCII text file. Others use their own custom file format to store this information.

3 *Package the master directory.*
If you are distributing on CD, write the master directory to a test CD. If you are distributing electronically, copy the master directory to a file server.

4 *Test the installation.*
Using the actual distribution mechanism, run a complete install of a single workstation. This will help ensure that you have not missed anything in your master installation.

5 *Notify and train the helpdesk.*
Issue a list of changes to the helpdesk, and provide training in the support of the process itself and of the new features/functions delivered.

6 *Release the package.*
If you are distributing electronically, move the package to the appropriate file servers. If you are distributing on CD, make as many duplicates of the test CD as are needed.

7 *Announce the release.*
Okay, so this probably goes without saying, but if you are releasing electronically and you intend for users to run the

(*continued*)

SOLUTION SCENARIO *Continued*

installation, you need to send out a notice telling them where to find the installation set and what to do with it.

RESULTS:

Although batch software installation sets are a fairly straightforward tool, their significant benefits make them an attractive option. They do not solve all workstation management issues, but they do a fairly good job of solving their well-defined set of problems.

Configuration Management

Configuration management is one area in which intranet applications differ very little from traditional client/server applications. It will always be necessary to get at least the browser installed on each workstation. That is not to say that it isn't getting easier. Most Windows machines, for example, come with Microsoft Internet Explorer preinstalled. Many machines also have Netscape Navigator preinstalled, and there are "Internet access" kits available that have all the software you need if your computer did not have a Web browser preinstalled.

The specter of the network computer has focused new attention on the issues of configuration management, since it is a major part of the *total cost of ownership* (TCO) equation, which for many companies runs from $9,000 to $11,000 per workstation per year. Microsoft and Intel have responded aggressively with a "zero-maintenance" approach that is a combination of hardware and software. The software components will begin appearing with the upcoming releases of MS NT 5.0 and the recently beta-delivered release of Windows 98, code-named *Memphis.*

But that covers just one aspect of client configuration management. Here we are dealing with everything that is not strictly specific to the business functionality of your intranet application. This includes the hardware (peripherals), operating system, network connectivity, and support software. We will address these areas from the bottom up, starting with hardware.

Hardware

Unfortunately, the problems involved with hardware configuration have not gone away with the intranet revolution. They've gotten marginally easier, as new applications tend to work on top of the existing hardware with little or no interference, but initially deploying the hardware for a large intranet can be a grueling task. At a minimum, you will have to deal with memory, hard drive, network card, and video card compatibility. If you will have remote workstations, add modems to the mix.

While the latest round of plug-and-play devices has made this easier, the best advice available is still: Record *everything.* Writing down or printing out obscure details like IRQ numbers and DMA addresses may seem tedious, but it is child's play compared to figuring out after a serious crash what those settings used to be. For this task, there is now a whole slew of tools available. If you are running EISA or MCA machines, print off the system configuration parameters, archive the information, and save those configuration disks! When you plan your hardware purchases, consider the availability of hardware configuration tools in your decision. Both Dell and Compaq provide hardware inspection programs that will record your configuration to disk or to printer. Microsoft provides MSD, a general diagnostic tool with many of the same features. Other manufacturers may well have similar offerings, but don't expect them from low-end clones: This is a feature you give up once you move into the cheaper market.

Another way to reduce your overall hardware headaches is to be consistent with your equipment. While it is not always possible to stick to a single vendor or a single product line, the advantages to doing so are tremendous. If all of your workstations are the same model, finding problems in any particular machine becomes much easier. Swapping parts, keeping spares, and learning the machines' peculiarities will all be significantly easier.

While these hints can make your job a bit easier, they do not resolve the fundamental problems of maintaining workstation hardware. There is some hope in sight, though. The industry is pushing toward a network PC or *network computer* (NC) that will (allegedly) reduce the potential for local hardware problems. The idea is that anything complicated or nonstandard will reside on the server instead of the workstation. This has already happened to some extent, with printers, scanners, tape drives, and even fax and modems moving from the workstation to the server and being pooled among clients. You can expect this trend to continue up to a point, but don't expect a panacea: The complexity will almost certainly be shifted instead to the server, and the trade-offs may not be pretty. A network PC with no hard drive will be useless if the server crashes, while today's PCs can be used right through a server outage.

Operating System

Managing the configuration of the workstation operating system is one area in which significant strides have been made in recent years and are being made right now. Microsoft's Systems Management Server has been used for years now to centrally manage the OS settings of workstations on large networks. Some of its features are available to the entry-level Windows NT/Windows 95 network as well, through remote registry administration and user profiles. For more information, see the SMS section.

DMI

It has long been an industry dream to have a consistent, cross-platform, reliable way to manage the hardware, operating systems, and software installed on desktop workstations from a central administration console. While this may seem like a pipe dream, a group of major industry players formed a consortium, the Desktop Management Task Force, to pursue exactly this goal.

In the past couple of years, the initial results of their efforts have emerged as the Desktop Management Interface, or DMI. The DMI is not a single application or package, like SMS, but, a protocol definition for how several types of software should work together. The various components that make up a DMI implementation must be obtained from different sources.

The core of any DMI installation is the administration console, or management application. This tool allows the administrator to gather information about the various DMI-enabled components installed on all of the workstations on a network and can also monitor those workstations for indications—messages from workstations that some information has changed. DMI management tools are available from a number of vendors and as a part of some common tools. SMS, for example, can serve as a DMI management agent.

The DMI management application communicates to a service layer installed on each workstation. The service layer collects information about installed components in a local database, which it then makes available to management applications. The service layer also gathers indications from the managed components and forwards them to the management applications.

To be managed by DMI, a component—whether hardware, software, or operating system—must itself be DMI-aware. A DMI-aware component defines a set of management information stored in a management information file, or MIF. This MIF is passed to the service layer, which adds it to the local database. The key point here is that the MIF is a separate file, custom-defined for each component. It is possible to create an MIF file for an existing non-DMI-aware application, but this is not a practical approach. (See Figure 2.2.)

Because of this requirement that each managed component be DMI-aware, DMI is gaining widespread acceptance very slowly. Although an increasing number of hardware vendors are adopting DMI and providing MIFs for their products, software vendors are not following suit. This limits DMI's overall usefulness, at least for the time being. As support for DMI does spread, however, it has the potential to become a powerful tool for taming workstation configuration issues. As this change can be expected to take place over the next several years, it makes sense to try to select DMI-aware components wherever possible, in preparation for the day when DMI's big payoff will be available.

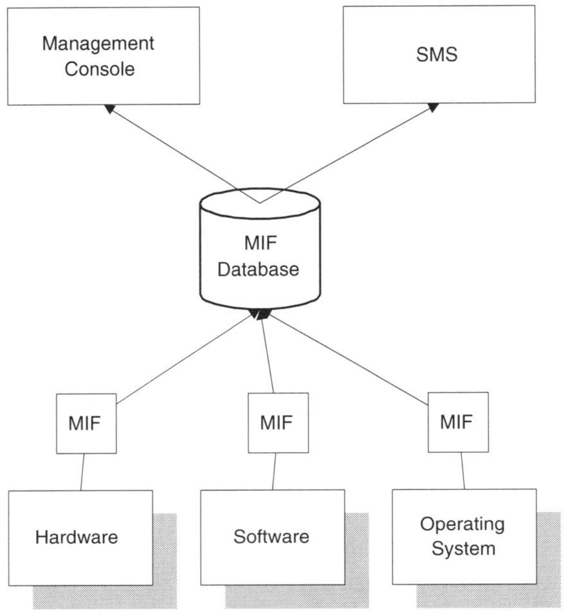

Figure 2.2 The DMI model.

SNMP

The Simple Network Management Protocol is the original TCP/IP suite protocol for managing network hardware and servers. Traditionally it has been used to provide up-to-the-minute status from widely distributed network components to a central monitoring station or stations.

Like DMI, SNMP is based on a management tool used to view information, known as the *SNMP monitor,* and workstation-based software, the *SNMP agents.* In SNMP, an agent represents a single component and communicates directly with the monitor, instead of through a workstation-based information consolidator. This means that any hardware or software component to be SNMP-enabled is required to provide an SNMP agent.

The original SNMP definition operated on a pure query-response basis: The monitor could request a particular type of information from a particular agent, the agent would return that information, and the monitor would display it. A later refinement of SNMP allowed for *traps,* which are messages sent out by the agent when it detects a problem or a change in information. Traps are received by monitors and can then be displayed to the monitor user. (See Figure 2.3.)

Unlike DMI, SNMP also supports updating configurations from the monitor: The monitor can send a message to an agent telling it to modify a particular setting. This makes SNMP a powerful tool for managing widely distributed network services. At this time, SNMP is most widely implemented in network operations hardware and software and in network server software. Most routers, gateways, file servers, Web servers, database servers, proxy servers, backup servers, high-end modems, and other service-oriented components already support SNMP, and many network managers use it as a core technology. However, SNMP support in workstation hardware and software is fairly rare still.

In spite of its similarity both in purpose and in function to DMI, SNMP complements DMI and the two can be used together if your

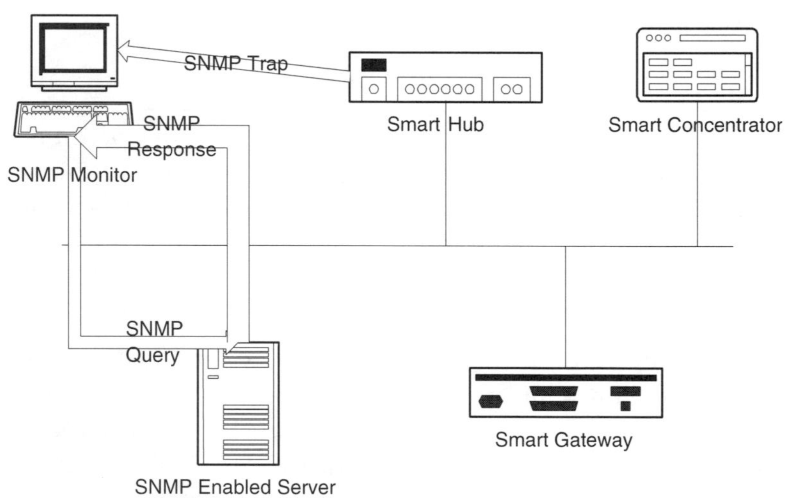

Figure 2.3 The SNMP model.

management tool supports both. SMS, for example, does support both.

As intranets gain in popularity, SNMP capabilities are being added to more workstation-oriented software and hardware. Choosing SNMP-enabled software and incorporating SNMP into your intranet applications will allow you to track every level of your intranet from a single console. These consoles are complex and expensive, but when implemented can provide tremendously effective mechanisms for managing a complex network. Generally, these managers are a must-have for the effective intranet manager.

SMS

Microsoft Systems Management Server (SMS) has the ambitious goal of providing a holistic approach to networked systems management. It promises to administer the hardware, operating system, network connectivity, and software configuration of your workstations. It promises to make coffee. It monitors changes to workstations, automates software distribution and installation, and allows remote control of workstations. It promises to fix Social Security. It also provides compatibility with DMI and SNMP for better industry standardization.

TIP *The complexity of this model imposes heavy planning requirements on an SMS installation. Effective implementation with SMS mandates an extensive planning effort—if you aren't going to do it, don't use it.*

That's a lot for one product! Let's look more carefully at what exactly SMS is and what it provides. To start with, SMS is not a single program. It is a family of programs designed to work together as an integrated whole. It builds extensively on the technologies provided by Windows NT and SQL Server, and relies on components on the SMS servers as well as on the managed workstations.

SMS operates through a hierarchy of Windows NT servers running the SMS application software (see Figure 2.4). These are known as *SMS site servers,* and they come in three varieties.

A *primary SMS server* uses a SQL Server database to store information about all of the workstations beneath it in the hierarchy. This includes all of the workstations managed directly by this server, as well as all of the workstations managed by any of this server's children. A primary server has a parent server to which it replicates all of the data it has.

The *root server* is a special instance of a primary server with no parent, and all managed workstations are its direct or indirect children. Because each primary server replicates its entire administration database to its parent, the SMS root server stores the configuration information for every workstation managed by the SMS installation. This has some rather severe implications for the drive space needs of the root server, as well as for the bandwidth requirements for its connections to its children.

A *secondary server* serves the same role as a primary server, except that it does not store its data locally. Instead, it acts as a

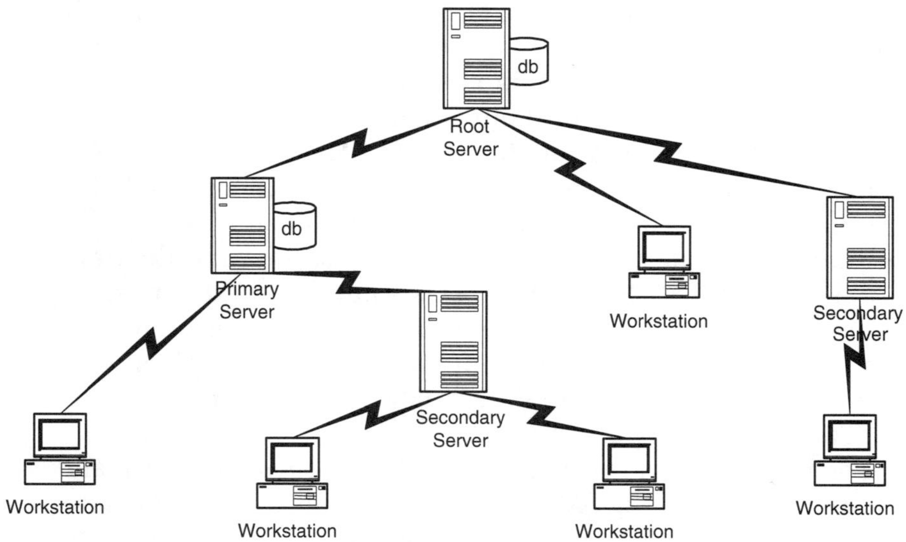

Figure 2.4 SMS installation hierarchy.

relay, passing data from its managed workstations to its parent primary server, and passing commands and batches down to its managed workstations. A secondary server cannot have children servers, and, because it has no local database, it cannot be used for administration. Administration of a secondary server's managed workstations is handled by its parent primary server.

An SMS *logon server* is not a site server, in that it has no role in gathering and distributing information about the managed workstations. Instead, these servers are used to log in each workstation and each user to the SMS infrastructure. This is done by modifying the user logon scripts stored on the logon server to install the SMS workstation programs and establish a relationship between the workstation and a site server. Because the logon server uses logon scripts, it must be a Windows NT domain controller (backup or primary). This is one of the few relationships SMS imposes between the SMS hierarchy and the Windows NT domain hierarchy.

One fundamental function of SMS is to gather configuration and software inventory information from the individual workstations and archive it in the SMS servers' inventory database. This is performed by an SMS component loaded onto the client workstation by the user logon script. This component detects installed software packages based on a master list of file names and sizes distributed with SMS. It then passes its inventory information to its managing SMS server. This information can be used by the administrator to track what software is installed where on a network and to plan the installation of new software.

In addition to software, the inventory component is able to identify certain types of hardware as well. It can identify installed cards, disk drives, memory, processors, and floating-point units (FPUs). In pre–Windows 95 machines the inventory cannot identify monitors, keyboards, mice, or other input devices. In addition, the inventory tends to miss duplicates: If a workstation has two 3Com Etherlink II network cards, the inventory will list only one.

The inventory is also able to collect files during the scan and send them back to the SMS database. This allows administrators to examine config.sys, autoexec.bat, and other configuration files. It could also be used to gather user-critical files in preparation for a workstation upgrade.

SOLUTION SCENARIO

Implementing Centralized Workstation Management Using SMS

PLANNING:

In planning an installation of Microsoft Systems Management Server, there are a number of issues that must be resolved. The planning phase is particularly important in an SMS rollout because of the complexity and variability of the SMS offering.

1 *Which sites will require local administration (and hence, SQL Server)?*
SMS servers come in two types: primary and secondary servers. Primary SMS servers maintain a repository (in a SQL server database) of the configuration information of each of their client workstations. Secondary SMS servers gather this information, but pass it up to a parent SMS server for storage. There is a special SMS server known as the root server, which has no parent. Other than that one server, each SMS server has a parent, and each replicates all of its data to its parent. A secondary SMS server has no administration features: It simply passes information only to and from its parent. Thus a site with only a secondary SMS server is managed remotely by the secondary SMS server's parent.

2 *How are the SMS sites to be distributed in the network, and what bandwidth will be required between those sites?*
Since all of the data on each SMS server is replicated to its parent, there is a fair amount of communication between the child server and the parent. Placing a server's parent on the other side of a slow network connection would result in network bottlenecks and serious performance impacts.

(*continued*)

SOLUTION SCENARIO *Continued*

3 *Will the SMS application share a server with other applications?*
SMS can use a lot of memory and processor resources. Hosting SMS servers on the same machines as other application servers may result in reduced overall performance, both of the SMS application and any other applications on the machine. One case in which SMS could coexist with another application is if the other application is used primarily during business hours, while SMS distributions take place mainly after hours. There would be less potential for resource conflicts in this scenario.

4 *How often should inventory information be collected?*
Every time inventory is collected, the information must pass from each workstation to its managing SMS server and from that server to its parent, on up the hierarchy. In a large network, this can result in huge amounts of network traffic. Collecting information too often can impact other network uses. Note that this is true even if information is collected only at night, since many other large processes tend to be scheduled to run at night: file server backups, large reports, bulk mailings, and software distributions.

On the other hand, collecting information too infrequently can make planning new distributions or other batch jobs ineffectual, because the current configuration of each machine and its status may affect your planning. Out-of-date information could lead to misinformed decisions.

5 *Will users be given the option of disabling remote control?*
Being able to remotely control a particular workstation can be a great aid to troubleshooting an installation or training your users. However, some users see this capability as a potential invasion of their privacy. If you allow the users to

(*continued*)

SOLUTION SCENARIO *Continued*

disable remote control, you may avoid those complaints, but you may find yourself unable to resolve problems without a personal visit to the workstation. Remote control is too useful a feature to give up easily, and we do not recommend disabling it. This issue is usually decided by some form of blanket corporate policy.

6 *Will users be given the option of choosing when to download new software updates?*
Updating software automatically at night works quite well in general, but there are reasons that users might wish to delay the update of their particular workstations. These range from disk space limitations (new software is almost invariably larger than old) to compatibility concerns (no new version is ever 100 percent compatible with its predecessor). You may want to allow your users to make these choices for themselves.

If you do so, you will have to contend with the problems of different versions of the software coexisting on the network. You may find your users having to save files in multiple different formats to be able to exchange with users of different versions of the software.

If you do not allow this choice, then you may have to contend with users complaining about loss of functionality or lack of compatibility. Generally, we find that tools such as word processors can be upgraded at the user's discretion within a maximum time window, but business applications should always be upgraded consistently across the organization.

7 *Is the network capable of supporting the communications required for remote control?*
As mentioned above, remote control of a workstation can be very useful when troubleshooting a problem. However, it requires the transmission of screen refresh and event infor-

(*continued*)

SOLUTION SCENARIO *Continued*

mation between the workstation and the SMS server console. This data can be voluminous, so remote control over a modem or WAN connection may not be feasible. It is important to know in advance where remote control will and won't be available, since that may impact your allocation of IT staff.

8 *How will the SMS architecture fit in with the NT domain architecture?*
Although most organizations construct their SMS architecture in some loose parallel to their NT domain architecture, this is not a requirement of SMS. SMS does require that certain types of servers be domain controllers, but that is about the only requirement. The SMS architecture is likely to reflect the structure of your IT support, while the domain architecture is more likely to reflect the structure of your organization as a whole. It is important to distinguish the two, since otherwise you may find yourself struggling to accommodate incorrectly perceived restrictions. With the constant evolution of the NT naming service, this needs to be looked at carefully and frequently revisited with any planned NT upgrade.

9 *Will the users run applications from their desktops or from a server?*
This trade-off is not at all unique to SMS, but it nonetheless has a strong impact on your SMS rollout plan. Applications loaded from the workstation's local hard drive tend to load faster and crash less often than applications run from a network file server. However, applications loaded from a network file server require less workstation disk space and can be updated more easily. These models can be intermixed on a network for different applications.

(*continued*)

SOLUTION SCENARIO *Continued*

TIME:

An SMS installation is neither a fast process nor an easy one. For the simplest networks, with one SMS server and a handful of workstations, a couple of days of planning and a week for rollout might suffice, assuming homogeneous workstations and a straightforward server configuration.

Enterprisewide SMS installations tend to be measured in months, and the planning alone in weeks. We implemented SMS to support four call-centers, each with 1200 seats, for one of the Baby Bells. It was three months before the planning team did its first dummy deployment. Running two test deployment cycles and rolling into production took another three months. It took a total of six months to get set up, but now their IT department can upgrade every workstation at the same time.

Again, SMS is a heavy solution. But once installed, it can pay off through significant reductions in management time and costs. Keep in mind that, once SMS is installed, it takes a continual commitment to keep it maintained and running smoothly. It is not a tool that you can install and ignore.

EFFORT:

Once the planning is completed, the steps needed to actually complete the SMS rollout follow:

1 *Install NT on all servers per NT domain architecture.*
This step is really independent of SMS and may in fact have already been done. We include it here to emphasize that SMS does not handle this task for you.

2 *Install SQL Server on primary SMS sites.*
Every primary SMS server needs a SQL Server database in which to store its workstations' configuration information.

(*continued*)

SOLUTION SCENARIO *Continued*

This can be on the same physical NT server as the SMS server, but it does not have to be.

3 *Install SMS servers on all primary SMS sites.*
The SMS software must be installed manually on each of the primary SMS servers. This includes configuring the SMS repository database.

4 *Create parent-child relationships between SMS sites.*
Once SMS is installed on all of the primary servers, the relationships between the servers can be defined. Don't worry that the secondary servers haven't been installed: SMS will handle that.

5 *Allow SMS to build required SMS secondary sites per the parent-child relationships.*
Once the hierarchy information is established, SMS can automatically install the appropriate components on each secondary server.

6 *Place the SMS end-user script into the login script of each client that will be using the system.*
In order for a workstation to be managed by an SMS server, special code must be added to the login script run by each user when attaching to the network. This is referred to as the *SMS login script.*

7 *Allow the SMS system to install each client per the logon script.*
As each workstation logs on to the network, the SMS login scripts kick in, installing the SMS workstation components.

8 *Configure each client with determined options.*

(*continued*)

SOLUTION SCENARIO ***Continued***

These options can be entered manually at the workstation at this point, entered manually at the server at this point, or preset in the installation script in advance.

9 *Begin using inventory and remote control functions.*
At this point, the inventory and remote control features of SMS are fully operational and available for your use.

10 *If running applications from server, configure the applications available to each user.*
Not all applications will be run from a file server. One advantage of doing so, however, is that you can control access to run those applications by protecting the file server share. This can be configured using SMS at this point.

11 *Build and test software download scripts prior to utilizing software distribution functions.*
Automated software installations will probably not go smoothly the first few times. Testing the scripts is critical, as is learning the peculiarities of the SMS system.

RESULTS:

A full-fledged SMS installation can greatly reduce your total time spent managing workstations. The larger your network, the more SMS should be able to save you. As mentioned earlier, though, it is not without its drawbacks:

- It is time-consuming to install.
- All of your operations must now be handled through SMS, to ensure stability.
- It requires significant network bandwidth, disk storage, and server processor overhead.
- It can be infuriatingly hard to diagnose problems with SMS itself.

A second important function of SMS is the ability to launch programs or batch files on each workstation. This function can be used to perform general maintenance (changing the default Internet Explorer home page on each workstation), to gather information (prompt the user for a phone number to be added to the SMS database), or install new software. The ability to use this feature for software distribution and automated installation is one reason SMS is so attractive to many administrators.

One final function of key interest is the ability to remotely control any workstation from the administration console. This allows a system administrator to take over a user's workstation remotely in order to troubleshoot problems or provide training assistance.

The SMS base product supports the entire Microsoft Windows family and, to a lesser extent, the Apple Macintosh family. Certain SMS features are not available for managing Macs. SMS can also be extended to cover UNIX workstations using software available from Digital Equipment Corporation. Again, not all features will be available to non-Windows workstations.

SMS operates over most common network operating systems and protocols, and can interoperate with other management packages via SNMP. Because it understands DMI information, it can take advantage of the information made available by components themselves.

Summary

This chapter has demonstrated that there are obvious trade-offs between performance and administrative overhead in the deployment of software to client desktops. Consequently, this leaves us with the same task we encountered in traditional client/server systems—a need to effectively and predictably manage the deployment of components. Using many of the same techniques and software that were developed for client/server, the next generation of Web computing should be able to benefit from the lessons we have learned.

CHAPTER THREE

Network Communications

Several years ago, someone in the computing industry (several have taken credit) said, "The network is the computer." It was presumptuous at that time, but farsighted. Today's distributed environments are making that statement a reality.

Most companies have elaborate network management tools in place for mainframe environments and similar facilities in place for other leased-line networks. However, few companies have applied the same level of operational discipline or resources to the development of an operations environment for next-generation systems, generally characterized by client/server and more recently by intranet designs.

The increasing dependence of distributed applications on the network requires a new look at managing the infrastructure. We are seeing a disturbing trend in intranet implementations whereby little to no accommodation is being made for this need. Much of this results from the conventional mythology that intranet systems can be done on the cheap, and the implementation approach in many companies that let lines of business (LOBs) implement intranet solutions independently. LOBs will direct their dollars to delivering a maximum amount of feature functionality and will usually disregard the operational need for effective network communications management. As a result, few intranet environments have an adequate network operations environment to support their deployment, resulting in unpredictable performance, as well as unpredictable impact on corporate networking resources.

There are a number of solutions that just manage the network itself, many of these provided by the network vendors. Companies such as Cabletron, Cisco, and Bay Networks all have products that allow users to map and monitor their network infrastructures. These tools, while adequate for their purpose, should not be seen as sufficient in the overall enterprise management scope. No single solution can solve it all, and designers should be prepared to have multiple solutions in place to manage different types of applications.

For example, if you are deploying a content-based system and lose a Web server, it is not particularly difficult to use a hardware product like Cisco's Net-Director to automatically route a user to another content box. The context of the link is low and can be readily captured within the browser. However, if you have an update transaction running on a back-end system and lose a connection, the state information of the transaction is complex. In this case, the network and the application need to work hand in hand to ensure that a server can fail and the service it provides will not fail with it.

The ability to handle this type of sophisticated programming is usually beyond the capabilities of most Web developers, especially the new crop that has flooded the market. Additionally, the complexity of these applications makes weekend construction unrealistic, regardless of what the tool vendors purport. In most cases in which Web systems fail to meet needs, it is because the construction was done by individuals with an inadequate understanding of the underlying physical network, the protocols that run on it, or the complexity of distributed objects and transactions in this environment. The intranet seeks to simplify and abstract the complexity of the underlying computing infrastructure further than any previous system design. The higher the level of abstraction, the greater the sophistication of the implementation and the greater the need for a high degree of skill in designing and engineering the solution.

Bandwidth Management

With the massive growth of network usage that has accompanied the growth of distributed applications, there is a need for more effective management of bandwidth usage. The nature of the IP-based intranet today is that all traffic has equivalent priority, meaning that the person loading a Dilbert cartoon has the same network priority as the one booking a new order for a customer. If it sounds crazy, it is. However, IP today really only allows traffic filtering at the Transmission Control Protocol (TCP) level. That means it recognizes TCP applications (FTP, etc.) and filters those protocols, but really cannot allocate bandwidth to them and knows nothing about your application. In the absence of this capability, physical design needs to take over and provide what the protocols today cannot.

One of the most common designs uses multiple network segments to which traffic can be routed. Paths are identified based on destination device, originating device, and/or protocol type. The process of traffic discrimination is one of prioritization, recognizing the application and user need for speed for specific types of data. Of course, all users want subsecond response time, but until the "theoretical $0 cost of bandwidth" becomes reality, you will need to educate users regarding the costs.

For one of our clients, we used an interesting design that not only separated traffic by type, but used a combination of purchased frame relay services and public Internet services to accommodate the differing types of traffic and their relative performance value to the company. In this case, we needed to support transactional access to a central Oracle database, provide tn3270 (Systems Network Architecture [SNA] in TCP/IP) access to legacy applications, NFS access to central image and source code repositories, File Transfer Protocol (FTP) access for software downloads from a central site, and support Notes replication between sites worldwide, which supported extensive document sharing.

The corporation's basic network infrastructure was a private frame relay network which was hubbed to a site on the east coast of the United States. A similar design was used to create a "European Hub" in Germany, which was then connected via frame to the various European sites. The two hubs were connected by a frame relay link across the Atlantic. The only connection to the Internet was via a T1 at the U.S. hub. (See Figure 3.1.)

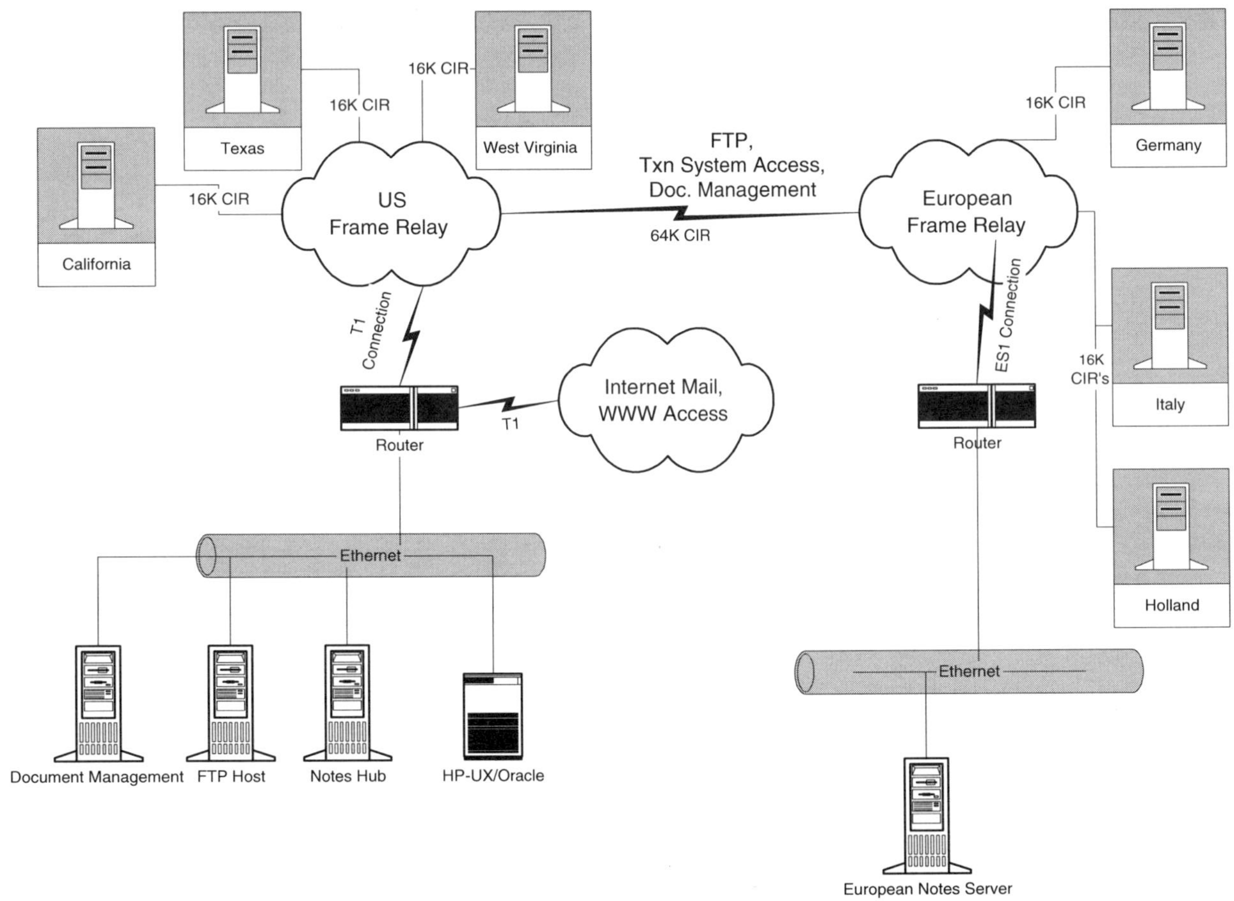

Figure 3.1 Initial network design.

The basic design forced all of the traffic across the singular frame link connecting the continents, which resulted in tremendous contention for network resources (E-mail traffic competed for network resources with transactional systems). In addition, Internet traffic from Europe came all the way across the ocean, which resulted in network saturation by applications as innocuous as Microsoft's Portfolio Manager or as deadly as PointCast.

In reviewing the design, we first looked at traffic types, characterizing the traffic as either *elastic* or *inelastic*. We realized that we were dealing with underlying protocols that had variable performance characteristics.

Elastic applications can adapt their behavior to changing network conditions. These applications generally use as much bandwidth as they can get, but they will run over whatever is available and can adjust dynamically. This concept is what enables you to play Doom over a modem from home or over a T1 in the office. Most TCP traffic, HTTP, FTP, NFS, and so forth, is elastic.

Inelastic is an expression applied to application traffic that cannot adapt to the changing conditions of the network. This usually represents real-time or transactional traffic flows. For example, a stockbroker's ticker information can be considered inelastic, since a delay in its transmission fundamentally changes the nature of the data itself. It goes from being accurate to indicative, and that difference matters!

Originally designed as a packet radio protocol, TCP/IP was built for the (relatively) low-speed and high-bit-error-rate networks of the 1960s and 1970s. Thus, TCP/IP was designed with an assumption of elastic traffic in mind—getting there was considered sufficient.

There are innumerable conditions that can affect inelastic traffic. Different applications have different tolerances for these factors.

- *End-end Delay:* End-end delay is the overall time required for a message to transit the network. In a simplistic model, this can result from the mixture of networking technologies. For example, a reservation system in a hotel accesses a local database that identifies availability of property rooms. However, when local rooms are not available, the application may wish to query other property databases in other nearby hotels in the same chain. On the LAN, the end-end delay for a message is 100ms, but when another property is accessed, just establishing the ISDN link to the other property takes an additional 2 seconds.

- *Jitter:* This is the variation in the amount of time it takes each message to transit the network. In routed networks, this can result from messages taking various paths through the network, which results in a different "hop count" between source and destination. The variable latency of routers also contributes, as packet forwarding rates decrease under load. Queuing in these routers is probably the greatest source of jitter. Why does jitter matter? Packet video is a good example. Frequently, packet video solutions use the previous frame as a reference point, often just sending the "delta," or change, to the previous packet, which decreases bandwidth consumption. Thus, the receiving node must have a sequence of frames before it can begin to decode them. A high jitter rate will result in a jittery presentation of the video, as the eye notes the difference in time between frames.
- *Bandwidth Limitations:* When bandwidth is limited, the ability to move data is fixed at a maximum rate per unit time. While this is not (usually) noticed in conventional terminal applications, bandwidth limitations place significant constraints on application design, data location, and process location in a distributed architecture. As we move toward more bandwidth consumptive component designs for rich and interactive intranet applications, bandwidth limitations become more apparent.

In our case, the tn3270 traffic and the Oracle traffic were considered inelastic due to business requirements and the nature of the underlying protocols. SNA has some basic time dependencies, which reflect an implicit design assumption of a dedicated, polling-based network. The Oracle traffic was also time-sensitive, since the nature of its use was online and interactive, and the underlying protocol was a synchronous RPC, which meant that the application was "stuck" until the RPC was fulfilled by the back end. The FTP, E-mail, and similar traffic was considered elastic and thus could use a less predictable environment.

The general performance model for this environment was not particularly "bursty"—that is, we had an estimated steady-state utilization of approximately 20 percent. We did note that the transactional systems were prone to broad increases—utilization would increase to 70 percent at key times during the course of the business cycle, such as at the end of a quarter or the end of a year. Thus, the business decision was to commit bandwidth to this application set, since the value of response time was measurable in the length of call center queues, the calls per hour being processed, and so on.

None of the other data met the criticality tests of the business or had the timeliness requirements discussed above. Thus, it was classified as noncritical data and was assigned a secondary priority.

How to solve this problem? Well, the solution had several aspects. First, the frame network between Europe and the United States would be constrained to only transactional traffic—that is, no E-mail, FTP, NFS, HTTP, or similar traffic would traverse the international backbone. Where did it go? Onto the public Internet! By adding a second Internet connection in Germany, the client was able to filter traffic at the local router. The ability to recognize the inherent difference in the value of timeliness in the data allowed this client to dramatically reduce their network costs on the expensive European link and improve performance for current applications. In addition, we took the opportunity to add firewalls to the network infrastructure, an important component in both security and traffic management, since the firewall provides the opportunity to identify traffic that can pass through in either direction. What did the solution look like? See Figure 3.2.

IP Traffic Management

TCP/IP has an inherent ability for communicating nodes to direct traffic to be throttled back in a busy network. However, it is the

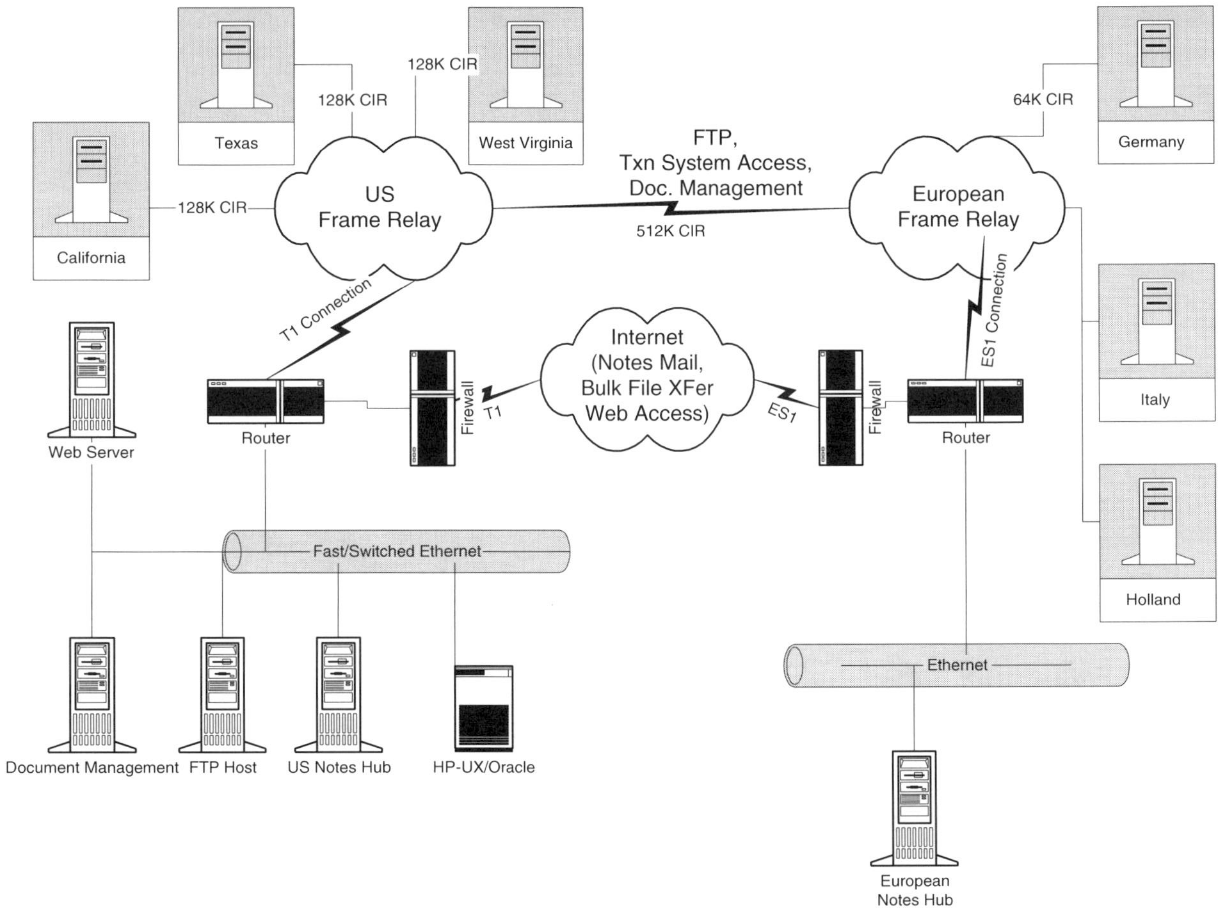

Figure 3.2 End-state network design.

responsibility of the end stations to handle this signaling, and in a congested net that can take as much as a second. That does not sound like a lot of time, but we are dealing with data moving at the speed of light, and a lot of data can flow between two nodes in a second. When an IP connection becomes congested, the application protocols can timeout, resulting in retransmissions. Retransmissions can result in a continued escalation of the problem by adding additional traffic to the network, resulting in a "death spiral," where routers flood, and so on.

TIP *In the past, large organizations generally exerted tremendous influence over their technology vendors because of their buying power. This leverage allowed them to dictate product directions and upgrades. However, today's market has changed radically, and corporate buyers have less and less power to influence vendors either directly or even through usergroups. Part of this diminished influence is due to the increasing importance of industry tasks forces and similar organizations. We recommend that larger IT organizations look at their technology environment and join key Task Forces. Some of these charge for membership, some simply allow you to join mailing lists. Some are open to individual memberships, others are only open to organizational membership. Several we think are worth looking at include:*

- *Internet Engineering Task Force: www.ietf.org*
- *World Wide Web Consortium: www.w3.org*
- *Object Management Group: www.omg.org*
- *Transaction Processing Council: www.tpc.org*

Participating in these and similar groups can provide you with an advanced knowledge of not only technology, but also provide you with insight into how various vendors are meeting the guidelines developed.

Several solutions are proposed for this problem, including:

Queuing Schemes: Various solutions allow for multiple queues to be maintained on a router and their servicing to be assigned variable priorities.

Increasing Router Buffer Size. Provides a mechanism whereby more data can be buffered in a router, which allows better accommodation of data destined for a downstream device in case the intervening communication link is congested. This should decrease packet throwaway and retransmission.

The Resource Reservation Protocol (RSVP). RSVP provides the ability to establish reservation information at each router along the path of a stream of data. This allows the routers along the path to make determinations about how to prioritize downstream traffic by placing a reservation for bandwidth through the entire network.

ATM vendors contend that these solutions won't solve the problem, since IP itself does not prevent congestion and these solutions are reactive mechanisms for dealing with it as it occurs. In part, they are correct. More sophisticated queuing schemes will result in more sophisticated software for routers, and that will require more hardware to preserve and increase packet transfer rates. This appeals to router vendors. Increasing router buffer size allows for less packet loss and should reduce retransmission rates, but any buffer can be overflowed. RSVP will supply the ability to provide capacity reservation through the network, but this is an add-on to an older protocol (TCP/IP) which is trying to stretch to meet today's needs.

On the corporate intranet, what does this mean? For most folks it means outlining an evolutionary path that implements IP-based solutions in the near term, since few applications in the market today can take advantage of ATM's QOS service. For most of our clients, we see an evolution that will likely move them to IP over ATM, using ATM's higher bandwidth combined with its more advanced QOS facilities, and then to ATM itself as the business requires, the technology allows, and the applications require.

Resource Reservation Protocol (RSVP)

For up-to-date information on this protocol, we recommend that you visit the Internet Engineering Task Force's (IETF) Web site (www.ietf.org) since progress on this is constant. However, the following provides a brief summary of RSVP.

RSVP is one piece of a broader set of services proposed by the IETF called the Integrated Services Architecture (ISA). ISA is a collection of services including queue management and some advanced congestion management techniques to manage (not eliminate) network delays and bandwidth consumption. RSVP is a protocol in this suite that allows reservations to be made through the network for bandwidth. In addition, it allows for policy development, which, similar to security policies, gives a device a set of rules to use in managing traffic. When a policy is violated, the device can consult the policy and take action to manage the situation, often without operator intervention. In today's widely distributed networks this type of network intelligence is critical to a practical, manageable evolution of the environment.

ISA provides advanced congestion management and queuing algorithms that limit delay, jitter, and bandwidth consumption in the network. It also includes protocols, such as RSVP, that make it possible to reserve bandwidth for particular applications. Together, these capabilities let IP networks handle real-time applications such as voice and video. However, it is still possible that protocols such as contention-based Ethernet used in combination with a routed network design will be unable to support this type of traffic. Unlike their deterministic brethren, they do not ensure fair use of the underlying media between nodes. Many are looking to a combination of Ethernet switching and higher-speed Ethernet technologies (Gigabit Ethernet) to provide the needed infrastructure.

Implementing RSVP requires making software and possibly firmware upgrades to switches and routers throughout the network. In addition, there are concerns about devices being saturated by an overwhelming number of small reservations. RSVP promises to be very consumptive of processing and buffering resources, and these requirements will likely increase with the number of reservations a router is handling. The packet classification schemes and the scheduling capabilities required to implement services for these reservations also will increase the amount of hardware required to service this protocol. ATM, a competing technology, was engineered with these QOS capabilities in mind and provides them in a more elegant fashion. Many see the extension of IP through devices like ISA as a Rube Goldberg attempt to forestall the inevitable. However, it would appear that implementing RSVP to support intranet applications that require rich media will require either significant upgrades to your current hardware and/or the addition of edge devices that will aggregate reservations and then use more efficient allocations within your backbone to manage the resource needs.

Umbrella Managers

When operating a complex distributed environment, there is a need to bring together the various elements of the communications environment and show their various outputs in a correlated fashion. While it is possible to buy or build a number of the tools required to monitor individual components, the umbrella manager provides a framework into which the various components can plug. This allows them to share information with each other and the manager to evaluate the various messages, assisting fault isolation by separating symptoms from disease.

These managers are discussed here not because they are specific to the subject of communications and networks, but because they generally emerged out of the network management space and continue to be network-dominant. They generally rely on the use of the Simple Network Management Protocol (SNMP), which gathers information from network devices. These devices use Management Information Base (MIB) information—structures that gather information about performance, errors, and so on.

In working with umbrella managers, there are two major designs: *best-of-breed* and *integrated*. Both have their benefits and drawbacks, and will be summarized here.

Best-of-Breed

Major players in this area include Hewlett-Packard, IBM, and Intel. While Intel may look out of place here, the company is constantly adding to its offerings in this area—although it is definitely the low end of the spectrum. If you are considering umbrella managers, we suggest you review their features and functions at the time of purchase, since the pace of innovation in this area is tremendous.

Hewlett-Packard: Openview—Operates on HP-UX, Solaris, Microsoft Windows, and NT. Openview is considered by many to be the leading SNMP manager, delivering enterprise management software for end-to-end service management in Internet computing environments. HP OpenView manages networks, systems, applications, and databases in order to improve service and reduce costs. OpenView consists of 11 applications that fall into the following categories: operations and problem management; network management; inventory, software, and user management; resource and performance management; and data and storage management. This platform has tremendous strength in the UNIX market, and HP's strong relationship with Microsoft has resulted in some tight integration with Microsoft's SMS product. Today, HP provides the OVWWW product. This has a read-only Web interface for the OpenView map, events, and MIB data, but no support for Java or SQL access to the repository data. At this time, the services are free to members of the OpenView Forum users group, however, your Openview reseller should be consulted regarding pricing. In addition, HP has the OpenView Professional Suite, which provides a read-only interface to the OpenView midlevel manager. Finally, InoTech (http://www.inotech.com) and Onion Peel Software (http://www.ops.com) sell add-ons that provide variously capable Web interfaces to OpenView.

Tivoli/IBM: Tivoli Management Environment (TME)—Operates on all major platforms including HP-UX, Sun-Solaris, Sun-OS, DECnet, NT, Netware, OS/2, OS/390 and OS/400. TME comprises 25 management applications that fall into the following five categories: deployment management, availability management, security management, operation and administration, and application management. With the integration of the Tivoli products into the IBM suite, Tivoli/IBM has an excellent but very complex product, which includes support for the 390 mainframe platform. For those looking at using the existing MF infrastructure as a Web platform, Tivoli and IBM provide a unique strength in the legacy platform areas. Tivoli provides the Tivoli TME 10 Netview product, a read-only browser interface. DEC's Polycenter Manager on Netview for NT is the same product as Tivoli's TME 10 Netview Server for Windows NT and should be extensible using similar techniques and add-on products.

While these solutions give extreme flexibility in the selection of components, this flexibility comes at a price in difficulty of configuration and complexity. In some cases, it may take six months or more for full implementation and integration of these tools in an enterprise. These tools should be implemented only with the help of an experienced systems integrator.

Integrated

The leading vendor here is Computer Associates with its UniCenter product. Over the last several years there were some concerns that CA was not committed to evolving this product, but the recent upgrade of the product demonstrates CA's commitment to this product line. The appeal of these products is simple, they are "pre-assembled," reducing the complexity and costs associated with the best of breed approaches. In addition, the user interfaces of the various application pieces are consistent, long a complaint of those who work with heterogeneous systems.

Computer Associates: UniCenter TNG supports TCP/IP, SNA, DECnet and IPX networks, and VMS, OS/400, UNIX, NT, and Windows 95 operating systems. UniCenter TNG provides end-to-end management of network systems, databases, desktops, and applications. It has an object-oriented, open extensible architecture with an interface that displays business process views and IT resources in 3-D graphics. The application's products fall into the following categories: security management, event/status/exception management, storage management, workload management, service/helpdesk, output management, database and application management, performance and accounting, network management, and job flow management. CA provides a free read-only Web interface to the UniCenter and UniCenter TNG repositories, and operates on platforms from NT to the mainframe. Interestingly, while CA's product does not support Java, it does support SQL access to the repository, something neither Tivoli nor HP provides.

Performance Management

What do we mean by *performance management?* Well, it is the ability to monitor the performance (throughput, queue length, latency) of each hardware and software component in the network application environment.

First some definitions:

Throughput

- The rate at which a processor can work, usually expressed in instructions per second
- The rate at which a network application component can work, usually expressed in transactions, jobs per hour, or some equivalent measurement of processed work over time
- The amount of data that can be carried by a communications channel, usually expressed in bytes or kilobytes per second

Latency

- The amount of time it takes a packet to cross a network from sender to receiver
- The amount of time a packet is held by a network device before it is forwarded on

Queue length

- The number of outstanding requests for a network device or application service

These concepts involve slightly differing issues depending on whether they are considered in the context of network hardware, network applications components, or actual bandwidth. These differing definitions result in differing ways of monitoring these characteristics.

Fault Isolation

Rapid fault isolation is almost impossible in the intranet environment. For example, a user calls the Help Desk because he or she cannot get access to an application. Is the failure at the browser, in an applet, in the network, in the Web server, or in the server OS? The key to fault isolation is correlated fault management, bringing together the information from the various elements and trying to isolate the various symptoms and find the disease. Many of the umbrella managers discussed provide much of the information needed to do this, but there is a level of application intrumentation that is necessary and not standard. This approach leverages readily available technologies such as SNMP to gather information about the state of the application, and can also gather information about services such as DBMS engines.

Capacity Planning

How do we plan for capacity? Well, the intranet is much easier to handle than the Internet. However, the key for designing in this environment is to build your applications with instrumentation, the ability to communicate with the underlying infrastructure and dynamically bring additional capacity online as needed. In concept, this is no different from the long-standing practice of starting additional CICS regions on the mainframe when the load on existing region resources becomes too great. This can be done manually if system monitoring is very effective; however, we believe that in today's dynamic environment it is best that applications work in concert with the underlying infrastructure to do this automatically. There continues to be a role for traditional capacity planning, but today's systems utilization is less predictable than previously. In many cases, content on the intranet is not developed by a central facility, so it is not possible to predict the needed capacity.

We recommend a basic design concept of the environment that additional capacity can bring itself on line as needed. This lends itself well to the use of multiple low-end servers, usually fronted with a load-balancing software environment.

Naming Standards

Naming standards are to provide a consistent way of identifying something. Naming standards are probably already used within your organization; for example, there may be a naming standard that is used when saving files to a common location on the network to aid coworkers attempting to identify the contents or author of the file. Most organizations today have naming standards for things like E-mail, directories, documents, user IDs, servers, and other devices. If two files on the network had the exact same name but different contents, there would be no way from the name to decipher which file was the one that you wanted. This is also true for machines connected to an intranet or the Internet. If two machines had the same name, there would be confusion as to which machine you meant to connect to. This is why naming standards are important for both an intranet and the Internet.

Naming standards need to be taken into consideration before creating an intranet. Many intranets are designed with a completely internal perspective. However, if the intranet is to be connected to the Internet, the name used internally or desired for external use may have been assigned to another organization. Stories abound of companies unable to get the names they desire, even though the names may reflect years of branding.

So far, we have described why it is important to have a naming standard, but we have not discussed why machines are given names instead of using their IP addresses. For example, if I want to connect to a file server in the New York office of Per-Se, a listing that includes BSG-CON-NYC is much easier for me to use than a listing that contains IP addresses. (See Figure 3.3.)

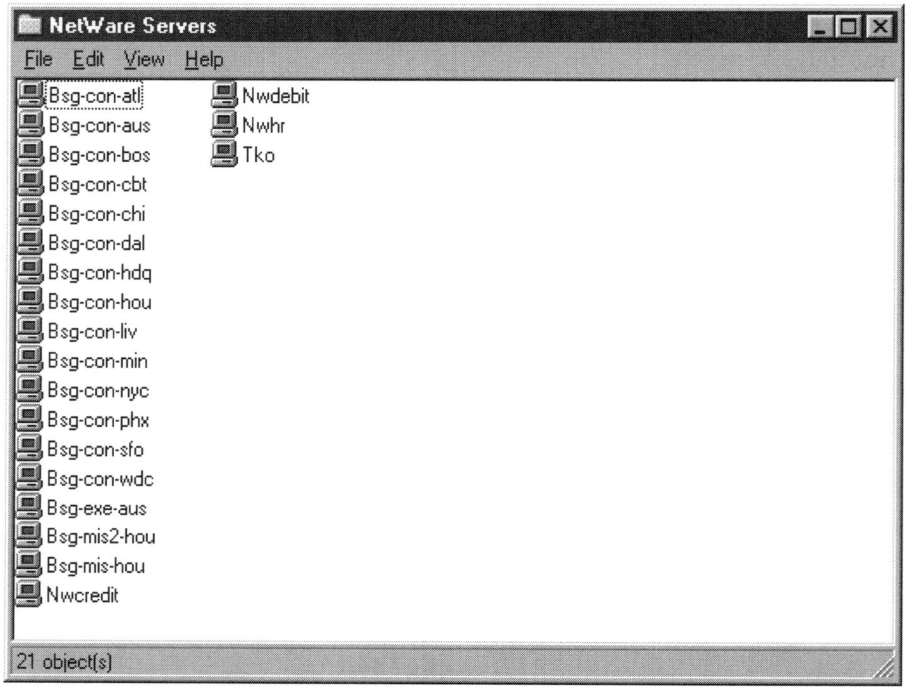

Figure 3.3 Listing of server names.

Another benefit of referring to machines by name rather than IP address resulted from the concept of *logical* addressing as opposed to *physical* addressing. This provides operators with tremendous flexibility in terms of locating, moving, and recovering services within the network environment, because users and applications (if well designed) do not deal with the physical addresses but the logicals. Thus, if the production SQL Server goes down and I recover it on another hardware platform, the user is isolated from the failure. Similarly, if my production Web server needs to scale, I can relocate to a new physical box easily.

There have been two primary systems so far that have aided in resolving names to IP addresses.

The first system was created when the Internet was a way for researchers and members of academic institutions to communicate and collaborate with each other. Network Solutions (the folks maintaining the nascent net) would receive a request for a machine to be added to the Internet. Network Solutions would assign an IP address and the requested name to the machine and would add them to a local hosts file that it maintained. Network Solutions would then distribute the hosts file to every machine on the Internet. This system worked for a while, but the hosts file grew too large to be maintained by one location and distributed to all the machines on the Internet. Even as an internal strategy this does not work. Today's intranet solutions are organic—they extend themselves at the need of the customer and business and IT cannot impose itself as an impediment to that evolution. The Domain Naming Service was developed to provide the scalability for naming that was required.

Domain Naming Service (DNS)

DNS is a hierarchical naming structure that uses a combination of text names separated by a period to develop a unique system name. For example, Bill Clinton could be "BigMac@Whitehouse .gov." While your internal DNS environment may not be very complex, it should be developed with a working assumption that it will be connected to the broader Internet environment, and this turns a fairly simple task into a fairly complex one.

DNS allows domains to be maintained at different group levels. *Domain names* are the names by which a domain is known to the network. Domain names consist of a sequence of labels separated by periods. For example, this fictitious machine name: u1.department1.companya.com. Today, Company A registers with Network Solutions on the server that maintains .com sites. Once Company A has registered, there is no longer any need for Network Solutions to be involved. The person responsible for Company A creates the domain department1. A person in department1 is now responsible for all machines in the domain. As long as the person responsible at each level makes sure that two domains do not have the same name, then the naming standard has been met, because two machines will never have the same name. This system allows the Internet to be broken up into more manageable pieces without the naming standards being compromised.

How To Name

One of the major issues to attack in building a naming structure is the appropriate use of functional, line of business, and operational parameters. What do we mean? Well, should Company A's finance database (DB) server be called:

accounting_system.companya.com
accounting_system.finance.companya.com
production_hp.finance.companya.com
production_hp.companya.com

There is no easy solution to this problem. However, naming systems for devices that are organizationally dependent tend to be the least optimal situation since changes to the organization can require extensive changes to the underlying naming structure. This results in such problems as addressing instability and errors. Generally, a functional specification such as the first naming option above gets our vote, although politics can play a significant role in naming. Frequently, lines of business that "buy" servers require that they be reserved for them alone and often mandate that the naming structure reflect their ownership. The best way to avoid this type of complication is to establish a policy early on.

What To Name

DNS is a hardwired environment in which *host names* are assigned to IP addresses and generally managed manually. With the rapid proliferation of TCP/IP to the desktop in support of the intranet, manually maintaining addresses for all devices is not practical. Instead, we recommend splitting devices into two groupings: *clients* and *servers, networking devices,* and *gateways.* Client machines are best handled with tools such as DHCP and bootp, since their names and addresses do not need to be static and well known through the machine environment. Server-class machines should have DNS entries, since they need to be well known and reliable. See Table 3.1.

TABLE 3.1 DNS versus DHCP Use

DNS Assigned	DHCP/bootp
File server	Desktop clients
Mail servers	Laptop clients
DB servers	Personal communication devices
Mail gateways	
Bridges	
Routers	
Switches	
Management consoles	
Mainframes	
Web servers	
FTP servers	

DNS and System Redundancy

The use of DNS to support servers has an additional benefit: supporting your contingency plan. By maintaining a server name/address centrally, a service can be recreated on another server quickly, and the DNS system will propagate the addressing change and reroute users to it. For example:

A client machine is using a Sybase "ini" file to point to a server called "hp_production.companya.com." In the DNS server, this address is mapped to 123.123.123.456. However, this server fails, and it is desirable that a replicated version on the server "hp_development.companya.com" (123.123.123.789) assume the role as the production server. In the DNS mapping, the entry for "hp_production.companya.com" is remapped to 123.123.123.456. Users who try to connect to hp_production.companya.com will now be directed to the new device.

This type of solution does not provide the nonstop environment that many applications need, but is often very appropriate for less critical environments where high-end fault-tolerant hardware/ software combinations are inappropriate. It requires users to reestablish their context (login) to the server, and DNS propagation delays (the amount of time it takes DNS servers to replicate changes to the hosts files) can result in some delays and inconsistencies in terms of what servers are hit. Thus, we recommend *DNS failover* as a solution for noncritical applications such as EIS/DSS and similar solutions. It should not be used for mission-critical transaction systems and the like, although it is often positioned that way for the budget conscious.

DNS has a round-robin assignment capability that allows traffic in the Web environment to be crudely balanced among several servers, but this solution does not scale well or provide balancing based on true utilization of the devices in question. Again, this is often touted as a way for people to get scalability in their environments, but we have found that the lack of integration to the underlying application environment makes this a poor solution for systems that truly have a highly dynamic use. While most current intranet systems do not, the idea of taking intranet-implemented processes and making them externally enabled (the *extranet*) means that your intranet architecture must be non-stop.

How DNS Works

A hierarchical naming structure, DNS also has a hierarchical name resolution process (see Figure 3.4). When a user makes a request for a named resource, the client IP stack first checks its local cache to see if the name has been previously resolved and, if so, uses that IP address for the request. It will also check a local hosts file, which is a local mapping of names and addresses. However, if the name cannot be resolved, the client will send the name to a local DNS device to see if it knows of the requested device. This can be the case if:

- The local DNS server knows the IP address because the machine is within its domain.
- The local DNS server knows the IP address because the machine was requested by another user recently and it is still stored on the machine.

In the case in which a local DNS entity does not have knowledge of the required address, it can query a higher-level DNS device to see if it knows about the device. As you can see, just

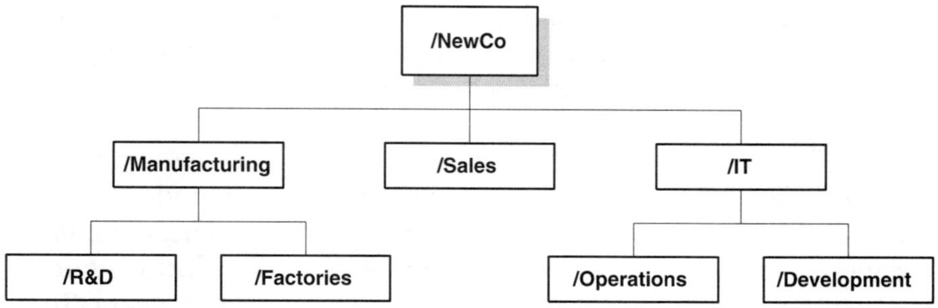

Figure 3.4 DNS naming hierarchy.

within a corporate intranet environment this means that naming must be managed at an enterprise level so that devices can readily exchange and keep current information.

Copyrights and Branding

The industry is rife with stories of companies that have tried to register a domain and found that another company or individual has taken the name. In many cases, it is alleged that these infringe on trademarks, copyrights, or well-established brands that have significant value to a company. While we will not debate the validity of the law, we will caution readers to include an external domain name registration in their intranet development and management strategies. While you may not think it is necessary today, every study we conduct and read externally shows that companies are hooking up to the Internet, and a naming policy that does not seek to manage to that eventuality is professionally irresponsible.

When considering such registrations, consider not only your company name, but any major brands you own that have value. To get an indication of whether such a thing exists in your company, talk to your CFO and find out whether you carry any value on your books for "goodwill" and what the justification for that is. In many cases a brand is considered an asset, and a lack of positive action to protect it can result in diminished corporate value and possible lawsuits by shareholders. While today that means registering within the .com domain, the next section will discuss some future directions of which you should be aware and which you need to consider in your intranet naming strategy.

THE FUTURE

Up until now, Network Solutions has been solely responsible for maintaining the list of Internet top-level domains. These domains are .com, .edu, .gov, .org, .mil, and .net. Network Solutions currently charges $100 to register a domain name for two years. To register a domain name with Network Solutions, contact http://internic.net.

In January 1997, the Internet Society (ISOC) ratified a proposal to expand the Internet top-level domains in order to add more machines and domains to the Internet. The proposal also called for new registries to compete with Network Solutions. The government believes that there should be more than one registrar to increase competition in order to reduce costs. Suggestions for new domains include .firm, .store, .web, .arts, .rec, .info, .nom.

Many companies are trying to reserve their current names in all of these new domains. The analogy we draw is to the 800 and 888 telephone implementations whereby companies had well-known numbers and mnemonic equivalents (800-FLOWERS, for example). When 888 came up as an extension to the toll-free numbering system, such companies were concerned that competitors could reserve the equivalent in the 888 code. However, if everyone simply runs out and reserves all of the domain equivalents in the new domains, we have made no progress toward developing a broader class of naming and probably none toward developing a more specific structure.

It is alleged by some in the industry that if a company does not actively pursue a trade name on every domain, a new company may select that name. The new company can claim that the old company did not actively pursue protection of its copyrighted name; therefore, the original company has no right to the name on the new domain, even though it may have copyrighted the name. We urge you to get your legal and marketing staffs involved in this process now, even if you are only working on your intranet implementation.

Many people in the industry believe that allowing other registrars to control domain naming will cause confusion and allow on the Internet many different naming standards that may not be able to communicate with each other. Many are afraid that the Internet will become a network of islands that will not be able to talk to each other. This issue was still in discussion as this book went to press. The authors advise that the resolution be researched before creating an intranet or attaching to the Internet.

IP Addressing

IP addressing is one of system management's most vexing but easily avoided problems. It requires planning, discipline, and process, irrespective of the amount of technology applied to solving the problem. However, many organizations grew their IP addressing schemes organically and, as a result, have created a nightmare environment for additions, moves, and changes. IP addresses are 32-bit numbers represented as ###.###.###.### where the digits in a field can range from 0 to 255. However, "0" and "255" should be avoided since these are reserved numbers with special meaning. By way of explanation, there are several different *classes* of address, only two of which (B and C) concern us here. Few companies have a class A address.

The class of an address is determined by the number of significant digits over which you have control.

- *Class B:* 123.123.###.###: Provides 64,534 addresses
- *Class C:* 123.123.123.###: Provides 254 addresses

An additional complication: We are running out of addresses! While it is now old news, most were shocked when the popularity of the Internet exhausted the pool of available addresses. Many companies with only several hundred clients got class B numbers early on. While class Cs are available, their restricted numbering range (254 nodes) makes it difficult to cobble together a manageable numbering strategy. What a conundrum—Class C's ranges are inadequate and Class B's are unavailable!

SOLUTION SCENARIO

Anticipating and Proactively Expanding Network Capacity

Figure 3.5 reflects the basic format of a dynamic, proactive intranet design. The high degree of redundancy allows for basic tenets of intranet planning to be followed: Losing a server does not render a service unavailable. The accent on a large number of less expensive machines runs through the design, where direct access storage devices (DASDs) are inexpensive and readily upgradable. Relying on SCSI systems allows the ready expansion of the disk infrastructure by adding an additional drive. Only in the case of persistent data such as a production DBMS, a security system, or other high-value storage is there a need to go to expensive redundant array of independent disks (RAID) and other systems. The availability is gained through running multiple instances of processes and having sufficient intelligence in the environment to detect and respond to a failure.

Elements in the architecture have, as appropriate, SNMP MIBs for the following components:

- Server OS: Monitors RAM, cache, threads, processes, disk I/O, queue lengths
- Network interface: Transmit/receive buffers
- Applications: Thread usage, RAM utilization, process queue lengths
- Network: Transmit/receive packets, device utilization, packet forward rate, CPU utilization, bandwidth utilization (backplane), bandwidth utilization by channel

(*continued*)

SOLUTION SCENARIO *Continued*

The design achieves its flexibility in several ways:

Additional capacity. Each component has a policy guideline for maximum usage; for example, if CPU utilization on an application server goes in excess of 75 percent for a sustained period, the console will instantiate another instance of the application server, pictured in Figure 3.5 as Application Server Instance #2. Similarly, if the Web server cannot locate an instance of an application, or the requested instance takes longer than the Web server is allowed to wait by policy, then the server will automatically route the request to the next registered instance of the application. Of course, this means that each component must be engineered to provide the interfaces to not only provide the requisite information, but also to respond to directives from the console.

Failover. If a component in the architecture fails, the effect of having multiple instances available allows for the ability to roll over to another instance.

The deficiency in the design shown in Figure 3.5 is one of state. In the case in which a transaction fails, there is not sufficient knowledge of the state of the transaction to make the switch seamlessly from the user's perspective. The architecture can be extended to have a state server coupled with the use of CORBA objects versus MS COM/DCOM components. These objects, having knowledge of their state, can make that state persistent. In case of a failure, the object can be automatically reinstantiated with full knowledge of its state. There is tremendous overhead in such a design, but the use of inexpensive hardware allows for these services to be provided in a cost-effective fashion.

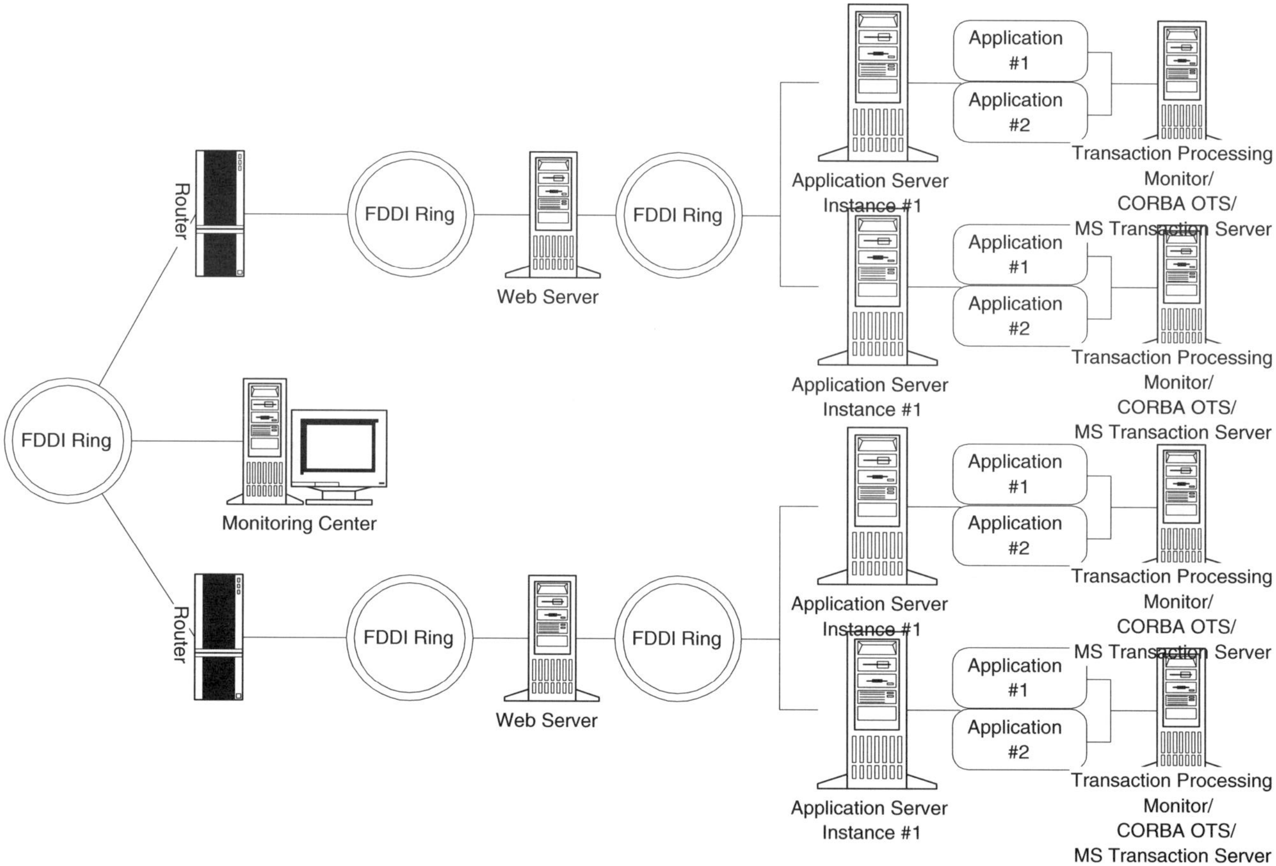

Figure 3.5 Redundant intranet design.

The IETF is working to resolve this by adopting IPv6, the successor protocol to the current implementation (IPv4). Part of IPv6 is the move to 128-bit addresses, and the specification provides for backward compatibility by embedding the 32-bit IPv4 address in the least significant bits of the 128-bit address. However, support for IPv6 is just emerging and the plethora of addresses does not diminish the need for a rational and disciplined approach to address management in the organization.

TIP *If you are considering moving to IPV6, plan, test and refine! There is no cookbook for making it happen, but here are some suggestions we have based on our experiences:*

1. *Read: Articles and books, white papers and IETF RFC's. Educate yourself about the changes in IPV6 so you can educate others about its value*
2. *Identify the Value Propositions: Going to IPV6 has to be pushed by more than getting more IP addresses for your company. When you think you have understood its scope and value, make a list of how the changes will provide value to your organization. Some of you will find security important because hooking your legacy systems to your intranet has been a goal, others will embrace RSVP or enhanced Multicasting/Anycasting support. Develop the business case, and identify the initial impact on your environment, paying close attention to platform and SW upgrades.*
3. *Build the Test Environment: Using the business case and listing of impacted systems, design a test environment that will truly prove the concepts and complexity on those platforms you think are critical. Do not fall victim to the practice of testing on a couple of PC servers and calling that sufficient. You need to prove the* reality *of the solution, that means good and bad.*

4. *Contact your host, network device and desktop OS vendors, and determine the dates for availability of IPV6. In some cases, they will be providing transition strategies like IP4 Tunnelling, find out the nature and limits of these solutions as well. For those of you with LAN servers handling "translational bridging" between heterogeneous LANs (Ethernet to Token Ring for example), make sure to factor your NOS vendor into the picture.*
5. *Revise your IPV6 address records as specified in RFC 1886. This will require updating a DNS server.*
6. *Contact the 6Bone, using their mailing list (send "subscribe6bone" to majordomo@isi.edu) or their web site www.6bone.lbl.gov/6bone, and determine how to configure your tunnel. The 6Bone is an IPV6 network which is maintained to assist in this transition testing effort.*
7. *Define an IPV6 test address using RFC 1897 guidelines, and configure the tunnel to the 6Bone.*
8. *Play, test, break, stress, plan and move forward with patience and persistence.*

As a rule, we recommend several guidelines for setting up an IP environment:

- Use dynamic addressing for clients; static addressing for servers.
- Get a legitimate, registered IP address from the InterNIC, your Telco vendor, or a similar external agency that has access to real Internet address ranges. If you cannot, then explore the use of a Network Address Translation (NAT)–capable firewall or router and use the reserved private network addresses (RFC 1918).
- Make use of the subnetting capabilities of IP to uniquely identify segments.

TIP *Many companies have implemented their own IP numbering schemes over the years. In many cases, companies have implemented IP numbering schemes which are not registered with InterNic. As a result, intranets which are deployed on this environment cannot be hooked readily to the public Internet, often limiting the ability to interconnect the two. For most companies, the costs and complexity of retro-fitting their existing environment is a barrier they cannot easily overcome. However, there are ways to handle this.*

One of the most effective transition mechanisms is the Network Address Translator (NAT). The NAT sits between the local network and the external network, and converts private internal addresses to registered Internet addresses. If NAT's sound like another router or firewall, it occupies a similar position in the network, and some of the router and firewall vendors are offering these types of services in their products.

NAT's are not a cure all, they can well support this type of translation for small networks. The NAT has to look into and change every packet that goes through, and this a tremendous load. In addition, some applications embed their addresses in the packet payload, up above the Network Layer. Significantly, the Windows Internet Name Service (WINS) can be problematic, as can certain Domain Name servers.

So, while we see a role for NAT systems in the evolution of your intranet, we do not see them as a long term solution. Use them judiciously, and make them tactical.

Dynamic Addressing

Dynamic addressing or address pooling is a critical component of an effective network management strategy, because it provides the ability to easily move physical devices with minimal physical intervention or reconfiguration. If you are using a network management tool that will automatically map devices based on their IP addresses, you need to be careful, since dynamically assigned devices will not always have the same IP address. This generally requires tracking physical devices using the Media Access Control

(MAC) layer address, which is burned into the network interface card (NIC) by the manufacturer. Collecting this information will likely require some changes to the current asset management and data collection process to ensure that the appropriate information is gathered at time of installation and as NICs are replaced.

Dynamic addressing uses a concept of *address pooling,* in which a series of addresses is given to a server that dynamically assigns them as clients come online. Those of you who implemented mainframe gateway products such as Netware SAA or Microsoft's SNA Server will recognize this process, which is analogous to the pooling and dynamic assignment of logical unit (LU) addresses in the Systems Network Architecture (SNA)/Virtual Terminal Access Method (VTAM) world of the mainframe. Dynamic assignment has many of the same benefits in the IP world, reducing management of the end devices.

Technology Alternatives

There are two major technologies at your disposal in developing a dynamic IP address assignment plan: the Dynamic Host Control Protocol (DHCP) and bootp protocols. Both provide address pooling, which allows a device's MAC layer board ID to be dynamically assigned an IP address, but DHCP, the newer of the two, provides more robust concepts, such as variable-length reservations, and is also natively supported in the Microsoft Windows 95 and NT environments.

BOOTP

bootp was originally designed to cooperate with a suite of IP protocols (TFTP, ARP, RARP, ICMP) as a transport mechanism for configuration information. With a UNIX genesis, bootp was the ubiquitous solution for the automatic assignment of IP addresses within many early adopters of intranet technology, and companies like Novell developed bootp server implementations. However, as the need for IP addresses expanded, bootp rapidly showed its age, and it needed to be extended. Nevertheless, bootp is still very common, especially among early-adopter shops that have extensive legacy investments in early UNIX hosts and/or workstations.

While bootp is not a bad solution, the successor to it, DHCP, is a much better engineered solution for a different scale of old problems and a different set of new ones. Most companies are finding a need to implement both to handle this transitional period, and we anticipate that need to continue for several more years as companies like Microsoft clean up their DHCP implementations and legacy OSs without DHCP support are aged out of sites.

DHCP

In response to the deficiencies of bootp, DHCP was born. There are two major differences between the two:

- DHCP provides for reservations on addresses, which supports the serial assignment to clients and the recovery of unused addresses.
- DHCP can provide all of the necessary IP configuration parameters needed in order for a client to operate.

As you can see in Figure 3.6, DHCP can do much more than simply allocate addresses dynamically. This client had no IP address, DNS server, DHCP server, or gateway specified at boot, yet it picked up all the requisite information by advertising for a DHCP server.

Thus, the ideal candidate as a DHCP client is a machine that will have a greater likelihood of relocation or one connected to the network from multiple points (transient client over multiple subnets). In addition, DHCP can help manage a small number of IP addresses by reclaiming them as client reservations expire. This latter behavior is one that bootp never had, and is critical for shops where addresses are limited.

In an effort to leverage as much of the bootp environment as possible and not require a DHCP host on every segment, DHCP can make use of *bootp relay agents,* a network host or router that can pass DHCP messages between a DHCP server and client. Thus, DHCP can be well managed into an evolutionary intranet strategy. The use of similar structures allows (in theory) bootp clients to interoperate with DHCP servers. However, this behavior is very vendor-specific, and DHCP server vendors should be grilled about

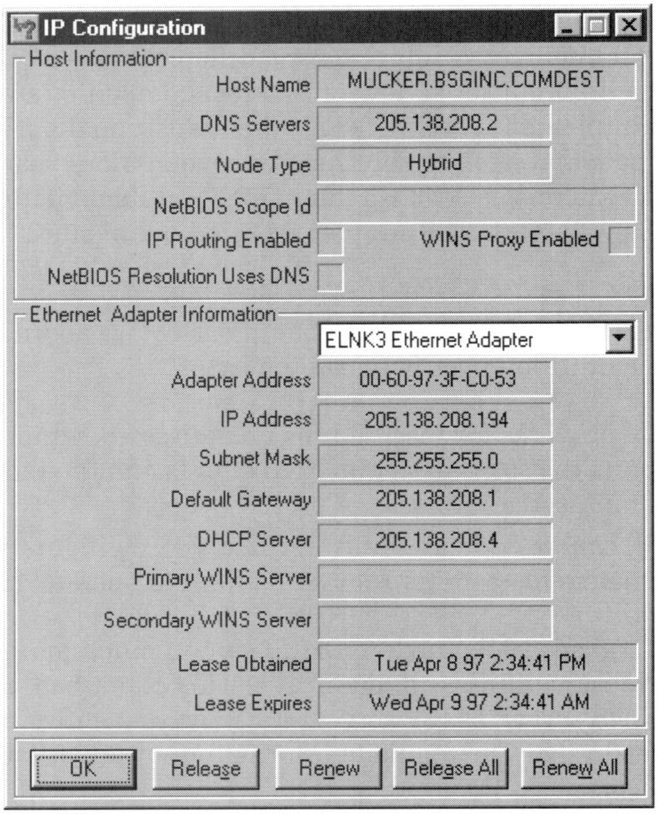

Figure 3.6 Sample DHCP screen.

compliance prior to a selection being made of a particular product. Surprisingly, OS/2 has one of the more robust and compliant implementations of the DHCP server, and Windows NT, in our last exposure, was very limited and oriented toward Windows client support.

Assigning Addresses DHCP has three ways of assigning addresses, but it is important to note that only the first will actually provide dynamic addressing. Most environments using DHCP will likely use a mix of these:

Dynamic allocation. The DHCP server is granted a pool of addresses by the administrator. When a DHCP client connects, the server grants an address to the client for some period of time (the reservation) or until the client voluntarily relinquishes the address. This allows for addresses to be periodically reclaimed and is the most common implementation behavior for DHCP in organizations.

Automatic allocation. The DHCP server assigns a permanent address to a client. This can be well used in conjunction with the DNS environment to manage logical and physical naming for servers and other static devices within your intranet.

Manual allocation. The administrator manually assigns IP addresses to the client devices, and the DHCP server is used to tell the client what that assigned address is. In this case, the DHCP server serves as a repository for addressing information, a necessary if limited role. Like automatic allocation, this can be well used with DNS.

Summary

Here we have seen that the same rigor and discipline that is typical of legacy system management is required to run an efficient intranet communications infrastructure. Of particular importance is the management of bandwidth, traffic, and performance, as all are crucial for reliable system performance. Granted, some of the issues of concern in an intranet appear new—especially concerns about IP addressing and DNS—but knowing how to recognize them will help you assess, address, and hopefully prevent them before they affect a mission-critical system.

CHAPTER FOUR

Hardware Evolution

When looking at managing a hardware (HW) environment, which includes planning its growth, there are infinite factors that need to be reconciled. There are infinite combinations of these factors, and there are not infinite other places you can find another job. However, we can cut through this maze of alternatives and focus on the several that really matter. You can, of course, make things more complex, but the following are the factors that need to be best understood to manage the complex interdependencies of the hardware platform:

- Server hardware platform
- Web server software
- Application type
- Network design
- Continuity of business strategy

Ultimately, intranet platforms need to be designed and built for tremendous scalability, if only because we do not know such things as how they ultimately will be used and how many people will use them. With an increasing tendency to use them as a way of wrapping legacy systems, the trend toward including robust components (Java/ActiveX), and the integration of voice, video, and other rich data, we cannot predict usage with a traditional level of discipline. However, that does not excuse the often irresponsible lack of planning we see in many ad hoc intranet efforts.

Frequently, the approach for building the intranet continues to be a pilot (read: "quick hack job using whatever tools can be downloaded for free and running on whatever machine is undefended") that rapidly grows into a production system. If this type of "evolution" is your institutional approach, then be prepared for rewrites, rehosting, rework, and recrimination.

Server Platform

When researching this chapter, we took the opportunity to talk with folks from a number of the major hardware vendors about the issue of servers and platforms. You should be happy to know that they all expressed a tremendous willingness to provide you with as much hardware as you need. In all seriousness, what they reinforced was that the spectrum of hardware alternatives continues to grow. With constantly improving processors, high-performance bus architectures, faster disk drives, and so on, the options are tremendous. Most companies already have a set of server hardware platforms that are standard—in many cases, one of these will be very suitable. In some cases, none will be.

For example, one of our clients had a rule that all NT boxes would be of a single Intel processor variety. This was because NT was positioned as departmental file server, and the growth model was to use cheaper servers. When an intranet solution was proposed and Microsoft's IIS was selected, it was impossible to get a multiprocessor Intel box through purchasing since there was no standard. The process for getting an exception required an appeal to the Technology Standards Committee (it was meeting in six weeks) and then approval by the CIO. We bought one on a personal credit card and carried it in one morning as a test machine, then let the business units fight with IS about it.

We can bring a little sanity to this process by trying to categorize the major HW platform types and providing some guidelines for their use. However, processors are changing every 18 months; bus architectures like PCI are evolving rapidly; clustering alternatives are emerging quickly. Do your homework before you buy; watch the market as you evolve. You never make the right decision in retrospect. Most of this discussion will focus on UNIX and NT platforms. I know, you can use the MVS mainframe for a Web server; you can use your AS/400. So we start our discussion with IBM.

IBM: Proprietary But Effective

Most of our clients have IBM or clone mainframes, and several have investments in AS/400 systems as well. Depending on which set of statistics you read, mainframe platforms contain about 80 percent to 90 percent of the mission-critical data and processes supporting business today. However, none of our clients have elected to use the MVS platform as their strategic direction for Internet- or intranet-based systems, in spite of their tremendous investment in and experience with the platform. Don't dismiss this solution out of hand for several reasons, including the obvious one that these systems have extensive management infrastructures and operations practices associated with their use and the more subtle reason that your IBM salesperson will likely call your boss and suggest the solution.

TIP *As this book was going to press, IBM made announcements regarding the re-positioning of the AS/400 as a Web Server, and a new release of the 390 operating system which also provided Web services. IBM continues to enhance these machines, and for many companies these announcements look attractive. In our experience, the 390 platform, especially the CMOS implementations, are much better suited to this use if you feel you must.*

The S390 CMOS boxes are fully participating members of the IBM environment, with excellent support for IBM's MQ Series, CORBA, and DCE. In addition, there is a much bigger integration market for MVS, with resultant support from vendors like Microsoft, BEA, Momentum, Peerlogic, and others. This makes integrating and leveraging the mainframe data and process very possible and highly facilitated through tools, and provides a longer life perspective on this platform in the overall architecture.

In spite of the recent announcements, we see the AS/400 as continuing to be oriented towards highly self-contained applications, not as a general purpose server. This feeling is supported by the Independent Software Vendors who continue to develop applications for the "Application Server 400", but do not seem to be producing enabling technology for its integration or its general participation.

The major reasons for using these legacy platforms revolve around security and integration. For years, IBM has been securing its customers' platforms. Many corporate customers, overwhelmed by the immaturity of most intranet companies and their products, see IBM as a company that has a reputation for delivering and supporting high-end solutions. In addition, IBM's centralized solutions eliminate a tremendous amount of near-term complexity from the management puzzle. However, we do not see this as a long-term direction for most of our customers and will not explore scalability in that model any further, since most IS shops know how to scale these systems. They have been doing it for longer than most Web professionals have been alive.

Hardware Architectures

Depending on the hardware architecture you choose, you have very different scalability solutions available to you. One of the key questions in considering these alternatives is your need to take forward your current software environment and use off-the-shelf products. Several of these solutions require specialized/optimized software solutions or have very complex operations requirements that require special hiring and supporting technologies. Some solutions are less mature; some more readily extensible; some have very different price points.

Hardware architectures are more than the processor and bus design. When considering a hardware platform, look for balance. Having four Pentium Pro processors chugging away is meaningless if you use 16-bit ISA disk controllers that cannot keep them fed. Conversely, a machine that can dish thousands of pages per second may be overkill if you are using a single Ethernet card to talk to the network. You get the point.

The following discusses four primary hardware architecture alternatives. No, this does not represent the entirety of all possible solutions in the market. Yes, there are unmentioned vendors and yours may be one of them. No, omission does not mean they are unacceptable or bad. Yes, we are only publishing information that is readily available in the public domain, since information we receive under nondisclosure is privileged and subject to change as the vendors move their products forward. Thus, when you begin to think about hardware management strategies, you should contact your vendor for an update on their strategy. Of course, you can always hire a consultant to come in and help you manage the process of reviewing vendors, solutions, and strategies. However, make sure, whatever you buy, that you have the knowledge base and tools in place to integrate it into your management infrastructure, not to mention the budget and time allowed in the work plan.

The major models are:

- Symmetric multiprocessing (SMP)
- Clustering
- Nonuniform memory access (NUMA)
- Massively parallel processing (MPP)

How are they different? Well, you can consider that the models vary by how much they share with involved systems. What do they share? Mostly the contention in a multiprocessor system is for access to the system bus and shared memory resources. See Table 4.1.

SMP—SYMMETRIC MULTIPROCESSING

SMP machines have been *the* scaling solution in LAN and workgroup solutions for the past ten years. SMP machines provided an inexpensive and relatively uncomplicated way to add power to a server platform with minimal operational dislocation or software changes. Of course, there was always some tuning to do when

TABLE 4.1 Hardware Architecture Comparisons

Architecture Model	Pros	Cons	Vendors	Cost
SMP	Common implementations supporting most UNIX implementations and NT/Alpha/Intel. "Commoditized" designs are well supported by software vendors. Large ISV product selection.	Limited scalability by vendor and OS.	Compaq Data General Dell Digital Hewlett-Packard IBM NCR Pyramid Sun Microsystems	$
Clustering	Implementations from major UNIX vendors. Failover capability provides good single-site continuity of business characteristics.	Administration complexity grows with each node added. Software needs to be extended/modified to effectively use clustering. Applications need to be architected/partitioned to effectively use hardware model, compensate for possible internode communications bottlenecks.	Digital (UNIX) Digital (Open VMS) Hewlett-Packard IBM Sequent Sun Microsystems	$$
NUMA	Extended SMP model allows leveraging of current technology knowledge. No changes to applications required when additional processors are added. Allows interconnection of commodity processors. High degree of scalability.	New technology means limited support for the technology in vendor, ISV, and consulting venues. Limited commercial implementations mean limited reference implementations. Dependence on high-bandwidth bus interconnection technology, which is relatively new.	Data General Sequent Hewlett Packard	$$

TABLE 4.1 *Continued* Hardware Architecture Comparisons

Architecture Model	Pros	Cons	Vendors	Cost
MPP	Massive scalability. Near-linear scalability for each additional node. Single-system view of all nodes irrespective of growth.	Applications need to be designed for parallelism. Highly skilled operators and programmers needed. Limited external support resources (ISV, consultants, vendors). Highly proprietary technology. Costs can start at approximately 2× NUMA costs.	IBM NCR Pyramid Tandem	$$$

additional processors were added to a system, but that was never an elaborate or even a required activity. In essence, SMP machines, especially in the early days of client/server, were a cheap insurance policy against outgrowing the selected application platform. This was a reasonable thing, since many of the applications being developed had no previous history and thus no predictability of use. We used to joke that most client/server systems failed because they were victims of their own success—that is, their value added to the business was so great it outstripped all the design parameters.

While several vendors provided us with their own test results on processor scalability, we found that their platforms were highly optimized and their numbers did not really reflect our experience. The numbers shown in Figure 4.1 correspond more closely to what we have seen in the field. This degradation results from the highly shared nature of SMP machine resources. Sharing ultimately means contention (just look at any playground). Because of this degradation, many of today's basic SMP architecture machines are limited to four- to eight-processor designs.

Managing this type of design is fairly easy, since the tools for it are mature. However, it is important to understand that SMP sys-

Solution Scenario

The best example we have of the value of the SMP architecture comes from a client in the gas industry in 1991. At that time, the Federal Energy Resource Commission (FERC) had ordered the deregulation of the gas industry, an action similar to that currently affecting the electrical utility industry. Working with a customer on a very tight schedule, we designed and built a system using PowerBuilder and Oracle running on a Compaq SystemPro running SCO UNIX. Since we were moving into a business that was new, there were no real metrics for sizing. The value of the open architecture and SMP was proven as the company moved from the SystemPro to a Sun SMP machine and then grew that to a four-processor implementation. This was not a painless process, but the ability to continue running the same application and scale it within a chassis without modification provided the business with tremendous value and continuity.

The lesson from this was what is referred to as "headroom." When buying SMP architecture machines, always look at the vendor's product line and whether there is additional scalability with binary compatibility. If you outgrow this box, does the vendor have another chassis that is bigger in terms of processor count supported, number of expansion slots, and performance of processors, or possibly a clustering arrangement that will allow you to move your application environment (binary portability) without rearchitecting? In short, when you look at your anticipated performance numbers relative to a box, how far away is the ceiling?

Of course, SMP machines are not a panacea. Since the processors share the memory bus, the additional horsepower provided by each additional processor is not quite linear. How that falls off is very dependent on the vendor's hardware

(*continued*)

SOLUTION SCENARIO *Continued*

implementation, operating system, and compilers. In essence, the problem is a simple one analogous to a traffic management problem on a highway. With a certain number of cars, a highway is an efficient place. While exits and entrances are finite, the contention between cars is such that traffic flow is unimpeded. However, at some point the contention between the cars as they try to use these facilities results in traffic backups and a rapid degradation of performance. A hypothetical graph for this might look like Figure 4.1.

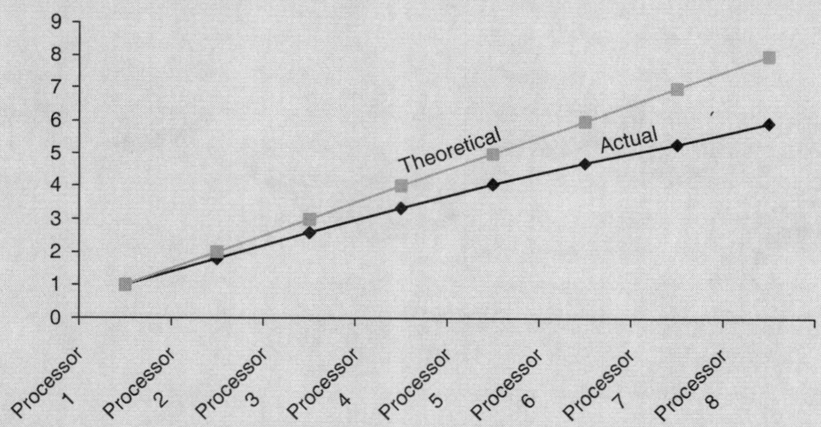

Figure 4.1 SMP processor efficiency graph (theoretical).

tems behavior is very operating system–dependent. The ability of SMP to provide services without requiring application changes results from the willingness of hardware vendors to put SMP services in their OS. That means that an SMP hardware platform that is currently running NT will exhibit different performance characteristics if that same chassis is used to support SCO UNIX or DEC's UNIX. Managing this type of hardware platform requires an excellent understanding of the underlying OS and how it operates. To extend the preceding example a little further, NT's thread management scheme and its interaction with the OS are very different from SCO's multiprocess scheme, and these behave very differently on the same hardware, even if they are still running Sybase 11. It is important that your hardware management team understand how the OS works, since that type of information is critical to effectively predicting bottlenecks in platform architectures and helping application developers make the most effective use of the underlying model. (See Figure 4.2.)

CLUSTERING

So you have a charter to build the new trading system for your company, but the twist is that it will be using Internet technolo-

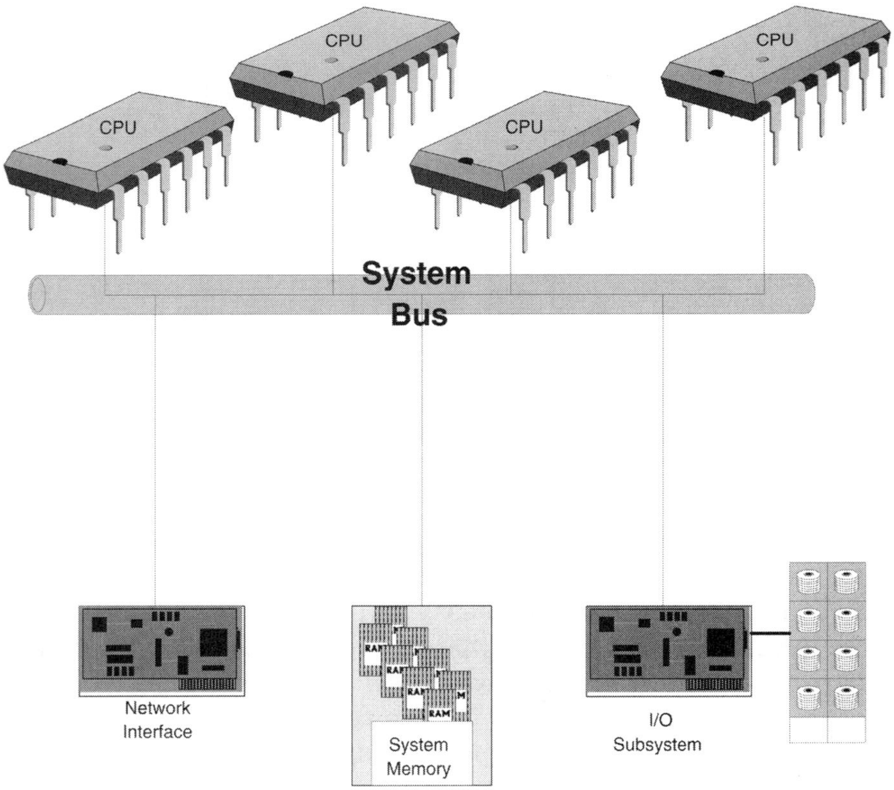

Figure 4.2 SMP architecture graphic.

gies. However, it must also meet the requirements of reliability, as well as scalability. What to do? You could send E-mail to the authors (aroehr@msn.com is one) but think about a clustering solution for hardware. Clustering allows multiple machines to be hooked together, creating a single system image to the application. Since these can be multiple SMP boxes, you can suddenly find yourself with the power of a "server farm" at your application's disposal. Therefore, how is clustering different from SMP? For purposes of this discussion, we will assume that a cluster has three characteristics:

1. Each node has its own copy of the operating system.
2. Each node has its own copy of the application.
3. The participating nodes in the cluster share certain resources, most commonly disk drives.

Contrast this model with the shared-everything SMP model we discussed previously. As you can see, clustering is really just ganging together a group of machines and implementing a software layer that can let them interact. Sounds easy, no? No. There is the issue of *coherency*. In a single-processor machine, a single piece of data (a *datum*) can be modified by only one processor. In a multiprocessor machine, the possibility exists that a piece of data can be modified by two processors at the same time. In an SMP implementation, the fact that all processors used the same shared memory and instance of the OS makes it relatively easy to keep processors from stepping on each other. Of course, each processor actually has its own local cache, which needs to be updated when a datum used by two processors and maintained in each cache is changed, but for purposes of this discussion let's assume the processors can make that happen. In actuality, most SMP designs can actually do this with hardware, making the process very fast but fairly expensive. It also makes porting applications from one SMP architecture to another a relatively easy process. In clustered systems, the complexity of maintaining coherency increases dramatically, since the processors do not share memory and the latency (delay) associated with interprocessor communications is much higher between network separated nodes. This is done through a complex arrangement of locks, which needs to be managed and maintained by the OS. This makes the process relatively slow as opposed to hardware designs, but makes it cheaper in hardware.

The conclusion that can reasonably be drawn from the above is that clustering systems tend to work best when used with systems that can be designed to minimize interprocess communications. Oracle's Parallel Server (OPS) is a good example of an application that was architected from the ground up to leverage this concept. In OPS, the server can send specific query components to the appropriate node, where the query is processed and the data passed back to a node, which then manages the joins and similar set manipulation. By using this approach, Oracle allows the nodes to work with maximum parallelism while minimizing internodal communications.

In addition to the obvious scalability benefits, clustering, with appropriate software, database, and application support, throws in the benefit of allowing the loss of one node without affecting the others participating. The brief illustration of OPS above points out a significant lesson: To operate effectively in a clustered architecture, the application must be designed from the beginning to isolate processes and minimize internodal traffic. This does not come for free, and it is not easy. Programming for a clustered environment is much more difficult than for an SMP environment. In addition, databases designed to run in a clustered environment require high-end physical data design experience, since optimizing the physical database design in a networked environment has to take into account the underlying node interconnect technology as well as the normal issues of indexes, number of spindles, and so on. However, the "Big four" database vendors (IBM, Oracle, Informix, Sybase) all provide DB implementations that will hide much of the complexity once the system is in, so, while the database administration (DBA) and operations staff need some really solid skills, the programming staff is generally insulated from the complexity of the underlying implementation.

In a multitiered model or distributed object model where multiple instances of a service can exist and can be brokered, clusters can be a great solution that provides scalability and high availability. This can become an excellent element in your continuity of business strategy. In this mode, a physical server can be lost without the loss of the services it is hosting to the overall environment, since the data that it is working with is on the shared device, and the brokering service of the transaction monitor or the object request broker can redirect the application to another instance of the service that has access to the state (data) of the failed process or object.

Figure 4.3 shows how a cluster might look. If you look at this picture, you see a circle in the center, which is the internetworking (here represented by an FDDI network symbol) that keeps these systems talking. Companies like Tandem and DEC have produced highly customized connection devices to provide the bandwidth that was required in years past, and today's solutions seem to be inclined toward leveraging solutions such as ATM or Fast/Switched Ethernet to provide the high-speed connectivity needed. Why? In the standard SMP model, CPUs are distributed across the shared memory bus, and this is really fast. For example, a four-processor Compaq Prosignia 5000 uses a *split bus* architecture, which provides high throughput with very low latency. In a clustered environment, those processors are now communicating through an entire network stack (all seven layers), waiting for network resources, and so on. Thus, the interconnection can obviously become a bottleneck. In addition, if the interconnect itself is not redundant, you can have a highly available architecture whose elements cannot intercommunicate!

What about Microsoft? As of this writing, there are several proprietary NT clustering schemes from vendors such as Tandem, NCR, DEC, and Data General. Vendors such as HP are moving their UNIX clustering products—for example, ServiceGuard—over to the NT environment to provide the robust features found in those products, and they are leveraging the hooks into products such as Open View to provide an operationally integrated cluster architecture. These vendors have committed extensive resources to building clustering into their implementations of NT to provide the scalability and high availability needed for some applications. Tandem and DEC are two of the oldest players in the clustering

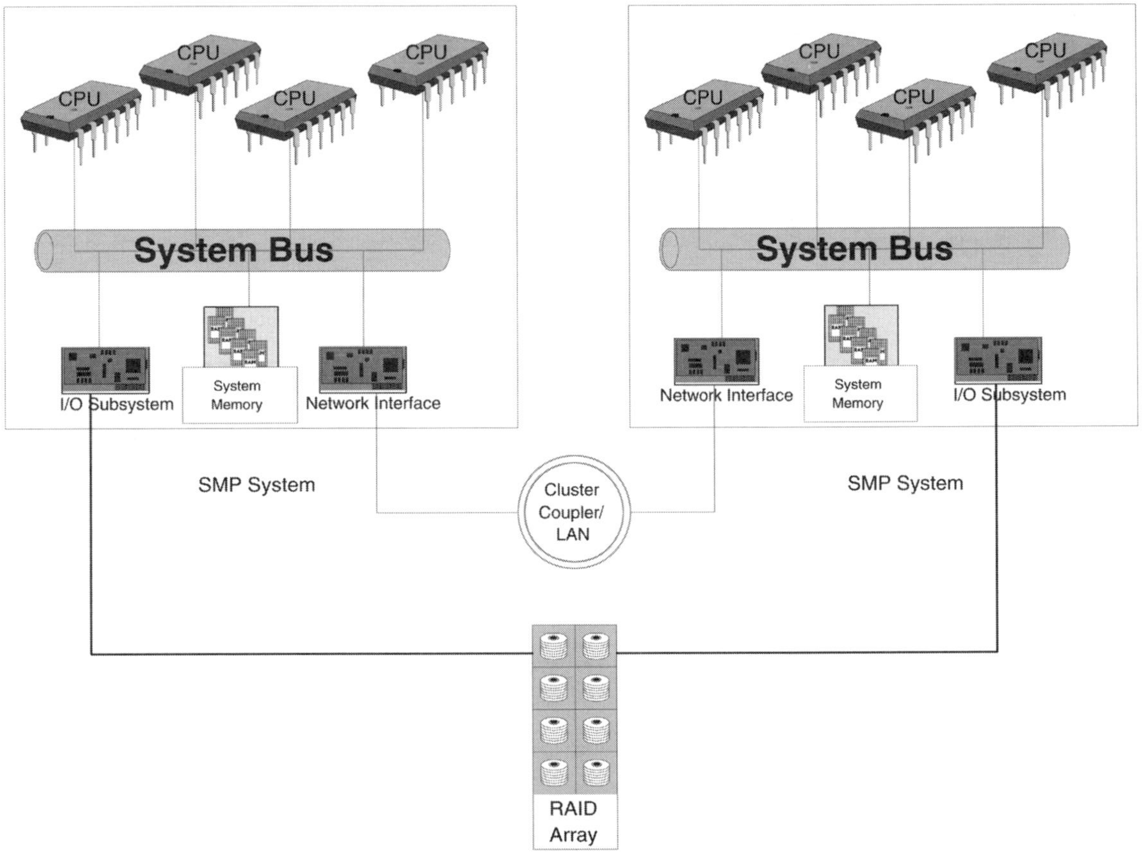

Figure 4.3 Clustering architecture.

business. Microsoft is also producing some technology, called Wolfpack, which has announced support from Compaq, HP, and a number of other significant Intel-based server companies. With the acquisition of Tandem by Compaq, we expect some very interesting solutions to emerge. Wolfpack support will be in NT 5.0, due in Q1 1998.

If clustering makes sense for you in the near term, you will have to go with one of the proprietary vendor solutions, and then watch Wolfpack. Ultimately, we do not recommend that you put a production system up on version 1.0 of Wolfpack while there are proven alternatives in the marketplace. Experiment with it if you are a heavy MS shop, but be diligent and make sure it meets your standards and needs.

NUMA—NONUNIFORM MEMORY ACCESS

NUMA, non-uniform memory access, can be confusing. However, it actually means what it says—that the amount of time it takes to get data from memory in this architecture is not always uniform. There are a number of NUMA variants, and we cannot consider each of them in this chapter. However, there are two primary designs: the *replicated memory cluster or shared memory cluster* (RMC/SMC) and the *cache coherent* (CC-NUMA). This does not mean there are not other competing alternatives, but these two seem to be leading the pack, with implementations planned or current from DEC, Sequent, HP, and Tandem. (See Figure 4.4.)

Replicated Memory Cluster RMC designs use memory transfer or replication mechanisms between independent nodes to move data between systems. When a processor needs data, it first checks the cache of other processors to see if they have the data already in cache, since getting it from memory is much faster (hundreds of times potentially, but your mileage may vary) than getting it from disk. These systems rely on very sophisticated middleware to establish and maintain connections between processors, and the ability to maintain these connections is critical. This pulling of data from other nodes' memory space results in the requisite *nonuniform* memory access latency, since the delay involved with getting data from another node's memory space will be different

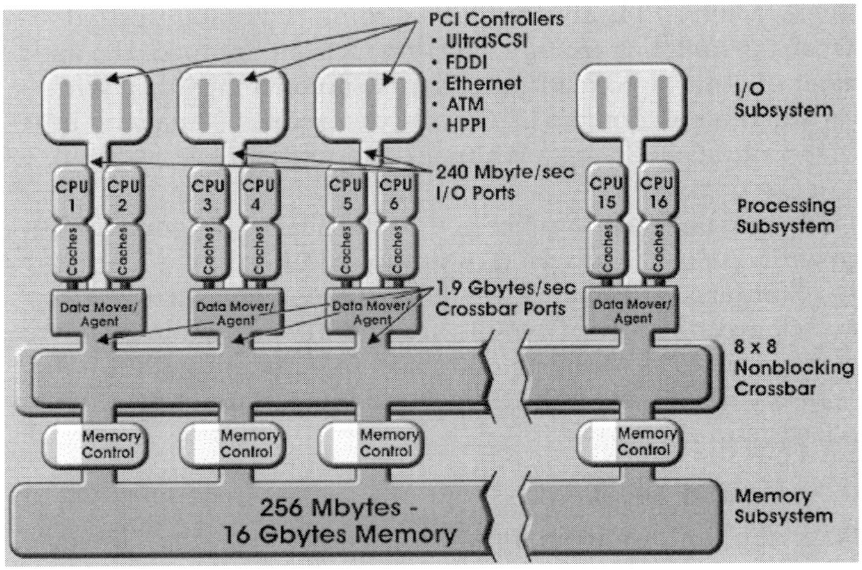

Figure 4.4 NUMA physical implementation.

from that associated with pulling the data from a processor's local cache.

It is important to realize that this is essentially a clustered model that maintains a separate copy of the OS on each node and a separate memory map for each node's OS environment. Through software coherency, the systems have knowledge of each other's memory contexts. Thus, the NUMA component is internodal. For Web sites where multiple Web servers are used, the RMC/SMC design has significant promise, since the odds of a Web page being in memory increases with every server added. However, if the site relies heavily on dynamic page generation, the benefits may not be overwhelming, since what is passed is a shell, which then requires additional work by the Web server or application server to instantiate in an appropriate format.

Cache Coherent NUMA CC-NUMA is very different from RMC, resembling an SMP design more than a cluster. This is because in a CC design, there is one copy of the OS that spans the several involved nodes, and this results in a single memory map. In essence, rather than being connected by a high-speed backplane in a box, the processors are connected by optimized hardware interconnects. This means there is no copy of data between memory contexts as in the RMC design, with an elimination of the associated software message passing. Coherence is managed in hardware, just like in an SMP box, with a resultant increase in performance.

What does this all mean? CC-NUMA designs supply a way of providing the single image that was the advantage of SMP systems, but with the ability to "organically" grow the compute environment by allowing multiple SMP boxes to be interconnected.

MASSIVELY PARALLEL PROCESSING

MPP systems are mentioned here simply because they exist, and a number of vendors are trying to position them as solutions in the high load dynamic intranet environment. We see this as overkill. MPP systems are shared-nothing designs. They require extensive customization of the application to operate effectively on an implemented hardware model and extensive changes to that application (potentially) whenever that hardware model changes. There is a possibility of using MPP systems as specialized processors to support the delivery of business and data services to the applications, since they are excellent at working over complex problems in parallel against vast amounts of data.

Unlike the SMP, clustering, and NUMA designs discussed above, MPP systems generally do not bother with cache coherency or shared memory. Each processor works independently and it is up to the programmers to ensure that their application logic uses the hardware environment most effectively. This requires a tremendous amount of knowledge on the part of the programmers, not only of the application, but of the operating systems and the hardware platform. In today's commercial environment, few companies can attract and retain that level of skill.

When working with statically partitionable data and with minimal internodal communications requirements, these boxes scream. However, the application design burden is immense and is usually well beyond the capabilities of most corporate DP shops to handle. In addition, most corporate applications—generally database-centric—do not lend themselves well to MPP implementations since the data and structures they use are fairly dynamic, and this requires extensive application management to readjust code and repartition data to avoid process contention (hotspots).

Web Server Software

This is a chapter about hardware; what does Web server software have to do with it? If your software choice is Microsoft's Internet Information Server (IIS), then you are going to work within an NT scalability model that is *horizontal,* meaning it adds more machines (as a rule) to your architecture. This requires an excellent plan for software distribution, failover, resource monitoring, and so on. While some companies try to hedge their bets by using the Common Gateway Interface (CGI) as the integration mechanism, this results in a real waste of horsepower on the server, since CGI requires kicking off processes for each CGI script, and NT is terrible at that. NT is a threaded OS, so if you are going IIS, then use ISAPI or NSAPI and get the benefits of performance. Using CGI will generally require about twice as much hardware for the same performance, and if you are structuring a server management model, that means more software, more complexity, more backups, more people. So why go MS? If you are standardizing on the COM/DCOM environment for your component work (note that we did not use the word *object*), then IIS has the best support for that solution in the market today. This provides you with ready access to a number of third-party solutions, advanced technology such as Microsoft Transaction Server for component pooling, and access to a broad base of developers who can get something done in a reasonable time frame. These are excellent business reasons for making this choice.

If you choose one of the multiplatform solutions such as Netscape, then you have an easier time in developing your hardware management model since you can go to really big SMP UNIX boxes, to clusters, or to a horizontal scaling strategy. However, we still suggest that you use Netscape's NSAPI as opposed to using

CGI. Of course, this will bind you to the Netscape platform, and we have been raving about the nightmare of "tight coupling" to our clients through years of two-tier PowerBuilder and Visual Basic application development. Why the switch? If you do it right and focus on making sure you wrap your business logic and data access logic in well-defined interfaces like CORBA, then your hit to moving to another server will be minimal. If you do not have a disciplined approach to your software design, then your code will end up tightly coupled anyway, and you might as well go for the best time to market you can manage and beg forgiveness after you have successfully delivered.

Application Type

How are hardware and application type related? Different types of applications have different availability and performance requirements, and this spills over into the hardware environment. Let's look at some different types of applications. In *Building the Corporate Intranet,* we identified several basic application types:

Content distribution (e.g., newsletters, forms, manuals). This architecture also serves as the basic infrastructure for all the other intranet architectures and is usually the first to be implemented. This was used by a client who had a large chain of restaurants and wanted to distribute the information on procedures and training throughout the chain in an efficient and inexpensive manner.

DBMS direct integration (two-tier or classic client/server). This was utilized by a chemical company that wanted to provide the sales force with access to a database of sales leads and status. The Web provided for easy access by a geographically dispersed sales force.

Traditional process integration (OLTP client/server). This is typically used by companies handling a high volume of transactional traffic, such as reservation systems.

Nontraditional integration—DBMS SPs (nontraditional DBMS). An example of this kind of system was implemented for a major pharmaceutical company that wanted to use the Web as a front end to a document management system.

Collaborative computing. This system is typically thought of as an alternative to Lotus Notes but can actually include much more, such as real-time conferencing (initially text-only but eventually, as bandwidth increases, using audio and even video).

When we look at these systems, we see applications with very different requirements for absolute performance, predictability of performance, and integration complexity. The third point, while interesting, is not critical to this discussion. The first two most definitely are. Systems should understand their own behavior—in this case, their performance—and be able to instantiate themselves dynamically to alleviate the performance bottleneck. This is called *application instrumentation,* and there is precious little of it going on in the industry. However, the highly unpredictable system loads associated with applications such as Call Center and Order Entry can swamp a highly planned server hardware model.

Building the Corporate Intranet advocates the philosophy that all systems should be built as logically distributed and physically partitionable. Of course, there are exceptions, but they should be tactical and business-driven, and should have a sunset date explicit in their genesis. That said, let's take two extremes, a content-based design and an OLTP (data integration) design, and see how their nature influences their hardware management.

CONTENT

A content-based system is responsible for taking static content and supplying it as required, dishing pages from a Web server. (See Figure 4.5.) Nothing fancy. Systems like this tend to get bound at the I/O level, since they are overwhelmed with requests for data from disk that they cannot supply fast enough. Thus, these systems, like database servers, benefit greatly from lots of memory. On many of these systems, your management console will report low utilization of the CPU, but will show very high network data transfer rates, high queue levels for I/O devices, and possibly high system bus utilization. In most cases, a system with

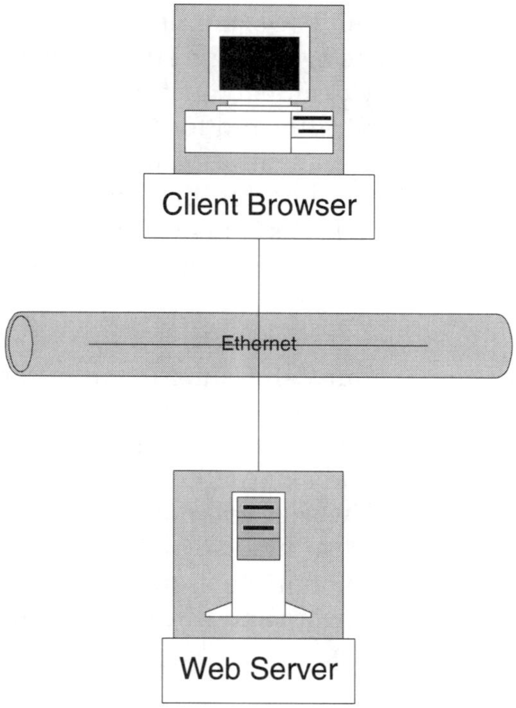

Figure 4.5 Content application platform logical design.

a single 10Mb/sec Ethernet card is not going to get bogged down dishing pages, since the data transfer rate from the I/O subsystem should be well in excess of 10Mb/sec. However, this illustrates the need for balanced design of disk subsystems, network architectures, and processor selection.

When working with this type of design, we generally find that systems with very large memories work best, since these sites have an 80 percent / 20 percent rule of use: 20 percent of the site sees 80 percent of the traffic. As a result, these systems should use a site management product that will track hits and provide a listing of the most commonly hit pages. This information, in addition to the regular information about how the server platform is being taxed, will provide you with great perspective on hardware tuning and possibly augmentation. For example, you may find that 80 percent of your traffic runs against the HR organization's Internet use policies. So, you may decide to host those on a separate machine to segment your traffic and load. Conversely, you may find that you have a high concentration of hits (80 percent) against a small percentage of pages, but find that your OS is reporting tremendous memory page faults. This would indicate that you are paging to disk and should increase the real memory in the system.

OLTP

So, you decided to put your Call Center on an intranet environment. By the way, this is not as insane as you might think, since a well-articulated design will allow you to then take those internally focused processes and externally enable them in a more intuitive presentation. However, you now have a requirement for a highly available, high-performance, highly integrated system—in other words, something of production quality. In looking at the relationship between hardware and this type of application, experience tells us several things:

- The database must be nonstop in its implementation.
- The load may be predictably seasonal, but unpredictable within a cycle.
- Response time must have 90 percent of queries returned in under four seconds.

TIP *Many companies building distributed on-line systems today are using Transaction Processing Monitors (TPM) to develop high performance, highly available solutions. However, what if objects are in your future? Classic TPMs do not support objects well, either as defined by Microsoft's COM (Component Object Model) or by the rest of the industry's Common Object Request Broker Architecture (CORBA). For companies looking at this problem, there are emerging migration strategies. In the TPM area, Transarc's Encina product is a good one to watch, since Transarc's engineers were very involved in the definition* *of Corba's Object Transaction Service (OTS). An alternative is BEA System's Tuxedo, with a plan to leverage their Object Broker environment in the future.*

Server hardware plays a big part in addressing this scenario, but it is not the totality of the solution. As Figure 4.6 shows,

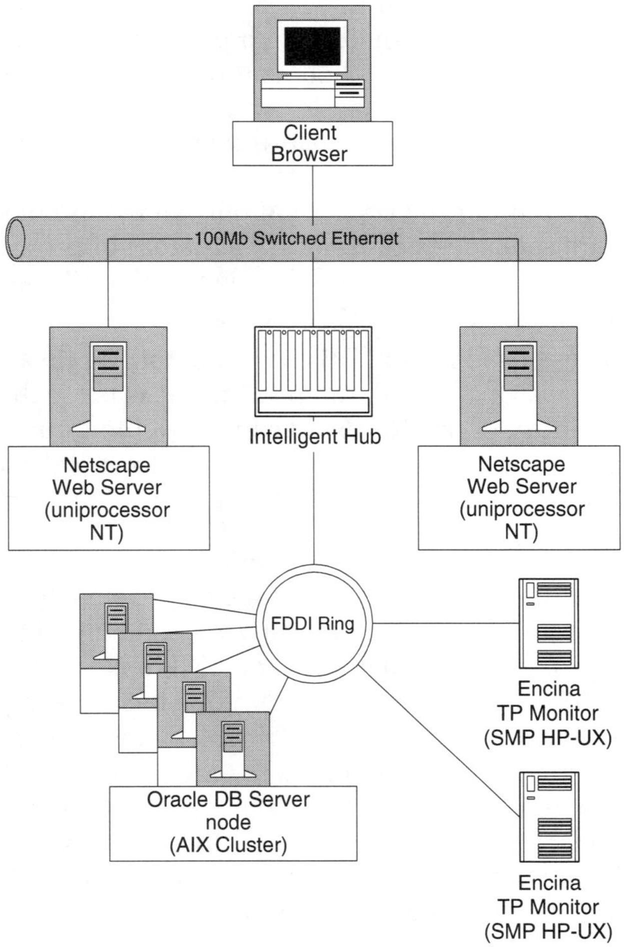

Figure 4.6 OLTP application platform design.

multiple types of server platforms will all play in your intranet design:

Uniprocessor boxes are used as Web servers to provide a high degree of simplistic scalability. The network is designed with switching to minimize the impact of adding additional servers and provide the highest bandwidth possible between the client and target server.

SMP boxes are used for the TP monitor. An operational guideline was established, which precludes a TPM from operating at more than 50 percent of its capacity for a sustained period (greater than ten minutes). This provides an effective load-balancing capability between the two servers and also provides the ability to use the TPM's failover capability to shoulder the additional burden in case one fails. HP boxes are selected because of HP's history of providing in-chassis processor upgrades, excellent reliability, and support for EMC's high-end DASD solutions.

A cluster is used for the DB environment. While a nonstop platform was examined, the price point was much higher and the flexibility of use for the hardware in the future was much lower. AIX was selected because of the long-standing IBM-Oracle relationship in the clustering area.

These systems front-end the application server environment, which will require a "brokering" service responsible for routing requests to services or objects that can service them. In this case, you should probably look to higher-end SMP boxes, since the possibility for parallel data access is great to fill a business request. Clustering at the app server level is not critical, since the failure of one server will result in routing requests to other services in the environment. Assuming that not a lot of state is maintained (logical unit of work managed in the client or the business layer's transactional semantics), we don't need shared disks or similar solutions at this level. Finally, the database can be implemented in a number of fail-safe designs, including a cluster, a backstop-failover, or a nonstop pattern. Which of these you choose will vary according to budget, mean-time-to-recover (MTTR) constraints, and so on.

The purpose of the preceding exercise was not to actually solve the problem, but to show how two different types of applications can have very different HW requirements and also how the applications make differing demands on the applications infrastructure and the operations infrastructure. Most companies are picking "an architecture" for their Web systems, and this is not an effective way to manage. If you are going to a massively redundant server farm model, then having a console tell you when one fails may be timely enough. If you are going to a small number of servers, then you will need to explore the possibility of including monitoring hardware on the servers to be proactive or expanding your operations model to include monitoring elements of both hardware platform and application environment.

Network Design

When looking to grow a hardware platform, one of the key questions is: How fast can I deliver the information? This is why it is critical to understand where your target audience is located. If we look at a basic implementation, you see that the bandwidth of one user community is T1, or about 1.5Mb/sec. The other community is using Switched Fast Ethernet to the desktop.

Let's do some quick math.

If a server is being used by the WAN group, the gating factor for load is the bandwidth of the communications infrastructure on the WAN. It makes little sense to build tremendous monitoring and management into a server whose single Ethernet interface provides 5 times the bandwidth that the WAN connection can use. In addition, it may make little sense to implement a multibus SMP machine with internal PCI bridging and other niceties when the bandwidth to the I/O subsystem is 30 times what the T1 can consume. However, that does not mean that the system does not need to be included in the corporate management infrastructure. It still should be monitored for use, but maybe to see if its discretionary capacity can be applied to another project or need. Remember, we want to rationalize the use of hardware whenever possible, since each additional machine has associated software maintenance costs, operations costs, and hardware maintenance costs.

Conversely, if the LAN group is to be the user community, then you have a different problem. The ability for a group of users to load such a system almost instantly would lead to a thorough management strategy for the platform, and part of that would be inclusion of platform performance and error data into the corporate management umbrella. In a high-demand system like this, correlated fault management becomes critical, and the ability to correlate an increased network load with a performance slowdown on the server or dropped packets from an overloaded Network Card becomes critical. In addition, such a design may require multiple replicated servers, a cluster of servers on shared DASD, multiple network interface cards, or another combination of solutions.

Most intranets are a hybrid of the two absolutes just described. As a result, very few systems can go in with a limited monitoring profile.

Continuity of Business Strategy

Continuity of business (COB) is the ability to continue to run an application in spite of things like hurricanes, tornadoes, bombs, and fire. You need a plan, and the plan is a major influence on your selection of hardware, whether initially or as the system evolves. In most cases, people do the first implementations of intranet systems on the cheap and then begin to worry when the project is a hit. However, taking some things into consideration up front will make the management of the COB a much easier process.

Some easy questions you should ask include:

> Is this system the sole source or repository for some information in the company? If no, then how long would it take to recreate the data from those sources? If yes, what is the impact of the data's loss?

TIP *When projects begin to go over budget, management has a clear protocol for how to get them back under control. This usually consists of shrinking analysis, training and "unnecessary" things like COB strategies. Recently, we had a client who made an interesting compromise, and got caught short. In their COB strategy for their DBMS system, they had a production server and a development server which could serve as a limited function backup in case of production failure.*

The development system did not need to be as big as the production system to handle development, but the several GB of RAM required to match the production system was an expense that was cut to accommodate adding additional functionality. In addition, the RAM purchased was not error correcting, that is, RAM smart enough that when it has a parity error it maps the offending memory out of use. The disk storage, rather than being mirrored, was RAID based.

When failure struck, it was insidious and costly. The concept in case of a failure was to take the memory from the production system, and put it into the development system to "upgrade it," and then unplug the disk drives and plug them into the development server. However, the failure here was low in memory, so when the machine began to try and load its Operating System the memory would fail and the OS could not load. A result of this problem was several days trying to recover the system, and an inability to process sales online for a week. The costs were well in excess of the $125,000 which would have been needed for the recommended hardware solution.

What is the user's expectation for planned downtime? What constraints exist on planning downtime? (Remember that downtime must be planned, especially with the rate of change of software in this business today.)

In the case of a system failure, what is the target mean time to recover that the business can accept?

Are there any contractual, regulatory, or other influences that constrain or otherwise modify the business's specified MTTR?

Does the COB strategy provide for secondary or tertiary backup or operations sites? If so, what restrictions are there on hardware/software platforms and the communications infrastructure provided?

Do you have a plan that accounts for necessary staff in case of a failure? This includes night-call training for operators on all shifts and automatic escalation procedures.

While all of these questions are important, the one that concerns mean time to recover is the most critical, because the answer to this will act as a major architecture constraint and will also have some significant cost implications. Make sure you and the users understand the difference between planned and unplanned downtime. Generally, a system may be classified in one of several categories for MTTR:

0 minutes: nonstop computing. This is the most extreme answer, and generally requires fully redundant designs. It is very expensive to acquire the environment, build the application architecture, and operate. However, this seems to be what people have in mind when they say "24-×-7" uptime.

10 to 30 minutes: high availability. In this model, the system is expected to be back online within 10 minutes of a failure. This can frequently be handled by using high-availability software solutions if the platform is UNIX or by using some of the NT clustering technologies. When working with UNIX or NT, be aware that the recovery of the file systems can often take longer than the 10 minutes allowed, especially as the volume of pages and so forth grows within the environment. Starting costs for HA solutions tend to be about half those for nonstop, and they can be less than that, depending on platform.

30 to 60 minutes: manual substitution. In this model, a system can be manually cut over to some alternative solution, for example the hard disks can be unplugged and plugged into another backup or development system. This usually reflects a low priority for the system, since this solution can use lower-end temporary spares, does not rely on expensive, dual-ported disk or similar hardware technology, and does not merit expenditure on supporting software.

Of course, you can go over an hour, but at that point a system is really being recovered at the data center's discretion.

In today's market, intranet systems in the first two categories are generally (not absolutely) UNIX-based, and this stems from UNIX's track record as a high-performance, high-availability system. Justifying the use of a Tandem as a Web server could be tough, so generally we suggest meeting the needs of the first category of COB profile by using multiple servers at the Web layer and putting the redundancy or nonstop quality solutions in the business services/transaction processing layer. However, if you do go with the multiple Web server strategy, an NT/Intel solution is very viable, since it has a price point for deployment that matches the technical and business need.

Summary

In this chapter, we looked at evolving the hardware and supporting environment. We looked at a number of technologies which are available today, and tried to provide some basis of looking at the pros and cons of the various solutions. While normally hardware is a discussion of boxes, we also looked at the implications of hardware selection in the context of the different types of applications you may build for your intranet. The essential message of this chapter is that one size, one box does not fit all. You can make it fit, which will result in sub-optimal implementations, but this is frequently contrasted with the operational costs associated with managing different chassis from different vendors. When identifying your hardware platform, make sure you use a Total Cost of Ownership (TCO) model to figure costs over 3–5 years.

TCO approaches can be found in a number of areas, including Gartner Group (www.gartner.com), Meda Group (www.meda.com), or Interpose (www.interpose.com).

CHAPTER FIVE

SERVER SOFTWARE

The fundamental software of an intranet is, of course, the Web server itself. For very simple intranets, there may be no need for any other server software at all. However, as an intranet becomes more complex, it can be called on to support multiple protocols and custom server-side applications. As the configuration of the intranet becomes more complex, so does the task of managing the server software components. We will begin this chapter by discussing the management of the two most popular Web servers: Microsoft's Internet Information Server and Netscape's Enterprise Server.

Figure 5.1 shows a typical intranet configuration with the various servers involved. Note that several of the servers connect to both the intranet and the Internet, but not all of them do. The proxy, news, and mail servers obviously must connect to the Internet in order to exchange documents for your users. The Web server and application server should connect to the Internet only if you want to give the public access to them. The database server should not connect directly to the Internet under any circumstances. The only way to fully protect your data from public access or corruption is to protect it from direct access. In Figure 5.1, not even intranet clients have direct access to the database server. Instead, only the application server can connect to it. All others must connect through the application server.

Although Figure 5.1 shows each piece of server software running on an independent machine, this is certainly no requirement. In fact, a small intranet could be run entirely from a single server machine. You will find, however, that splitting the server software onto multiple machines will provide greater flexibility to address

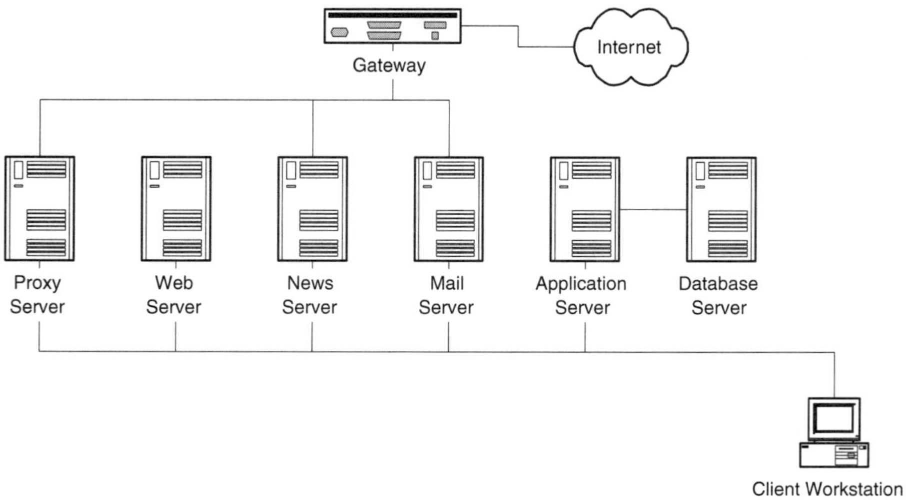

Figure 5.1 Intranet servers.

performance and security issues. There is also no restriction against running the same server software on multiple machines on an intranet. One of the most effective ways to scale up an intranet is to duplicate hardware. If the application server, for example, becomes a performance bottleneck, you could simply add a second or even a third.

Web Server Software

The basic role of the Web server is to field requests for HTML pages and other files, retrieve them from the hard drive, and return them to the requesting browser. Most Web servers, however, provide much more functionality than this. Most support advanced security to control access to served files. Most also support some type of server-side programming, such as CGI, to produce HTML and other documents on the fly. And many support server-side scripting, allowing the Web server to act as an interpreter for a simple scripting language. In this section we will discuss the management of two of the most popular Web server packages.

Netscape Enterprise Server

The Netscape Enterprise Server is the most commonly installed server in the Netscape family of Web servers. Others include Netscape FastTrack Server and Netscape Commerce Server. This section focuses on Enterprise, which differs only slightly from the other members of the Netscape family.

In the Netscape conception of the Web, incoming HTTP requests are for objects, and the Web server's job is to find the requested object, check whether the requestor has rights to see the object, and, if so, return it to the browser. To provide the object, though, the server actually makes use of a *service function*. Which service function is invoked depends on the type of object requested, the location of the object, and, potentially, the results of other processing.

The server has built-in service functions to handle certain types of service requests. For example, one service knows how to return a file from disk. This service is used to retrieve and return HTML, text, and image files, and is all you need for simple Web sites. Another service knows how to invoke external programs using the Common Gateway Interface and return the output to the browser. This is Netscape's way of handling CGI programming. A third service can load a Javascript file from disk, interpret it, and return the results. This implements Netscape's LiveWire functionality.

The server itself acts as a sort of skeleton, or framework, which fields requests, looks through an internal set of these services, passes the request to the appropriate service, captures the result, and returns the result to the browser. You can add additional functionality to Netscape servers by implementing service functions in C or C++ using Netscape's NSAPI libraries, and then configuring the server to load and execute your handler.

The Netscape servers read their configuration information from a set of files stored in each server's home directory. There are three basic files for each server. When a Netscape server loads, it reads in the file "magnus.conf." This file, whose name is a relic from an early code name used by Netscape, controls settings for the framework itself, including which service functions to load. It can also specify other files to load. The default magnus.conf loads the file "obj.conf," which defines object-handler mappings. The third file, "mime.types," is used by the file service to return the correct mime headers for a file based on its extension.

Although it is possible to edit these files directly—indeed, it may be necessary to do so in certain circumstances—Netscape provides a much more friendly interface in the form of the Netscape Administration Server. This is a separate Web server service, running on a special port, which presents a set of HTML forms for administering all of your Netscape Web servers. This server makes copies of your configuration files, makes modifications to those copies for you, and then, when you are ready, stops the servers, updates the originals, and restarts the servers. Clearly, this is far easier than editing the files directly.

Whether you are configuring your server through the user interface or directly through the files, the options fall into a number of logical groupings. Network settings control how your server interacts with the network. Here you control what port your server listens on, how it resolves network requests, and related parameters. Of particular interest is the reverse name lookup setting. When a client machine establishes a connection to your server, only the machine's IP number is known. To determine the client's name, your server has to make a DNS query across the network based on the IP number, receiving back the machine's name. While this can be a useful analysis and security tool, it is a slow process and can hurt performance.

TIP *Determining the name of a machine making an HTTP request can take significant time, especially on the Internet. Disabling reverse name lookup can improve your Web server's response time.*

Another group of options controls access to your server. These let you enable access control, choose the method of access control, and allow or deny specific users or groups of users access to your server. This access control falls into two broad categories. One is address-based control. Your server can be set to allow or deny access immediately, based on the originating address of the request. One of our servers is connected to the Internet but is not really intended for public access. It is not a critical server, so it is not protected by a firewall, but nonetheless we have it configured to respond to queries only if they originate from a machine whose IP number falls within a specific range. Thus, computers on our own networks can access this server, but no others. This type of access check is very fast: There is no need to go through the process of checking usernames and passwords. Once a user's connection is established, another layer of security allows screening based on usernames and passwords, or potentially some other scheme. This second layer of checks is slower and places more load on your server but it allows finer control, mapping specific users to specific directories.

The last two groups of parameters control the content of your Web server. One controls mappings of URLs to content directories, and the other controls mapping of URLs to CGI scripts. These together determine how files and scripts on your server are presented to users. It would be possible to create an entire Web site with files stored in only one or two directories, but such a site would quickly become an unmanageable muddle. It is important to invest time in the initial layout of your directory structure. A clear, logical structure is needed to facilitate the growth of your site.

With Netscape servers, there are two approaches you can take toward designating script files. Normally, an incoming request for a URL is translated into a local directory path and file, and that file is sent as the response. However, you can indicate to Netscape that certain files are to be executed and their output to be sent as the response. You do this either by designating certain directories as CGI directories or by designating certain extensions as CGI extensions. In the first approach, all of your scripts would be grouped together in one or maybe two directories. Those directories would be flagged in the configuration files as CGI directories: Any request for URLs that map to those physical directories will cause the server to execute the requested file, returning the output. To use the second approach, you must specify which extensions represent CGI scripts. Common ones are .exe and .pl, for Windows executables and Perl scripts. Another common one is

.cgi. Any URL that maps to a physical file with a designated extension will result in the specified file being executed. This allows you to place CGI files with the associated content instead of in separate directories. There are good arguments for each of these approaches, but overall we recommend the CGI directory approach, just because it makes a clearer distinction between what are really fundamentally different types of files.

TIP *URL to physical path mappings for Netscape servers are handled as simple text substitutions, allowing such odd mappings as this: /DEMO/1 can map to /cgi-bin/demo.exe/1. These can be very helpful in maintaining compatibility with older versions or with existing standards.*

Some members of the Netscape server family have special configuration groupings in addition to those already mentioned. They control special features such as LiveWire and database access. They are subject to the same general comments we've made already, especially those following regarding version control. Netscape's handling of configuration files makes keeping them under version control particularly easy, so you should be sure to take advantage of that ease.

Microsoft Internet Information Server

Microsoft's Internet Information Server (IIS) is really more of a framework for servers than a server in itself. A basic installation of IIS supports WWW, FTP, and Gopher. Additional plug-ins allow IIS to act as a proxy server, a server-side script interpreter, and more. Here we will focus on the basic WWW server features of IIS.

The configuration options available for IIS are largely similar to those for Netscape servers, although they are grouped a bit differently. One of the most significant differences is in parameter storage. IIS reads its configuration information from the Windows NT registry and not from configuration files. It is possible, nonetheless, to record its settings in files by using the registry's import/export feature (see the section on version control).

WARNING *Unlike the Netscape servers, IIS cannot be stopped or started from within its Web-based management tool.*

IIS provides two user interfaces to its management functions: one a Windows-based application, the other a set of Web pages. They provide roughly the same functionality, but with a slightly different layout. The first tab of each controls the network and general configuration of the server. This tab allows you to determine which security mechanisms (standard or challenge-response) your server will accept, and whether it will allow anonymous access.

When a user connects to your IIS server, the server impersonates the user to perform operations on the user's behalf. If you are using Windows NT challenge-response security, this is straightforward. If you are using normal security, the name and password supplied by the user are used by the server to impersonate the user. If you allow anonymous access, then the server has no user to impersonate. This is why you must supply a default username and password for the server to use to service anonymous accesses: Every NT process must have some identity to assume. This means that anonymous users will have access to whatever files and/or services to which the default user has access. By default, IIS calls this user "IUSR_machinename." Unfortunately, a number of software packages get confused by spaces and underscores, so we recommend dropping the underscore.

The next tab in both management applications controls content directory mappings. IIS does not completely differentiate between HTML directories and scripting directories. Instead, each mapping specifies a physical directory location for the given URL. The properties of the mapping control whether the contents of a given directory should be readable or executable. For a file to be returned to the client, it must be readable. For it to be executed and its output returned to the client, it must be executable. If it is flagged as both, the behavior is not clearly determined. Most URLs will be treated as requests for the file. Appending a "?" to the end of the name will cause the file to be executed.

Another feature of this tab allows the specification of virtual servers. Normally, a request for a URL received by a server with multiple IP numbers is processed no matter which IP number received the request. However, if you specify a virtual server for an address mapping, that mapping will be used only for requests that come in to that IP address. This allows one machine to serve two completely different sites simply by having two IP numbers. The number of IP numbers a machine can have is limited only by Windows NT.

The final tab controls first-pass access control. Using this tab you can have your server respond only to requests from specified IP numbers or ranges or have your server respond to all requests except those from specified IP numbers or ranges. As with the Netscape servers described above, this provides a first line of security at a fairly low processing cost. Note that changes to these configuration parameters do not take effect until they are applied and that some may require stopping and restarting IIS.

One significant set of configuration parameters you might expect to find in these applications is not there: access privileges. IIS relies on underlying Windows NT file security to control access to individual files. Once the server impersonates the user—or the default user for anonymous connections—it has access only to files to which that user would have access if logged in locally. Thus you control individual access to files and directories by assigning file permissions to groups and users using Windows Explorer.

Related Server Software

Only the simplest intranets will rely solely on Web servers. Most intranets will use other server software to supplement their Web servers. This may include support for Internet E-mail and News, an RDBMS for corporate data access, or a proxy server for secure

Internet access. This section covers some of the additional server software you might need on your intranet, and the management needs of each.

FTP Servers

In recent years, many FTP sites have been supplanted by Web sites. There are, however, specific functions that can be provided by FTP that are difficult if not impossible to provide using HTTP. In particular, file uploads and high-volume or large-file downloads are handled especially poorly by HTTP. Therefore, if you plan to allow users to upload files or if you wish to distribute software through your site, you should probably run an FTP server.

The UNIX operating system has many very good FTP servers, and they all integrate very well with UNIX security. In the Windows NT world, the Microsoft FTP server built into IIS is a fairly good option. Like its UNIX counterparts, it integrates well with the operating system's security.

When users connect to an FTP server, they can log in using an individual username and password, or they can log in as an *anonymous* user. You should decide whether to allow anonymous user access. In both NT and UNIX, you perform most FTP security configuration through the file system itself. The FTP server will grant the user access to whatever the file system allows. This includes creating files, creating directories, browsing directories, and deleting files. Lock users out of a file in the file system, and FTP will be unable to return it to them.

In both NT and UNIX, you can control the apparent identity of anonymous users. Effectively, you create a fake user, often called Anonymous, to represent anonymous users. You can block anonymous users from certain actions by blocking the user Anonymous.

Most FTP servers allow the creation of *index* files for each FTP-accessible directory. When users switch to a new directory, the index file is displayed by their FTP client. The name used for these files varies by server package, but .index and read.me are common ones.

There are two sets of configuration options for FTP that are particularly worth noting. The first allows control of the number of simultaneous users. It can be especially useful to limit external FTP users during peak business hours. Good FTP servers support scheduled access levels: You could allow 100 simultaneous users from 6 P.M. to 6 A.M. and only 10 from 6 A.M. to 6 P.M. Other servers also allow limitations on FTP traffic. These would allow you to limit FTP bandwidth to, say, 56K during peak time and 128K after hours.

Proxy Servers

Proxy servers allow you to create an indirect connection between your intranet and the Internet at large. The proxy server software runs on a server machine that has one network port connected to the Internet and another to the intranet. Either or both of these ports could be a dial-up line instead of a network connection. Web browsers on the intranet are then configured to access Internet sites using the proxy server. Each HTTP request from the browser is received by the proxy server, which then requests the page from the actual server on behalf of the browser. Once the page is received from the real server, the proxy server returns it to the browser. (See Figure 5.2.)

Proxy servers provide several key features to the intranet. A proxy server can be configured to buffer pages, so that if multiple users request the same page, the proxy server requests it only once. If the connection from the proxy server to the Internet is slow or expensive, this can be a real plus. A proxy server can also be configured to access only specified sites. The intranet administrator can restrict browsers from accessing any sites not in a preapproved list or block specific sites known to be objectionable.

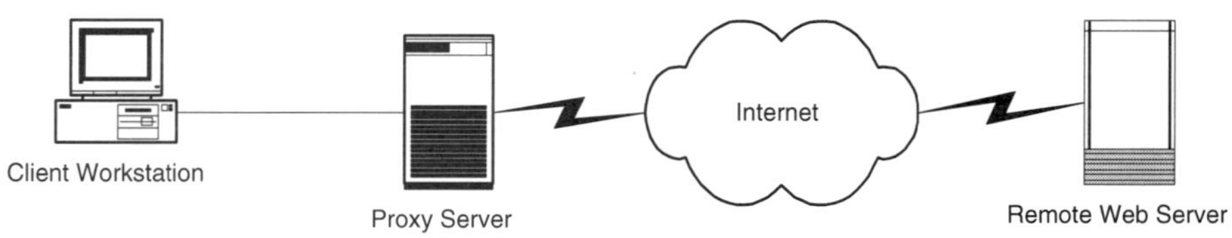

Figure 5.2 Proxy server in action.

Last, the proxy server can be configured to allow access using only certain protocols. Attempts to access the Internet using other protocols would simply fail.

With all of these options available, of course, configuring a proxy server can be an immense task. Although proxy server software packages differ in the range of capabilities and configurability they provide, they do all share certain common elements. Therefore, we will focus on a single software package, Microsoft Proxy Server, for the rest of this section. Microsoft Proxy Server is an add-on for Microsoft IIS 3.0. It can handle not only the HTTP protocol, but also FTP, SMTP, NNTP, POP3, and a number of other protocols. It is configured from within the Internet Services Manager.

The first group of settings control the proxy server's connection to the Internet. Here you can control which protocols should be proxied, as well as which outside sites can be accessed. Certain proxy servers, including the Microsoft offering, allow you to control caching of pages here as well.

The range of machines allowed to connect to or through the proxy server can also be configured. This allows you to restrict access via the proxy server to machines connected to your own intranet or even a subset of your intranet. This is generally done by entering a range of IP addresses, or a network address and subnet mask.

It is important to note that, while most Web browsers support access through a proxy server, most other client software does not. Configuring a proxy server to handle POP3 and NNTP, for example, is just half the battle. You must then install proxy-enabled mail and news clients on each workstation on your intranet. Such software should become more common over the coming months, as proxy connections between intranets and the Internet become more common.

Mail Servers

Managing a mail server involves three fundamental tasks: maintaining connectivity, configuring user mailboxes, and monitoring the flow of mail to and from the server. (See Figure 5.3.) Of course, different software packages provide different tools to perform

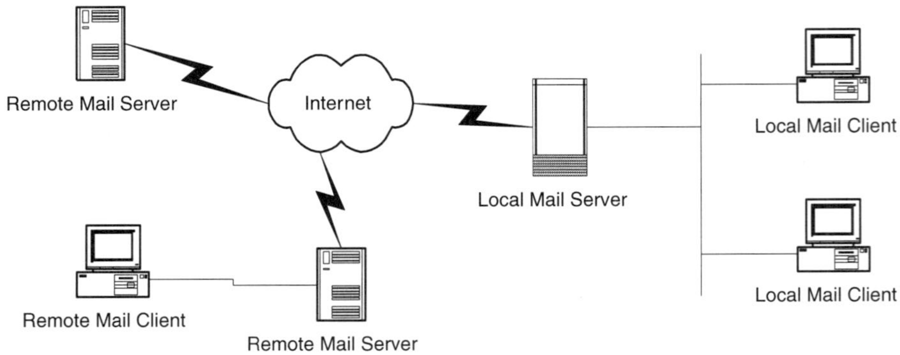

Figure 5.3 SMTP mail.

these tasks, but the tasks remain the same from a standard UNIX installation to the latest release of Microsoft Exchange Server.

New mail messages are created by a mail client, and are then transferred to the local mail server for delivery. The mail server determines the destination server based on the recipient's address and transfers the mail directly to the remote mail server. The remote server holds the messages until the remote client logs in and retrieves them. Mail messages are transferred over a direct connection between the originator's server and the destination server—they are not relayed from one server to the next like news messages.

Connectivity for a mail server means connectivity to the Internet to exchange mail outside of your intranet as well as connectivity to the intranet for access by your users. Note that mail systems use very different protocols for transferring messages between servers and for accessing messages on the server from a client.

The Internet standard for transferring mail between servers is the Simple Mail Transfer Protocol (SMTP). All Internet mail servers support SMTP, but there are a number of mail systems that were not originally intended for use with the Internet. These include Lotus Notes and Microsoft Exchange, among others. Many non-Internet mail servers now include an SMTP component, and there are add-on SMTP gateways available for virtually all mail servers. Notes and Exchange both support SMTP directly in their latest versions, but older versions required third-party gateways.

There is very little to configure regarding server-server mail transfer. Most servers do allow you to specify whether new mail messages are sent immediately to their destination servers or are held and sent in a batch. The only reason to send messages in batches is if your intranet does not have full-time connectivity to the Internet. You may wish to schedule an hourly Internet connection for mail transfer rather than establish that potentially expensive connection each time a new message is entered. Some servers also allow the connection to be made based on the number of waiting messages.

If you do try to use this scheme, you will have to decide how to handle incoming mail. If your Internet connection can be activated by an incoming packet, then each inbound SMTP transfer will bring up your connection. This essentially means your mail server will always be available, but at a cost in terms of connect time. Alternatively, some Internet service providers (ISPs) will provide *store-and-forward* service, whereby incoming mail messages are stored on a server at the ISP site and forwarded to your mail server only when the connection is active. This can be a good compromise for a part-time connected intranet.

Typically, mail addresses refer to "user@domain.com," rather than "user@server.domain.com." For this type of address to work, a remote mail server must be able to determine which server in your domain is the default mail server. This is now handled by the Domain Name Service (DNS). If your intranet is connected to the Internet, either you or your ISP will almost certainly be running DNS for your domain. If your mail server is called "mail," you will need to add a mail record to the DNS tables to indicate that mail addressed to "user@domain.com" should be forwarded to "user@mail.domain.com."

Clients access their mail either through direct file access, POP3, or a proprietary mechanism. In a UNIX environment, it is typical for mail readers, such as pine and elm, to access the mail spool directly. From a management point of view, this is an easy mechanism. It simply requires making the mail spool available on a network drive and configuring the users' logins to have access to that drive. Configuring a UNIX mail reader is usually as easy as setting a couple of environment variables in the default user configuration.

POP3 (Post Office Protocol) allows users to access their mailboxes over a network without direct file access to the spool. POP3 is used by programs like Eudora, Netscape Mail, and Microsoft Internet Mail to access mail servers across a network. Although not all mail servers support POP3, a growing number do. One of the great advantages of POP3 is that it allows a single mail client to access mailboxes on widely disparate mail servers. Configuring a mail reader for POP3 access is also quite simple, requiring only the name or IP address of the mail server.

The few mail programs that do use proprietary protocols tend to be small pieces of larger packages. A classic example is Lotus Notes. Although Notes certainly does act as a mail reader, it is really a more complex groupware system. We will not go into the details of these proprietary mechanisms here, except to note that it is unusual for a proprietary client such as Notes to support POP3. The current release of Microsoft Exchange is an exception to this rule. Exchange does support POP3 mail readers and also includes an Active Server Component that provides Web browsers with access to mail. This feature can be used to avoid having to install and configure a mail reader on every user workstation.

Mailbox configuration varies tremendously from one mail server to another. The simplest UNIX servers automatically create a mailbox for each user account. There is generally an additional mailbox for a fake "Postmaster" account, to which undeliverable mail can be forwarded. More complex servers allow the independent creation of mailboxes and the creation of mail aliases. Most intranets will not need all of the features provided by most mail servers. The best rule here is to keep it simple: The simpler your mailbox structure, the easier it will be to manage.

News Servers

Running a Usenet news server on your intranet can be a demanding proposition, both in terms of equipment and in terms of management effort. Like the mail servers, news servers must be configured both to transfer articles with other servers and to allow clients to post and retrieve articles. (See Figure 5.4.) Unlike mail servers, news servers use the same protocol, the Network News Transfer Protocol (NNTP), for both types of communication.

Usenet news works by replicating articles between news servers. When a user enters a new article in a news reader, the news reader posts it to the user's news server. The article is added to the server's news database and is sent on to the server's upstream server, downstream servers, and news readers. This has some immediate performance implications. Once posted to the local news server, an article will not be immediately available on all servers. Indeed, it can take many hours for a new article to propagate across the entire Internet. Also, a copy of the article is stored on each news server that provides that newsgroup. This can lead to enormous disk space requirements. Last, the transfer of articles and article lists to news readers themselves can be a resource-intensive task.

Configuring communications for your news server is fairly straightforward. All news server software allows you to specify your upstream news feed. Because of the bandwidth needed between a news server and its feed, this should be as logically close as possible. Most companies use the news server of their ISP as their upstream feed. This usually means no more than two hops between the servers, allowing for maximum throughput.

Once you have specified your upstream server, you will need to specify a news transfer schedule. The flexibility provided by different servers varies, but most allow you to perform transfers on a

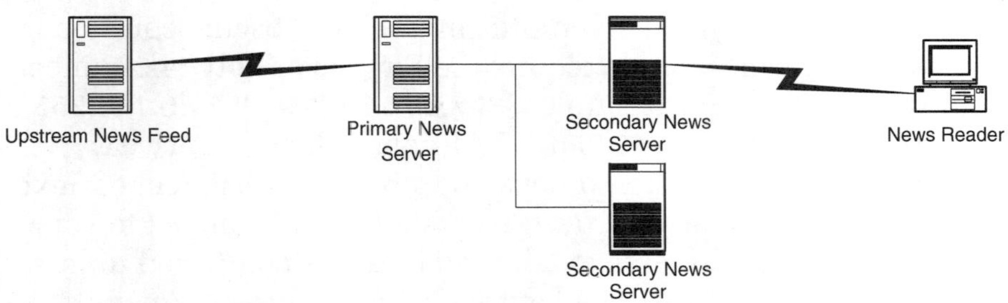

Figure 5.4 Typical Usenet news server configuration.

timed schedule or based on the number of articles waiting to be transferred. In addition, many upstream feeds can be configured to initiate the transfer if they have incoming articles for your server.

If you operate a small intranet, you are unlikely to have downstream servers. However, larger intranets may find it useful to maintain multiple news servers. Since transferring articles from the upstream feed to each local server over your ISP connection is likely to be inefficient, the most common approach is to have a single primary server replicate with the upstream feed and have the secondary servers replicate from the primary server. This limits the amount of traffic to the outside network and yet allows multiple machines to share the load of providing news service.

Each downstream server will need to have a news transfer strategy. A straightforward strategy for larger intranets is to have secondary servers push articles posted by their users to the primary server, but wait for the primary server to initiate transfers of incoming articles. This allows optimization of the transfer schedules on the primary news server without having to deal with interfering transfers from other servers.

Of course, each server also must be configured to handle client access. This can be a very simple task, in the case of open servers. If you do not need to limit or monitor access to your news server, there is no additional configuration needed. However, if you do need to control access, you have two options: You can limit access by address or you can limit access by user.

Limiting access by address is the easier option. Most servers allow you to specify a set of workstation names, with wild cards, which can access your server. This might be "*.bsginc.com" or "*.ny.bsginc.com." Others require an IP range or network number and subnet mask. For example, "207.86.146.129–207.86.146.255" or "207.86.146.0, 255.255.255.*." Although this is a very easy mechanism to administer, it does not provide a great deal of flexibility. Any user on an approved workstation can connect to your server. You will be unable to tell which user is connected unless you can track which user had a particular IP address. You will also be unable to limit access by user.

To limit access by user, you will need a news server capable of supporting authentication and news readers that support your news server's authentication scheme. In theory, this should not be so difficult. Most intranets use some sort of authentication scheme already. In practice, though, integrating your news server into your intranet authentication scheme can be complicated. UNIX-based news servers tend to integrate well with standard UNIX account security, but outside of the UNIX world, good integration is scarce. A pleasant exception to this is Microsoft Exchange.

Among its many other uses, Microsoft Exchange 4.0 can serve as an Internet/intranet news server. As a news server, Exchange's main advantages are tight integration with Windows NT security, a common management user interface, and accessibility via Web browsers.

The NT security integration can be very important if you are implementing an NT security infrastructure across your intranet. An important note is that users do not necessarily need full network accounts in order to use Exchange as a news server. You can create an anonymous access account that would allow "guests" to access your news server, but restrict them to reading or posting to a small subset of your groups. This makes a lot of sense for customer service groups or new product discussion groups. For users who need individual access to news but do not need access to the rest of the intranet, you can create stripped-down accounts with rights to read and post news but not to log in locally or access the file server.

The ability to use Exchange through a Web browser can be very helpful. Not every user, especially on an Internet site, will have a news browser configured. Microsoft ships an Active Server Page package that allows a Web browser to read mail and news stored in Exchange. This requires no configuration on the client workstation and can greatly improve your site's accessibility.

We've discussed a number of problems associated with running a news server on your intranet. But if you need to provide news access, what are your options? First of all, many ISPs operate news servers of their own, and you may be able to arrange for your ISP to provide direct news access for your users. This can greatly reduce your administration load, of course, but for a large number of users this may result in excessive bandwidth demands. Additionally, you will be dependent on your ISP's customer service if there are any problems.

If you have to operate your own news server, you will probably want to limit the resource demands it creates. There is one final area of configuration that can assist with this: content. You do not necessarily have to carry every newsgroup. Indeed, there are many, many newsgroups you will want to block. Some are inappropriate for a corporate intranet. Others carry very large binaries. Others are so chaotic as to be useless. Limiting the newsgroups you pull from your ISP can significantly improve your news server's performance. Note that each server can only carry newsgroups that its upstream feed carries.

There is one exception to this last rule: A news server can provide its own local newsgroups. You can, and probably will, define newsgroups that you do not wish to replicate out to the world. These can be shared and replicated among your own news servers and yet never be passed out to your upstream feed. In fact, it is becoming increasingly common to find intranets hosting their own mini-usenet, with no replication at all with Usenet at large. If you only need to provide news to support your own locally defined newsgroups, you can have much greater control over the usage and performance of your news servers.

Database Servers

Obviously, a database server is not strictly a piece of intranet software. However, most corporate intranets do include some form of access to corporate data, usually using a database server. There are many choices of database server software, and we make no attempt here to examine them. Our point here is simply that a database server in an intranet environment must be carefully secured, especially if your intranet is connected to the Internet. We discussed this briefly in the introduction to this chapter, and here we wish simply to reiterate: a database server should have no direct connection to the Internet, in any form. Often, we even recommend that the database server have no connection to the intranet, either.

There are three levels of database server security you could provide. The worst would be to have the database server directly connected to the intranet and the intranet directly connected to the Internet without a firewall. Don't do it. The next step up would be to install a firewall or a proxy server. In theory, this should adequately protect your database server. However, no firewall is completely impenetrable, and even proxy servers can be misconfigured enough to make you intranet vulnerable. Generally, the risk created is minor (see Chapter 6), but your corporate data deserves as much protection as you can provide.

The final level of protection is to disconnect the database server from the intranet altogether. We recommend installing a second network card in the application server or Web server and establishing an isolated mini-LAN between it and the database server. Not only will this protect your database server from direct access, but it will also improve network throughput on both the intranet and the database mini-LAN. In fact, this last benefit is enough to justify installing such a mini-LAN even if other considerations require you to have a direct connection from the database server to the intranet as well.

Intranet Application Server Software

Custom applications developed for intranets can take a number of forms, and each form imposes different management and configuration constraints. This does not attempt to cover the development of intranet applications, but rather the installation, configuration, and management of custom intranet application software.

CGI

CGI programs are perhaps the most ubiquitous type of intranet applications. CGI programs are fully independent programs that are invoked by a Web server and return their output to the Web server for return to the browser. The important points to note about CGI programs are that they run in their own process space, they receive their input either through the environment or through *stdin*, and they return their output using *stdout*.

Because CGI programs are launched upon each request, they must be kept fairly small in order to load fast enough to provide reasonable response time. If your Web server is suffering from poor performance, excessive use of CGI or inefficient CGI could be the culprit. Because CGI programs run in their own process space, it is uncommon, although not impossible, for a crashed CGI program to also crash the server. Note that as long as any instance of a CGI program is running, its executable image on disk will be locked. For this reason, it is often necessary to stop your server in order to install new versions of CGI programs or libraries used by CGI programs.

A serious limitation of CGI programs is in error handling and reporting. Since they are launched by the server, they have no access to the computer console. They therefore have no way to report error conditions directly to the screen. Unfortunately, a number of application frameworks have default error handlers that attempt to report errors directly to the screen. At best, this message is simply lost. At worst, the entire server can be hung up while the error handler is waiting for a response, which it can never get. Therefore, you must provide a custom error handler to handle all potential scenarios. Common ways of reporting error conditions are to a file, to the server itself, to the Windows NT event log, to a network console, and to SNMP. All of these record the error condition and allow the administrator to view it later. CGI is notoriously difficult to debug because of these limitations.

NSAPI

NSAPI is used to extend Netscape servers. This is done by implementing special functions in dynamic link libraries (DLLs) and then having the server load those DLLs. These DLLs and the functions within them are usually referred to as *NSAPI plug-ins.* NSAPI plug-ins tend to be extremely efficient. They run within the server's process space, only one instance is needed to handle multiple requests, and they remain loaded as long as the server is running. They also have direct access to data used by the server.

Therefore, if you are encountering application performance problems caused by CGI, porting them to NSAPI is a good option.

NSAPI suffers many of the management problems of CGI. NSAPI plug-ins cannot be updated while the server is running. They are difficult to debug because they cannot be run interactively. And they have no access to the screen for error reporting. This last issue is less important for NSAPI plug-ins because they can report errors directly to the Netscape server through an application programming interface (API) call. Errors reported this way show up in the Administration Server's error log.

ISAPI

ISAPI is the Microsoft equivalent of NSAPI. It can be used in many of the same ways, although its functionality is slightly different. Like NSAPI, ISAPI has an advantage over CGI in that scripts are implemented as extensions to the Web server, which run in the server application's program space. This is a great advantage in terms of performance, but it comes at the cost of manageability. Like NSAPI extensions, ISAPI extensions cannot be updated or modified while the Web server is running. IIS preloads all of its ISAPI extensions on start-up and keeps their files open until it is shut down.

Because IIS runs its extensions in its process space, it is much more vulnerable to bugs in extensions than to bugs in CGI programs. A bug in an extension can easily bring down the whole server. For this reason, ISAPI extensions must be tested much more thoroughly prior to deployment than CGI applications. Testing ISAPI extensions can also be considerably more complex than testing most other software, because they must be run from within IIS itself.

Although ISAPI extensions are often installed beneath the Web root, we do not recommend this approach. We find it clearer to consider ISAPI extensions as separate projects, outside of the Web application itself. A good example of this approach is Microsoft's ASP engine. The interpreter that handles Active Server Pages (see next section) is implemented as an ISAPI plug-in, yet it does not install into the Web root tree. Its source code is undoubtedly in a

SourceSafe archive back at Microsoft, but that archive has no relationship to any Web project anywhere. Essentially, ISAPI extensions, like many other server-side components, should be treated as their own independent applications, whose eventual consumers will be Web-based applications.

ASP

Microsoft Active Server Pages are a mixture of HTML, server-side scripting, and client-side scripting. Active Server Pages leverage Microsoft's OLE/COM technology set to allow easy integration of components written in any language that supports OLE/ActiveX. We discuss ASP in more detail in Chapter 7. For now, the important issues involve file access. For users to have access to an ASP script, they must have read access to the file containing it. In addition, for users to have access to ActiveX servers (OLE servers), they must have execute access to its .DLL or .EXE. Inappropriate permissions are the first place to check if you are having any sort of trouble running ASP scripts.

LiveWire

Netscape's LiveWire is similar in concept to Microsoft's ASP: a server-side scripting language interpreted by the Web server itself. The LiveWire language is roughly Java-based, but is generally less powerful than ASP. Because Netscape's servers do not integrate into Windows NT, they do not have the permissions concern previously mentioned.

Version Control

No matter what sort of application programming model you use for your intranet applications, a significant portion of your maintenance costs will come from tracking the versions of various components on your production servers. In fact, this can well apply to your HTML and graphics as well, if you use multiple servers for improved performance. Implementing a solid version control strategy from the beginning can be a real time-saver. Note that where the compiled components are concerned, we mean version control of the executable binaries, not source control of the code to build the binaries. The latter is assumed as part of your standard software development process.

There are essentially two strategies for intranet version control software. The simplest approach is to use a stand-alone version control package to maintain your version archive. To do this, you would create a working copy of your Web server's entire directory hierarchy, including binaries. Changes are made to this working copy, then checked into the archive. Once a set of changes is complete and tested, the production copy of the files is updated from the archive. Multiple servers can then be updated from the same archive, guaranteeing consistency.

While this approach provides all the functionality needed for solid version control, it can be quite cumbersome. Not every file can be handled this way, since some need to vary from one production server to another. Updating production servers must be a manual process, since each server must be stopped before the files can be updated. To overcome these limitations, a number of new Web-centric version control packages have been developed. Two in particular, Microsoft's SourceSafe (combined with FrontPage Server) and PVCS, have made the task of Web site source control much easier.

Both have a somewhat narrow conception of what needs to be controlled in an archive. All current Web-oriented version control systems consider the Web to be the content of the Web's root directory. This is nearly adequate for simple Web sites, consisting of HTML, image files, and maybe a few CGI scripts. But even a very simple Web site is impacted by more than its immediate files. Most server software is controlled by configuration files, and those are rarely stored in the content directories. Other files, such as server-side ActiveX files, come into play on a more complex Web application, and, again, these do not generally reside beneath the Web root. It is our feeling that almost any file that affects the operation of your Web site or application should be kept under source control. If a problem arises because of a change in a setting in a configuration file and your configurations files are not kept under source control, you'll have a hard time knowing what changed. One of the great advantages of source control is the ability to roll back to a previous version of your application to hunt down problems. In a Web-based application, your server is part of the application. If you can't roll back your configuration files, you are not truly re-creating the old environment. In fact, one of the disadvantages of IIS compared to Netscape's servers is that IIS reads its configuration information from the Windows NT registry, precluding source control. You can get around that by exporting the IIS registry key to a file and archiving that. This same file can be imported from source control as well. This extra step is an inconvenience, but is well worth it.

No matter what version control strategy you are using, even if you are using some form of manual version tracking, it is very important to be able to determine which version of your application produced a particular HTML page. During the system testing phase of one of our projects, we used up to six servers for testing. Every time a set of problem reports was resolved, we rebuilt the binaries and re-deployed to each of the testing servers. After one round of fixes, a tester complained to me that a bug he had submitted several rounds earlier had been continuously ignored. Our particular method of version tracking allowed me to view the source of the offending HTML page and see the revision numbers of each of the files (including C++ source files) that went into the creation of the page. One particular file seemed to be quite out of date. Upon further examination, we determined that the developer who had fixed the bug in question had neglected to check in the corrected file. Without the version information, finding this oversight would have taken much more time.

In the example above, the problem turned out to be in C++ source code, but in a Web application there are many, many places for such mistakes. An active Web site undergoes fairly continual change. In a Web site using style sheets or a Web-based application, several files can go into building a single Web page. Keeping track of the changes—and, more importantly, bug fixes—in this environment can be extremely difficult. Clearly, Web-based application development demands the same source control needed for standard application development.

Distribution

Distributing intranet server software is usually an easier task than distributing client software, because the number of servers used on a given intranet tends to be limited. However, a complex application may require a number of testing servers, and certain applications may be deployed on many smaller servers instead of a single large one. One of our applications was designed to run from small servers at each of our client's branch offices, to reduce WAN usage. The application was not expected to change much: More dynamic functions were to be handled from a central server. For this type of scenario, the techniques discussed in Chapter 2 work quite well. In our case, we put together a distribution CD, which included the Web server software, our custom CGI programs, and an installation program that generated appropriate configuration files based on the server environment.

For larger, more centralized applications, especially applications that see frequent updates, you may want to combine your distribution function with your source control mechanism. We detail this method in Chapter 7.

Managing Logs

Nearly all intranet server software generates copious logs not just of errors but of access in general. Some track connections and usage by user, others by workstation. Some track the full details of what a user did in a particular session, others simply summarize the connection statistics. Whatever data your software does make available to you in its logs, it is important to handle it consistently for it to provide its full value.

There are basically three ways that a server program can record logs for the system administrator. The most common is to generate log files on disk, usually one for errors and one for accesses. This technique is common mainly because it is easy and relatively quick. Making sense out of that data, however, is a much more complex issue. For starters, searching through a potentially quite large plain-text file is not nearly as fast as simply appending to it. For this reason, administrators tend to rotate log files: They move the logs at the end of the day into an archive and start logging to a new file. This makes the individual files easier to deal with, but does nothing for the whole set.

Many servers also support SNMP. Using SNMP, a server can send log information to a centralized SNMP monitor that will gather and store the information from many servers. This simplifies certain server monitoring tasks, and makes processing the log data into useful information much easier.

Last, many servers will record their log information to an Open Database Connectivity (ODBC) database. This can make the data much easier to process, without requiring the infrastructure needed by SNMP. Writing a custom program to process logs from a database is much easier than either SNMP or flat files, but keep in mind that writing to the database will still require some processing time.

Summary

In this chapter we took a look at some of the management issues surrounding the two most common Web servers: Microsoft's IIS and Netscape's Enterprise Server. We also looked at managing third-party packages for other services such as mail and news, as well as some application server–specific issues. In the following chapters on Content (Chapter 6) and Application (Chapter 7) Management, you will notice some overlap in the administration of server software, client machines, content, and applications. This is only to be expected as the distribution of client and server components—as well as dependencies on underlying hardware and services—can vary greatly depending on your implementation. Just remember our 10-Layer Model from Chapter 1 and that the bottom line is that each activity (or service) must be accounted for at some point, regardless of where it physically lives.

SOLUTION SCENARIO

Performance Tuning

Performance tuning of intranet servers is complicated by the number of layers involved. Assuming no application layer, or at most a very light application layer (see Chapter 7), performance problems could result from network bandwidth, processor speed, processor cache, memory size, hard-drive size, inappropriate server configuration, poor connectivity among intranet servers, or even malicious tampering!

After working with a particular machine, a software package, or a configuration for a while, you will develop a sense of what changes of behavior are caused by what bottlenecks. Power users of Microsoft Windows know that if their hard drives are being accessed a lot when there is no apparent cause, they probably have too many programs loaded into memory, resulting in excessive page-file activity. To verify this, they could run the Performance Monitor and watch the "Page Faults per Second" indicator. If this was excessive, and closing a program or two caused it to drop significantly, they would have their answer. This is a very good place to start with an intranet server as well.

We once noticed a severe drop in performance on an HP LaserJet running TCP/IP print services. After a bit of packet analysis, we discovered that a rogue process somewhere out on the Internet was trying to establish an FTP connection to our printer! This failed, of course, but the attempt was repeated every second. We blocked our printer's IP address on our firewall, and performance returned to normal. You really cannot rule anything out when investigating performance problems.

The most important step in resolving intranet performance problems must be taken long before the problems arise. In

(*continued*)

SOLUTION SCENARIO *Continued*

order to fix problems, you will need a suite of tools to help analyze the symptoms. While these can theoretically be installed at any time, you will be much better equipped to analyze problem behavior if you have observed the normal behavior of your intranet environment. It is hard to tell if a machine is swapping virtual memory excessively if you do not know how much swapping "normally" occurs.

Thus, in our performance tuning solution scenarios, the preparation phase is critical. The exact tools you choose will depend on your particular intranet environment, but there are a few common classes. High-level tools will allow you to view the overall performance of an application, a service, or the network. These may not give great detail, but they are fast and easy to use, and can provide a sort of triage stage before you attack problems with low-level tools. The low-level tools provide great, often bewildering, detail about a particular network protocol, processor usage, memory usage, and disk access. These are used when the high-level tools have either narrowed a problem to a limited area or failed to help at all.

If you are developing custom intranet applications, providing application layer performance tools may be up to you. In general, a performance monitor for a custom application should at least be able to record the number of simultaneous connections, the number of connections per second, and the time taken to service each request. How exactly these concepts translate into numbers will depend on your application.

In one of our applications, there were two very distinct types of connections: queries and requests. Essentially, a query was a database query resulting in potentially hundreds of records returned. A request resulted in an insert into the database and a small amount of back-end processing. Our initial optimization efforts went into requests, because they

(*continued*)

SOLUTION SCENARIO *Continued*

seemed to require the most processing logic. In the initial version of the performance logging function of the application, we made no distinction between the different types of transactions. We noticed quickly, though, that transactions fell into two ranges. Our intuition was confirmed when we added functionality to the performance monitor to differentiate between the types of transactions: Queries were much more frequent and were returning far more data than expected. As a result, we refocused our optimization efforts around a variety of schemes to cache the results of very common queries. Adding this sort of instrumentation to an existing application can be much more difficult than designing it into the application from the beginning.

If your intranet is based primarily on standard services (Web, FTP, News), you will be able to use the performance monitoring functions of those services. The facilities vary among software packages, but in general you should be able to measure requests per second, simultaneous requests, bytes per second, and some sort of success/failure count. These measures are useful mainly in the initial design and deployment of an intranet, when the configuration and placement of files is still in flux.

In one of our applications, we observed many more graphics transfers than we expected. Looking more closely, we discovered that in some of our HTML pages, we referred to graphics files with lowercase letters, and in others we used uppercase. Of course, this made no difference to our servers, but it confused the caching algorithms in certain Web browsers. As a result, those browsers requested each graphic twice, even though the same graphics were used on every page. This doubled the load placed on our servers by those browsers.

(*continued*)

SOLUTION SCENARIO *Continued*

In another intranet, we used a secure server and an open server. The load on the open server was quite low, while the secure server was barely managing its work. Analysis of the secure server's logs showed that it was expending considerable computation encrypting noncritical graphics files (logos, banners, etc.). By pointing all our references to such files to the open server, we were able to cut the load on the secure server by 30 percent, avoiding a costly hardware upgrade.

Not all intranet load can be monitored easily at the application or service level. Often, the bottleneck is in the network itself. Resolving such issues can require extensive work with a network traffic analyzer, or *packet sniffer.* But these tools, while powerful, can be very difficult to use. Some problems can be found using higher-level tools, so it is always best to at least try that path first.

There are two ways to use a packet sniffer to trace intranet problems. If you have an idea of what the problem is but need to verify it, a sniffer can help isolate the evidence that you need. In this mode you would configure the sniffer to trap only the specific packets that you were looking for. If you have no idea what the problem is, you will want to see all of the traffic. Here you would configure the sniffer to trap all traffic. As you can imagine, this can generate a lot of data to sift through. To make the data more useful, you should try to limit the traffic as much as possible (without, of course, affecting the problem you are trying to isolate).

The former usage is usually easier and more effective. It was this technique that allowed us to trace the mysterious LaserJet problem mentioned above. Since we knew that the traffic we were looking for was targeting the LaserJet, we set our packet sniffer to watch for traffic on port 515 (the printer

(*continued*)

SOLUTION SCENARIO *Continued*

service) addressed to the IP number of our printer. Even though we could see traffic on the network (our hub's lights were blinking), we saw no traffic in the logs. So we broadened the parameters, sniffing for all traffic to the printer's IP number. The logs then showed a packet every second to port 21, the FTP port. Examining a couple of these packets, we were able to determine that an outside machine was attempting to establish an FTP session with our printer.

As an example of the latter usage, one of our intranets was connected to the Internet only by a dial-on-demand proxy server. This was implemented using Microsoft's RAS and Proxy Server. Whenever any browser on the intranet requested an external address, this request was handled by the Proxy Server, which dialed out to our ISP. This worked fine, except that occasionally the Proxy Server would dial for no apparent reason. None of our users even had their browsers running, and yet the Proxy Server dialed out. Running a packet sniffer initially proved useless because there was a huge amount of intranet traffic to sift through. Even though we knew what to look for (a packet referencing an external IP address), we couldn't find it in the nearly 1GB of logs. So we turned off one machine at a time, making sure at each step that the problem still recurred (yes, this did take a while). Finally, we were down to just three machines: our Web/Proxy Server, our database server, and our Lotus Notes server. Running the packet sniffer again resulted in a more manageable log, and we found our problem: A misconfiguration in the database server was resulting in a spurious request every 15 minutes back to our office. This was not at all what we had expected, and since it was not on the standard HTTP port (80) we might not have found it using the first technique above.

(*continued*)

Solution Scenario *Continued*

Some performance problems on intranets may have little to do with the network itself. The various software components of your intranet may not function exactly as expected, especially in concert. If the techniques reviewed above prove to be no help or do not seem to be the right direction, you may need to examine the processor, memory, and/or disk usage on your servers. Most operating systems have built-in facilities for this type of analysis. In Microsoft Windows NT, you can use the Performance Monitor or the Process Viewer for most of this information.

The process viewer can be especially helpful in tracing problems involving CGI programs or multithreaded server plug-ins. In one of our early C++-based CGI intranet applications, performance was fine for the first hour or so after the machine was started, but degraded rapidly after that. The only way to restore performance was to reboot the machine. We all immediately suspected a resource leak of some sort. Somewhere in one of our scripts, we must be allocating memory and never freeing it, or something similar. Eventually, this consumed available memory, causing the server to swap to virtual memory on disk. Looking through our code and running memory leak analyses on it found nothing. We finally ran Process Viewer on a stripped-down test machine and discovered that the entire script was remaining loaded! There were thousands of instances of one particular script that were never unloaded from memory. As usual, fixing the problem was quite easy once we found it.

That particular problem was quite unique to the way we were using CGI, but similar problems arise in most multithreaded, object-oriented environments. Using Microsoft's Active Server Pages and ISAPI technologies with ActiveX servers can produce problems with object references. This is

(*continued*)

SOLUTION SCENARIO *Continued*

especially true if your objects reference each other. Normally, COM (the technology behind ActiveX) tracks references to objects and frees them when they are no longer referenced. One of our ActiveX servers, though, was remaining loaded even after the last of our users had disconnected. The oddity of the server remaining loaded led us to inspect memory usage with the Performance Monitor and Process Viewer, and we found that no instances of a particular pair of objects were ever being freed. Further inspection showed us the problem. The first object, when instantiated, created an instance of the second class, which established a reference back to its parent. When our ASP script released the reference to the parent object, the child still had a reference to it. This left an active reference to each object (the parent referenced the child, the child referenced the parent), and COM did not unload them. If you must have such circular references, you will have to have some way to break the circle. We added a *cleanup* method to the parent, which, when invoked, cleared the reference from the child to the parent. In our ASP script, before we released our last reference to the parent, we invoked the cleanup method. This broke the circle and allowed COM to free the pair of objects.

The last point of analysis to discuss is disk usage. In general, a smoothly running intranet server should not access its disk frequently. This is both an observation and a recommendation. When planning your intranet, you should allow enough memory on your servers so that they can cache virtually all the files they need. Ideally, they should have to access the disk only to write logs, to record submitted information, and to load changed scripts or pages. Obviously this ideal cannot always be achieved—but the less your servers access their hard drives, the better they will perform. Exces-

(*continued*)

SOLUTION SCENARIO ***Continued***

sive hard-drive access can be a sign of a poor configuration. Your Web server may be configured to use less memory cache than it could. Or it may be configured not to cache at all. Excessive disk access should definitely be viewed as a symptom of a potential problem, and should be investigated thoroughly.

A final note on performance tuning: We mentioned earlier that recognizing problems is easier if you are familiar with the normal behavior of your servers. A certain amount of this is simply intuition. Something about the behavior of a machine or group of machines may not feel right. But don't completely rely on intuition. You should periodically record logs of important performance parameters. Once you are comfortable that your intranet is in a stable state at optimal performance, record a few minutes of logs showing memory allocation, processor usage, disk access, and network traffic levels. If your intranet has different usage patterns at different times of day (maybe you run batch account balancing at night and data input during the day), you should record sets of logs representative of the different usage patterns. You will find these to be very helpful as a reference later if things do go wrong. You won't have to ask yourself, Am I imagining things, or is the server particularly slow today?

CHAPTER SIX

Content

The management of content in an intranet is an issue of growing complexity for administrators and Webmasters. As intranets evolve from Web servers that provide simple documents to complex systems delivering wide varieties of valuable content, the need to *effectively* manage that material becomes increasingly important. Doing this, however, is not as clear-cut a task as one would initially imagine. In the past two years we have seen our clients' content grow tenfold or even more depending on how they choose to use this new distribution and information-sharing medium. As such, the need for defined methods for managing content has escalated.

In this chapter we will share recommendations for organizing your intranet content to keep it manageable by using some simple tools and techniques, and setting standards for developers and administrators. We will also look at some of the latest version management tools available for content developers and Webmasters, as well as how Push technology may be used to deliver content in real time.

Organizing Content

The first step to content management is making sure it is organized. We have developed some tools to help ease the maintenance burden for both the content developers (e.g., department writers, artists) and administrators when planning and managing intranet content applications. The following sections describe several that may appear obvious but are often forgotten or omitted due to time constraints. We would caution that—as always—careful planning and documentation of your intentions are your best assurance of success and long-term manageability.

Site Maps

The first thing that, surprisingly, is missing from many applications is a logical schematic for the Web interface. By this, we mean a map of Web pages and their relationship to each other—often known as a *site map.* Although an intranet application is not technically a site in the ordinary sense, it is often represented in a manner similar to Internet applications.

The use of site maps in intranet application design and management will, of course, need to be altered, depending on the type of application being built. Typically, a site map is a very shallow, two-dimensional representation of the browser interface of the application. If there is logic within the HTML code, the application layer, or elsewhere, it will not be directly represented in the site map. The purpose of the site map is to help the Web administrator understand the organization of the pages and manage the content for which he or she is responsible.

Figure 6.1 shows a site map for a simple application drawn with Visio Technical. It was drawn during the planning and design stage, long before any coding was started. The reason the site map was created *first* is that it illustrates the general activity of the site so that users, functional designers, and technical designers can all discuss the application within a common, visual context. It shows the total number of pages, the number of each type of page at each level in the structure, and their dependencies. At this point, page-level linking is not necessarily depicted, although it may be if desired.

TIP *The "depth" of your site will influence its usability. A site map will help determine if the organization of a site promotes usability based on the number of levels in its hierarchy. The structure should be such that no part of the site is more than two to three mouse-clicks away from any other*

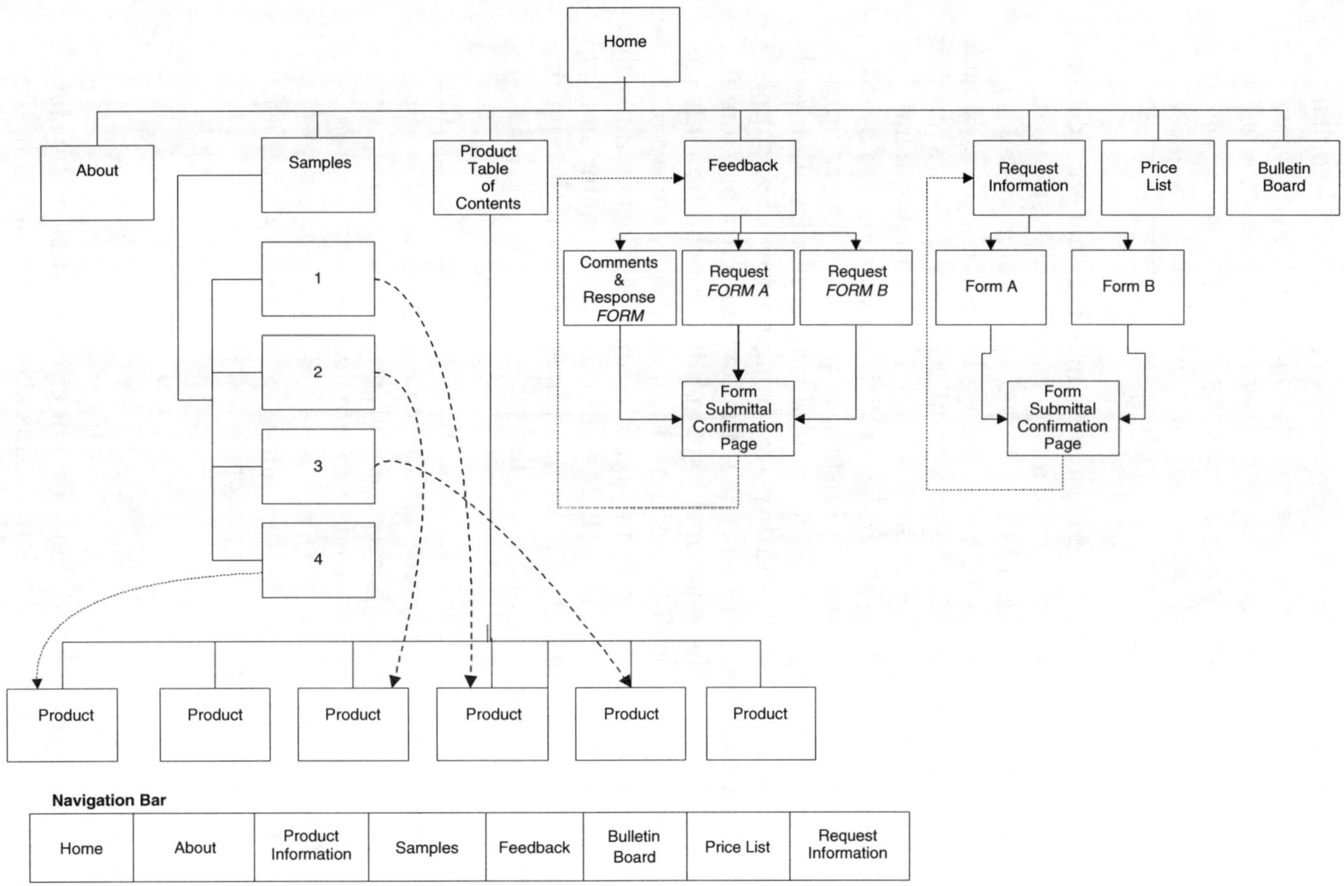

Figure 6.1 Generic application site map.

(usually drilling down through pages) and organized so that a user can intuit where to find sought information. As the application is expanded and enhanced over time, administrators will want to avoid organizational complexity by keeping their site structure logical and as shallow as possible.

We use this mapping technique for single intranet applications, for an application that is part of a larger family of systems, or expanded to encompass all the planned applications in an intranet. Each site map for a smaller application simply ties back into the larger schematic at some point. Figure 6.2 shows another map of interrelated applications within a single department.

Luckily, maintaining site maps in Visio is not required over the long haul if you have an administration package that provides mapping or file relationship for you. If your administration package does not have such a utility, we strongly urge either supplementing or upgrading to a package that includes it. For example, Figure 6.3 shows the relationship of application components as viewed with Microsoft Developer Studio. It shows quite a bit more detail than our sample site maps, including all objects with which an item is associated. As such, it gives the administrator an excellent idea of what objects are involved in each part of the application and how they are related or linked.

TIP *Post your application site maps in accessible (or password-protected) portions of your intranet management site. This will help new designers and administrators understand how others are using the tools, as well as allow everyone to access management documentation with ease—a valuable way to share designs and integration points.*

Functional Maps

Of course, intranets and their content are not managed by site maps alone. Functional relationships also are important to the administrators responsible for developing and maintaining

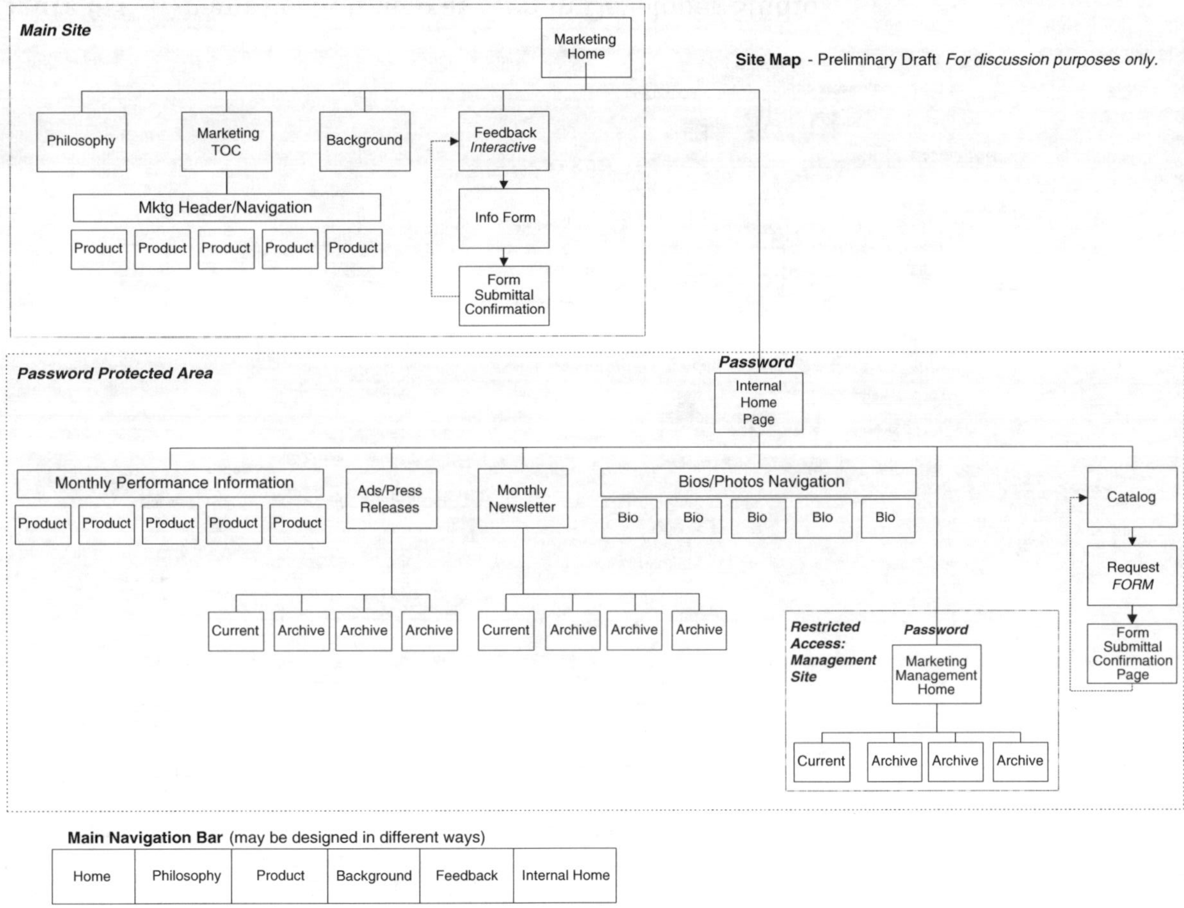

Figure 6.2 Multipart application site map.

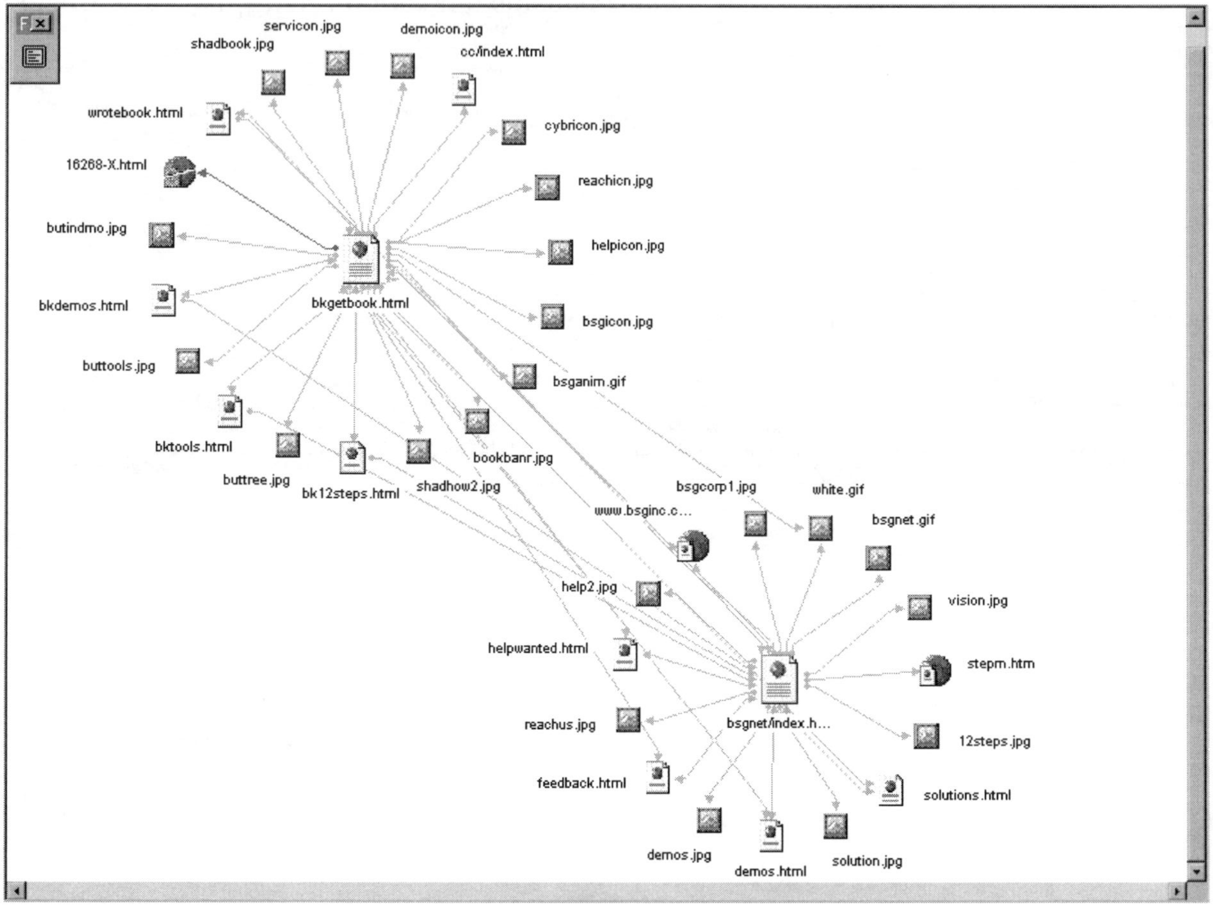

Figure 6.3 An application map as seen in Developer Studio.

applications, however they are best when used in conjunction with other background information and schematics that are part of the full documentation of an application.

Figure 6.4 is a functional information flow for an intranet application that tracks forms (note that it is given in a very generic form to show how the drawing technique is used). The flow is from top to bottom, with the components of the application as logical units of work (LUWs) shown in the boxes for each system user. On the left-hand side, the other parts of the application are shown, which will basically represent what will be the buttons in the application navigation bar at a later iteration of the design.

As an application develops over time, through enhancement and other changes, functional relationship diagrams and supporting documentation are extremely useful to administrators. It helps them understand how the application is meant to perform so that critical functionality is not altered unwittingly.

Interface Design Documentation

Interface design documentation is another important tool for Webmasters to have. It helps them understand how pages should be layed out and how their design correlates to the rest of the application. This in turn helps them keep the design intent consistent and usable as the application is updated.

We recommend using empty browser frames—essentially screen shots—when beginning page interface designs. When working with users and designers, we simply bring a stack of photocopies of blank browser frames upon which we can sketch. Then we can lay out sections of the application and how it will function—how the user will move from one page to the next—on the table or pinned to a corkboard so that everyone in the discussion can see how the design is shaping up.

This information is then documented by the development team and kept on file for administrators and content developers. When they need to see how and why the application was built the way it was—basically to understand the look, feel, and flow of it—they can then reference these documents and diagrams.

Figure 6.5 shows an empty browser frame just as we use them in design sessions, whether for a new application or when updat-

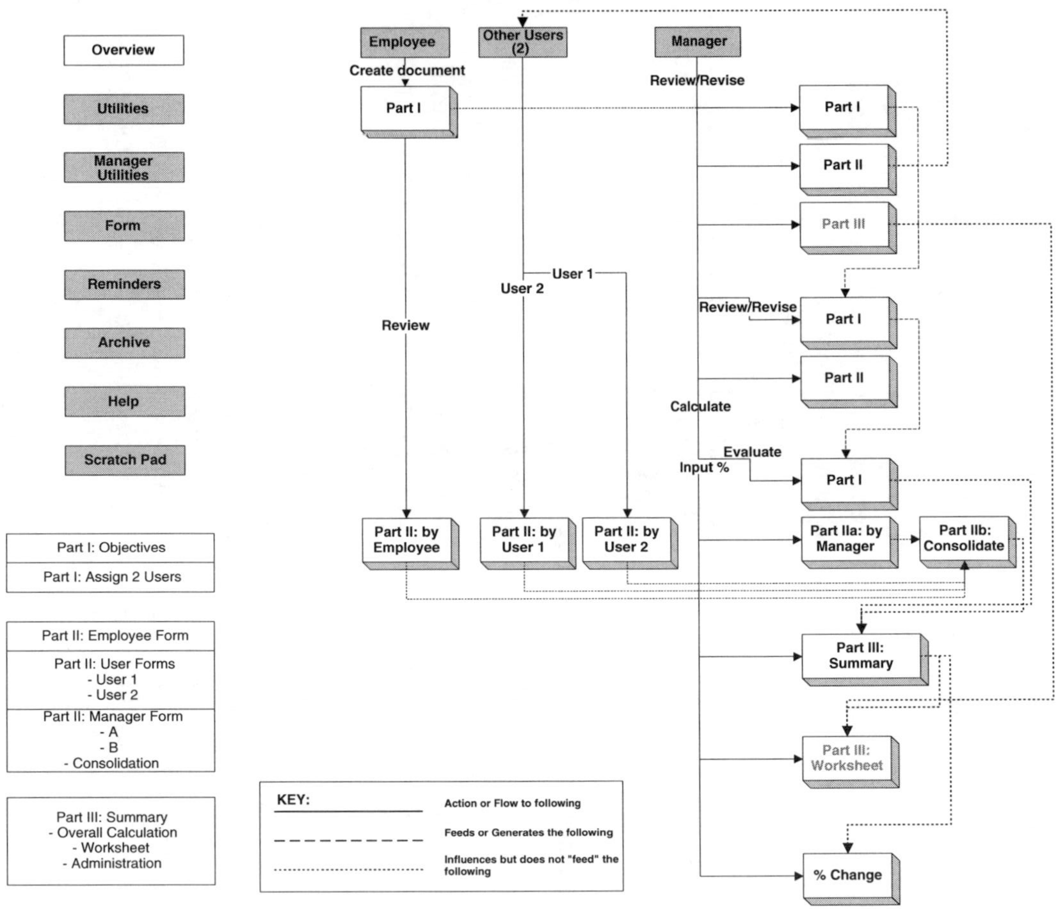

Figure 6.4 Sample application functional flow.

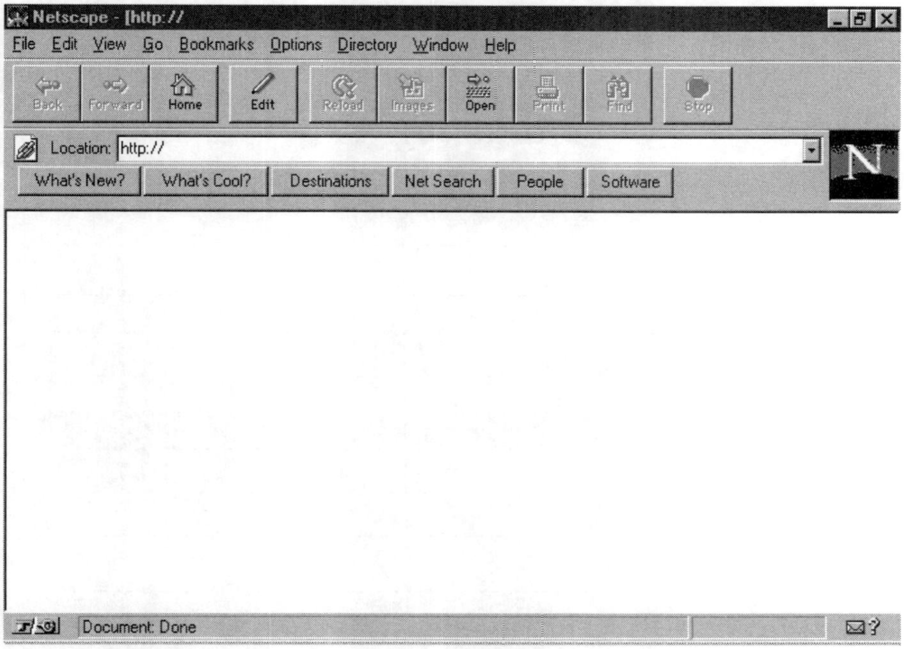

Figure 6.5 Blank browser frame for sketching application interfaces.

ing an interface for an existing application, and Figure 6.6 shows a documented design at first iteration.

TIP *As your application content and designs change, be sure to keep track of your old versions in a safe archive. This is good for reference as well as recycling! You may be able to harvest pieces of old designs in other applications or in later iterations of current ones.*

Editorial Calendar

As anyone who has created a content-rich application knows, the creation of meaningful, interesting content is a true challenge.

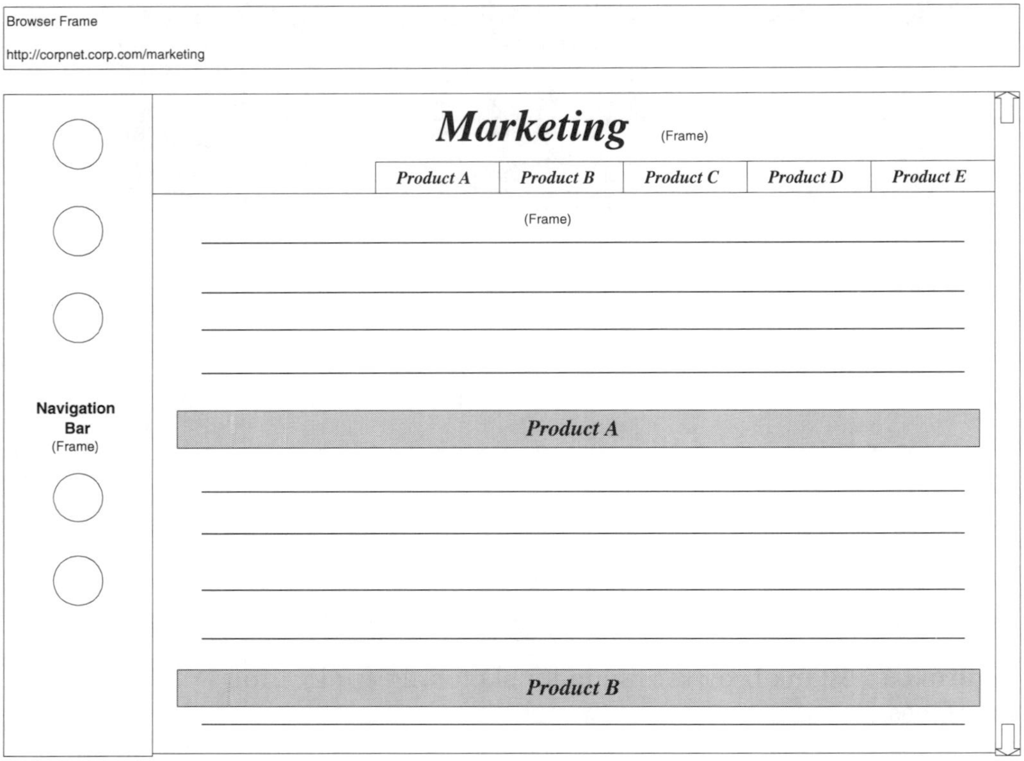

Figure 6.6 Sample interface layout (first iteration) as documented for administrators.

Unfortunately, it is not a challenge that goes away once the application is built; to the contrary, the creation of meaningful, useful content is the ongoing, never ending responsibility of good application owners and administrators. Users want to see fresh, relevant content that answers their need for reliable information. Intranet applications that fail to provide this will only frustrate users and garner negative reputations in the corporation (like any less-than-satisfactory application).

To offset this potential problem, we use an *editorial calendar* as part of our planning and management processes. If you are somewhat familiar with publishing or communications fields, you probably have a good idea why we use such a tool for managing intranet content. An editorial calendar is a document on which planned content is scheduled for easy reference by everyone on the team. At a magazine, for instance, the editor of each section keeps a calendar that lists the columns and sections for each issue of the magazine planned for the year (or longer). As story ideas and contributions are suggested, the content for each is planned far in advance so that writers and artists can plan their pieces and have them delivered in time for layout and printing.

In an intranet application, content can be managed in a similar fashion. First, the owner should determine how often the content needs to be updated. This will very likely change from page to page, as some will have longer life spans than others. A news page may need to be updated daily or weekly, whereas corporate policies and procedures may require changes only when the policy itself is modified—perhaps once a year or even less.

A generic editorial calendar can look something like Figure 6.7. We have found that the most logical place to store this information so that it is easily accessible is—you guessed it—as an HTML page on your intranet. Most commonly, it may be in the IT application in the intranet administration files or in the reference and administration documentation for the application it supports.

Regularly updated content usually is text-based material that is replaced periodically, without the rest of the page layout being

Calendar for (*department name*) (*application name*) **on** (*intranet*) **located at** (*URL*)

Application Owner: ______________ Webmaster: ____________________
Content Approver: _______________ Legal Approver: _______________

Date	File Name/ Reference Locator	Content Section	Update Required	Developer/ Content Provider	Completion

Figure 6.7 Blank intranet editorial calendar.

affected. However, the graphics and layout should also be updated occasionally, depending on the function of the site.

Figure 6.8 is an excerpt from a monthly schedule for a small IT application. Larger applications with lots of changing content would be longer and possibly more detailed so that a reader could follow it. Just as each application in an intranet is different, the editorial calendar for each will be different as well.

You may find that you need many different people, as shown in Figure 6.8, to participate in the creation of content for your application; on the other hand, you may need only the owner and administrator to participate. You may also want to supplement your plan with the participation of other roles (for instance, other IT persons or the marketing department) depending on how your intranet is organized (see Chapter 1). Ultimately, it is the owner's responsibility and liability to ensure that the appropriate people are involved in the proper capacity.

Standards

In addition to site maps and editorial calendars, everyone creating applications for an intranet should have a common set of standards and guidelines from which to work. As intranets have grown, the lack of standards in many organizations has led to haphazard development of pages in wildly varying styles. Users are never sure how a particular application will perform or how it will navigate, because there is little or no agreement among Web administrators to implement consistently.

This is a time when the overall owner of the intranet—which may very likely be IT or the marketing department—must take a stand and set expectations, guidelines, and standards to be used by anyone who wishes to develop for the intranet. Once again, this may be easier said than done.

In some companies that we have visited, we have explained that there needs to be a single accountability point for the success of the intranet—one that can set standards and enforce them as necessary. Ad hoc, haphazard development of applications can only lead to later confusion, inefficiencies, and maintenance nightmares. Unfortunately, the intranet managers with whom we

Calendar for IT Notes & News on CorpNet at http://corpnet.corp.com/IT/News

Application Owner: Elizabeth Jones, IT Director   Webmaster: Tim Barnes, IT developer

Content Approver: Dan Greene, CIO   Legal Approver: Claire N. Sapp, In-House Counsel

MARCH 1998

Date	File Name/ Reference Locator	Content Section	Update Required	Developer/ Content Provider	Completion
3/02/98	default.html	Start	Weekly IT News	Elizabeth Jones, writer Tim Barnes, HTML	
3/9/98	default.html	Start	Weekly IT News	Elizabeth Jones, writer Tim Barnes, HTML	
3/16/98	default.html	Start	Weekly IT News	Elizabeth Jones, writer Tim Barnes, HTML	
3/16/98	usage_policy.html	Policy	Policy Update from CIO/I-Net Review Committee	Dan Greene Claire Sapp, Reviewer Elizabeth Jones, Editor Tim Barnes, HTML	
3/23/98	default.html	Start	Weekly IT News	Elizabeth Jones, writer Tim Barnes, HTML	
3/30/98	default.html	Start	Weekly IT News	Elizabeth Jones, writer Tim Barnes, HTML	
3/30/98	feedback.html	Feedback	**New Section: Customer Feedback	Elizabeth Jones, writer Tim Barnes, HTML	
3/30/98	hd_main.html	Helpdesk	Monthly Helpdesk Update—Facts, Figures, Tip of the Month	Carrie Swinson, Helpdesk Supervisor Elizabeth Jones, Editor Tim Barnes, HTML	
3/31/98	ALL	ALL	Incorporate New Layout Guide-lines from Marketing	Tim Barnes	

Figure 6.8 Sample intranet editorial calendar.

meet often feel unempowered to make such definitive statements; they fear they will be ignored and the departments will continue developing in whatever manner they choose. Managers may also express concern that there will never be consensus on standards for everyone to use, because each developer will want to do it his or her own way, thinking that is the best way.

We understand this concern—we deal with it frequently. However, there is only *one* answer to this conundrum. Go up the corporate food chain to find a sponsor who *can* make decisions that will be respected and get that person's backing. This may mean going to the CIO, CFO, or even the CEO to get buy-in that intranet consistency is a long-term critical success factor and that they must support you in implementing it. You must convince them to support an *organized* intranet operation, just as they support organized manufacture of other products or the organized recording and reporting of financials. With this support then, the intranet owner can do whatever it takes to make sure standards are set in a timely manner and used by anyone who wishes to be part of the intranet.

The culture of your organization will probably influence how strict your standards should be. Some companies have very detailed standards on everything from coding to look and feel to the rate at which content must be updated, whereas others simply distribute design suggestions that need not be followed.

Basic Development and Administration Standards

At a minimum, you will want to make sure that all intranet applications have some common features that will make them understandable and usable by your user community. Which features you think should be standard will probably depend on the sophistication of your users. If you are building for store clerks with an average eighth-grade education you will probably have very different considerations than if you are building for NASA scientists.

However, the following are some basics that are recommended to everyone building and managing intranets:

Standard navigation providing direct access to the intranet home page and other major applications or sections should be included. These days most intranet applications are designed for frames-enabled browsers, so a navigation bar at the top, bottom, or left side of the browser is used to provide quick and easy access to other parts of the intranet. For navigation within a departmental application, a supplemental bar may be added to the main one or another standard may be suggested. In many companies, this decision is a collaborative effort between IT and the marketing department so that the resulting standard is both usable and attractive.

Standard information about each page should be included so that users will be able to assess the timeliness and accuracy of each, and know how to contact the appropriate person if they have comments or questions. As part of the standard header or footer on content pages we suggest including:

- Document source
- Department
- Author name and E-mail address
- Administrator or Webmaster E-mail address
- Creation date and date last modified
- Guidelines for using alt-tags behind graphics
- Page titles for all documents (you may wish to suggest a format)

Size limits for certain types of files. In general we recommend that no page should be more than 50K, with an average page size of 10–15K. We encourage page authors to learn to lay out pages in such a way that graphics can be minimized or eliminated. Your environment may be such that larger or smaller files should be standard, depending on your bandwidth, standard hardware, software, and expected usage.

Tips for selecting color palettes and simplifying images to keep them at a manageable size will make the administrator's job much easier.

Suggested layouts with corresponding font and color styles should be included. Typically, you should have standards for at least five types of content:

Start page or table of contents page. The design for an opening page of an application or the header of a section of an application. Typically this is used to logically segment portions of the application for easier navigation.

General contents page. Basic layout for pages with explanatory text, graphics, and links to other resources.

Raw information wrapper. Layout for pages that contain some sort of raw data such as spreadsheets or press releases. These typically have few or no graphics or linking beyond the standard navigation tool, and do not follow that typical content page layout since they merely present data.

Multimedia. When a large graphic is desired there should be a standard method for displaying the information (e.g., as a GIF file without a full HTML page around it). Sound files should also have a standard file format (e.g., WAV for short clips, RealAudio for streaming audio) and recommendations for when to use AVI or MPEG.

FTP. There should be a standard method for linking and storing downloadable files. This should include size, format, and FTP directory.

In addition, it is wise for the intranet owner to create basic guidelines for creating applications. When a department is considering developing new or expanded functionality, there are some fundamental considerations that should be undertaken. We have put together a sample of some of the ones we use most frequently, starting on page 195, which you may wish to supplement or reduce according to your own needs.

Creating Templates

In addition to having development policies and procedures, creating templates that content developers and administrators can pattern their work upon will save inordinate amounts of time and effort in content management. This can help ensure that applications have a degree of predictability and consistency that otherwise could not be achieved unless the same developer(s) created all the pages for your intranet.

You can create templates easily and then simply distribute them on your intranet to developers. Some companies are going so far as to create *wizards* to make the process truly idiot-proof. A wizard is a small application that guides users through a set of questions to help them determine the information that will be contained in their Web page (see Figure 6.9). When users are finished, the wizard creates the actual HTML code and the pages are ready to go with minimal edits or changes required. The Microsoft

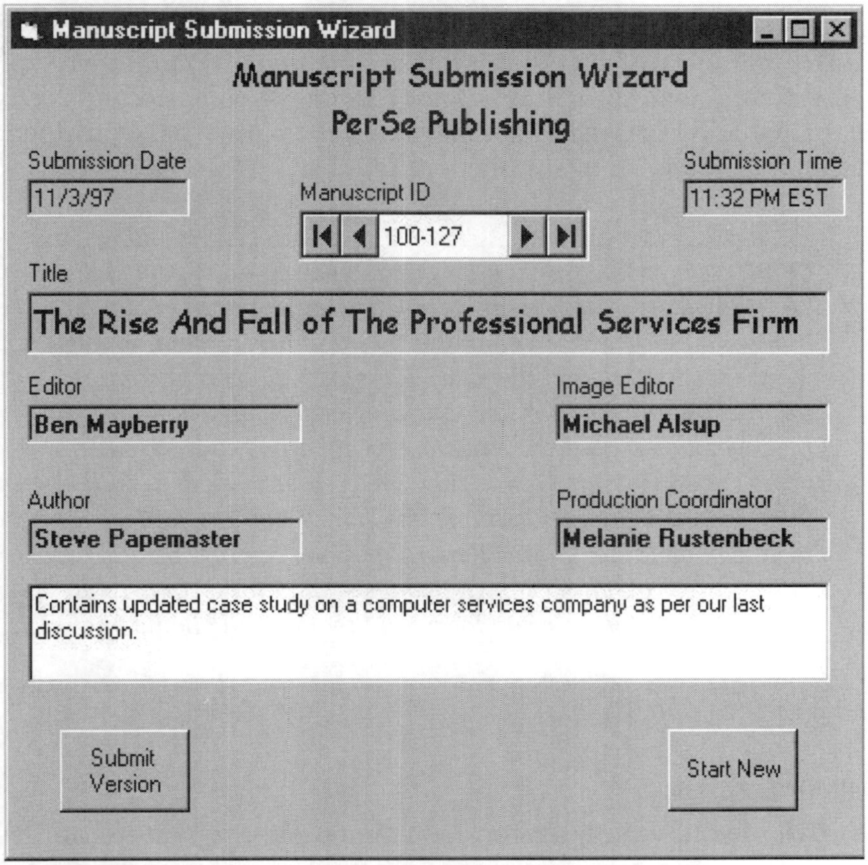

Figure 6.9 Wizard for creating content pages.

SDK for building wizards in Front Page is fairly straightforward; however, it is basically unsupported at the time of this writing. (For more information, see the Microsoft Web site.)

Keeping Documentation and Records

Every good Web administrator or Webmaster should keep a directory with relevant site information, probably as part of a password-protected intranet application. If you are responsible for setting management standards in your organization, you should require that all Web administrators keep consistent documentation and records for their own reference, for IT's, and for later administrators.

The following list is the minimum documentation that we typically recommend for administrators. If your Webmaster is very technical and responsible for more duties than we have outlined here, you may wish to supplement this list.

TIP *As your intranet grows and expands—and especially if it involves people from many different departments in key roles—you may wish to create some standard intranet management toolkits that include shared or stand-alone repositories for tracking information. For our projects we have migrated the management Toolkit that we created in Lotus Notes several years ago to Domino so that they are Web-accessible as well. Ours includes Project Documents, Change Control, Issues, Meeting Scheduler, Status Reporting, Code Share, Specification Repository, Database Change Requests, Standards, and Team Address Book (as we often form joint teams with clients and partners).*

WHOM-TO-CALL LIST

As part of your administrator documentation, a whom-to-call list for all team members to reference should be created and stored on the intranet for easy access (see Table 6.1).

Sample Guidelines for Developing Intranet Applications

1. Establish the business case for the site or application. Although it can be brief and to the point, the business value should be clearly stated before undertaking any sort of technology investment. This includes identifying:

- The target audience for the end product
- The expected return on investment or business need that will be satisfied

Then the project needs to be reviewed to ensure that net-based technologies are the most appropriate for deployment. In some cases, another solution class may be advisable.

2. Identify the project stakeholders from the appropriate functional, technical, and business areas that will be impacted and/or involved in the project. This is also the time to assign project roles. Additionally, it is important to:

- Recruit a project sponsor with executive-level authority to ensure success.
- Gain consensus from stakeholders to promote and contribute to the project.
- Identify the owner and project manager responsible for day-to-day operations and project completion and establish a project plan.
- Identify content developers and administrative staff (e.g., a Webmaster) responsible for managing the daily operations of the project.
- Identify the content and legal approvers for the project.

(*continued*)

3. Notify the IT Intranet Group to discuss plans and coordinate with any relevant companywide efforts or initiatives. This ensures consistency and communication between the various departments. IT may have useful recommendations or tips/tricks learned from other efforts that can aid the development and implementation process.

4. Decide on the technical design for the application. (*Note:* If there are corporate application design standards—for example, tools, techniques, languages—they should be referenced here.)

5. Assess development needs. Determine what the hardware, software, personnel, and supporting component requirements are for the application. With the rapidly evolving pace of technology, each net-based application should be revisited to ensure that the proposed technologies are in line with the evolving set of corporate standards. Make especially sure that communications needs are adequately addressed including network bandwidth, Internet connectivity, and routing. This activity should be coordinated with the IT Intranet Group prior to initiating the procurement process.

6. Complete the application design and prototype. In designing the application it is suggested that a series of site maps and editorial calendars be used to facilitate the process and manage content development. For transaction-based applications, business process mapping and functional design should precede database, business object, application, and screen designs. In many cases, a simple HTML prototype may speed the consensus process. It is strongly advised that application test scripts be written early in the design process to ensure that expected results are achieved.

7. Proceed with development. Execute the plan, including the architectural components, application design, database

(*continued*)

configuration (as appropriate), and application development. Please refer to existing corporate guidelines covering development of custom applications for further information.

8. Do testing and get approval from the project team and department content approver.

9. Obtain approval from other content approvers (i.e., the marketing department for external material), the legal approver, and the project sponsor, as necessary.

10. Deploy the plan. The application administrator should have a deployment plan and live date prepared prior to the release of the final product. This plan must be approved by and coordinated with the IT Intranet Group.

11. Plan for maintenance, backup, and recovery. Be prepared for high activity at initial installation and to provide maintenance and support as necessary. A plan for adequate support must also be enacted; most intranet systems require 24-×-7 support and must be carefully examined to make sure they meet the design goals for mean time to recover (MTTR). Business applications must also follow corporate guidelines for disaster recovery.

12. Plan for quality assurance and review. Have a mechanism for soliciting and recording feedback and suggestions from users, and incorporating this information into the next iteration of the application. Have a plan for continuously updating and improving the site; an editorial calendar and updated site map may be helpful.

TABLE 6.1 Whom-To-Call List

Name	E-mail	Phone	Group	Role
Mitra Miller	mmiller@bsginc.com	212-632-1700, X	BSGnet Team	Project Manager, Owner
Ben Bernard	bbernard@bsginc.com	212-632-1700, X	BSGnet Team	Architect, Advisor
Andy Roehr	aroehr@msn.com	212-632-1700, X	BSGnet Team	Director, Approver

SOLUTION SCENARIO

Using Wizards for Content Development and Management

At a publishing house, the need to create and manage content can take on new proportions compared to what the ordinary business deals with. One client of ours decided they needed to give semi-computer-literate users, such as book authors and journalists who are external to the corporate network, the ability to publish content on their intranet so that the rest of the community of editors and publishers could share access to the material. Doing this, however, was obviously a tricky task, as the client was certain that the most that could be expected from their user community was a basic understanding of word processors and the ability to connect to the Internet and use Web browsers. A two-prong solution was proposed that involved the following steps.

First, a demilitarized zone (DMZ) would be provided between the intranet and the public Internet, in which authors and editors could share content. Two firewalls would be used to provide a secure space for posting manuscripts and other files to be shared by the internal and external communities. The basic configuration is shown in Figure 6.10.

The idea of a DMZ is to provide a secure space for shared work between the two communities without jeopardizing the security of the corporate intranet by allowing access to nonemployees. In the case of this example, only users from within the organization were allowed to go outside the second firewall and return data—no access was allowed through the second firewall by entities external to the organization (a proxy at the firewall was used to manage internal IP sources in this arrangement). This client felt the security risk was such that a firewall with username and password authentica-

(*continued*)

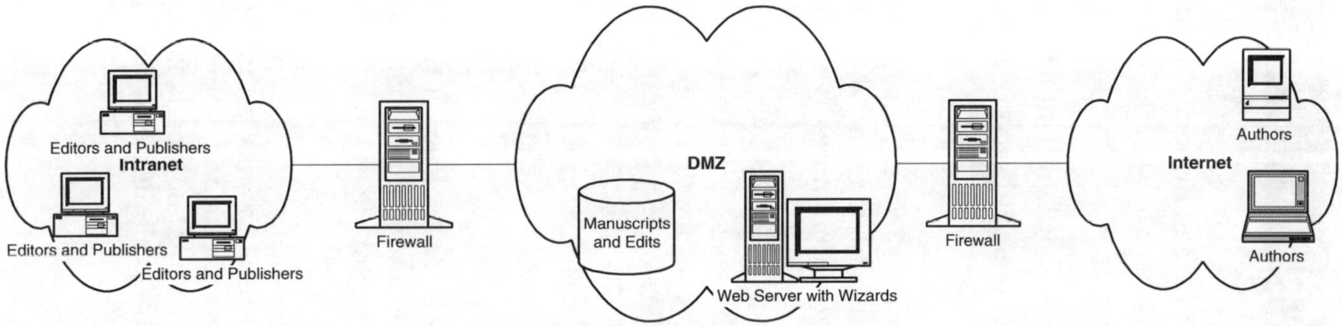

Figure 6.10 Creating a demilitarized zone (DMZ).

SOLUTION SCENARIO *Continued*

tion was sufficient security to access the DMZ (although certain areas of the DMZ had additional challenge/response criteria). However, for added security, the following measures could have been used:

- Username and password authentication
- Certification of clients and servers using the X509.3 standard
- 128-bit encryption using Netscape Secure Sockets Layer (SSL) version 3 (*Note:* This is for domestic use as there is still at this time a restriction on the encryption of data internationally to 40 bits or less.)

Second, wizards (such as the one in Figure 6.9) would be provided for generating pages with embedded documents and links to other appropriate directories and pages. These wizards would use a series of questions to guide authors through the Web page creation process and store their work in the appropriate location on the intranet for editors to access.

PLANNING:

The planning for this effort took about two weeks of effort on the part of an architect and a project manager, including the building of a wizard prototype as a proof of concept.

TIME:

The actual duration was six weeks, although that included the configuration of hardware and software for the environment. The effort was also intentionally encapsulated to get a quick-hit win prior to developing other services.

(*continued*)

SOLUTION SCENARIO *Continued*

EFFORT:

The development was performed by a team of four lead application developers, a part-time senior technical manager (responsible for the firewall and quality assurance of other architecture components), and a full-time project manager who doubled as a functional designer and QA.

RESULTS:

The wizard was a straightforward implementation process, as was the creation of the DMZ. The trick was the additional management overhead to the network administration staff to have all the users configured properly by the time the applications were ready for release (many required new or changed user accounts).

One strong recommendation is to give extra time for iterative feedback on the wizard from real users, not just from the team working on the project. Because wizards are supposed to be intuitive, designing them can be challenging unless a knowledgeable designer is involved. In this effort, the users were consulted on an almost ongoing basis, and then a set of usability tests were performed on a small, random sample from other parts of the organization.

Version Management

Integrity—the concept of the proper file or program being in the proper place at the proper time to keep a system functioning—and version control are as important to content development and management as they are to code development. Content on an intranet really can be thought of in the same manner as components of client/server applications—it needs to be tracked and administered carefully because of interdependencies of documents, other objects, and links between them.

The need for good version-control software has not gone unnoticed by vendors, especially Microsoft and Netscape. (*Note:* Independent vendors are providing some excellent options here as well.) Both vendors have recently developed new suites of tools to help Webmasters and administrators manage their content and publish it reliably. Although we like much of what we see in these tools, they are not yet as streamlined as they should be. However, considering the obvious importance of content management to administrators and managers across the globe, you can be reasonably confident that the tools will grow more and more robust.

Regardless of the tool that you choose, you should look for the following features in your software, to be of maximum assistance to your administrators:

- It should provide a common repository for storing content.
- It should provide a check-in and checkout facility with username and date-time for each file.
- It should provide versioning of files, allowing different states (versions) of documents to be used by different users when desired.
- It should provide visual link management across sites and applications.

We discuss other aspects of version control in relation to more complex applications in Chapter 7.

TIP *The Working Group on Versioning and Configuration Management of World Wide Web Content has a page of resources at www.ics.uci.edu/~ejw/versioning/. Although it is hard to know exactly how the group's work will affect the products on the shelf in the long run, it has identified the following basic capabilities that should be in a tool (check out the site for more good information):*

> Policy-neutral versioning. *The methods defined for accessing, modifying, and locking entities should*

allow multiple versioning policies to be built on top of them.

Retrieval of a stated version of an entity. *Any given revision of an entity should be accessible, thus supporting links to stated revisions of entities.*

Writing to a given version of an entity. *Once changes have been made to an entity, versioning policies often dictate that the changes be written into a new, stated version of that entity.*

Parallel development support. *Since it frequently occurs that several people edit the same entity simultaneously, this type of activity must be supported.*

Browsing within a collection of entities. *Often, multiple entities together form a logical grouping—for example, a collection of HTML and GIF entities that comprise online documentation for a software product.*

Retrieval of derivation relationships between versions of an entity. *The ability to trace the development and ownership of an entity provides visibility into the development of that entity and is frequently useful to the user.*

Visibility control. *Through the user agent, it should be possible to control the external visibility of an entity.*

Types of group work supported. *These should include single and parallel asynchronous, and not parallel synchronous.*

Content Approval Processes

The ability to publish information on an intranet gives great freedom to your user community; however, it also may expose the organization to risk if content is posted that misrepresents the company or its interests. You may have heard of companies with

SOLUTION SCENARIO

Using Visual SourceSafe for Content Management

The issue of managing content within in an intranet has several layers of complexity. At the most basic level, it is necessary simply to track versions of files, including Web pages, multimedia clips, and artwork, as they migrate from the developer desktop to the intranet.

To do this, a tool such as Microsoft's Visual SourceSafe can be very useful. The typical configuration is something like Figure 6.11. In this example, a developer is working at his workstation, developing content first on the local working directory. He probably is running a personal Web server in addition to his HTML editor—in this case, MS FrontPage—so that he can develop and test the files locally before migrating them into the intranet environment.

On the intranet there is a Web server (in this example, it is Internet Information Server, or IIS) and a FrontPage Server, located on the same server machine. Visual SourceSafe (VSS) may also be running on this machine or on another server within the environment.

As the developer completes files, he checks them into VSS. When a user requests that file from the Web server (IIS), IIS/FPS requests the current version of the file of VSS and caches it locally in its Master Directory for future use.

The next time the file is edited by the developer, he checks it out of VSS, which logs the pertinent who/what/when information about the file checkout. When he returns it to VSS, he checks it in as a new version and the old can be archived. The next time the file is requested from IIS, it checks the version of its cached copy of the file against the VSS version to determine if a new copy is needed; if so, it retrieves the new copy and sends it to the user.

(*continued*)

SOLUTION SCENARIO *Continued*

This very simple configuration of version control software is most useful for small, very controlled intranet development environments. It is recommended as insurance against developers mixing files (and accidentally overwriting each other's work) and as a way to track versions.

PLANNING:

Plan the version control software to be used, the hardware it will run on, and who will administer users and their permissions.

TIME:

Implementing the software is easy, assuming you have the base operating system and Web server (e.g., Windows NT and IIS). Installing VSS should take only a couple of hours. The overhead is in designated users and their permission levels for files, which can take less than an hour or considerably more if there are many users.

EFFORT:

One server administrator is needed to install and configure the software.

RESULTS:

This is very easy to implement at this level for a relatively small group, and the benefits in long-term reliability and integrity of files clearly outweigh the costs.

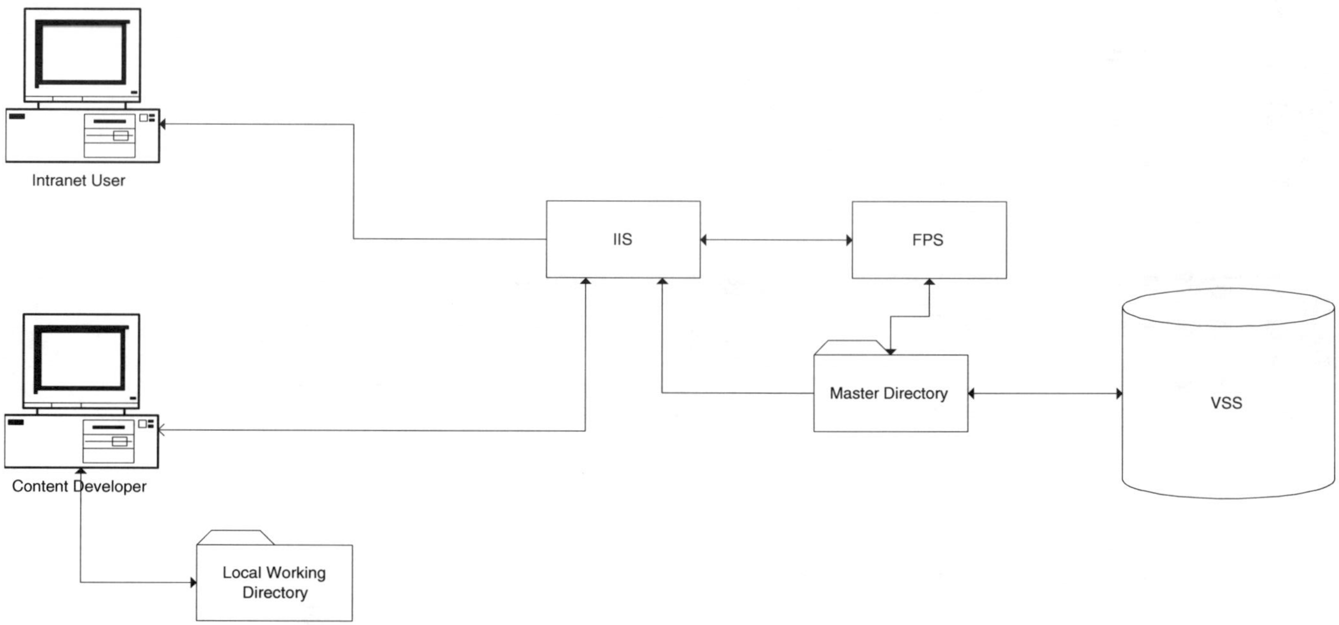

Figure 6.11 Basic use of version control software.

departments posting confidential information on renegade sites without proper approval. Although no maliciousness was intended, this sort of practice can expose the organization to risk.

Thus, many companies are migrating approval procedures into their intranet operations. This process can be completely user-driven by exchanging files between individuals using E-mail or the like. However, this quickly becomes inefficient as the number of content producers and approvers grows with the information being produced. We have found that using a common paradigm once again from the development environment is useful to facilitate the process. Use separate development and production environments for producing, testing, and migrating content as well as code. The scenario looks something like Figure 6.12.

Once again, a developer checks out a file from the repository (in this case, we are extending the Microsoft example cited above) and edits it locally at the workstation. He tests it on his personal Web server until he is satisfied that it should be migrated to the development environment. He then checks the file back into the development environment. In the case of Visual SourceSafe, a project can be set up as the development environment, such as "Corpnet-dev." A separate project is set up as the production environment and named something like "Corpnet-prod." When the file is checked into Corpnet-dev, it does not affect the live intranet on Corpnet-prod; however, it can be accessed via a development Web server for the content developers and approvers. The content approver can then see the file in the development environment, test it if appropriate, and decide if it may be migrated to the production environment.

Visual SourceSafe has the capability for file sharing between projects. For instance, once the file "index.html" is approved in Corpnet-dev, then index.html in Corpnet-prod can point at the same physical source code. When the next version of index.html is migrated to Corpnet-dev, it will not affect Corpnet-prod, which will continue to point to the old version of the file until told to do otherwise.

This ability to point to particular versions of files is called "pinning," and gives administrators the ability to have greater control over code that is migrated into production.

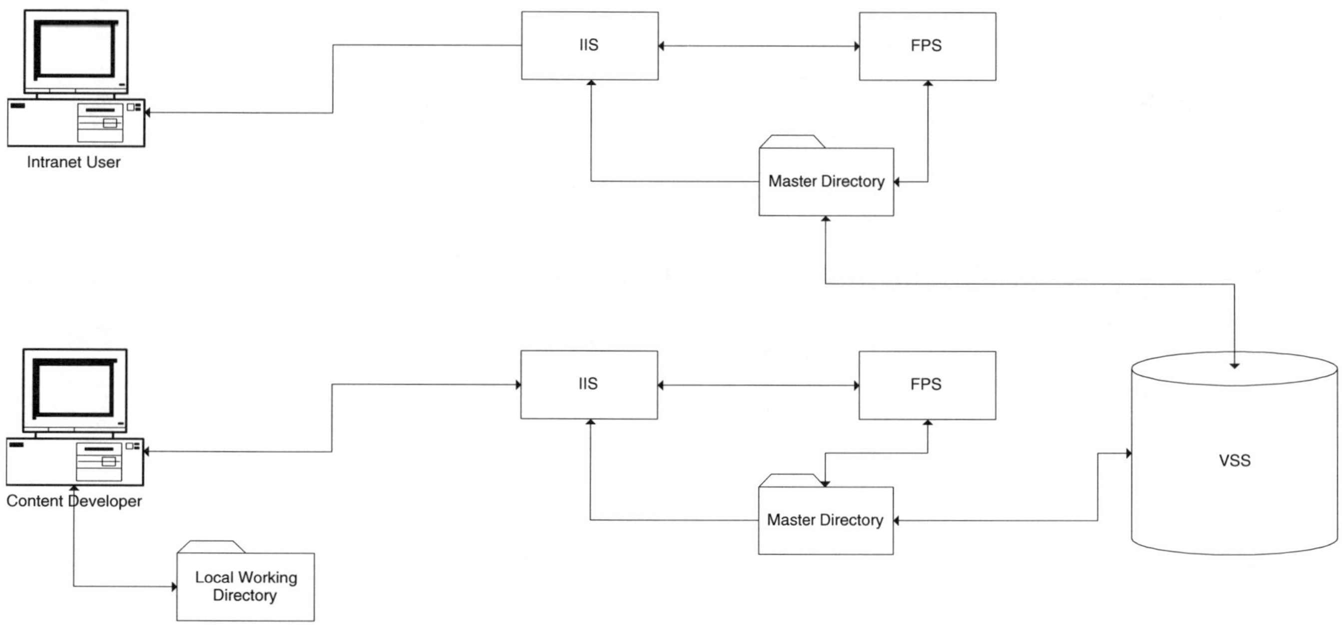

Figure 6.12 Separate development and production environments.

Extending the Development and Approval Environment

This same concept can be scaled to include multiple development, test, and approval environments as it makes sense for the organization. Depending on the size and distribution of your content development staff, it may make sense to have additional environments.

Figure 6.13 shows the use of separate development and test environments prior to the migration of code to an external site in a demilitarized zone or the Internet. Notice that the content is a *one-way* migration of code out to the "external" server, and nothing is allowed back through the firewall. All development, edits, and revisions of content are performed inside the organization and then an administrator moves it to the outside site when ready. Once again, file sharing and version pinning can be used to control source file approval until ready for publication.

TIP *Test new software in your development environment prior to using it in production. By testing new software packages and tools in your development environment, you can save yourself time and headaches in deployment to the rest of the organization, and prevent having to back out modifications because of unknown conflicts. To do this effectively, however, you will have to keep firm control of the development environment so that it is a very close mirror of the production environment that you seek to simulate.*

Other good tools for content and source management include the following:

Intersolv, the makers of the PVCS line that is used in so many development shops, has a new product called PVCS Tracker for Web Teams that is specifically designed to allow for Web content control and version management. PVCS Tracker automates an approval-based change control process, a good feature for intranet organizations that have many content authors submitting to one administrator or webmaster. This allows the application owner and administrator to agree on

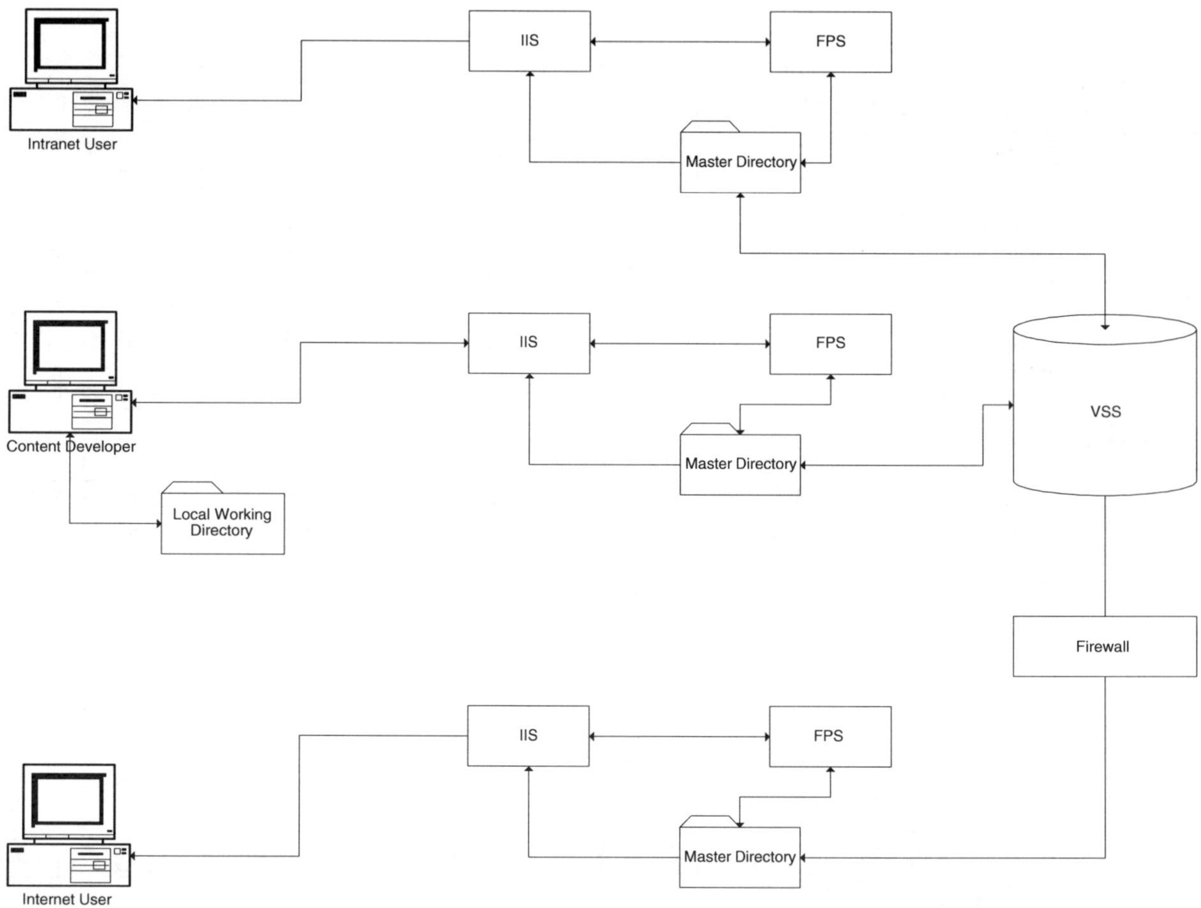

Figure 6.13 Internal development and production environments separated from an external or DMZ environment.

their processes and have technology enforce them. The tool also has some canned reports that track change requests to your intranet content. (For more information see www.intersolv.com/products/pvcs-webteams.htm.)

Mortice Kern Systems (MKS) is one of the leaders in the area of software management tools. Its new Web-based product, Web Integrity (www.mks.com), is designed to record new versions of Web pages while maintaining easy rollback capability. Netscape has chosen MKS as its technical partner, with the core functionality of Web Integrity integrated into the Netscape Enterprise Server. MKS also has a strategic technology partnership with Informix Software and has developed an object management DataBlade for the Informix Universal Server.

TIP *For more information and the latest recommendations on Web versioning issues, check out the page from the Internet Engineering Task Force's World Wide Web Distributed Authoring and Versioning Working Group. The purpose of this group is to set functional requirements and drive standards and recommendations for the industry. Read all about it at www.ics.uci.edu/~ejw/authoring.*

Link Management

Link management seems like an obvious need for any intranet site or application, but it can present more challenges than you would think, especially as the intranet expands and the files to which you link are beyond your control (e.g., files in other departments or on the Internet).

As mentioned before, link management is a feature in many Web site management packages. (See Figure 6.14.) One well-known package is WebMapper from NetCarta, now owned by Microsoft and renamed Site Analyst, which performs automatic

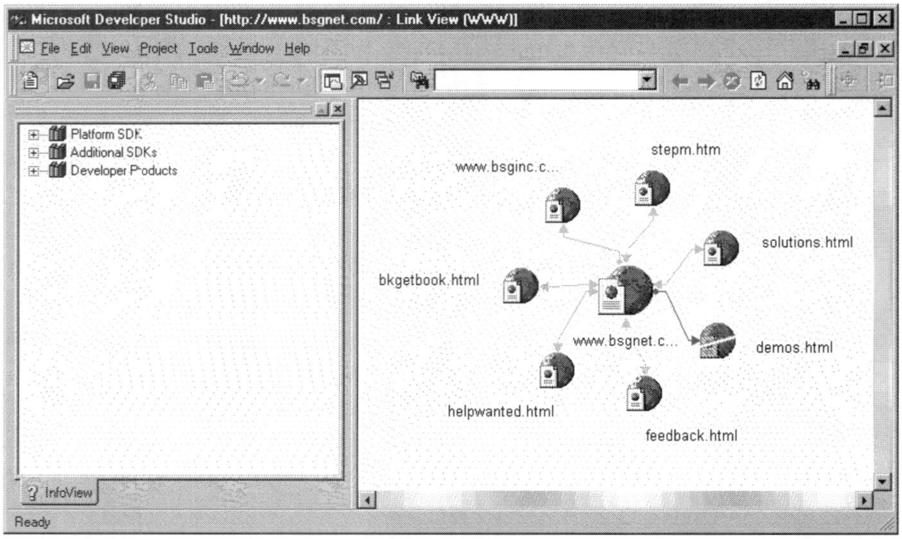

Figure 6.14 Link Management: Fixing a broken link is vastly simplified with a tool that spots them.

link validation on a selected site. Site Analyst is available as a component of Microsoft Commercial Internet System (MCIS) 2.0, Site Server 2.0, and Site Server, Enterprise Edition. For more information on these products, see the BackOffice Live web site at www.backoffice.microsoft.com.

In Netscape's Enterprise Server there is integrated link management built in to maintain and update links, helping administrators avoid broken links on their Web sites as documents are moved, renamed, and updated. The NetShare toolset provides views that make it easy to find and correct documents that do have broken links, and also incorporates revision and access control. Visit Netscape at home.netscape.com for more information.

Usage Analysis

There is an old adage that the three critical success factors in real estate are "location, location, location." The same could be said of intranets, where the crucial issues are "content, content, content."

What is the point of providing information to people if they do not like it and consequently cannot or will not read it and use it?

In order to assess whether a site or application is accomplishing its objective to provide useful information to people, the administrator should regularly assess its usage. Effectiveness may be measured in raw number of hits per page (i.e., user requests for a given page) and many other criteria that can be derived from the information tracked in the log files of your Web server. Some that are commonly suggested include:

- What pages are users accessing most often?
- What are the most common entry and exit points of an application or site?
- Which user groups are accessing which applications and at what time of the day? (When are the peak times?)
- Where are the users and departments located? (Especially valuable in a geographically distributed organization.)
- What client operating systems are being used? (If you have a heterogeneous environment, this can be useful.)
- What browsers are being used? (If you give your users a choice of browsers, this may tell you if your licensing is paying off.)
- What forms are being submitted and in what volume?
- What scripts are being run and when?

An analysis tool will review the log files created by your Web servers and provide you with valuable information about your sites and your users. A couple of our favorite tools for this function are as follows.

WebTrends is an easy-to-use third-party package compatible with log files created by any Web server. Reports generated by WebTrends include statistical information as well as colorful graphs that show trends, usage, market share, and much more. A free trial download (which is what convinced one of our Webmasters to use it) is available at www.webtrends.com.

Microsoft includes a Usage Analyst in its Site Server tools that is based upon the recent acquisition of Intersé market focus. Usage Analyst provides usage analysis capabilities to generate the information needed to measure return on Web investment. Both administrators and managers responsible for the intranet can use the preconfigured analysis reports available with Usage Analyst to learn about how frequently and how long content is viewed. The standard reports can also reveal request and visit trends, navigational patterns, and server load patterns, among other things. With this information, administrators then can make necessary adjustments to the site to better serve their users.

If you prefer to create your own reports to analyze your sites, you can simply have them run against your server log files. You might check out the following free scripts and log analysis tools available at http://awsd.com/scripts/index.shtml for ideas. Just be aware that freeware is *not supported.*

See Figure 6.15.

Using Push Technology for Content Distribution

Currently, one of the most talked-about methods of managing content on intranets is through the use of Push technology. Up to this point we have mostly referenced Pull applications—ones that provide information and data to users via a server from which they can browse or download information at will. This means that users are in control of what they see and when. Until recently, this sort of information access has been sufficient because users typically know what is available to them and how to access it. However, the rush of all kinds of valuable information and content has overwhelmed average users. They no longer know what is available to them, much less how to find it.

This presents the intranet owner and application designer with a new problem. If there is valuable information that the population should have, how can you make sure that they have easy access to it? Various methods have been used. One is mass E-mails

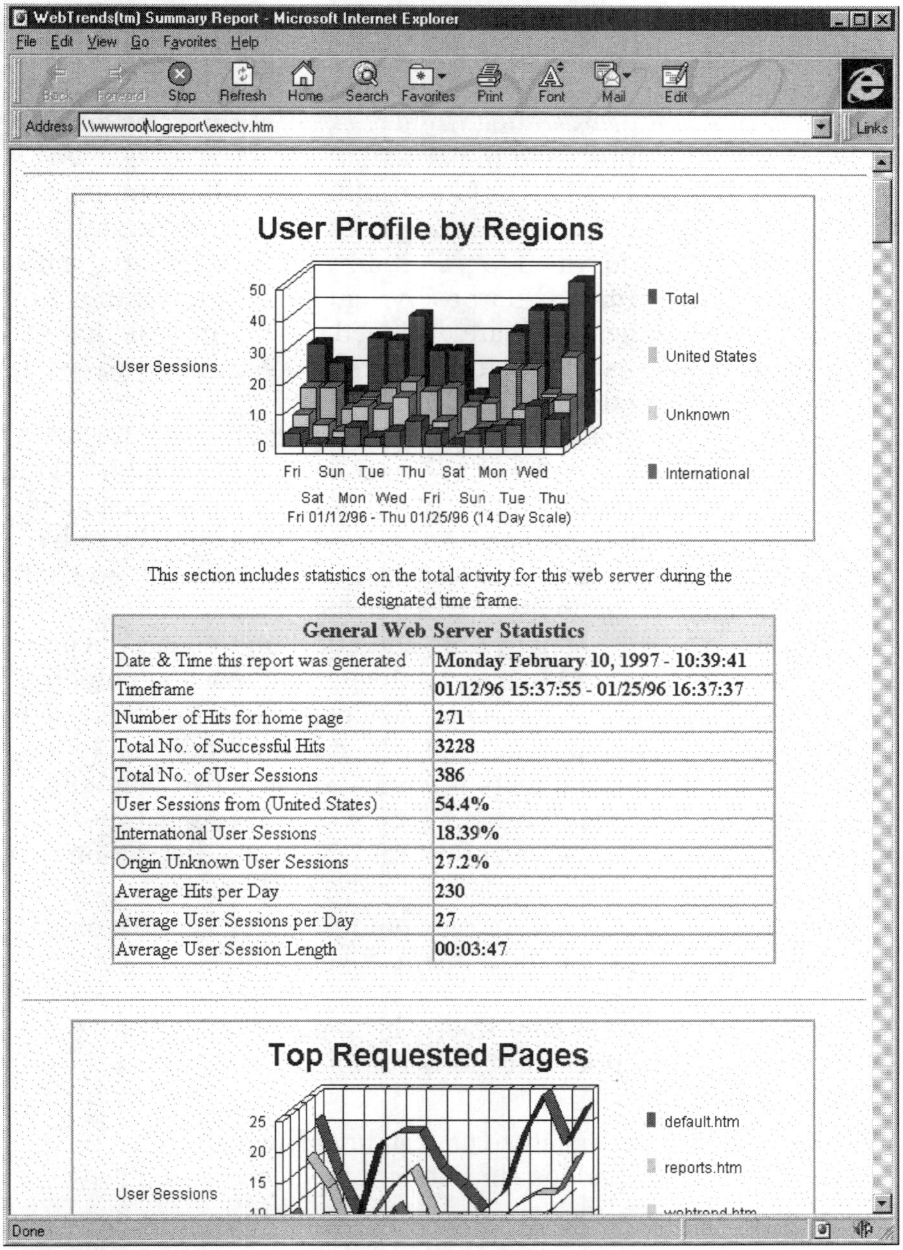

Figure 6.15 Usage analysis report as produced by WebTrends.

that have produced as much junk E-mail as the United States Postal Service ever delivered. Another is new organization of information through shared databases, bulletin boards, newsgroups, and repositories so that users can access information directed at people interested in particular subjects.

Push technology is different from traditional Pull technology in that it is information delivered straight to customers' computers, rather than waiting for them to pull it down from a server. It most resembles E-mail, which is purposely sent to someone, although Push software packages now are designed to send information in many other forms as well, including screen savers, pop-ups, wallpaper, and scrolling tickers.

The use of broadcast technology has the potential to improve company communication by allowing companies to send breaking news throughout an organization in a quick, predictable manner. In addition, it can help reduce printing and production costs by distributing more information electronically with the added confidence that the information will be seen and read.

However, the investment of time and effort on the part of content developers to make Push technology useful has the potential to be onerous. Content authors may feel compelled to sift through piles of information to publish that which is most relevant to the organization. In addition, there is a real danger of overwhelming users with yet another information source. A dizzying array of pop-ups and news flashes may turn into more of a distraction than a community service.

To keep a broadcast application from becoming a source of information overload, we recommend that:

- The intranet owner coordinate the application owners' efforts so that information is not duplicated or contradictory,
- Application owners agree on a standard way to capture, organize, and condense bulletins into succinct, unobtrusive messages, and
- Channels are programmed to meet the needs of the communities within and across the organization.

If this commitment is made, Push technology can be very valuable to many companies. We recommend that you spend some time looking at the bells and whistles included in the top software packages and selecting one that most closely suits your needs. New releases are coming out all the time, so instead of evaluating the versions available to us at this writing, we will simply recommend the packages that look like the strongest contenders.

PointCast I-Server. Probably the best-known product in this category, PointCast I-Server is server software that extends the communication capability of the trendy PointCast Network to intranets. It gives companies the ability to broadcast news and information directly to an employee's computer over the intranet. Publishing content on a company "channel" is possible by filling out supplied Web forms or by writing a standard HTML document. Only authorized administrators can create and broadcast content, and all internal content is broadcast behind the company firewall, so company information remains secure. (www.pointcast.com)

Marimba's Castanet. Marimba's Castanet is composed of a *transmitter* (server software) and *tuner* (client software), which send and receive channels of information, software, and other content in an organization. As with several other packages, users subscribe to a channel that carries a particular type of content and then receive updates on that topic from the server. In return, the server receives data back from the user community about usage of the various channels. (www.marimba.com)

BackWeb by BackWeb Technologies. BackWeb's server channels parse information into *info packets* that are sent down to user machines as bandwidth is available. When all the packets for a particular piece of information (which can be in multiple file formats including software as well as documents) have arrived, they are then assembled and disseminated as a whole to users via one of several communications mechanisms. These include Info Flashes (little pop-ups that appear in corners of the screen, that can be expanded to show detail when the user clicks on them), screen savers, wallpaper, or direct access via the client software interface. To measure usability, the administrator can receive feedback about usage of info packets, once deployed. (www.backweb.com)

Wayfarer Communications QuickServer. Wayfarer's products are designed to provide high performance and personalized, interactive, and secure applications across an intranet. Developers can use familiar tools, platforms, and protocols to develop and deploy Wayfarer applications, which provide personalized information collection and delivery as well as performance levels. (www.wayfarer.com)

Push technology is still growing in popularity, but our guess is that it eventually will be a standard component of every intranet. You may or may not be ready to invest in the software or, more important, the content development just yet, but Push is definitely a technology to keep on your watch list if you aren't already an ardent user. (See Figure 6.16.)

Search Engines

Any chapter on managing intranet content would be incomplete without the mention of Web search engines and crawlers (see Figure 6.17). They are truly invaluable additions to an intranet, giving a semblance of order to what would otherwise be an HTML wasteland of untapped data.

Search engines are software that is designed to allow users to search for keywords and concepts in listed documentation. As the administrator of the software, you can determine what the users are allowed to search—a department site, the full corporate intranet, or the World Wide Web as well. You may wish to offer all of these options, depending on your bandwidth concerns (larger searches require greater processing and data transfer).

E-zines (electronic magazines, also known as Webzines) and paper periodicals frequently rate and rank the best search engines and crawlers. So we recommend reading their surveys for the best new features. However, the ones that continue to have strong

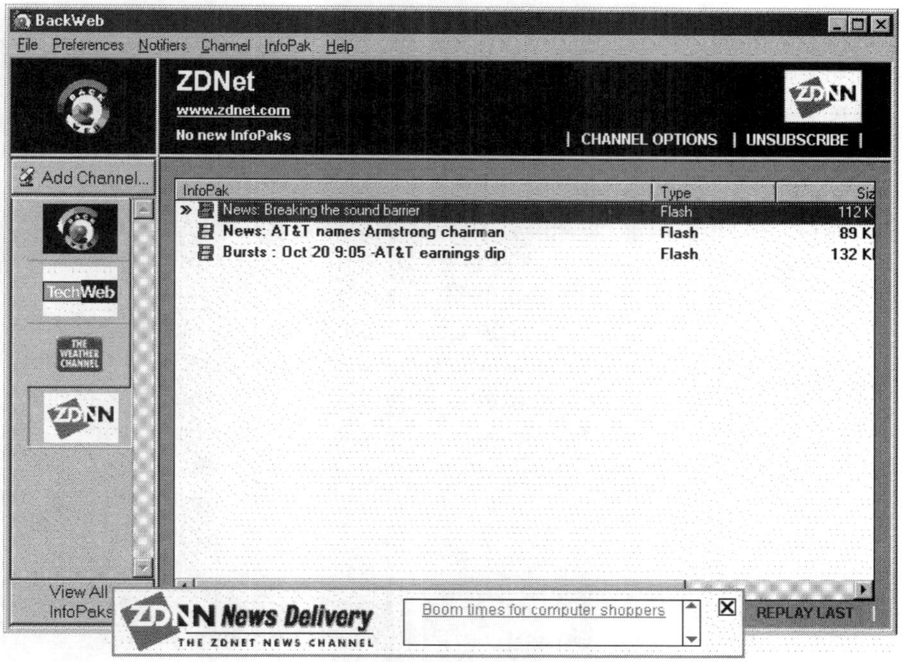

Figure 6.16 Push Technology: BackWeb user interface and "pop-up".

showings include AltaVista (www.altavista.digital.com), Excite! (www.excite.com), InfoSeek (www.infoseek.com, http://ultra .infoseek.com), and Lycos (www.lycos.com).

TIP *Be sure to look for a search engine that will automatically catalog documents found on your intranet so that you do not have to constantly update your indexes. This is a popular feature on software and is well worth the investment.*

Summary

Having presented both tools and techniques for helping to manage and administer content in this chapter, now is a fitting time to

SOLUTION SCENARIO

Using Push for Content Distribution

A large financial institution had a large, thriving intranet, but it was mostly pull-based information that users had to search (with the exception of mass E-mail, which was starting to border on junk mail in quantity as well as quality). In particular, there was a need on the part of several departments to be able to send stock evaluation reports and market research directly to various constituents in a timely manner. The current system was to send most of the weekly, monthly, and quarterly reports through interoffice mail or via FedEx to clients across the globe (at very high cost) and some of the research by electronic mail attachment composed by an administrative assistant.

The solution that was settled on was to use a Push server to distribute the information. Because of their commitment to provide strong technology as opposed to content, the software that was chosen was BackWeb. This particular product was able to not only program multiple channels of information to which users could subscribe, but it allowed for software distribution as well. Via a hook into a database (such as Oracle or SQL Server), specific content generated for an individual customer or user could be Pushed to that user via the BackWeb engine.

PLANNING:

The decision to use Push technology was fairly easy, but how to implement it was trickier. In the end, a quick prototype was built to illustrate how the product would interface to the user community, and then the actual installation was performed.

(continued)

SOLUTION SCENARIO *Continued*

TIME:

Preparation of the prototype took four days—basically, two days to understand a very basic functional flow (there was not much complexity to the need as the reports were already being generated and stored in a database; we merely had to propagate them out) and two days to develop the interface. The setup of the Push server took another day to install, test, and configure.

EFFORT:

The effort mostly involved one lead programmer for one week with some supervision and quality assurance.

RESULTS:

Although the programming involved here is not particularly difficult, deployment cannot be instantaneous. Because this is a change for customers and users, some change management issues were involved as well, especially explaining to users how and where they could now receive their reports. This requires a bit of marketing and communications, as well as help desk support to make the transition as smooth as possible.

encourage publishing and publicizing them on your intranet. Use your own guidelines and policies well and modify as the needs of the organization change. Other departments will look to you as an example, and your "walking the walk" will help them accept and adopt the principles that will facilitate long-term management. Most commonly, we have developed a section of the IT application on the intranet to house the development and operational policies and procedures. Regular user policies (such as usage guidelines and so forth discussed in Chapter 1) are usually kept in a sister directory.

Figure 6.17 Search engine.

In the next chapter we will look at some of the more complex issues that arise as you go beyond content management into full-scale application management issues. Some of the same techniques used in this chapter can be expanded and leveraged, and some will have to change to accommodate the added complexities of multitiered applications.

CHAPTER SEVEN

The Application Connection

In this chapter we will take a closer look at how to manage the operation, growth, and diversification of intranet applications.

There are really four categories of issues faced by the intranet application manager. The most mundane is the day-to-day management of the application. Like a client-server application, an intranet application is not so much released as deployed. Once installed on a server, an intranet application can require daily maintenance intervention. Unlike a client-server application, though, this intervention is generally server-side only.

All the other categories cover changes in the application itself. Change in the application layer comes in three complementary flavors: changing usage patterns, changing business needs, and changing technology availability. If any one could be pinned down, the others would be much easier to manage. But none are static, and they will always compete for attention. It is important, as we will discuss later, to recognize these as different types of change. In most organizations, changes in business needs and usage patterns should drive changes in the intranet, not changes in technology availability. The exception to this is an organization for which making use of the latest technology *is* a stated business goal. More on that later.

At some point after your intranet has been up and running for a while (or, potentially, even before your intranet is up and running), somebody will come to you and say, "Can't we add the ability to . . . to our intranet?" Maybe it's a new application. Maybe it's extended functionality. Maybe they want to give the public access to a heretofore internal-only application. Whatever the change, being prepared ahead of time is your best defense. When designing intranet applications, it is very important to look not only at their intended uses, but also at their potential uses. One intranet tool we designed for a client was originally intended for use by their top executive management team. High throughput was not, therefore, one of its design factors. But the executives were so pleased with the information it provided that they decided to make it available to the entire 100+ management team. We were able to meet this change with only minimal changes to the application, but only because it had been designed from the beginning to allow for scalability.

If your intranet application accomplishes its purpose, it is likely to find a larger audience than originally anticipated. Whether this means deployment across the company or to the Internet, the load and throughput requirements will change dramatically. Planning for this expansion and accommodating it when it does happen are the subjects of the second section of this chapter.

Very few intranet applications can initially satisfy all of the business needs of their users. It is not usually even desirable to try to do so, as such a large, monolithic application would likely never reach deployment in the first place. So once an application is deployed, its users are quite likely to request new features or changes to existing ones. These types of changes tend to be much easier in an intranet application than in more traditional—even client/server—applications. Most such changes can be accomplished at the server end with no need to meddle with the clients at all.

The Internet is best known for its pace of technology change. It is quite impossible for an intranet to avoid the impact of this change. It can certainly be a good thing: A new technology can become available just when you need it. It is more likely, though, to be a bad thing: New versions of browsers don't tend to be fully compatible with older versions. New technologies may offer features that tempt you to switch technology sets at an impractical phase of a project. Or new technologies may make your perfectly effective and usable intranet applications seem obsolete before their time. Managing the impact of technology change is one of the greatest challenges facing intranet managers.

Ideally, building intranet applications would follow a time line similar to other application development efforts. This time line is detailed in our book, *Building the Corporate Intranet,* and it is perfectly viable when first building an intranet. You analyze your business needs, assess your technology alternatives, choose your technology set, gather application requirements, design the applications, implement them, deploy them, and maintain them. As already stated, this works fine when initially building an intranet, or when an intranet is small and centrally controlled, but this model doesn't fully handle the complexity of maintaining a growing intranet. Intranet applications are very much living systems. Requirements will change, usage patterns will evolve, and intranet technology is never static from one day to the next.

Daily Management

The tasks involved in the daily management of intranet applications are naturally as varied as the applications themselves. We cannot claim to cover every potential task here. However, there are certain tasks that seem to be common to most applications and certain attributes common to most tasks.

The foremost concern for many intranet managers is security. Whether this means protecting data from loss or corruption through backups or protecting sensitive organizational data from unauthorized access, maintaining data security can be a demanding task. Most of the issues involved are covered in Chapter 8, but there are some concerns that are truly unique to the application layer.

It is important to note that intranet applications generally present three layers at which data can be protected: A user can be prevented from running a particular piece of an intranet application by setting the Web server security to deny access to that script; an application can deny the user access to particular data based on their security rights; and the database server can refuse to return the data to the application itself based on the user's security rights. All three of these mechanisms are valuable, and your security needs may require that you use all three of them. The cost, however, is in tremendously increased maintenance complexity. The three mechanisms may not integrate well, and you could find yourself having to maintain three separate sets of security information for the three layers.

One way to avoid this is to use more tightly integrated security models. The mechanisms provided by Microsoft's Windows NT, Internet Information Server, and SQL Server work together particularly well. By creating Windows NT accounts for each of your users, assigning those users to groups, and controlling each group's access to different resources, you are able to centrally manage the individuals' access rights. This technique does require a significant initial time investment to set up the groups' access, but adding new users becomes as simple as adding the users to the proper groups.

You can control a group's access to a particular program by controlling its access to the files that make up the application. In CGI, this means the HTML and executable files; in Active Server Pages, this means the ASP files and potentially ActiveX server .EXE and .DLL files. If a user does not have execute access to these files, IIS will not process any requests for them. Once a user has gained access to a script, the script itself can make calls to security functions within the Win32 API. These calls can further refine a user's access rights, permitting a script to allow certain users full access while limiting others to basic functions. Last, SQL Server 6.x allows the use of integrated NT security. This means that access to tables and views in your core database can be granted or denied based on a user's membership in Windows NT groups.

The initial setup cost mentioned is the time spent establishing each group's permissions. Ongoing maintenance is generally limited to adding new users to groups, moving users between groups, and removing them altogether. Of course, any change in your fundamental security rules may require considerable adjustment to the privileges of the groups, but at least you only have one set of groups, instead of three.

One disadvantage of this approach is that SQL Server does not really use Windows NT group membership information. Instead, it provides a mechanism for importing this information from the NT security database to its own. This is done for performance reasons, and its only impact is that you will need to repeat that import every time you change the NT group membership. The second disadvantage is that the NT challenge-response security scheme is proprietary and is currently supported only by Internet Explorer. Again, the impact of this is minimal, as IIS does support the standard security used by most browsers. If standard security (using clear-text passwords) is not sufficient, you may be able to use Microsoft's Certificate Server, which should be available by the time this goes to press.

Many other combinations of security mechanisms are possible, and many of these combinations may become better integrated over time. The three layers of security (server, application, and database) will remain, however, and the complexity of your management task will depend on how you cover these layers.

An oft-neglected aspect of intranet application security is auditing. Again, this topic is covered more generally in Chapter 8, but there are specific issues with auditing intranet application usage. The biggest of these issues is that unless you specifically design your applications with auditing in mind, it can be quite difficult to perform. You can, of course, use your Web server's access logs to provide some auditing information, but this is usually of limited value. Trying to reconstruct a user's session from server logs can be excruciatingly cumbersome and is really a possibility only in the simplest of applications.

If auditing is important to your organization, facilities should be designed into each intranet application deployed. This could mean adding triggers to your database that track each change made by a user. Or it could mean adding functionality to each script to log each user's actions. You may wish to provide a way to enable and disable such logging so that it does not hurt performance, but can be available when an attack is suspected.

Whichever options you choose, keep in mind that the audit information has two purposes: to help spot security breaches when they do occur and to help spot patterns of behavior that constitute a security concern even though the individual actions do not. You may, for example, need to allow your IT department access to the personnel department's records, but you'd want to know if someone in IT was snooping around too much in personnel files.

Intranet applications have the same need for regular backups as any client/server application. However, the complexity of the process is affected by the many layers present in an intranet application. Most of the components are likely to change only infrequently. The database portion of your application, though, is likely to require nightly backups or potentially even RAID protection. You will also want to protect changes made to the security database.

Performance monitoring is another feature that should be designed into an application from the very beginning if it is needed. For very simple applications, the performance-monitoring features provided by the Web server, the database server, and the operating system may suffice. Most larger applications will benefit from specialized monitoring functionality. It is often difficult to predict usage patterns for intranet applications, and monitoring can help establish these. Once usage patterns are understood, further optimization of the application can be targeted at those areas that will benefit the most.

The most useful performance data to gather are frequency of requests, response time to requests, and volume of data returned in responses. This data can be used with data collected from other layers of the intranet to help solve existing performance problems or to plan for expansion, as detailed in Chapter 5.

The mechanism used for performance monitoring of your applications will depend largely on the mechanism in use for other layers of your intranet. Gathering and processing the performance data will be much easier if you use a consistent mechanism throughout. In particular, logging to SNMP is complex enough to warrant use only if your Web server and other components are already logging to SNMP. The simplest logging approach is to simply write logging information to a flat file as it is gathered. This is quick and easy to implement, but be warned: Writing to disk could slow your scripts' response times (you'll want some kind of caching, which adds complexity), and the format of this data will be of little use for programmatic analysis. More complex, though only marginally, would be writing the performance data to a database. This will allow better programmatic access, but still suffers from the potential for delays while the application writes to the database.

Many operating systems provide some native support for performance monitoring. Microsoft Windows NT, for example, provides a sophisticated performance-monitoring API. This can allow an application to provide extremely detailed performance data, which can be viewed together with the performance data of other programs. The problem with this approach, though, is that these APIs do not tend to be straightforward. It can be very expensive in terms of development time to add such sophisticated features.

Expansion

It is relatively common in the life cycle of an intranet application for its usage patterns to change significantly. You may design an application for ten users, only to find an audience of hundreds. Or you may design for hundreds and find thousands. You could design for intranet users and have to extend to the Internet. Or to a roaming, dial-in sales force. Usage changes could also mean volume changes: Your dozen-order-a-week online catalog could find itself processing hundreds or thousands of orders a week (the kind of problem we all dream about). There are two approaches to planning for intranet application scalability. You can design your application from the beginning to scale up, using additional hardware if necessary. Or you can design your application to meet the current need and then reimplement it if its capabilities are exceeded. It is a clear gamble: If you expect your application to gain usage significantly, then building in scalability is a wise choice. But if you are unsure of its audience, or if getting it up quickly is key, you may not want to make such a large initial investment. Either way, it is important to consciously make this choice and to be fully aware of its implications to avoid being caught off guard later.

Changes in application usage can affect security as well as performance. A LAN-based intranet application may not need the sophisticated security systems that Internet-based applications need. But if you build your applications without Internet-quality security, you will be in a bind if you ever do go live on the Internet. The gamble is really the same as described above, and the best advice is also the same: Document the decision you make and its implications so that you are not caught off guard later. If you deploy a nonsecured application and later your organization connects to the Internet, somebody needs to know that additional security steps need to be taken.

Extension

Changes in functionality are common and expected in all types of applications. Most organizations have procedures already in place to deal with such changes. With a good understanding of your organization, you should be in a fairly good position to anticipate the types of changes that will be needed. This may seem impossible, but actually there are a number of very well defined types of business changes that could hit you. If you are lucky, only some of them will. If you are unlucky, they all will. You do need to plan ahead so that your applications can adapt.

The real problems arise, though, when the desired changes in functionality cannot be achieved within the current technology set. Then you are faced with a number of undesirable options: Defer the changes, approximate the desired changes within the existing technology set, reimplement the application in a different technology set, or implement the changes in a different technology set, creating a hybrid application.

The advantages and disadvantages of most of these options are fairly clear. The last option, though, is something that is much more of an option for intranet applications than for others. An intranet application does not have to rely entirely on one technology set. Indeed, it does not even have to reside entirely on a single computer or even within a single operating system. One of our applications currently under development relies heavily on Microsoft's Remote Data Services (RDS) for access to data residing on an NT SQL Server database. This is no problem for our production environment, which will be entirely NT, but our development environment is Windows 95 using Personal Web Server on each developer's workstation, and RDS's server-side components do not support Windows 95. For a nonintranet application, this problem would be solved using stubs and wrappers and similar patches. For our purposes, though, we simply have the application running on the Windows 95 "servers" reference the RDS components running on a central NT server. After all, we have no need to debug RDS. This has allowed us to avoid the headaches (not to mention expense) of upgrading a dozen developers' workstations to Windows NT.

TIP *Microsoft's Advanced Data Connector (ADC) was renamed Remote Data Services (RDS) between release 1.0 and release 1.1. Release 1.1 is compatible with release 1.5 and vice-versa, but release 1.0 is not compatible with either. This means that IE 3.x running RDS 1.1 or IE 4.x running RDS 1.5 cannot access IIS 3.x running ADC 1.0. In addition IE 3.x running ADC 1.0 cannot access IIS 3.x or IIS 4.x running RDS 1.5. This type of incompatibility problem can be hard to track down in an I-Net environment, and may well become more common as more tools span the browser/server divide.*

A word of warning about this approach: Intranets are inherently layered. We often refer to the "10-Layer Model," but sometimes that model is more conveniently divided into fewer layers, sometimes more. Every layer that is added is another layer of complexity and interaction management. Splitting an application across multiple servers adds a layer. Splitting an application across multiple technologies adds a layer. So does splitting an application across multiple operating systems. Proliferation of such splits can rapidly lead to pure chaos, especially if different splits are being made in different applications. This technique is a powerful tool, but like all powerful tools, it can cause as many problems as it solves. Be very, very careful how you use it. One way to mitigate the risks involved is to align your splits. If several applications need to be split, try to split them the same way so that you have fewer configurations to keep track of. If you are splitting an application across multiple servers, do so at some clear, logical point. Consistency is a very desirable attribute in this case.

Technology Change

More than anything else, managing an intranet means managing change. And this is true of intranet applications more than any other part of the intranet. If you choose to install a conferencing system, you simply have to decide on a software package, plan the deployment, purchase the software, and install it—in all, a delay measured in days to weeks. If you choose to implement a custom online order entry system, you must go through a much longer process, sometimes measured in weeks, but usually in months. The degree of technology change during the course of development of an intranet application can be immense. As a result, the degree of uncertainty about your technology choices can be paralyzing.

One of our intranet projects was initially proposed in mid-1996, when CGI was still a very common intranet development mechanism and the future of server-side plug-ins using ISAPI or NSAPI was uncertain. Because of this, we proposed a system developed in C++ using a library we had developed to allow a program to run under CGI, NSAPI, or ISAPI. By the time the contract was awarded, nearly six months later, intranet application development tools had advanced considerably, and we had to reassess our technology choices. We finally settled on Microsoft's Active Server Pages in combination with some business-logic-specific ActiveX servers implemented in Visual Basic 5.0. The project was developed using Visual InterDev, with testing performed under Microsoft's Personal Web Server. Not one of these products had been available when we performed the initial technology assessment.

The project was completed in late 1997, by which time new versions of all of the products we were using and several new products besides were available. Internet Explorer 4.0 was in production by then, bringing with it Dynamic HTML. We cannot be sure if we would have chosen to use DHTML if it had been available earlier, but clearly it was too late to switch courses. If you try to switch to each new technology as it becomes available, you will never have a completed project.

Choosing an Initial Technology Set

We are careful to discuss technology sets and not single technologies, because intranets, more than any other computer environment, consist of multiple coexistent technologies. One of the great advantages of an intranet is that it can meet many different business needs. Any intranet that nears this goal will surely do so by relying on many technologies. So when you choose your technologies, the important question is not "Should we use X versus Y?" but "If we need both X and Y, how can we make them work together?" Unfortunately, this can often prove to be the tougher of the two questions.

In our intranet planning methodology, we recommend that organizations allow their initial technology choices to be driven by their most important (presumably first to be implemented) applications. This does not mean completely ignoring other applications that may be planned for later; it simply means that emphasis should be placed on those applications that are most likely to be implemented, that will see the most use, and that are most critical to the success of the organization.

Because this issue is covered in greater detail in our previous book, *Building the Corporate Intranet,* we focus here on the issues that most affect ongoing intranet management. Once you have decided which of your applications will be the first implemented, you will need to decide which technologies are appropriate for each application. You may find some that can be implemented very simply using existing CGI tools, others that really need their own server-side plug-ins, and others that could go either way. Or you may find that all of your applications require custom Java programming. The important thing here is to be sure you know all your options.

Once you have your technology options outlined, there are two extreme approaches you could take. You could choose the technology or technologies that meet most of your requirements, adopt them, and force-fit all other applications into that model. Or you could implement each application using the technology set that is most appropriate to that application. If you are really lucky, the same technology set will be most appropriate for each application. The rest of us have to find a compromise between these two approaches.

Trying to force all of your applications into a single technology set may work initially, especially in a small intranet. As new applications are requested, however, the chances that this approach will remain viable diminish rapidly. On the other hand, using a different technology set for each application can (and will) lead to unimaginable management nightmares. Troubleshooting within a single technology set is hard enough. Once a half dozen are interacting on an intranet, it can be nigh impossible. The compromise? Obviously, this will vary based on your environment. We usually use some form of the 80/20 rule. That is, we try to select a primary technology set that will satisfy the requirements for 80 percent of the expected applications. The remaining 20 percent are implemented using the smallest possible set of additional technologies. Keeping the 20 percent down to one or two other technology sets will go a long way toward reducing management headaches later.

Planning for Change

In the I-Net arena, technology is changing even faster than business needs are. It is inevitable that, at some point, the technologies you have used to implement your intranet will begin to seem a bit outdated. If you are lucky, you will have already deployed your intranet by the time this happens. Don't count on being lucky. Whether pressure is coming from above—management worried about corporate image—or from below—users wanting the latest and greatest multimedia features—the pressure to adopt new technologies will come.

There are, however, things you can do to prepare for this technology evolution. One is to have some defined process for adopting new technologies, discussed in more detail in the following section.

Setting Some Ground Rules

On a small intranet, it is usually possible to centrally coordinate the adoption of new technologies. For some readers, this may be a one-person task. Others may have a small team that assesses and selects technologies. For larger intranets, however, ideas for changing technology can come from all directions. A large corporate intranet, with a number of departmental applications, may be besieged with requests for an expanded technology set. Maybe your PR department wants streaming video. Or your direct marketing department wants push features or mass E-mailing. Or some hack in engineering has been using HTML 9.0 on a personal Web site and can't understand why the corporate intranet is so far behind.

The exact nature of this sort of input is impossible to predict, but not its presence. There are two keys in dealing with it: Never adopt a new technology without some sort of assessment, and, if at all possible, have somebody else at least start the assessment. We are not trying to suggest a way to shirk your responsibilities, but simply recognizing an important fact about intranets: The only way to keep any central control of an intranet is to allow a certain amount of distributed flexibility! Issuing an edict saying that all new technologies must be assessed by the intranet management before use is the fastest way to ensure that new technologies are adopted willy-nilly across the organization.

Instead, we recommend a *guided growth* approach. If PR people want streaming video, let them experiment with it on a small scale first. Make it their responsibility to assess its business value and impact by running an internal server accessible to only a limited audience. If the pilot is successful, and they still want a full production version, then begin the full assessment process.

Allowing departments to add new technologies experimentally can greatly reduce the number of new technologies you are forced to assess. Once they actually deal with the process of providing streaming video, PR may decide that it's neat, but way too much work. Its business benefit may not justify the outlay of their, and therefore your, time.

Once a technology has passed the pilot phase, it is still important to assess its impact on the intranet as a whole. Streaming video, for example, places a significant load on your network bandwidth. Making it available across the organization could cripple other applications that require speedy network response. For this reason, it is still important that the central intranet management play a role in even experimental technology deployment.

Dealing with Change When It Hits You

Transitioning between technology sets is a task with which most intranets will have to deal at some point. The pace of technology change in the industry is such that no amount of analysis and planning can completely protect your intranet from the need to adopt new technologies or possibly to even completely convert to a new technology set. While no intranet manager looks forward to these efforts, there are ways to handle the transition less painfully.

One advantage that intranet applications have over other applications is that they tend to be divided into clear layers. It is possible to completely overhaul the server side of an intranet application without modifying any of the client-side user interface. Conversely, you may be able to extensively modify the user interface without significantly altering the server-side functionality (although this is trickier).

When To Say No

As mentioned in the introduction to this chapter, a major pitfall in a rapidly changing technology environment is succumbing to the temptation to use every new technology that comes along. Often, organizations adopt Internet and intranet technologies in part because they want to be on the cutting edge. We do not deny that this can be a business driver; but if it is, it should be factored in along with other business drivers.

SOLUTION SCENARIO

Managing IIS Applications Using InterDev

The Visual InterDev components of the Visual Studio development suite from Microsoft are designed to facilitate the development, distribution, and maintenance of Active Server–based I-Net applications. In fact, though, this toolset can be used for any Web-based application, from the simplest case of a mostly static Web site (which we discussed in Chapter 6) to more sophisticated applications using CGI, Java, or some even newer technology. This solution scenario explores the use of InterDev to develop and manage changes to an ASP and ActiveX–based application.

PLANNING:

Because of the complexity of the development and deployment environments for this type of application, it is important to clearly plan out the roles played by each machine. In order to do this, the different roles need to be understood. From a deployment perspective, the most important machines are the production servers. These are the computers that will run the Web servers accessed by the end users. In a small I-Net application, you may have only one production server. In a very small I-Net application, your production server may double as your development server (although we discourage this approach). In larger applications, you are likely to have multiple production servers.

New applications and changes to applications need to be tested before they are deployed. The role of the testing server is often filled by one of the development servers, but this has the same inherent risks as using the production server for development: Files are more likely to get out of sync and a problem with a script under development can bring down the

(*continued*)

SOLUTION SCENARIO *Continued*

testing server. It is common for large development efforts to have multiple testing servers for the different stages of testing.

The changes themselves are generally made on a development server. Again, small projects might be able to get away with a single development server, but the consequence of multiple developers changing different files simultaneously on a single server is chaos. We recommend that each developer have his or her own development server. This does not mean that each developer needs a Windows NT Server. Both Peer Web Services for Windows NT Workstation and Personal Web Server for Windows 95 provide excellent options for the development of ASP applications. In fact, this book is being composed with the help of IIS on an NT server and a Personal Web Server running on my notebook.

In Chapter 6 we presented a solution scenario using InterDev, IIS and Visual SourceSafe to manage the content of a Web site. Managing a full-blown application is more complex, but it shares much of the fundamental structure. We recommend that you look back at the Chapter 6 solution scenario before continuing.

For the application in question, our environment consisted of a production server, an integration testing server, and individual development servers for each developer, as described above. The production server and the testing server used IIS 3.0 running under Windows NT Server, and the development servers used PWS running under Windows 95. The primary SourceSafe archive was located on a file server. The development servers and the testing servers all ran the FrontPage Server Extensions with SourceSafe integration, allowing them all to access the common SourceSafe repository. Installations to the production server were handled using file transfers (either through the FrontPage Server Extensions,

(*continued*)

SOLUTION SCENARIO *Continued*

ZIP files, or FTP). The production server did not use Visual SourceSafe integration. It was connected to the other servers by a 28.8 modem, and SourceSafe does not perform well over slow or unreliable network connections.

Figure 7.1 may seem needlessly complex, but let's examine its pieces to see why. This model is very different from most

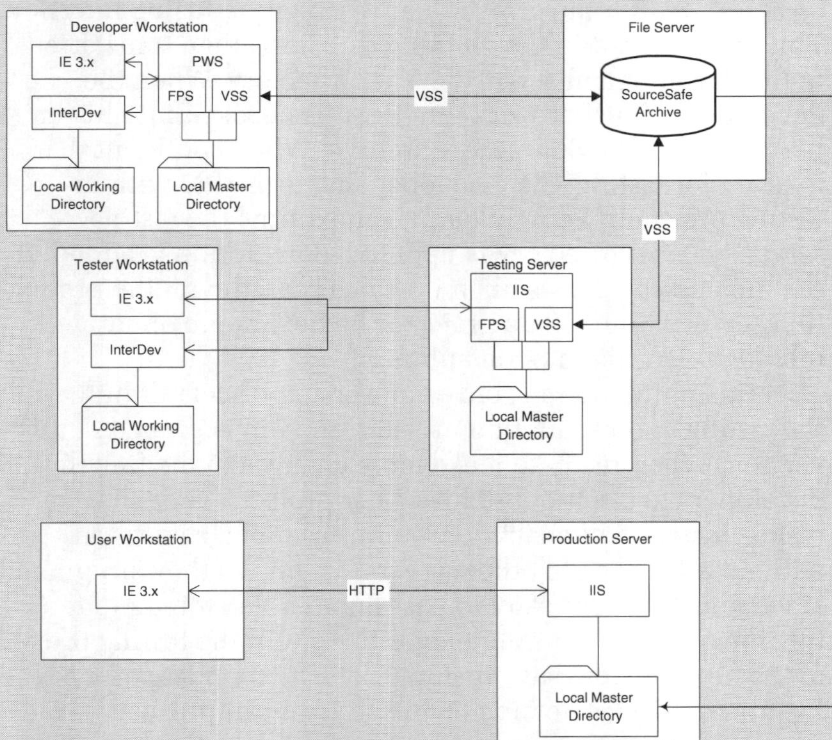

Figure 7.1 ASP development under InterDev.

(continued)

SOLUTION SCENARIO *Continued*

Web development models. At its core is the SourceSafe archive, and not the production Web server itself. The SourceSafe archive is roughly configured to mirror the structure of the Web master directory, in multiples: For each server, there is a mirror of the directory structure. The files are shared between the parallel directory structures, using pinning or branching to control which version is used on each server.

Let's follow a single file through its lifetime. A developer creates default.htm on his or her workstation, using InterDev. This file is stored in the working directory, then transferred to the development server's master directory. When the developer is finished with the file, it is checked into his or her project in the SourceSafe archive. When confident that it is ready for testing, the developer shares the file with the testing project in SourceSafe. The next time the testing server's master directory is updated, default.htm is added. If the file passes its tests, then it is also shared with the production server's SourceSafe project. The next deployment will include this version of default.htm.

At this point, there is only one version of default.htm. In the testing and production projects, the file is pinned at this version. When ready to make more changes to the file, the developer checks it out of his or her project. He or she can make changes and check in versions as much as desired without affecting the other servers, as long as they are pinned at version 1. When ready to pass another version on to testing, the developer simply moves the pin in the testing project to the new version, say version 5. The next update of the testing server will get version 5, and the test can proceed. If the file passes the test, then the production project's pin is also moved to version 5, allowing this latest version to be deployed.

(*continued*)

SOLUTION SCENARIO *Continued*

TIP *To integrate the FrontPage Server component under PWS for Windows 95 with Visual SourceSafe 5.0, you must have DCOM95 from Microsoft installed on your Windows 95 machine. See www.microsoft.com/dcom95.*

This technique can be used for any file which is part of the web project itself. This can include images, Java classes, and even ActiveX controls and .CAB files. We do not, however, recommend this for compiled server-side executable components. Compiled components in general differ from others in that they have source code that does not really belong in the Web root tree. The resulting executables may belong in the Web project, in the case of client-side components and CGI, or may not, in the case of most other server-side components. ActiveX servers, for example, do not need to be a part of the Web project. They need to be installed on the server, assigned the correct file permissions, and registered with OLE using regsvr32.exe, but they can be stored anywhere on the server. ISAPI extensions need to be installed on the server and registered with IIS, but they also do not belong in the Web directory. The same is true of NSAPI extensions.

We have referred to the different layers of an I-Net application a number of times. One reason that the layer model works so well is that each layer is built on top of the lower layers. The business objects depend on the database, the application depends on the business objects, and so on. In ASP, the ASP pages themselves are the customers of the ActiveX business components—thus the clear separation

(*continued*)

SOLUTION SCENARIO *Continued*

between the server-side interpreted ASP pages and the server-side compiled ActiveX components.

This does not mean that development of the ActiveX components has to be completely independent of the ASP development (although there are reusability reasons why that is desirable), simply that they should be maintained as separate projects within SourceSafe.

In Figure 7.2, the highest-level projects each represent a server-specific tree. The Web project represents the master directory on each Web server and is associated with the proj-

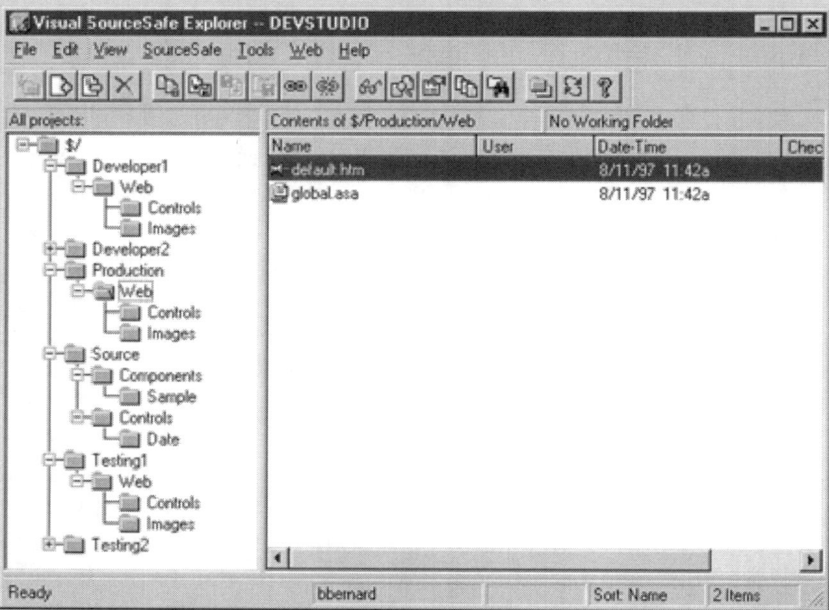

Figure 7.2 SourceSafe project structure.

(continued)

SOLUTION SCENARIO *Continued*

ect in Visual InterDev. The projects within the Source project each represent a compiled component. In this case, they are all Visual Basic projects and are accessed through the SourceSafe integration features of Visual Basic, but they could as easily have been Visual C++ or any other OLE-compatible language. Note that the Controls project produces a .CAB file, which is shared into the Controls directory of the Web project. This is distinctly different from the Sample project, which produces a .DLL, which is not shared into the Web project. The .DLL is an ActiveX server, and as such is not deployed as part of the Web. Instead, it is incorporated into Sample.Exe, a self-extracting installation program, which must be run on each deployment server.

Now that the process is understood, you need to assign servers to roles. It is possible for certain roles to be served by the same computer, but that is best avoided. It is especially important that the file server not serve any role that might cause it to crash. In our scenario, we have two development workstations, a file server, a production Web server, and two testing Web servers. The file server also serves as the database server.

For this scheme to work well, you will need to communicate the procedure to all of your team members. Preparing a set of instructions like the following will help your team understand the configuration and the procedure, and should facilitate any changes to the structure or procedure you might need.

TIME:

Clearly, establishing this type of development and distribution environment is time-consuming. For a simple three-server environment like the one described above, planning

(*continued*)

SOLUTION SCENARIO *Continued*

and configuration could easily take a week. You should add in an extra day for each additional server, and up to an extra week for each tool with which you are not already familiar. The tools to which this applies are FrontPage Server, Visual InterDev, Visual Studio, and Visual SourceSafe. Each is complex enough in its behavior and light enough in its documentation to cause troubles on its own. In a full development environment, they can really get things twisted up.

You need an ongoing SourceSafe administrator to ensure that the procedures detailed above are followed and to sort versions out if they are not. This person can fill other roles as well, but anticipate that the person will be spending between 20 percent and 50 percent of the time dealing with SourceSafe and FrontPage Server issues, depending on the size of your project.

EFFORT:

Although most of the work for this approach seems to be in the planning and setup, there is a significant overhead imposed by the need for developers to keep such careful track of the status of their files. This is really quite unavoidable in an application development effort, but it may be hard to justify if your application is viewed as a Web site instead of an application. This is an unfortunate misperception in the industry. In reality, Web sites need as careful control and status tracking as applications, but many Webmasters do not have the management or software engineering background to recognize this.

Besides the SourceSafe management mentioned above, the significant effort required by this approach is all in coordination. This includes the daily coordination of testing the various server installations on developers' workstations and the testing servers, as well as the significant coordination of each

(*continued*)

Solution Scenario *Continued*

new major release. The instructions below outline the procedure for using SourceSafe in this scheme.

1. *Creating the SourceSafe structure.* From within SourceSafe, create a top-level project for each of the Web servers needed. Within one of these, create a new project, called Web. Within that project, create subprojects for the folders of your Web server. Drag the Web project into each of the other server projects to establish your shares. Create a new top-level project called Source. This will hold the source of your compiled elements.

2. *Adding a Web server to the SourceSafe structure.* Create a top-level project for the new Web server. Choose the Web project of the server that is closest in function to the new server. If nothing else fits, choose the production server. In SourceSafe, drag the chosen Web project into the new top-level project you've just created. This establishes the new share, with each file pinned at the same version as the chosen server. You may need to adjust the pins to match the purpose of the new server.

3. *Attaching a Web server to the SourceSafe project.* Be sure that SourceSafe is installed on the Web server, with integration and FrontPage Server, but without a SourceSafe database. Be sure that the srcsafe.ini file in the VSS directory has an include line referencing the SourceSafe archive on the file server. Be sure that nobody has any files checked out of the Web project! In InterDev, create a new Web project on the target server. If any files or folders are created automatically (default.htm, global.asa, Images), delete them. From the Project menu, choose Enable Web Source Control. When prompted for a project, enter $/serverproject/Web. This will retrieve the project from SourceSafe to the Web server and add its information to the local workspace.

(*continued*)

SOLUTION SCENARIO *Continued*

WARNING *Be very careful using the InterDev command "recalculate links" if you have multiple Web servers sharing a SourceSafe archive. If any files are checked out, how those files are handled is unpredictable. Check all files in before using the "recalculate links" command.*

4. *Creating a new Web file.* In InterDev, choose File/New to create your file. Be sure that it is added to the right folder of the right project. This file is not yet available to others. You can check it in to your Web project and test it on your Web server as much as you like. When this file is ready to be shared with other servers, open SourceSafe. Drag the new file from your Web project (or subproject) to each of the other Web projects. You should also pin the file at the current revision in each of the other Web projects.

5. *Creating a new control.* From within Visual Basic, create your new control project. When you save it, answer Yes when asked whether to add to SourceSafe. Add it to its own subproject of the $/Source project. When the control is ready to test for the first time, use the Setup Wizard to create a .CAB file for it. This .CAB file should be added to SourceSafe, and shared to a subproject of your Web project, usually called "Controls."

6. *Creating a new component.* From within Visual Basic, create your new component project. When you save it, answer Yes when asked whether to add to SourceSafe. Add it to its own subproject of the $/Source project. When the component is ready to test for the first time, use the Setup Wizard to create an installation set for it. This can be

(*continued*)

SOLUTION SCENARIO ***Continued***

stored on floppy, on the file server, or in the SourceSafe archive.

7. *Updating a Web file.* To update a Web file, simply get a working copy in InterDev. Note that you cannot get a working copy of a file that is pinned in your server Web project. You can check it back in without affecting others. When you are ready for others to have your file, either tell them to move their pins or move their pins yourself.

8. *Updating a control.* Make whatever changes are needed by checking out the source files. When you need to test on your server, you must first build the control, then the .CAB file. The .CAB file is pinned just like any other Web file, so when you are happy with your changes, you must be sure the pins are adjusted in other projects.

9. *Updating a component.* A component is updated independently of the Web project. Check out the source files, update them, rebuild the component, and rebuild the installation set. You have to install this new version on each server, as detailed below.

10. *Deploying the Web.* Deploying the Web to a server with SourceSafe integration is a simple matter of executing the "Get Current Version" command on the Web project. Deploying to a server without SourceSafe integration is done from within SourceSafe on a server with access to both the SourceSafe archive and the Web directory of the target server. SourceSafe's Deploy feature will copy the current versions of the entire Web project to the target server.

11. *Installing the components.* Compiled server-side components will need to be installed separately. To do this, simply run the setup program created above on each of the target servers. If the setup program does not run regsvr32.exe for you, don't forget to do it yourself. Also be sure to check

(*continued*)

SOLUTION SCENARIO *Continued*

permissions on the resulting .dll, since users must have execute rights to it in order to use it at all.

RESULTS:

Once this approach is completely adopted, the results should be clear: Reproducing reported problems should become easier, making and testing fixes should be less chaotic and should cause less downtime to the production servers, and the total cost of system modifications should be significantly lower.

A final note about this scheme: The method described for deploying the Web can deploy to an FTP server as well as a file share. This could allow you to deploy your Web to non-Microsoft and non–Windows NT servers. In fact, if your components are all portable, you can build your Web under IIS using InterDev, FrontPage Server, and SourceSafe, and then deploy it to a pool of UNIX machines running Netscape servers. We have used a similar scheme in other cross-platform development efforts. In addition, this scheme could be easily adapted to a less integrated toolset for development and maintenance on a non–Windows NT server. The basic concept of how we are using SourceSafe could apply to any version control package. You may have to do more of the steps manually with other packages, but by the time you read this there may be packages for UNIX and Netscape that integrate well.

Solution Scenario

Migrating from CGI to ASP

There are many disadvantages to developing I-Net applications using CGI. As a result, most intranet managers are moving away from CGI to more usable and manageable application interface mechanisms. Because of its integration with Microsoft's visual tools suite, many are reimplementing CGI applications using Active Server Pages. This is the case with some of our earlier I-Net applications. One in particular was implemented initially using the CGI version of our Web Framework. While the technology set we used (C++, Netscape Enterprise Server, the Web Framework) made sense for the initial implementation of the application, we felt that further work on the application would be facilitated by converting it to Active Server Pages. This scenario is based on that conversion effort, which has yet to be undertaken.

PLANNING:

Planning for migration or reimplementation really needs to start when the application is initially developed. Granular, modular design and careful documentation of the initial implementation will enable a more successful migration. Unfortunately, the realities of project time lines often limit the amount of time spent designing and documenting the application. For the purposes of this scenario, we assume neither a thoroughly modular design nor a thoroughly documented implementation.

We do assume, though, that the CGI implementation of the application uses the typical CGI state model (see Figure 7.3). That is, the server maintains no state, relying entirely on the client to pass state information. This model is very different from the ASP model for maintaining state. In ASP, the server

(*continued*)

SOLUTION SCENARIO *Continued*

maintains most state information in the Session object. The client simply keeps track of its session ID, which it passes to the server in its cookies collection. The ID is used to locate the particular user's state information within the collection of Session objects maintained within the Application object.

This fundamental difference between CGI and ASP will be the largest obstacle to overcome in your migration. In a typical CGI application, the server is entirely stateless: The server's response to a client request depends entirely on the content of the request. If the same request could be stored (in the browser's shortcut menu, for example) and reissued later, the response would be the same (unless the application has a time dependence or its response is based on data affected by other users). This means that when the server generates each page, it must package state information within the page. This is usually done using hidden fields, browser cookies, or serial codes added to the URL path.

While it is possible to implement an ASP application using this model, to do so would be to ignore many of the benefits of Active Server Pages. In our example, the front end of the application consisted entirely of pure HTML

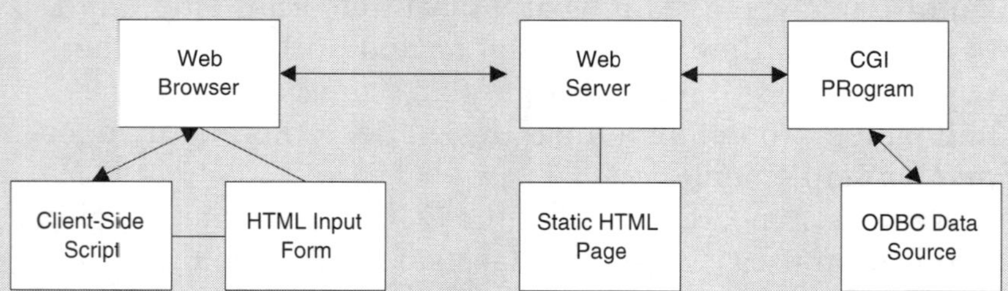

Figure 7.3 The CGI model.

(continued)

SOLUTION SCENARIO *Continued*

forms (no client-side scripting) produced by CGI scripts using Web Framework templates. The conversion to Active Server Pages did not require any changes to the layout or operation of the forms themselves, except for the change in the form action, to reference the ASP files instead of our CGI scripts.

Since the HTML was produced based on templates that were stored in separate files, isolated from the business logic of the application, producing ASP equivalents of those forms would have been quite easy. In fact, because the template language used by the Web Framework was designed to be compatible with standard HTML editors, its structure was quite similar to that of Active Server Pages files (with less server-side scripting). The challenge would have been migrating the business logic.

In the Active Server Pages model (see Figure 7.4), there were two places we could have implemented the business logic: in server-side scripting within the ASP files themselves or in stand-alone ActiveX business components. The original logic was implemented in Visual C++ 4.x, using RogueWave's Tools.H++ and DBTools.H++ libraries. Moving that logic into the ASP files would have meant throwing away the entire

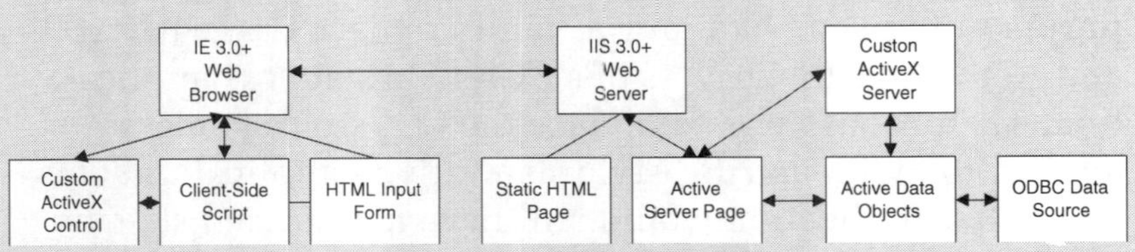

Figure 7.4 Potential elements of an Active Server–based application.

(*continued*)

SOLUTION SCENARIO *Continued*

business logic layer and reimplementing it in VBScript or JScript. Neither of those alternatives appealed to us much.

Moving the logic into separate ActiveX components, however, would have allowed us to reuse large amounts of the original code. The ActiveX components could easily have been implemented in Visual C++. The expensive process would be separating the presentation layer logic (which would have to move into the ASP files) from the true business logic (which remained in the components). Even with the use of HTML templates within our original CGI code, there was still significant intermingling of presentation logic (which essentially selected and populated the templates) with business logic.

We felt that the cost of this separation would be justified by the improved modularity we would gain. Once the business logic was moved safely into the business components, it would be more (but not completely) immune to the sort of change we were dealing with. We felt that the future of ActiveX was sure enough that any new technology we might need to adopt would probably allow us to continue using our ActiveX business servers.

Of course, once the conversion described above was done, we would still have accomplished only half the task. The purpose of the conversion was not to replace C++ with ASP and ActiveX as the drivers of a CGI-style stateless application. The purpose was to replace the CGI-style stateless application with an ASP-style state-driven application. Our converted application would still have maintained state by passing values in hidden fields to the browser and retrieving those values back from the browser's posts and requests.

The next step would have been to move the state information from the hidden fields to variables within the Session

(*continued*)

SOLUTION SCENARIO *Continued*

object. This would have reduced the amount of data passed from the server to the browser and back, it would have allowed us more flexibility in our optimizations, and it would have allowed us much more freedom to cache data on the server side.

As of this writing, the conversion project described above has been planned but not yet performed. The anticipated changes that would necessitate the conversion are not yet certain enough to justify the expense to our clients. As mentioned in the technology section above, we feel strongly that adoption of new technologies, like ASP, should be driven by real business needs and not simply by the availability of new technologies.

TIME:

Our time estimates for this type of conversion effort focus on the three facets described above: the HTML, the presentation logic, and the business logic. The time required to convert the HTML of a CGI application into ASP files depends on the complexity of the HTML and the degree to which the HTML is embedded within the CGI program code itself.

In our example, most (not, unfortunately, all) of the HTML was generated from template files. These files consisted of standard HTML 2.0 with a half dozen special *template tags* added. Many applications developed in CGI used a similar strategy, as did other non-CGI-based approaches, such as Microsoft's Internet Database Connector. Converting any form of templatized HTML to Active Server Pages should be a straightforward task. Our estimates ranged from 3 hours for some of our simpler pages to around 12 hours for more complex pages. If your initial HTML is not templatized but

(*continued*)

SOLUTION SCENARIO *Continued*

instead is mixed in with your CGI code, you should probably double those estimates.

In Active Server Pages, the presentation logic is usually handled by server-side VBScript embedded within the ASP files. This means that, unless your original CGI application was implemented in Visual Basic, you will have to reimplement most of the presentation logic. In our application, as in many I-Net applications, the presentation logic was not particularly complex. There were some pages whose layout varied based on the user's security privileges and others whose layout varied depending on the amount of data returned by a user's query. Most of the others had little or no presentation logic at all. We still estimated between 1 and 2 hours for reviewing the presentation logic of even the smallest scripts, because we wanted to be very careful to distinguish between presentation and business logic. For larger scripts we estimated 4 hours to handle security issues and anywhere up to 12 hours to handle volume issues.

We initially anticipated a great deal of trouble moving the business logic from C++ CGI scripts into C++ ActiveX Servers. This was largely based upon past experience of trying to use RogueWave's class libraries, Tools.H++ and DBTools.H++, with Microsoft's class library, MFC. Since each library introduced its own overhead and each had a slightly different programming model, using only one would have been preferable. The existing code relied quite heavily on RogueWave's libraries, so removing them would amount to rewriting the application from scratch. But implementing ActiveX components in C++ without using MFC was a daunting alternative. While it was possible to implement COM and OLE components in raw C++, or even in raw C, the potential scope of such an effort was not attractive.

(*continued*)

SOLUTION SCENARIO *Continued*

Fortunately, this was about the time Microsoft introduced ATL, its non-MFC approach to implementing C++ ActiveX components. The lightweight ATL did not seem to pose any of the risks of conflict with RogueWave that the heavier MFC had. This was one of the cases in which the pace of intranet technology change actually worked in our favor. Since many of our scripts worked together in longer processes, we felt that two or three scripts might be consolidated into a single component. And figuring between 30 and 60 hours to create each component, that left us with between 10 and 30 hours to migrate each script.

EFFORT:

For this type of conversion, the planning phase truly is the most important. If the authors of the original application are not part of the conversion team, it will be necessary to place even more focus on preliminary analysis and planning. The process of actually implementing the conversion should follow in a number of clear, discrete steps.

The first step is to convert the HTML forms into ASP files. This may mean converting templates from some other template language to ASP, or it may mean extracting the HTML embedded in CGI code. It is important, though, that these HTML-only ASP files be complete. Adding the presentation logic into an ASP that is missing pieces of HTML would be an extremely frustrating process.

The second step is to extract the business logic. Really, these two processes are independent and could proceed in parallel. Either your business logic or your HTML forms may be clearer than the other. We recommend starting with the clearer of the two. If your CGI scripts were implemented in a language that supports ActiveX, you may be able to reuse

(*continued*)

SOLUTION SCENARIO *Continued*

much of your initial code. Otherwise, you will need to reimplement most of it, if not all.

The third step is to add the presentation logic to the ASP files. This step is nearly impossible to do without the HTML and business components in place. The presentation logic essentially knits the two together: It is the glue, and it must have something to bind. This is also likely to be rework, as it is tied heavily to the business components and will have to be in either VBScript or JScript.

The final step is to move the application state information from hidden fields or cookies into the Session object. This step is not strictly necessary, but it has its advantages. The one significant drawback of changing to the Session model is that each user session consumes server resources, even while the server is not actively processing a request. For large applications or for those that need to scale without significant changes to server hardware, you will want to minimize the amount of data stored on the server for each session. In those cases, you may prefer to pass state information to the browser instead. You are trading network throughput for server resources.

RESULTS:

The clearest benefit of this entire process is to move your application a step toward a more modular, extensible implementation. Our example application would have gained a much simpler mechanism for making changes to the behavior of its front end. The business logic of the application was well defined and was (and is) unlikely to change very much over time. Implementing that logic in C++ made sense because it was stable and performance-critical. The front end, however, has been subject to more flux. Implementing the

(*continued*)

SOLUTION SCENARIO *Continued*

front end in VBScript in Active Server Pages would make it much more practical for our client's staff to make their own changes to the UI, and much easier and faster for us to make those changes for them.

The largest benefit, though, is in the improved development and debugging tools available to us. CGI applications were notoriously difficult to debug because they ran in the Web server's process space. The server-side VBScript used by Active Server Pages suffered from a similar problem, but with the release of Internet Information Server 4.0, Microsoft introduced server-side-script debugging tools for use with VBScript.

Summary

Much as we have seen in previous chapters, the effective and efficient management of the operation and growth of intranet applications depends on setting guidelines and then using strong techniques to facilitate that process. The toolsets, on the other hand, change from season to season. To help you understand what you are facing, we have given you some examples of how we have managed change of application on some of our projects; we encourage you to look more closely at the *techniques* that were employed rather than the tools (the technologies are listed so that you can get a clearer idea of the exact situation). Just as we do within our own consulting ranks, you can take this experience and leverage it over other toolsets and set expectations appropriately.

CHAPTER EIGHT

Security

Securing your intranet is a seemingly hopeless task. After all, if you make it secure enough to let you sleep, you will probably be up all night handling pages from people who cannot get connected. Your mission, if you choose to accept it, is to reconcile legitimate expectations for security with legitimate needs for access. By the way, the ground is shifting beneath you. How do you keep up? There are an enormous number of resources available to you. By way of an example, take a look at RFC 1244, the *RFC Site Security Handbook.* This is in the public domain and, along with a number of other documents, is available at www.internic.org. At the end of this chapter there is a listing of additional resources that we find helpful to us in our day-to-day work and that we used in researching this book.

This chapter is *not* meant to be an all-encompassing discussion of intranet security. As a matter of fact, firewalls are not even mentioned. In this chapter, we have tried to delve into some of the less obvious issues of securing the intranet, and there are 10,000 books out there about firewalls. If you really need some advice on that subject, here it is: Buy a firewall and hire professionals to help you implement it. Make sure it supports filtering of content at the certificate level, so signed applets can be passed through. Don't use freeware solutions—you don't want to be in the software support business.

Most of the information in this chapter is based on security for the UNIX environment. We do not mean to imply that NT has no security problems—that would be irresponsible and untrue. However, NT as a major Web server platform is just coming into its own, and there is not yet the body of findings on it that exist for the UNIX environment. However, the issues cited in this chapter often have their NT equivalent, and NT administrators can use the approaches and guidelines we set forth here as a way of structuring their own environment. We have found that most security breaches arise from ignorance on the part of the implementor and that ignorance is not platform-dependent.

It is important that we not lose sight of one important and indisputable fact: that the majority of security breaches result from *internal* employee actions. People are the biggest security risk, be it in formal industrial espionage, accidental disclosure, or malicious damage or destruction of data assets. Thus, a highly formalized technical infrastructure may only lure you into a false sense of security if it is not supported with effective policies for monitoring and managing the human factor. This includes clear policies on appropriate use, proactive monitoring of use, and the development of clear disciplinary actions including dismissal and possible legal action. We find that most companies that implement intranets do so in an ad hoc fashion. This is a recipe for disaster. Be thoughtful; be thorough. Build policy and procedure to support an effective operations model. Invest in technology to help you do this, since you will never manage it manually. Finally, read, research, and retain experienced or broader-based consultancies to help you with this. The intranet today is very different from what it was a year ago, and the security and risk management approach must change accordingly.

The Times They Are A-Changing

When we wrote *Building the Corporate Intranet,* the primary implementation was using secured, private network environments to deliver HTTP-based systems. Today, we are faced with a different environment in which the presumption is that the corporate intranet is connected to the public Internet, and we are passing around applets and components that encapsulate business logic and are active in the client environment.

Our client base is shifting its focus from deploying over private internal networks to building *virtual private internets* (VPIs), private nets deployed over the public Internet. We see two prime motivators for this shift:

- *Cost.* Deploying in the public Internet can be less costly than the private alternative.
- *Access.* Using the public Internet provides a ubiquitous mechanism that can be used to integrate vendors, customers, far-flung offices, telecommuters, and the like.

This makes security, well executed, a major business differentiator and a competitive advantage for a company seeking to operate in this environment. It is also a major point of exposure, since a breach of security can make your company an undesirable partner, thus limiting business opportunities.

If security is so important, why is it so often poorly done? In most companies with whom we work, intranet security has been implemented in, at best, a haphazard fashion, usually because of the organic nature of the environment. Like the early client/server systems, many of the intranet systems have been built on the cheap as proofs of concept, which required maximizing business functionality and leaving good design and security implementations for a later phase. When we audit many of these systems, we quickly find that they are not only inadequate in their security, but in many cases they provide holes in the corporation's current security model, especially when they move from Content class sites to integrating with legacy systems and other data repositories. It seems that, in our rush for modernity, we have left our common sense and experience as data processing professionals behind. What is needed is an approach that can clearly define *sufficiency* and the associated risks with any implementation.

In Search of Sufficiency

What does sufficient security mean in the corporate intranet? Well, there are several criteria for a secured intranet environment, as shown in Table 8.1.

TABLE 8.1 Goals for Intranet Transaction Security

Goal	Description
Authentication	Identifies the partners in a transaction or communication session.
Integrity	Ensures that data has not been modified while between the two parties.
Access control	Provides for discretionary access at an individual level so the identity of a participant is well know and access can be easily revoked.
Privacy	The content of the communication should be encrypted so only the participants can read it.
Nonrepuditation	Interactions between the participants must be certified, such that neither party can deny the sending or receiving of a communication.

These goals are not achieved through the use of a single product or vendor solution. In fact, achieving these goals is an application-to-application issue that should reconcile the needs of the business and the legitimate obligations of IS. The goal is not absolute victory for either party, but rather a search for sufficiency. Sufficiency is determined by looking at several factors:

Financial exposure. What is the possible financial impact of the information being released to an unauthorized individual? In the case of financial institutions, this is not only their own information but the information of their customers. Processing credit card transactions is well understood, and there is an entire legal and technical protocol that protects from fraud. However, when a company begins to handle institutional-size investment transactions over its intranet, the financial implications run into the billions of dollars.

Regulatory exposure. What are the regulatory requirements for handling this information? While many of these are well understood for development, transportation, storage, and access to paper content, what happens when the intranet becomes involved?

Legal exposure. This is always a sticky issue in today's litigious society. The Internet and electronic content liability is all a brand-new area in law, and what is acknowledged to be sufficient for paper content may not apply to electronic content. For example, in a commercial bank where we worked, the Customer Call Files were secured and available only via sign-out sheets. These files contained call comments, financial information, and so on, which was highly proprietary to the customer. By policy, the files could not be taken out of the bank, since one had come back after being left on a subway car. However, when those files went online via the intranet, what liability attached to their interception?

Public relations exposure. This occurs after we finish with the lawyers. What is the possible damage to the company in the public's eye if a breach takes place? For example, remember the CIA's Web site? In many cases where no legal, financial, or regulatory issues arise, security may be driven entirely by the need to tightly control access to information in preservation of the corporate image.

Environmental interaction. What level of interaction is required with corporate data assets? In many cases, nodes in the intranet environment have very different access needs. For example, the human resources department might have a policy and procedures site that is strictly content-based and another site that interacts with the HR database to allow people to look at pension status. In this case, a differing level of sufficiency is self-evident.

Operations integration. What level of integration with the overall operations environment is required? In many cases, intranet nodes are autonomous and are not included in the enterprise contingency planning or disaster recovery plans. When a node is to be included in the operations model, its associated security must comply with the operations standards.

Much of what is required to implement a sufficient security environment is not technological but operational. However, the ad hoc nature of many Internet environments, the shoestring budgets, and quick-time-to-market business drivers usually actively exclude the development of effective security. In addition, most of the content-focused shops, the contractors, and college kids do not have the knowledge of such areas as data processing, security, and auditing required to make the corporate intranet part of the enterprise computing environment. Most user organizations see security as an operational imposition, and if any process is applied without thought it will be, at best, inappropriate. However, all systems attached to the corporate network should meet operational standards for security below the application layer if there is no interaction with corporate data involved, or all the way through if there is.

The Network

What many do not realize is that systems within an organization tend to trust each other, and once a hacker enters a single system, the hacker's ability to penetrate other systems is greatly increased. Within our own company, for example, we have a corporate site and a site used by our Web practice. Our IS organization has been adamant that these two networks will not talk, and thus we maintain a separate network for our Web practice clients and servers. They are physically separate; they never meet. Even the machines on them cannot be attached to both simultaneously. Within an organization, this concept of trust can result in major holes.

It is often surprising that a study of a network security problem seems to ignore the physical design of the network. Since security is a question of managing access, what better way to manage that problem than by closely analyzing the nature of the connection between two parts of the network? We tend to work with a presumption that all points of a network are connected as peers—usually individual segments connected to a backbone by routers, bridges, or switches. This design assumption made perfect sense in the closed network environment and allows a great deal of flexibility in locating users. It can be dangerous in today's interconnected designs.

TIP *It is generally accepted that NFS is a major hole in any security system, and our general advice is "don't use it." With solutions like DCE's distributed file system, which uses Kerberos-type security, there are better solutions. However, we increasingly are hearing requests about "Secure NFS." This is a secure RPC mechanism that validates and manages user/host access to NFS services. While this approach is better than the use of User IDs in traditional NFS to control access, it is still NFS, and thus vulnerable to denial of service attacks, play-back, and other methods of breach.*

Unless you plan on running NFS through an encrypted Virtual Private Network (VPN) to a remote site, we do not suggest that you pass NFS through the firewall, even the so-called Secured NFS solutions. This is still NFS, with the usual concerns over the number of service ports which need to be opened to handle this traffic. Note that these can be reduced if you run NFS over TCP instead of UDP, but not every vendor supports this, and the performance tends to degrade due to the additional overhead of the TCP protocol.

This brings up a second set of issues with NFS. Without the security problems, NFS in a WAN environment still will generally provide poor performance for users, as well as cause excessive loading of valuable network links. Even in the LAN environment, the addition of NFS traffic to an already heavily loaded backbone or local segment can have tremendous and unpredictable performance impacts.

The following design reflects a simple network. This client has used a single high-speed router to connect multiple segments to segregate traffic for purposes of performance. No use is made of traffic filtering between segments, the most common situation in which we find our clients. After all, in the hierarchical network designs that most of us implement, we structure for access to two things: enterprise shared services such as E-mail and legacy applications, and local services such as an accounting package, EIS, or a file server.

In many cases, the constraints put in place at an organizational level are not reflected in the network design, and this can open many companies to litigation. For example, one of our clients was a commercial bank seeking to develop an investment banking capability as well, in response to the relaxation of the banking laws. Working diligently, the bank developed an organizational structure in which employees of one were not employees of the other and even went to the extreme of securing the investment employees in a separate facility. However, in an effort to manage costs, the current infrastructure was used, which meant running the traffic of both businesses on a single network. In addition, the hierarchical nature of the trust relationships between the file servers required to support universal administration resulted in a situation where individuals from one area could gain access to the files of users in another area. Why was this shared network ability a problem? In addition to the obvious ability to access files, the more insidious concept of *snooping* the network allowed the individuals in one area to examine traffic flowing to and from another.

Snooping

It is rather simple to snoop or sniff a network. Network interface cards are driven by software drivers that are designed to disregard packets not sent to their hardware address. However, putting a card into what is called *promiscuous mode* is very simple, and companies like Network General, Hewlett-Packard, and Novell all provide tools that can be used to snoop the network, gathering all traffic and putting it into readable format. Using these tools, someone can intercept passwords or gather actual data—for example, a list of customers with their current Demand Deposit Accounting (DDA) balances or their account numbers. In other cases, sessions can be intercepted and then played back later.

The increasing volumes of data on corporate networks seem to provide their own solution—after all, with data volumes rising so dramatically, how can a snooper possibly decode and decipher that much data and find relevant or damaging traffic? Good thought! Bad news. With the increasing power and decreasing cost of CPUs, there is more than sufficient horsepower available to decode vast amounts of data. Worse, this can be packed in a laptop computer and carted to almost anywhere, making physical security of network wiring closets and the like critical. The only possible saving grace is that the volume of data that needs to be captured if someone is on a fishing expedition is vast and needs to be spooled to disk for later analysis. With my laptop, I can fill the entire hard disk in just an hour in a major corporate network—assuming I capture everything. However, good snoopers are not going to do this. Rather, they will briefly analyze the network and identify the machines that have heavy traffic patterns. Servers can be readily identified by looking for machines with a high output-to-input ratio, reflecting the transmittal of data in response to requests from clients. In many cases, gaining access to a desktop for a few brief minutes will provide sufficient information from reading router tables to provide snoopers with the information they need for a targeted attack.

How do you avoid this problem? In many cases you cannot. Most companies need to snoop the network on occasion to determine the nature of problems. As consultants, we frequently ask for permission to do so, since we require information about response times, systems loads, and so on, which can only be gained at the wire level. In addition, we have used snooping software to actually disassemble packets and make sure the SQL sent to an application is correctly optimized or the result sets are suitably ordered, trying to separate a front-end from a back-end problem.

TIP *As we have discussed, there is no real way to detect an interface in promiscuous mode unless you are on the box itself. In that case, you can usually look at the definitions of the network cards and make the determination. Even then it can be difficult, and once a box is compromised to this extent the only way to clean it up it to rebuild it from scratch. In addition, knowledgeable sniffers will even make sure that traffic does not get logged on the machine but gets routed elsewhere to avoid telltale signs like file volumes rapidly filling with data.*

If you are really paranoid, buy hubs with eavesdrop protection. One vendor we know that can provide this is 3COM. The way it works is that the hub does not send the packet to all ports, but rather to the specific port. In order to do this, it has to keep a list of MAC addresses for the hub, which does add a little overhead. In addition, it issues a "jamming signal" on all ports during a transmission so Ethernet's Collision Detect service works and multiple cards do not try transmitting at once.

Some effective ideas include the following:

Physically secure your network wiring centers. Most companies have one or more network wiring centers on each floor. In many cases, these were colocated with telephone wiring rooms and/or electrical wiring rooms and, while protected by keys, there is no log of entry/exit. In addition, this multiuse nature means that data, telephone, and electrical contractors all have access to the facility. We recommend putting your data wiring in a secured facility, accessible only through the use of smart entry cards and with a proactive entry/exit log review procedure.

Use secured network wiring. For example, the use of 66 blocks for data wiring provides convenient connectors to which alligator clips can be readily attached. Category 5 and similar copper wiring solutions are all easily tapped. The use of multiport dumb hubs allows anyone with physical access to the hub to attach a device and snoop the passing traffic. In some cases, the use of induction detection devices can be used to actually snoop copper wire without any need for physical connectivity. The use of fiber-optic wiring is recommended in secured environments for both the horizontal or desktop solution as well as the backbone. Induction snooping is impossible with fiber.

Encrypt traffic. If the information is sensitive, encrypt it. This can be accomplished with any number of tools; however, Kerberos, X509.3 certificates, or other public/private key and encryption schemes are readily available. During the time this chapter was written, there were some major changes in this area, as the U.S. government relaxed the export constraints on the length of encryption keys for financial institutions. We anticipate that relaxation across the board is a matter of time.

Physically separate networks. Where traffic is sensitive to the point that release would result in regulatory or other legal sanction, you may want to physically separate the networks, moving any interconnection points to a managed 24-×-7 facility with highly managed access. In some cases, the pressure of the market may warrant this type of segregation even if not mandated by law or regulation.

Perform background checks on your staff. In many cases, the shortage of staff has resulted in more casual hiring practices, including an abandonment of background or even reference checks. Where operators or technicians are going to have access to monitors that can capture real-time data flow or to network facilities, extensive background checks should be conducted. If you are dealing with an outsource vendor relationship, make sure that such checks are the responsibility of the outsourcer and that your contract is written to indemnify you in case of breach by one of the outsourcer's employees.

In Figure 8.1, the router simply handles the redirection of packets between segments and does some basic filtering between segments to limit broadcasts. Each segment, conveniently, corresponds to an organizational unit. Security in this figure exists only at the application layer, provided by application passwords. All entities are equally trusted—that is, it is assumed that no individual would have reason or motivation to attack the data assets of another group, although they have network-level access to them.

In looking at the trust diagram in Figure 8.2, we can see that most of the organization does not trust the users and systems in other organizational components. The data center is considered to be trusted by all. If you look at the executive environment, you will note that it trusts the data center and is trusted by the administrative organization. However, administration is not considered to be trusted by the executive component, since people in the executive offices have access to data and information (strategic

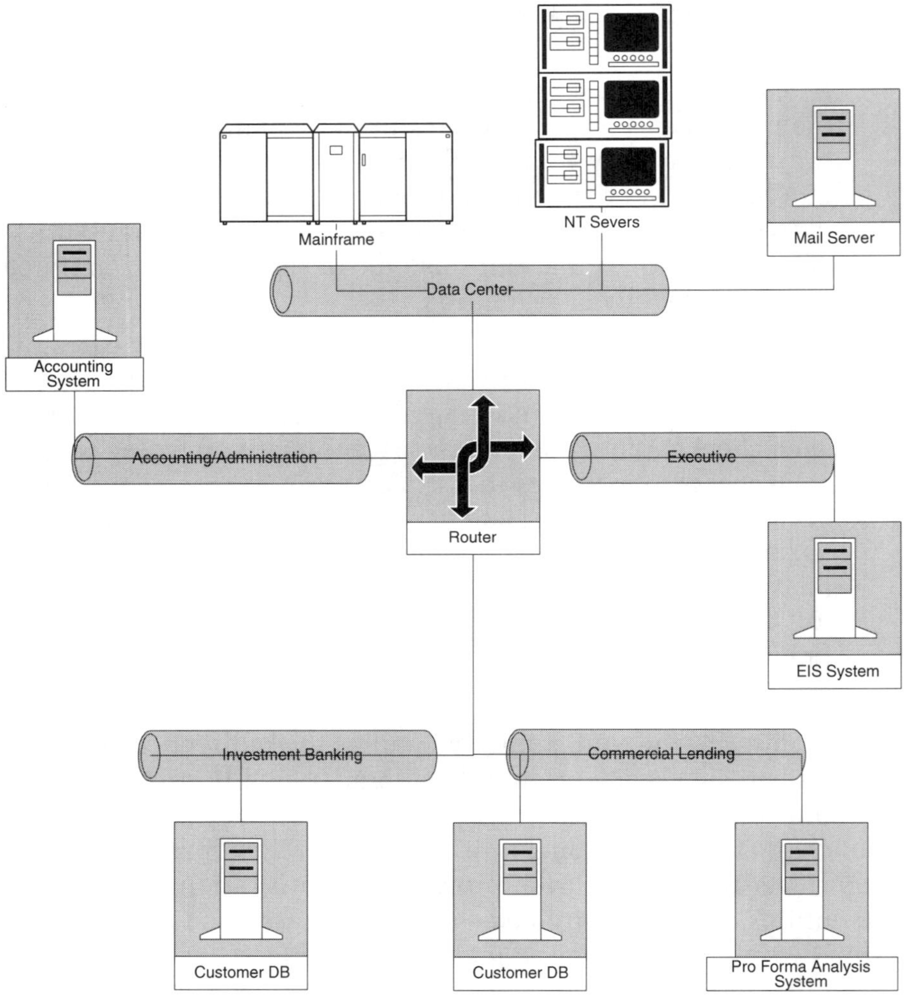

Figure 8.1 Initial network design.

planning, profitability, salary, succession planning) that is a superset of that originated by administration and is not within their need to know. When this model is reviewed, the concept of "need to know" at the business level translates to "needs access to" at the application level and ultimately to "needs connectivity between" at the network design level.

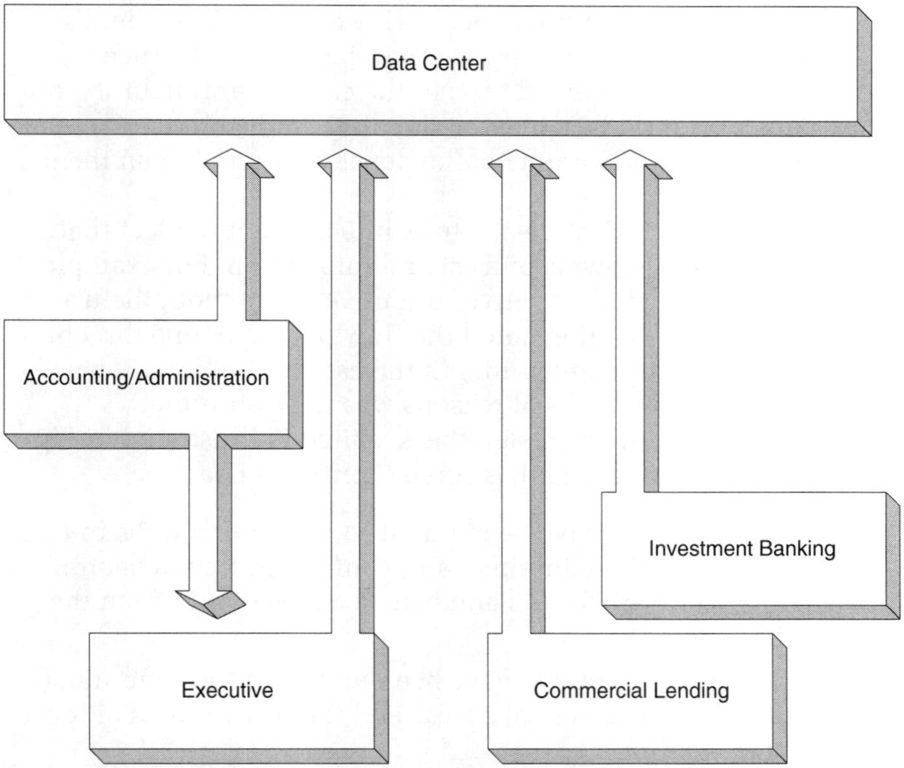

Note: An arrow points at the "trusted" environment, indicating that the system originating the arrow trusts the computers in the organizational component pointed to.

Figure 8.2 Organizational trust diagram.

In the preceding situation, the indicated separations result from either a legal/regulatory framework, as in the case of the separation of investment banking and commercial lending, or through policy, as evidenced by the separation of the executive and administrative components. Does the network design policy reflect this? In the case we are describing, the answer was no. The ad hoc nature of the growth of the intranet environment had all the traffic on the single backbone segment and through a single router, where it was available for easy snooping—something we demonstrated by taking a client network manager on a trip to a wiring closet, where we quickly pulled a list of account names and balances from the wire in about five minutes. The client's position had been that the application security met the needs. However, the client realized that, in the case of legal liability, the access model should be driven to the physical level, so a lapse at the application or operations policy level would not open them up to legal liability.

The resulting physical design took into account the fact that there were differing levels of trust and interaction. For example, in the case of the administrative/executive interaction, the use of a network device that prevented the flow of data in one direction was considered sufficient, while in the case of the lines of business, the separation for legal reasons was to be absolute.

The physical network design that resulted is illustrated in Figure 8.3. The overall design has some significant changes:

The wiring hubs have been replaced with smart hubs in which ports are maintained and configured from a central facility. Ports are locked and can be enabled only from the central site.

All bridges and routers have been moved to the central data center, limiting physical access and the possibilities of local reconfiguration.

The wiring runs in the executive suite have been converted to fiber-optic cable, providing maximum security against physical penetration of the network.

All long-haul wiring runs between the wiring closets and the data center have been replaced with fiber-optic wiring. The use of fiber provides for longer runs without the need for repeaters and provides security against physical tampering.

The connection between the administration and executive areas is handled using a dedicated bridge and dedicated segments. This provides absolute control over traffic between these areas and also precludes snooping on the common network of traffic between these two organizational areas.

The data center backbone Ethernet topology has been replaced with a fiber-optic FDDI ring. This provides a higher level of redundancy than the Ethernet design through the use

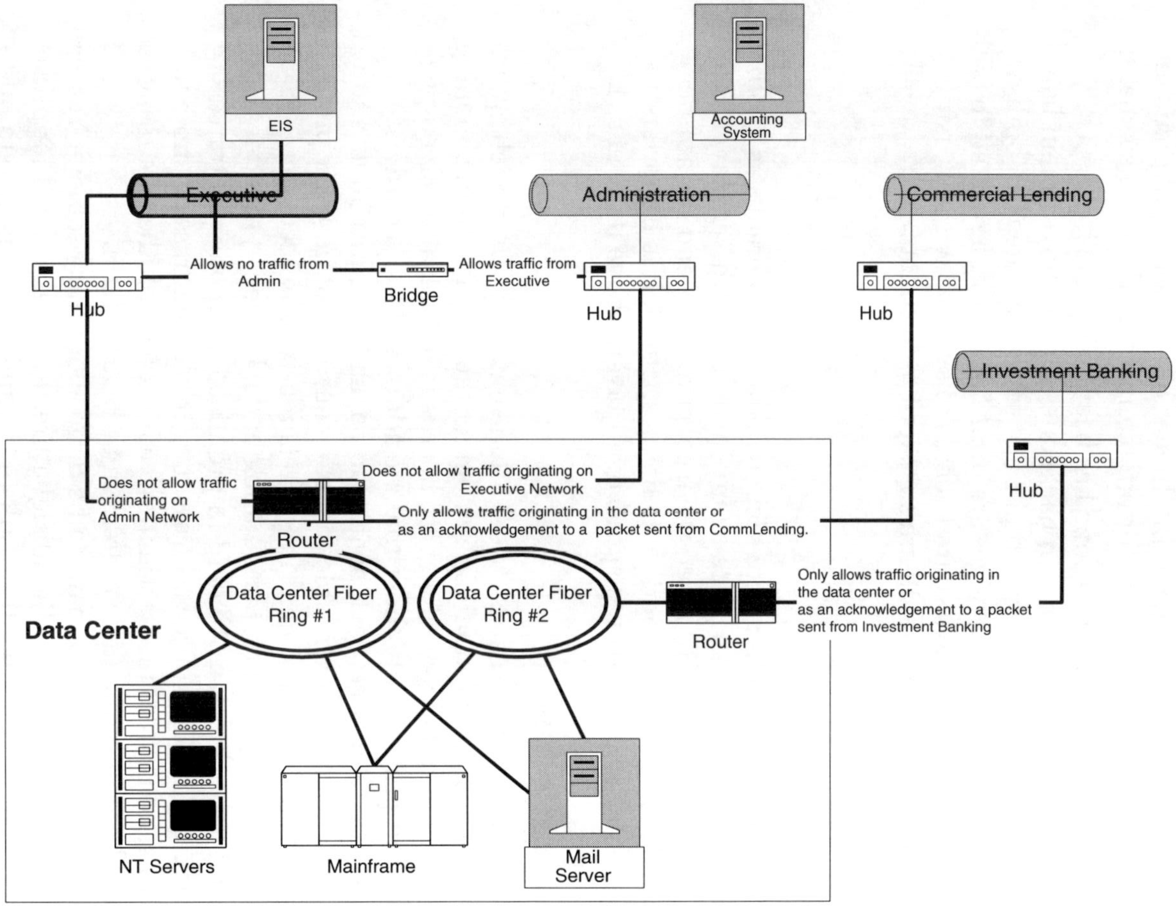

Figure 8.3 Secured network design.

of dual counterrotating rings. An alternative would be the use of an ATM environment or the use of a *collapsed backbone,* in which a high-speed intelligent hub uses its backplane to provide the backbone for interconnecting the local segments.

The data center backbone has been duplicated, physically separating the common backbone from the investment banking backbone. Servers that must communicate with both or provide shared services are *dual-homed* or connected to both rings. This allows shared access to systems without using shared media, which are susceptible to snooping.

Spoofing

Spoofing is a situation in which a device masquerades as another device. This can take place at any layer; the hardware layer, the data link layer, the IP layer, the transport layer, and the application layer are all susceptible to being spoofed. It is important to note that when a layer is spoofed, all layers above it are at risk.

HARDWARE ADDRESS

Network interface cards (NICs) all have unique IDs, which are set by the board vendor. If you remember the discussion of snooping, the standard behavior for these boards is to look at received packets and process only those that are addressed to its hardware address. Of course, each board can be made promiscuous, and we know what kind of trouble that can cause! Most network protocols trust that the source field in packets received is accurate; it is the real address of the real originating node. However, this does not need to be the case. A board in promiscuous mode can trap a packet, alter the source address to match its address or another, and send it on to the destination, with the result that the response will be sent to the new address in the source field.

There is not much that can be done about this problem. You can encrypt data and use digital signatures at a higher level (application layer), which would result in the spoofer being able to intercept but not read the traffic. An example of this is the use of X.509.3 certificates, like Nortel's Entrust which would provide trusted relationships and end-end encryption. Products such as SSL and SET also can provide services in this area.

Spoofing at the hardware address layer is a little more difficult than other forms and requires penetration of physical security (or it should if your network is adequately secured). It is almost impossible to trace spoofing at this level, although the use of secured ports can limit the ability of a spoofer to casually attach to the physical network itself. These hubs are usually active or smart hubs from companies such as 3COM, Cabletron, HP, Bay Networks, and IBM, and they frequently are found as higher-end switches. While the cost per port is much greater than that of a dumb Ethernet repeater, the control available to you is much greater and the resultant security is also much greater. However, to use these devices effectively you must be committed to developing the operations policies for configuration management and monitoring. Otherwise, the investment is wasted.

ARP

The Address Resolution Protocol (ARP) is the perfect place to masquerade. It is not, as commonly thought, part of TCP/IP, but is really part of the lower-level protocols like Token Ring (yes, it still exists) or Ethernet. When a packet is ready to go out on the wire, ARP is used to match a hardware destination address to the IP destination address. The source node sends out an ARP message to all local clients with the IP address and asks the client with that IP address to return the corresponding hardware address. This association is stored in cache on the host and is aged out over time. This makes sense, since you expect the logical (IP) address to hardware address relationships to change over time, and the caching decreases the level of ARP traffic in the network. Interestingly, all of the devices listed in Figure 8.4 have the same physical address, because, when a device is remote to the requester, the hardware address of the intervening router (in this case) is used.

ARP spoofing can be accidental or intentional. If two users set the same IP address, one might respond to the first ARP, setting the association in the requesting host's cache. When that entry ages out, a subsequent ARP might result in keeping the response from the second machine. Assuming the services, data, and so on

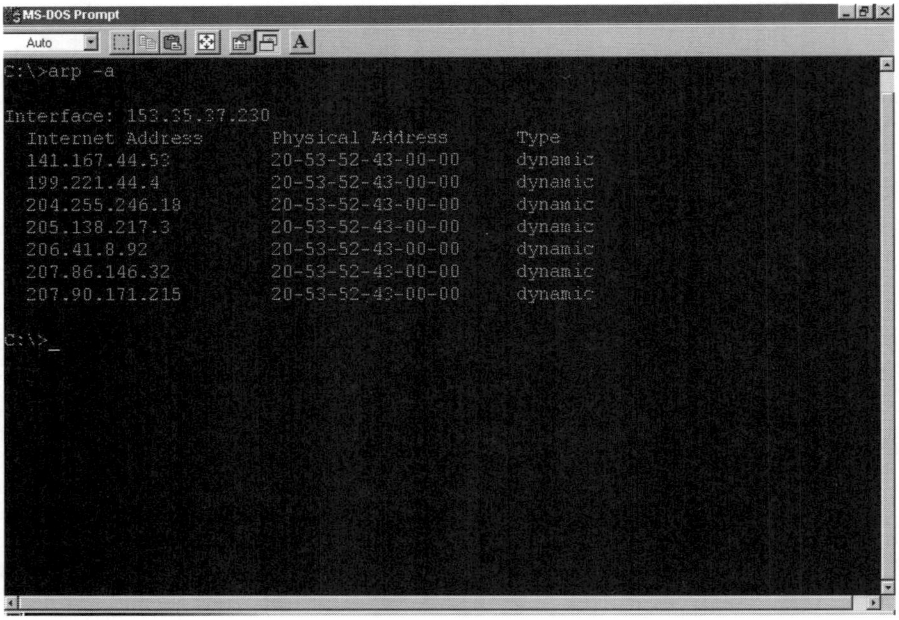

Figure 8.4 Example ARP list.

local to these two machines are different, your requesting application will likely fail.

Intentional ARP spoofing can be done in a way to make the spoofing machine either the first or last respondent to the ARP request. The easiest way to do this is by making it the only respondent. This can be done in several ways:

Change the legitimate machine's address. Probably the least disruptive and thus hardest to catch technique, this allows someone with access to the host machine to change the IP address. This requires either physical or remote access to the system, and admin or superuser privileges.

Disconnect the legitimate machine from the network. This does not require access to the machine itself, but does generally require access to the physical wiring plant. This can often be caught by alert console operators, assuming that

RMON, SNMP, or a similar proactive management facility is in use.

Down the legitimate machine. This is difficult to do in data centers or similarly physically controlled environments but not at all difficult to do in physically distributed environments or widely dispersed environments such as branches or franchises.

ARP spoofing is a tough problem because it is almost impossible to detect until after the breach has occurred, and it is difficult to prevent unless ARP is entirely disabled. The fact that the legitimate holder of the IP address being spoofed is trusted by the target machine is problematic. In many cases, trusted machines in a distributed environment have access to a number of things, such as NFS mounts, which can expose data. There are several possibilities for managing this problem:

Servers that extend trust to others based on IP address should have ARP disabled, since these types of relationships are usually between well-known servers. These entries can be manually maintained in the server ARP tables, which provides permanence (such entries do not expire from cache) and will avoid the possibility of ARP spoofing.

Locate trusting machines on a highly controlled segment. This prevents a spoofer from gaining access to that segment, powering down one of the machines and assuming its identity.

Use routers to control ARP flow. They are generally secured and can prevent ARP requests from traveling off of a trusted segment or responses from coming onto it. This forces the spoofer to have physical access to a machine on the trusted segment and/or the segment's wiring plant.

Have hosts periodically ARP for their own address. If a response is received, then the machine should notify the console operators, who can investigate and see whether it is a purposeful spoof or an accidental configuration problem. This simple trap can be evaded by sophisticated hackers who can program their machines not to respond to such requests, but it will thwart the less sophisticated. Since many OS kernels actively monitor for address duplication, just paying attention to the existing system alerts can go a long way toward managing this problem.

Leverage SNMP facilities. Most systems today ship with SNMP MIBs, and these can be tweaked to report the contents of the local ARP cache periodically to a server that is responsible for examining these for anomalies.

Use a promiscuous mode collection agent. This can collect all ARP traffic on a segment and look for anomalies. If you have a widely distributed network, you would need to deploy RMON devices on every segment from which you wanted to collect information, which can be an expensive proposition unless your hubs provide that ability.

There are also downsides to this measure:

- In case of failure of the destination system, the source system will not re-ARP for a new IP/hardware pair, but will continue to send data to the permanently coded ARP address.
- Operational complexity increases, since any legitimate changes to the IP/hardware pairing will require manual changes to the ARP tables. If you do not have an excellent operations management model, this type of complexity will generally cause more problems than it will solve. In addition, active monitoring for deception means developing an incident management model that assumes a high level of operational sophistication.

ROUTERS AND ROUTING PROTOCOLS

Today's networks are often held together by routers. These interesting devices run a number of protocols that identify and track the routes between networks, and provide the ability for these devices to dynamically determine the optimal routes as bandwidth and utilization change. This section discusses several of the protocols that make this possible and how they can be "spoofed."

ICMP By now you have realized that anything that relies on dynamic addressing is a target for being duped, and routers are no exception. The basis for router spoofing is simple: When a host sends a packet to a destination, the default router is used. However, in a complex network there may be several routes to a destination. When a router knows a better route to a destination, it uses the Internet Control Message Protocol (ICMP) to send a message called a *redirect* to the originating client to alert that client to the alternate route. The normal behavior for a machine receiving such a notification is to update its local routing tables so subsequent packets to that destination will use the optimal route, while the packets in flight will be delivered using the default router so nothing gets lost or retransmitted. It is possible to turn off ICMP processing on some machines, which simply results in suboptimal delivery of packets. In addition, many companies have several paths between sites, which can be adjusted to force certain routing behavior. Machines that disregard ICMP messages will ignore these directions.

Several methods are used for ICMP spoofing, including:

- ICMP fraud in which invalid ICMP messages are sent to a machine that invalidates the local router table and results in outbound packets not reaching their destination. This is malicious and annoying, and is generally termed a *Denial of Service* attack.
- ICMP fraud that invalidates the local router table and allows a spoofer to masquerade as a router, intercepting traffic.

Several methods exist for preventing ICMP attacks, but, as always, when you give up the flexibility provided by these dynamic protocols, you are stepping up to an operational burden. Solutions include:

- Turn off ICMP processing. This is not really possible for Windows clients, since we know of no shrink-wrapped IP stack for NT or Windows 95 which supports this. Some UNIX SVR4 implementations will allow the introduction of a packet filter with no manipulation of the kernel; however, you need to check with your vendor and make sure your release will support this.

- Make sure that router ARP entries on hosts are hard-coded and not dynamic. This prevents an ARP spoof of the router.

RIP Other routing protocols such as the Routing Information Protocol (RIP) are frequently used in the network environment and are also susceptible to spoofing. RIP is a *vector distance* protocol, which is actually based on work done at Xerox's Palo Alto Research Center (PARC) in the development of Xerox Networking System (XNS), a set of network protocols that provided the intellectual basis for Novell, Banyan, and others. A host using RIP gathers routing information from each router on the network, which describes its knowledge of destination networks and the *hop count,* or number of routers between the router and the destination. A locally attached network has a value of "0"; an infinite distance is designated by "16," which means "can't get there from here." This results in RIP being limited to networks with a maximum of 16 routers between any two hosts. When this information is received, the host processes the information and determines which router is best used for which destination network.

Any machine which is a so-called passive participant (just listening) in the RIP environment is a candidate for a route spoofing attack, since RIP is listened for on well-known port 520. If security on the system does not prevent access to that port, or if operators or other users with sufficient access desire, they can send false routing information to the device. If routers in the organization are also passive participants in RIP, the disruption can be extreme, as the routers disseminate the incorrect information across the enterprise.

As you can see, the problem here is not really RIP, it is the trusted relationship that is assumed between devices. A passive RIP participant accepts information from any active RIP participant. This, while noble, can be disastrous, especially if RIP is used at a border with another company or with the Internet itself. The normal RIP listener, or *daemon,* has no constraints on who is trusted, but there are more rigorous replacements for it. GateD, a replacement developed at Carnegie Mellon University, consults a configuration file on the host when it starts, which includes information on the IP addresses of trusted RIP partners. CMU is no longer responsible for GateD, that responsibility having been transferred to the GateD consortium. Information on GateD is available at www.gated.merit.edu.

Many router vendors also provide proprietary or alternative mechanisms to GateD and similar solutions, and some OS vendors that provide secure kernels even provide OS-level alternatives. You want to work with those vendors to determine what they provide, what they support, and where they are heading. Whenever possible, you should use commercially available, supported software and not freeware or similar patches. See Figure 8.5.

DNS

The Domain Name System (DNS) is covered elsewhere in great detail, but here is a brief recap. DNS is a distributed naming service

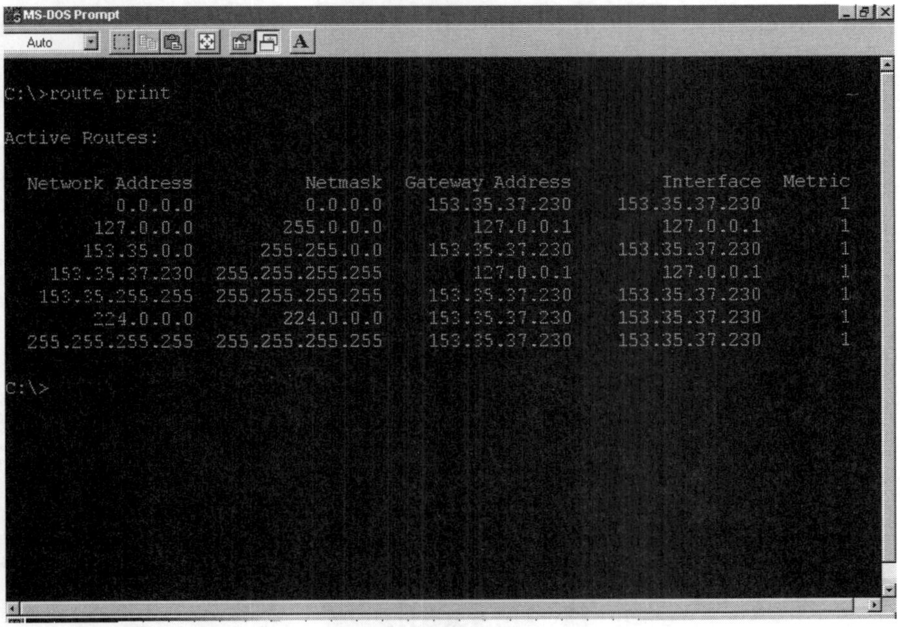

Figure 8.5 Example router table.

that matches IP addresses to a name. For example, my IP address might be 123.123.123.123 and my name might be "mucker.bsgnet.com." It is much easier to interact with "mucker" than with the IP address. DNS is a service that provides this translation using a domain-based, hierarchical, distributed data structure. A company's DNS hierarchy might look something like Figure 8.6.

The hierarchical nature of this design allows subdomains such as "R&D" to manage themselves and create subdomains without the intervention of some central naming authority. Given the issues involved with getting domain names from the InterNIC today, can you imagine if they had to assign all the subdomains as well?

Assume for a moment that each of the subdomains listed has a DNS server. When queried by a client within its domain, a DNS server can issue either an *authoritative* or *nonauthoritative* reply. If the data is kept in that DNS server's portion of the database, then the reply is considered authoritative. If it is not local, then the server can make one of two types of replies: recursive or iterative.

The more common of the two, a *recursive* reply occurs when the server forwards the request on to a DNS server it believes to be more authoritative than itself about the requested information and returns the result and the name of the servicing DNS server. This allows a request to be passed way up the internal hierarchy and even out onto major DNS servers within the Internet itself. When an authoritative response is received by a DNS server, that

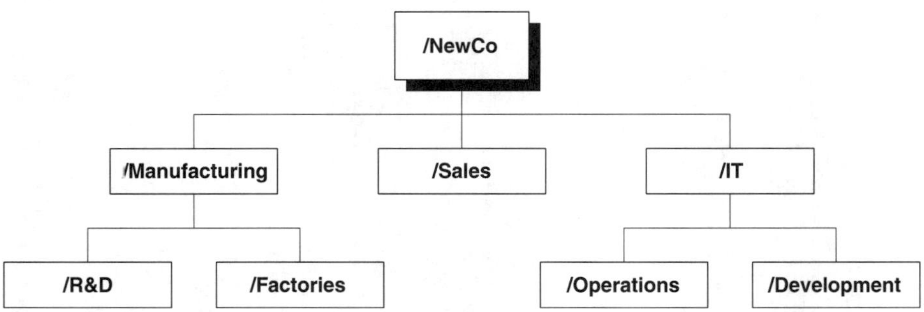

Figure 8.6 Example DNS hierarchy.

response is cached with a *time-to-live* parameter in a manner similar to what we discussed with ARP entries previously. This reduces network traffic, but you can already see the issues of trust creeping back into the picture.

An *iterative* request is serviced by simply passing back to the requesting client the name of the authoritative DNS server the queried server would have passed the request to and allowing the client to interact directly with that server.

With all this name resolution going on, there exists lots of opportunity for spoofing all over. A DNS server address can be ARP spoofed; DNS traffic can be router spoofed—and it can be DNS spoofed. When a server receives an authoritative response, that response and the data it represents are trusted to be accurate. If a domain's server has been compromised, it will return false information to queries, and that information can rapidly spread through the network. So, if a DNS lookup is remapped to direct a request to some other machine, it will happen. Conversely, if a reverse lookup takes place, a server can be fooled into believing that the IP address of a requesting client corresponds to a legitimate and authorized client. Finally, the nature of the time-to-live parameter means that such data will persist in the network even once the problem is detected and resolved. Unfortunately, there is nothing of which the authors are aware that can be done about this problem within the DNS environment. Suggestions are welcome. Some ways that people have tried to work around these problems include:

Cross-checking. In the DNS world, this means that all *reverse* lookups are checked by making a forward lookup. In English, this means that the IP address of the prospective client is used to issue a name lookup on that IP address. Then a lookup is done against that name and the returned IP address is checked against the originating address of the prospective client. If it fails, you have a client with an identity crisis.

Forcing iterative responses. As discussed above, an iterative response passes the client the name of a purportedly more authoritative DNS server. If the queried server is compromised, then it can claim a level of authority with regard to a domain that it does not really have. One way to avoid this is to query a *root-level* domain server for the addresses of name servers that it considers authoritative at the next level, and so on. This is slow, and if the root is compromised then the truth is meaningless.

Forcing multiple queries. As pointed out previously, DNS is distributed and it is also replicated. It is mandated that DNS content be replicated on multiple systems, and those systems cannot have a single point of failure. This means they cannot reside on the same hardware, share DASD, be attached to the same network, or use the same power drop. Most companies observe this level of redundancy with Internet solutions, but the same discipline should be applied to intranet solutions. In this fashion, it is unlikely that an intruder will have compromised every instance of the DNS information if you catch it soon enough. The domain structure recognizes a domain master–secondary relationship, and when a change is made to the master it periodically gets passed to the secondaries. So, if you catch an intruder and take your master DNS node offline before the corruption gets passed along, you will be able to contain the problem.

DNS is such a part of the intranet that the ultimate solution—turning it off—is wholly impractical. Windows users have the ability to use WINS as a partial solution, but the best solution is just keeping your DNS server up to date. As issues are discovered, DNS is constantly being enhanced. This is one of the best reasons to use a highly reputable vendor for your DNS services, since you want the software updated frequently. CERT, COAST, and others are working actively with vendors to improve DNS. Be careful if you are running so-called freeware DNS servers—the price is great but the cost can be really high! Many companies do this with their first intranet experiments, but if you are looking at this book, you are moving beyond experimentation—you are using the intranet as a fundamental component of the enterprise computing platform. Don't cut corners!

Encryption

Encryption is the process of taking *plain-text,* or the raw text, and applying some algorithm to it that generates *cipher-text,* or the encrypted output. Encryption is like a lock on your door: It will not prevent someone from coming in; it will simply make the process of getting in so odious that the burglar will go elsewhere or prolong the attack so long that the information being sought is no longer valuable. Like security, encryption is a way of managing risk, not eliminating it. For example, RSA has posted rewards for individuals able to break its 40- and 48-bit keys, and also posted a reward for breaking the government's 56-bit data encryption standard (DES) system. All of those have fallen so far to coordinated, distributed hacking solutions, which, in the case of the DES break, harnessed the power of tens of thousands of computers across the Internet to process sets of possible solutions in parallel. While there were some 72 quadrillion possibilities to be tried, the distributed cracking model was able to process almost seven billion keys per second. The solution was found after only 25 percent of the possible keys had been tried.

The conventional wisdom that long guided encryption policy in the United States was: How big a machine would be needed to crack this? However, the rise of connected computing and the Internet will require a rethinking of this philosophy. After all, these participants volunteered, but what about someone who sends out a work that runs quietly on attached systems without permission?

First, some terms need to be introduced:

Public key. A solution that permits publication of a key for use in supporting the encryption/decryption process. Both pretty good privacy (PGP) and X509.3 certificate systems use this type of solution based on technology licensed from RSA www.rsa.com.

Private key. A solution in which the same key is used for encryption and decryption and is helped by both partners. Probably the most common of these solutions is the data encryption standard (DES) developed by IBM and endorsed by the U.S. government.

Asymmetric key. A system in which two keys are generated for a user. The holder of a key can decrypt a message encrypted by the other key. This can result in a private/public solution, in which a key is held private to the user and a public key is published for those who interact with the user to use in the encryption/decryption process.

Because of all the possible solutions in the market, this section will focus on two sets of solutions: RSA and DES. But first, a word from the lawyers.

ENCRYPTION AND THE LAW

In the United States, the National Security Agency (NSA) is the government watchdog and think tank on encryption. The budget and activities of the NSA are highly secret, as are its true capabilities. What is public knowledge is the tremendous intellectual talent and computing horsepower the agency has and the actions it has taken to block the granting of patents in the area of encryption as well as to prevent the export of encryption technology. In addition to the actions of the NSA, excerption technology is also regulated by the U.S. Department of Commerce and the U.S. Department of State. These actions, while not always appreciated by the business or academic community, are supported by a number of laws including the Invention Secrecy Act of 1940, the National Security Act of 1947, and the International Traffic in Arms Regulation.

Currently, encryption export laws are changing dramatically. The Clinton administration moved to allow the export of stronger encryption to banks and other financial institutions working overseas. In addition to this relaxation, the Clinton administration has also put forward the concept of *key escrow,* in which stronger encryption could be used but the keys would need to be put in escrow with the U.S. government and could be given to law enforcement officials by the courts. The jury is still very much out on this process, and there is tremendous resistance from foreign companies and countries who object to the U.S. government having this level of access to information.

The essence of the preceding discussion is that you need to be careful about the technology you use and the assumptions you make about the technology you can use. Finally, be very careful about the countries in which you try to use encryption. While China may be an obvious suspect for banning encryption, would you believe that France is another? Also, watch the nuances. While 56-bit keys can be exported for authentication, only 40-bit keys can be used for encryption.

ENCRYPTION SOLUTIONS

The world is full of encryption technology, and Congress is doing its confused best to destroy the U.S. leadership in this area. In this section, we discuss two of the most common solutions available today.

DES—Private/Secret Key The data encryption standard was designed to be implemented in hardware, which makes it very fast. Using 56-bit keys, base DES effectively implemented was long considered unbreakable. Today, *triple DES* continues to advance the state of the art in this area. While DES is almost never allowed for export, there are a number of DES products that are built on U.S. designs and are interoperable with U.S. software.

DES is often referred to as a *bulk* encryption solution—that is, it works well for large data sets and uses a 64-bit data block design to support this need. Currently, DES is considered sufficient for most solutions, although there is some doubt as to whether it will be recertified by the U.S. government in its current form. So-called triple DES is a much strengthened implementation and theoretically seems impervious to cracking at this time. However, DES does not seem to be winning the vendor war, where most solutions seem to be moving to the more popular *public key* solutions. One of the major reasons for this is the need to find a way to move the shared key in a secure fashion. If the private key is sent in clear text, it is fairly worthless as an encryption mechanism!

RSA—Public Key In the early 1980s, several patents were issued to mathematicians for a concept called *public* or *symmetric key security.* In this model, a seed is used to generate two keys. The trick to the system is that what one key encrypts, the other can decrypt. Unlike the need for finding a way for secure transmission of keys imposed by secret key solutions, public key solutions allow for the transmission of public keys in the clear.

Let's say you want to send an encrypted E-mail message to someone. You look up his or her public key, use it to encrypt the message, and then send the message on. The recipient uses his or her private key to decrypt the message. This system has been widely accepted by a number of vendors and is the basis for the encryption of pretty good privacy, the security of Lotus's Notes product; the use of X509.3 certificates by companies like Verisign, Microsoft, and Netscape; and the encryption technology for the SET protocol being used by Visa, Mastercard, and American Express for secured credit card transactions. This approach of public keys seems to be much better suited to the casual interaction model of the Internet, where two parties may want to exchange information with no prior knowledge of each other, and is the leading solution among our client base.

Certificates With the rapid growth of casual interaction on the Internet and intranet, many companies are turning to a specific implementation of public keys to provide a trusted relationship. Especially in instances where the interaction with your intranet will take place across a public Internet connection, this trust becomes more important. To meet that need, the concept of the *trusted third party* or *certificate authority* has emerged. One of first major certificate systems was implemented by Per-Se in 1996 to support the trading of electrical transmission capacity on the U.S. power grid. Valued at about $22 billion a year, security was an issue. The following example illustrates how this works for the SET system being implemented by the major credit card vendors.

1. The cardholder initiates a request for a transaction.
2. The merchant sends back a digitally signed response along with its certificate and the certificate of the payment gateway.
3. The merchant decrypts the cardholder's request and validates the certificate with a certificate authority.

4. The merchant processes the transaction, sending it to the payment gateway.
5. The merchant acknowledges the payment to the cardholder.

For additional information on the use of digital certificates, you can look at the following sites:

- www.visa.com
- www.verisign.com
- www.nortel.com

Resources for Security Information

There is a lot of information available to you in researching security—probably too much. Table 8.2 is a list of resources we find useful. These include organizations whose charter is to deal with security, public newsgroups where security is the topic, and Web sites with relevant white papers.

TABLE 8.2 Security Newsgroups

Group Name	Group Description
comp.security.unix	The primary group for security, with comments from expert and novice alike
comp.security.misc	More chatter than the previous, but not bad
alt.security	Noise factor here is getting too high, not recommended
comp.security.announce	Posting area for CERT bulletins
comp.security.firewalls	Discussion of firewalls
sci.crypt	For those who enjoy it, lots of theory on cryptography
talk.politics.crypto	Lots of discussion on cryptography
comp.os.ms-windows.nt.admin.misc	A general area for discussion of NT administration; has some discussions of security but lots of other noise
comp.os.ms-windows.nt.admin.networking	Focused on NT networking; does deal with security issues but not as a primary subject

The following sections discuss organizations that provide security information. In most cases, these organizations are set up with a specific purpose in mind, such as serving the Department of Defense. However, they often make their alerts, bulletins, research, and so forth available via E-mail and/or Web sites. We also recommend looking at your vendor's Web sites and making aggressive use of your support contracts. In many cases, these contracts provide for some hours of consulting from the vendor—security is a great way to use those high-end hours.

Computer Incident Advisory Capability Group (CIAC)

The Computer Incident Advisory Capability Group (CIAC) is part of the Department of Energy and is primarily based in the DOE's Lawrence Livermore site. It provides E-mail advisories to anyone on the Internet, and also has both an FTP and a Web site. This is an excellent reference site for those knowledgeable about security and looking to leverage the great work done here.

FTP: ftp://www.ciac.llnl.gov/pub/ciac

WWW: http://ciac.llnl.gov (NB: If you use the "www" prefix, you will get a "site not found" error message.)

E-mail: ciac@llnl.gov

Computer Operations, Audit, and Security Technology (COAST)

Run by Purdue University, COAST is an organization committed to the improvement of network security. It has an excellent FTP archive, with an extensive collection of documents and tools that are invaluable to the security management process. Its Web site is solid, with not only excellent local content but excellent links to other sites that can help direct and target your research. Through its work with government agencies and some major corporations, COAST has also developed some very good studies on network security, which are available through the site.

FTP: ftp://coast.cs.purdue.edu

WWW: http://www.cs.purdue.edu/coast.html

E-mail: coast-request@cs.purdue.edu

U.S. Computer Emergency Response Team (CERT)

Founded in 1988 by the U.S. Department of Defense, CERT is an organization whose mission is to protect the infrastructure of the Internet. It is located at Carnegie Mellon University and has several functions, including responding to Internet users about security issues, producing bulletins about known problems, researching Internet security issues independently, and working with vendors as appropriate. CERT is probably the best known of the Internet watchdogs, since it is also has the role of dealing with the media to address and, where necessary, publicize concerns while educating.

CERT has a comprehensive mailing list, with well over 100,000 subscribers as of this writing, and it permits anyone to subscribe. The FTP site contains all of CERT's bulletins, so as a new user we suggest that you first look to the FTP site as a source of information about problems or issues. In addition, CERT maintains a number of security programs in the FTP archive and posts its bulletins in comp.security.announce. CERT will usually delay announcing a problem until it has had a chance to work with vendors to deal with it, so usually its postings are helpful not only in alerting you to the vulnerability, but in providing you with real solutions to it.

FTP: ftp://info.cert.org

WWW: http://www.cert.org

Email: cert@cert.org (Subscribe by sending a request to cert-advisory-request@cert.org)

DOD SECURITY CLASSIFICATIONS

The U.S. government has its own method of classifying secured systems, and this system is often cited by vendors in defining their security levels. The Department of Defense documents these in the *Orange Book,* which was published in 1985. The multiple hierarchies are represented by A, B, and C levels, which have a numeric hierarchy within them. Most major operating systems claim to be at least C2, and most UNIX vendors, like Hewlett-Packard, offer patches or in some cases "Secured OS," which can

SOLUTION SCENARIO

Security

A client intranet site is up and running, providing a content solution to the company. However, as the solution matures to data integration solutions, the issue of security becomes more important. In addition, the client needs to allow access to its intranet over its Internet connection. The client deployment environment is a UNIX platform running Solaris with Netscape's Web Server supporting both HTTP and HTTPS. Connectivity to the Internet will be provided by the client's long-distance vendor. The proposed physical architecture is illustrated in Figure 8.7.

TIP *In many companies, the development of the intranet has sparked requests for access to the Internet. With email and similar services becoming ubiquitous, this was inevitable. However, many companies have legitimate concerns about controlling access to make sure productivity is not affected, to make sure that unprofessional or offensive content is not brought in, and to make sure that viruses are not introduced. In a number of our clients, this has resulted in a policy of no interconnection between the internal and external network, and several provide the needed services to users (Web access, email, etc.) via dial-up services to an ISP.*

We do not recommend this. Once a client is connected to the Internet over a dial-up line and connected to your LAN, you are exposed to unopposed infiltration from the Net.

So, our suggestion? If you are not able to afford a permanent connection to the network, buy a firewall and a

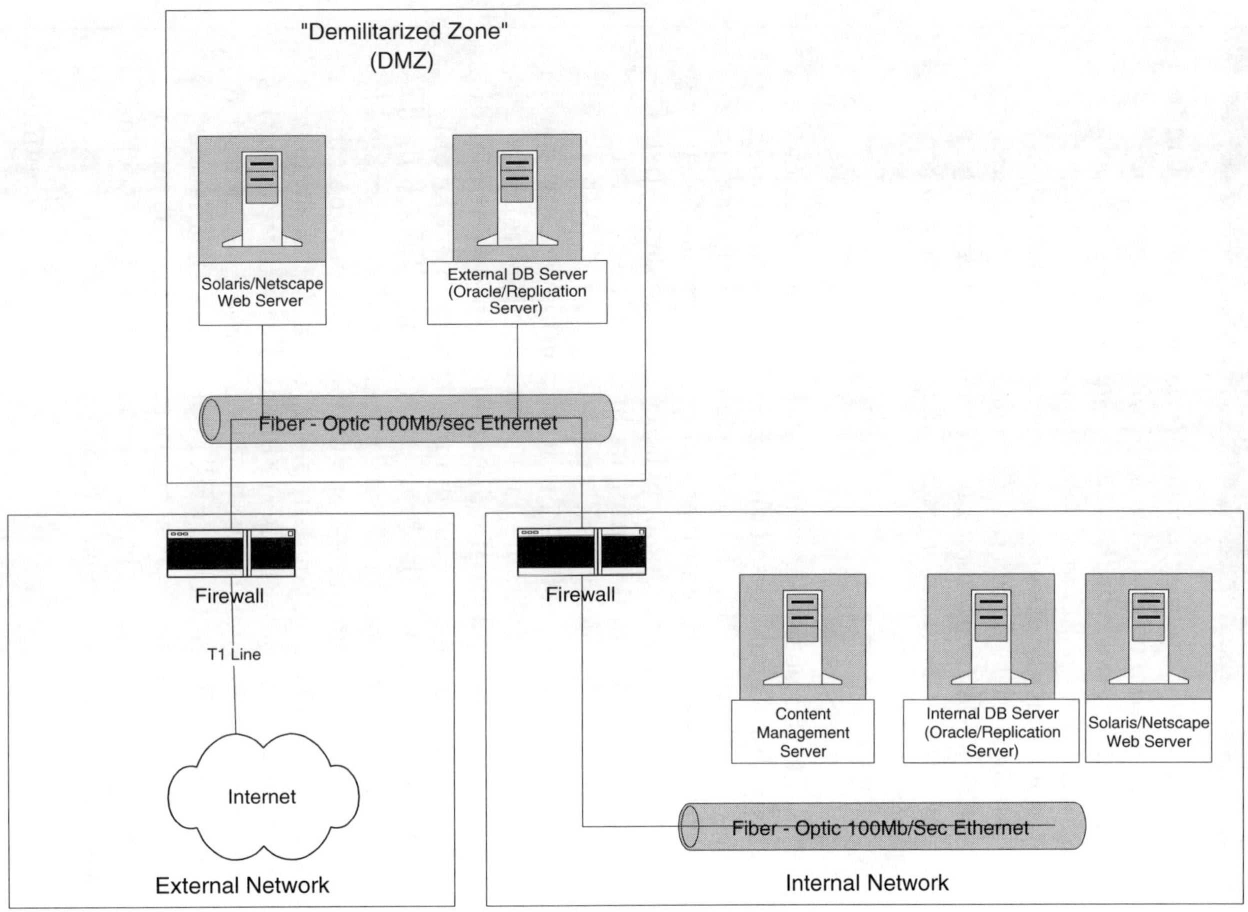

Figure 8.7 Security solution network architecture.

SOLUTION SCENARIO *Continued*

router with dial-up capabilities, ISDN preferred. This can be a shared service on your LAN, which will connect to the ISP as needed by the user, but still provide the protections of the firewall to the broader network environment. In addition, the use of a router can allow further restrictions on use by filtering traffic from unauthorized users. While ISDN is not absolutely ubiquitous, it is generally available in most major metropolitan areas, and can be very cost effective.

First, it is important to understand that there is a range of security threats, and based on their security you will need a range of responses. The following table will help categorize the risk and severity, and that should help you focus your efforts on eliminating the more egregious problems first. The classifications we find helpful are listed in the table, in descending order of severity.

Vulnerabilities in classes 7 to 9 are considered most severe and usually result in immediate disconnection from the Internet or other source of vulnerability. Since vulnerabilities in this range assume a connection to the Internet, the only protection available is the firewall. A security breach in the firewall will often result in the immediate disconnection of the site from the Internet—not a casual decision when this means disconnecting your suppliers, clients, and employees. When SATAN or other tools are run against a firewall in this situation, a zero-tolerance policy is important; no identified holes can be allowed to exist. For companies that have a need to occasionally relax security to support some exceptional interaction, we suggest a second Internet connection with an “airwall” between it and the corporate network.

(*continued*)

SOLUTION SCENARIO *Continued*

Threat Class	Threat Class Description
9	Users remote to the site can gain access across a firewall and have write and/or execute access to files owned by non-"root" or "admin" on the host system.
8	Users remote to the site can gain access across a firewall and have write and/or execute access to files owned by "root" or "admin" on the host system.
7	Users remote to the site can gain access across a firewall and have read access to files on the host system.
6	Users remote to the host on the same network can get write and/or execute access to files owned by "root" or "admin."
5	Users remote to the host on the same network can get write and/or execute access to files owned by non-"root" or "admin" or transmitted across the network.
4	Users remote to the host on the same network can get read access to files transmitted across the network.
3	Users local to the host can gain write and/or execute access to files owned by "root" or "admin."
2	Users local to the host can gain write and/or execute access to files owned by non-"root" or "admin" users.
1	Users local to the host can gain read access to files.
0	"Denial of Service" attack prevents users from accessing a device or files.

Class 4 to class 6 vulnerabilities are slightly less severe, since the majority of members of an organization can be considered as trusted. In addition, almost all internal systems exist behind at least one firewall, if not several, and have fairly disciplined operations and security methodologies applied to them. However, breaches in this range can result in the automatic shutdown of a system.

Class 1 to class 3 leaks are even less severe, since the physical proximity of the intruder to the system allows for elements of physical control. In addition, most breaches in this class are not malicious; they are found by interested users

(*continued*)

SOLUTION SCENARIO *Continued*

who want to test the limits of the system or do not know how to use it appropriately and stumble on a breach. However, breaches of this type should be investigated with speed and rigor, since a disaffected employee is the highest security risk in the organization.

The nice thing is that there are several tools—SATAN being one of them—that allow you to look for vulnerabilities in the range. Do not underestimate attacks ranked in class 0. While these generally do not compromise the integrity of your data, they can shut down access to a business-critical system and keep your company from operating. In 1996 a New York–based Internet service provider was the target of a Denial of Service attack that shut it down for days until a team from CERT, the FBI, and several other agencies was able to help defeat the attack.

be upgraded to B2 classifications and beyond. Upgrading the security can radically affect the services a host can support, as well as the usability of the environment. As of this writing, we know of no high-end secured implementations of Microsoft's NT environment, so the majority of systems in that class of solution are still using UNIX systems. This is not to say that NT cannot be made secure, but as a relatively immature OS, a greater frequency of holes are being found.

So the hardware is purchased, the Internet connection is in, the clock is ticking for deployment. How do you evaluate the site to see if it is secure enough? Here is how we would go about it. There are three basic sources of risk against which we need to guard:

- Malice (intentional)
- Ignorance or accidents (unintentional)
- Disasters (acts of God or nature)

Emulating an Attack

The best way to look for holes is to emulate an attack. If you don't want to do this, then most of the major consultants can provide an "ethical hacker," who can work with a team to break into the system and spot holes for you. Per-Se has provided this service to several clients over time, and the following three-step approach, while simple, is based on the approach we use. It is very straightforward.

STEP 1: A FOOT IN THE DOOR

Have you walked by a desk in the office recently and seen a couple of little yellow stickies with passwords listed on them pasted to a computer screen? If your company is like most, this is the rule and not the exception. At one client's offices, the director of human resources was shocked when the hired ethical hacker handed him a list of names, salaries, and other personal information. He was red with embarrassment when told that the source of the breach was the hacker getting to the office one hour early and simply logging in with the various passwords on the desk. Remember, if someone is given an ID on a system it means there is some element of trust in that person, and once an intruder gets into an existing account, the intruder is now "trusted" by the system—usually enough to begin to bend the rules without setting off alarms.

There are more sophisticated ways to crack a system, but most work with the assumption that people use simple-to-remember mnemonics or other common words for their passwords. People also tend to use a base password and vary it with a numeric sequence such as "ROSS01." When you realize that most passwords are this simple, it makes it easy to write programs to process a file of passwords and decrypt some. One of our favorite tools for doing this is called Crack.

Crack is a program available over the Internet—take a look at the CERT FTP and Web sites. By taking a password file, usually from /etc/password on a UNIX box and using a dictionary, Crack can often find the first password in several minutes. More obscure passwords may take several hours or even days.

How do you manage this vulnerability?

In many cases, we recommend password standards that are politically difficult to enforce. After all, if you make passwords too hard to remember, then people will just write them down. So we recommend several strategies:

Widely publish a clear policy on password security and enforce it. In most organizations, senior management people are the biggest offenders, often giving their secretaries their passwords and IDs so they can check their E-mail and the like. It should be clear that a zero-tolerance policy is followed throughout the organization. The first flogging should be very public and, with luck, senior enough to make the point.

Use a 10+ position password. Passwords should not be repeatable, nor should they be sequenced. They must be composed of numbers and letters.

Use single sign on products like DCE or messaging architectures, which authenticates the user to the environment. This can limit the number of user passwords significantly and allow the single password to be more complex.

Use secondary challenge response technologies. With the increasing use of smart cards, tools such as DES and the ability to use card-generated one-time passwords become more cost effective for a company.

Have the operations department regularly scan the password files using tools like Crack to find passwords that are vulnerable, and work with the owners to avoid breach-supporting behavior.

Restrict and log access on a time basis. In most companies, people work fairly regular hours. As a result, time-based security that denies a user access outside of some band and alerts an operator to access outside of that band in real time can be a powerful ally.

Be Careful What You Crack In 1995, Intel hired a well-known security expert, Randall Schwartz, as a consultant. During his tenure with Intel, Schwartz ran Crack against an Intel server *with-*

out specific authorization from Intel. Schwartz was convicted in an Oregon courtroom of an unauthorized breach. So, before you run Crack on your company's systems, make sure you have written authorization from your DP audit or similar authority. While it might be tempting to run Crack, SATAN, or other tools and look like a hero by finding holes in the environment, you could be jeopardizing your job. If you are a consultant doing security work, make sure you develop standard contract wording (this will vary on a state-by-state basis, so work with your lawyer) that will cover you in case you are asked to perform a similar ethical attack.

STEP 2: GETTING TO THE ROOT OF THE MATTER

The holy grail of hacking is "root" or "admin" access on a host. In most environments, root has unlimited power and is usually highly trusted by other systems as well. There are a number of ways to get access to root. One of the most common is to exploit services like NFS, which are frequently configured by less knowledgeable users with root access to read/write. In other cases, administrators set up NFS in this mode to provide software distribution between nodes and simplified administration. SATAN is a tool that can help you find problems at this level, but we suggest running COPS, a tool from the same folks. One of the most common ways of hacking root is to look for a script that grants these rights. On many systems, administrators have such scripts, which they can use to change the rights of a user or their own when they need to. Usually, it is such a convenient thing that gets you into trouble.

Following are some suggestions about how to manage root-level vulnerabilities:

- Monitor newsgroups and mail lists for news about breaches and aggressively test your system for them. Learn from the mistakes of others!
- Rotate root passwords every two weeks, and immediately change all passwords following notice of resignation by or termination of individuals who have root.
- Log all root access, and audit logs daily!

Maintain records about your host software configurations, since most breach points are known to root operators and are fixed by patches from the vendors. Knowing your vulnerability to a problem can be simplified by knowing what you are patched for already.

Be prepared to apply vendor patches as they become available. In many cases, this means having a test machine with a software configuration identical to your production platform where you can install the patches and run a formal test process, *including regression testing,* on the patch. As with any OS or application fix, these patches will often fix one problem but cause another, especially in the behavior of applications that may have made assumptions about access to system services.

Do not run a system with a service having root permissions. Frequently, we see companies in which the Web server, DB server, or similar service is set up with root access. In most cases, this is not the result of malice, but ignorance. However, neither is excusable.

SPREADING OUT

Once people have root access, they have a field day and you have a big problem! If you remember, we discussed trust in Chapter 3. The point of that discussion was that systems tend to have some inherent level of trust of each other, and once you are at the root or admin level, you are, in essence, the system. One of the major drawbacks at this level is the ability of users to alter the log files and audit trails on the system, hiding their trail until they get greedy for cycles or information goes missing. In other cases, tools are available that will actually mask the user's activities. One of these is called *rootkit* and runs on the UNIX environment. We will not provide a pointer to this tool since legitimate administrators don't need it and we don't want to help hackers. Rootkit can actually replace significant system executables with its own versions that help them hide. For example, "ps" will not display the processes being executed by the intruder. If you can't find them, how do you know whether an intruder is spreading out onto your systems? Some signals include the following:

Nonexistent programs are executing. Frequently, an intruder will attempt to run some of the UNIX "r" commands, most if not all of which you should have removed from a production server. If requests for those files begin to appear, they should be traced immediately, since those commands are a favorite shortcut to another system.

Performance behavior changes. This can have several manifestations:

- The system slows down but the monitoring tools show normal behavior.
- The system shows a change in usage pattern. For example, if a system drops to low use after batch normally but changes behavior to show high use during off hours, this should be investigated. It may be as innocuous as someone running Doom; it may be someone running Crack on a system.

Network performance changes. Most systems, like DBMS or Web servers, show patterns of network use by time and ratio of inbound to outbound traffic. In one case, we spotted an intruder who had hacked into one host and was now using the host's root privileges to suck files off of others. This showed up as streaming data outside of normal network use on the system console and set off several operator alarms.

CATEGORIES OF THREATS

Like any good consultants, we like to characterize things. This gives us and you a way of separating the crisis from the catastrophe. In the next section we try to provide a framework for grouping these threats, which can provide a checklist of sorts for you in examining your own vulnerability.

Physical Threat You should be alert to the following forms of physical threat:

Intruders gain physical access to a facility and remove a machine—not impossible with increasingly small machines. This can also include the removal of the hard disk(s), which can be small enough to slip into a shirt pocket, or the removal of an unsecured backup tape from a drive. This threat can be managed using a physical access control program, including access cards, retinal scanners, palm scanners, and similar techniques.

Intruders gain access to a site and note ID/password information written on Post-it notes or otherwise in public view. This can be managed through staff diligence, a well-documented security policy, and the application of security audit policies.

Intruders search site trash for password notes, documenting E-mail messages from wastebaskets, and so forth. This can be managed through the use of incinerators, shredders, and other destructive measures.

Intruders steal computers during business activities (travel, conferences, etc.). This can be managed through the use of physical security measures such as door locks, device cabling, and device tags.

Disaster This category includes earthquake, flood, and bombing, resulting in either destruction of computing platforms or a denial of service due to lack of access and an absence of an alternative site. Generally, this is managed through the development of adequate disaster recovery plans, including a "Hot/Warm" site contingency plan.

Mechanical Failure Mechanical failure in general is best managed through redundancy. Let's face it, stuff breaks no matter how much we spend on it. However, today's technologies provide some great solutions, including server clustering and RAID technologies, which can allow for the loss of a device or even an entire server without impacting a user. Of course, this type of protection is not free, but you need to do the homework to figure out the cost of downtime and thus the value of redundancy. Some of the major points of failure you need to accommodate include:

Hard disk. Can be managed through the use of RAID technologies or, in some high-end cases, the use of products like EMC's Symmetrics products, which can provide disk shadowing between sites.

Disk controller. Can be managed through the use of mirrored controllers.

Power supply. Usually managed through server failover, although some high-end boxes provide redundant power supplies.

Processor. Multiprocessor boxes generally will crash if a single processor fails. Some will reboot themselves when a processor fails and come back up with the processor out of the loop; others will be down hard.

Memory. Error-correcting memory will cost a little more, but it is often worth it. When an error in memory is detected, the memory can be mapped out and the system can continue to operate.

Electronic Signals Signals sent over the network can be intercepted, corrupted, and rerouted. This subject is discussed in detail in Chapter 3; however, major threats include:

Snooping. Intercepting, decoding, and either misusing or retransmitting corrupted information.

Spoofing. Masquerading as a server or client to collect information destined for the legitimate device.

Programmed Threats These threats include the following:

- Misuse of security tools and toolkits (see list of tools at end of chapter)
  - SATAN
  - COPS
  - ISS
  - PINGWARE
  - SPI
  - Tripwire
  - Tiger
- Infected files from outside sources
  - E-mail attachment
  - Downloaded programs

- Java applets
- ActiveX components
- Programmer backdoors and trapdoors, which are undocumented bypasses of system security and audit facilities
- Viruses

External Connections Threats from external connections include:

- *Physical communication lines.* In many cases, the least secure place in a company is the shared communications closet, especially in buildings where a wiring facility is shared by several companies.
- *Routers.* Router configurations should be managed centrally, with highly secured passwords and a careful use of SNMP.
- *Unprotected floppy disks.* Probably the source of more misery and damage than any other unintentional security breach through the passing of viruses that can destroy data.
- *Firewall breach.* Similar to the control of routers in close management of their configurations. However, the ability to filter by protocol, port, and, in some cases, content requires a greater level of sophistication, which many network management organizations do not have.
- *NFS exports to arbitrary host.* The use of Network File Services (NFS) is pervasive, especially in UNIX environments; however, it was designed to be used in a trusted environment and as such allows great flexibility. In most cases, we recommend turning off NFS.
- *NIS password file accessible from arbitrary host.* Allows access to the password file from any host.
- *REXD access from arbitrary host.* Allows the remote execution of host commands from any host.
- *Remote shell access from arbitrary host.* Allows a remote system to start a session on a host with the privileges of a local user.

Arbitrary file accessible via TFTP (Trivial File Transfer Protocol).

Writeable anonymous FTP home directory.

Unauthorized or excessive information access via Web server (Spiders, Alta Vista, InfoSeek, Lycos).

- Web robots
- Web agents
- Web spiders

People (the Threat from Inside) Like it or not, the biggest source of risk is people, and those inside are the biggest violators. Unfortunately, there is little that can be done to keep people from feeling disaffected. However, by having firm controls, good audit processes, and constant monitoring, you can detect a breach before the trickle becomes a flood. Remember, most employees will try something small at first, then move up to something more serious, so early detection of something untoward will generally preempt something disastrous. Watch for:

- Unauthorized access to privileged files or data
- System tampering, including changes to configuration files
- Password breaking
- Alteration of audit information

Summary of Security Action Items (Checklist)

The following list is provided for general reference. You should supplement it with additional items for your particular security needs.

- Procedural tactics (security policies)
  - Using assets accountability management
  - Assigning data use accountability to users
  - Complying with laws and regulations
  - Establishing a computer management committee
  - Keeping computer system activity records

- Confirming receipt of documents
- Obtaining cooperation of computer security officers
- Correcting maintenance of production systems
- Establishing courier trustworthiness and identification
- Using data classification
- Using data file and program backup
- Destroying discarded documents
- Using EDP auditing
- Establishing employee identification on work products
- Providing financial loss contingency and recovery funding
- Employing human subject review
- Mandating independent computer use by auditors
- Inspecting personnel data input and output
- Isolating sensitive production jobs
- Keeping security reports confidential
- Using magnetic tape erase
- Minimizing copies of sensitive reports
- Monitoring computer use
- Obtaining participation of users at critical development times
- Printing a proprietary notice on sensitive documents
- Establishing a remote use agreement
- Establishing the separation and accountability of EDP functions

Physical protection to prevent direct access to important resources

- Areas where smoking and eating are prohibited
- Courier identification and background checks
- Delivery access control (physical access restraints)
- Electronic equipment protection

Electronic power shutdown and recovery
Inspection of incoming and outgoing materials
Isolation of sensitive production jobs
Minimal traffic and access to work areas
Passwords for access from workstations and terminals
Physical access barriers
Physical security perimeter
Programming of library access control
Remote terminal physical security
Security for sensitive areas during attended periods
Tape management (avoid labels)
Universal use of badges
Validation of authorized versions of production programs

Technical security, including both hardware and software
Maintaining separation
Isolating users
Setting levels of sensitivity
Leaving auditing trail
Backing up passwords
Restricting remote access
Using encryption
Controlling access
Tracing unauthorized access attempts
Protecting security provisions
Checking the security features of all the equipment you buy
Keeping computer program change logs
Using password file encryption
Logging trouble calls from users
Controlling data file access

Backing up data file and program
Reporting exceptions
Validating data input
Using passwords for work station access
Restricting display of privileged information
Protecting data used in system testing
Establishing auditor participation in setting requirements
Assigning responsibility for application program control
Suppressing incomplete or obsolete data
Establishing telephone access universal selection
Establishing workstation login protocol
Using cryptographic protection
Using data classification
Establishing dynamic password change control by users
Enforcing limited transaction privilege from workstations
Establishing limited use of system utility programs
Monitoring computer use
Using automatic password generation
Keeping file names secret
Separating personal identification data
Separating test and production systems
Using personal identifiers to govern database
Using workstation identifiers
Establishing a data recovery plan
Being prepared for emergencies
Maintaining an alternate power supply
Encrypting passwords that are transmitted over the network
Associating passwords with time stamps and adapter address
Providing password-protected screen lock

Requiring users to sign on again if the server becomes unavailable

Requiring users to sign off when they leave their workstations

Forbidding sign-ons when the system is being maintained

Defining file access rules for both physical and logical drivers

Supporting file name wild cards with file level security

Limiting LAN administration to a single server

Reporting all access attempts to the resource owner

Preventing all input to the server without a valid ID

Use disk mirroring for quick recovery

Emphasis on people, not technology

Getting employees involved

Providing security training for DP and audit professionals

Managing resistance to change

Fighting the vengeful ex-employee

Some Existing Security Tools

Some of the existing security tools include the following:

NID—Network Intrusion Detector (from CSTC)

Courtney—Monitors the network and identifies the source of machines of SATAN probes/attacks (from CIAC)

Gabriel—SATAN detector (from Los Altos Technologies)

COPS—Checks for a number of known weaknesses of password systems and alerts the administrators (from Purdue University)

CPM—Detects snooping (from Carnegie Mellon University)

ifstatus—Similar to CPM (from Purdue University)

ISS—Checks security holes in sendmail, improperly configured NFS file sharing, and so on

SPI—Security profile inspector
Tiger—Similar to COPS
Tripwire—File authentication tool (from Purdue University)
Argus—Transaction auditing tool (digital signature)
Netlog—Traffic logging for TCP and UDP
NOCOL—network monitoring tool
See also ftp://info.cert.org/pub/tech-tips/security-tools

CHAPTER NINE

Legacy Systems Integration

Increasingly, companies are leveraging their intranet infrastructures to deliver more than static content; they are becoming application delivery environments. There is no single way to perform this integration, and most enterprise architectures will require several of the models we discuss in this chapter.

According to Christopher Bird, "A legacy system is any system which has reached the stage of System Test in the Systems Development Lifecycle." Using this definition as the basis for a chapter on legacy systems integration, we obviously have a lot of ground to cover!

Architecting for Integration

When looking at any application, one of the most important questions to ask is: How can I integrate to it? It has been our experience that some of the most effective integration scenarios arise when looking at mainframe systems. The lowest grades for integration go to the two-tier client/server applications. Many are shocked by this statement, but if you understand mainframe architectures the reason is evident.

There are three logical integration points to almost any application (see Figure 9.1). While this is a simplification, it quickly illustrates that the integration point you choose has several implications including:

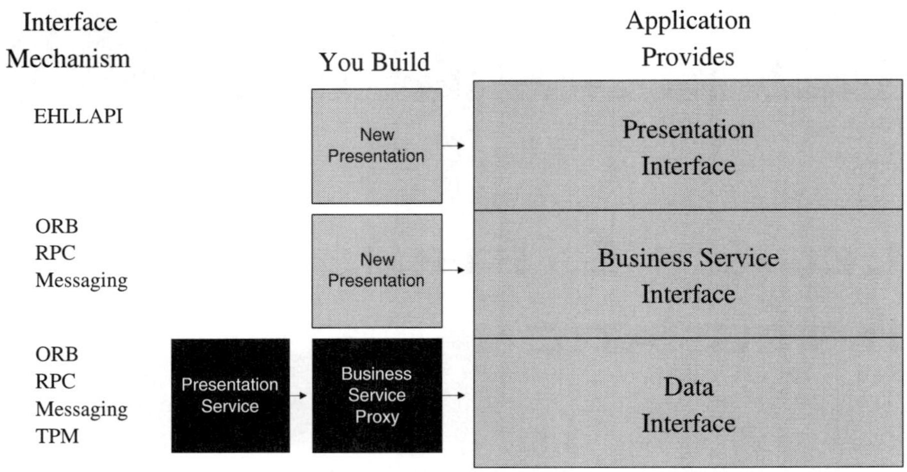

Figure 9.1 Application integration: three points of entry.

Cost of construction. The deeper you dig in the integration stack, the more it costs to deliver the application. This results from several things, including the cost of enabling integration technologies and their supporting hardware, the cost of more highly skilled staff to do the development, and the actual cost of development, which results from the increasing effort at each point. Reducing construction cost is often done by limiting design, but this generally results in higher maintenance costs, especially in an environment as dynamic as an intranet.

Cost of maintenance. It is interesting that the least costly application to construct can be, in some dynamic environments, the most costly to maintain and least reliable. Maintenance costs in an integrated environment are best managed by focusing on the interfaces between the layers, minimizing cohesion between them as much as possible.

Time to market. The more you build, the longer it takes to deploy. The more you buy, the less likely it is to reflect the way you do business today. Buy-and-integrate has some interesting business implications. Many companies execute business processes today in a fashion dictated by their current technology's limitations. However, for many people, that has become *the* way of doing business. When looking at new packages, many companies fall victim to the temptation to reimplement the current processes in the new package. This delays time to market and also generally diminishes the value of the package itself, since the processes it enables were designed to work together.

TIP *So, what is Microsoft up to in the middleware area? Microsoft has two major products addressing the middleware area: Microsoft Transaction Server (MTS) and MSMQ. These products provide transaction management and reliable message-based queing to users of Microsoft's ActiveX/DCOM services.*

With MTS, Microsoft is trying to provide a very simplified interface to a fairly complex concept, that is the instantiation and execution of components within the context of the COM environment. MTS' Transaction Coordinator has several critical roles including:

- *Atomicity, regardless of failures (node crash, network crash, misbehaved resource manager or application)*
- *Race conditions (transaction starts to commit while one resource manager initiates an abort)*
- *Availability (a resource manager prepares a transaction but never returns)*

Microsoft's Message Queue Server (MSMQ) is the messaging side of Microsoft's middleware solutions. It is based on ActiveX. Relatively new, it was only released to manufacturing in September 1997, and is not expected to be in common use until the appearance of NT 5.0 in 1998. Microsoft is positioning the product in scenarios where one or more of the following situations exist:

- *Store-and-Forward: When sending and receiving applications are expected to run at different times, often used to integrate new online systems to existing batch systems*

- *Defensive: In environments that are normally available, but the cost of message loss or interruption is high like stock trading*
- *Asynchronous: When sending applications need not wait for responses before moving on to other tasks, for example, a credit authorization in a customer care situation*
- *Journaled/Audited: In cases where requests for services must be logged, audited, and possibly reprocessed to recover from failures*
- *Connectionless: When connection-oriented communication (i.e., that involves shared state) between a requestor and a receiver (or receivers) is not practical. In some messaging applications, the ultimate receiver of a message may not be known in advance (as in publish and subscribe applications).*

Getting It Together

It has been our experience that the best entry point is at the business process layer. However, this is probably the least common entry point in legacy client/server applications and can be difficult in legacy mainframe applications as well. Integration at that level makes the most sense in the context of your intranet, since the Web interface provides a flexible presentation layer. It can be developed quickly, and changes to it to include new features or functions have minimal impact on the underlying business services. However, let's look at the integration options by layer.

Presentation Layer Integration

Integration at the Presentation Layer is nothing new (see Figure 9.2). We have been using screen-scraping technologies for a dozen

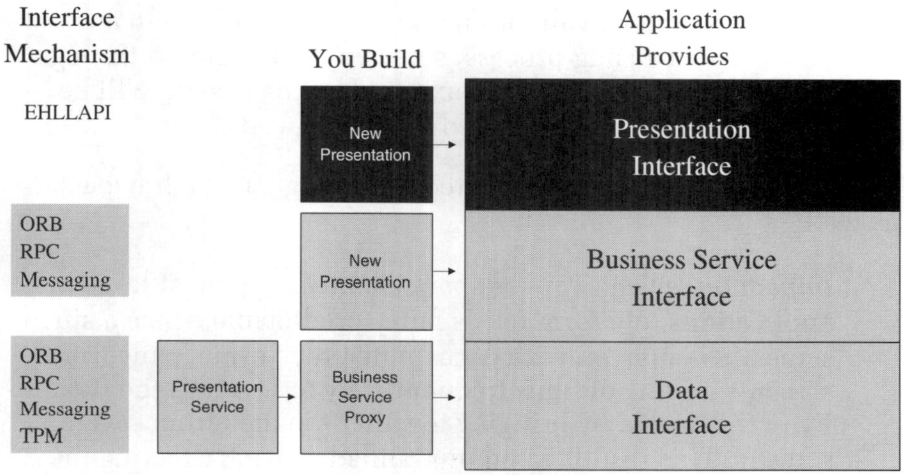

Figure 9.2 Application integration—presentation layer.

years, mostly leveraging IBM's High Level Language Application Programming Interface (HLLAPI) and Extended High Level Language API (EHLLAPI). This solution has several distinct advantages, including:

High potential for leveraging legacy code, data and platforms, and experience. Using technologies like CICS on the mainframe or on another platform integrated to the mainframe, this solution can make leverage easy.

Generally quick time to market. As we discuss in the Solution Scenario, the use of tools that can wrap the Presentation Layer can reduce time to market tremendously and also provide some insulation from changes in the back end.

Simplicity of the tools required. With the use of tools such as Visual Basic and PowerBuilder, the libraries required to screen-scrape can be readily integrated into new presentation or into components, which can then be accessed using Active Server Pages and similar solutions.

Additional cleansing of data. The use of tools like Visual Basic allows for the development of more robust or new edit masks and screen validations. This can contribute to an overall legacy cleansing process, since any data entered through the system or existing data accessed by the system will be subject to these additional edits when saved.

However, like all solutions, screen scraping has its drawbacks as well:

Impact on legacy platform performance. In most legacy applications, platform use is fairly predictable, since a single screen is displayed with each "enter key" cycle. However, screen-scraping designs frequently try to leverage the flexibility of the design by bringing together the data from several screens. This results in an unplanned impact: Creating the new Web-based customer screen may hit three to four legacy screens, so your realized transaction load on the legacy platform is much greater to support the same or modified business function.

Integrated maintenance requirements. Screen-scraped designs are positional; that is, they scan the incoming data stream from the legacy platform and pull out the data between one point and another that corresponds to a new screen field. As a result, changes to screen positioning can "break" your intranet front end. In one extreme case, the shift was subtle enough that the data being entered was still numeric; however, it was coming from the Social Security Number field instead of the amount field. As you can imagine, this created some very odd results and extreme frustration.

Limited scalability. Processing and scraping screens is much more processing-intensive than just processing result sets, and this means decreased scalability for the platforms. More platforms can mean more complex and expensive systems management, so the application's time-to-market savings can readily be consumed by its operations costs. However, few organizations seem to do effective total cost of ownership tracking, so doing a quick job means the data center eats the support cost. This is often an encouraged behavior in some companies.

SOLUTION SCENARIO

Legacy Web Integration

A large, international trucking firm, with hundreds of agents in the United States, had a large investment in legacy technology. With competition heating up, the firm needed a way to support access to this information. The task: Do it fast, do it right, and train the client staff at the same time. The system ultimately had to support some 50 concurrent users and a total of 1,500 users overall.

The information needed to feed the application already existed on the mainframe, and in examining the application we realized there was a need for real-time information and near-real-time information. This segmentation gave us the opportunity to limit the transactional impact on the legacy platform by periodically moving new legacy data down to a SQL Server platform, which resulted in improved performance and provided greater future flexibility for such functions as dynamic reporting. The transactional information was a bit more of a task. This required real-time access to the legacy information. This information was already manifested in the legacy application via 3270/CICS, and we had a predisposition to reuse the transactions and the business processing wherever possible. See Figure 9.3.

The solution for the mainframe integration was to use IBM's CICS for NT. At $1,500 or so it was a bargain, and it provided two important facilities:

External Call Interface. Provides the ability to interact with the mainframe via LU6.2 calls. Handles login and session management, as well as direct invocation of CICS business transactions where available.

(*continued*)

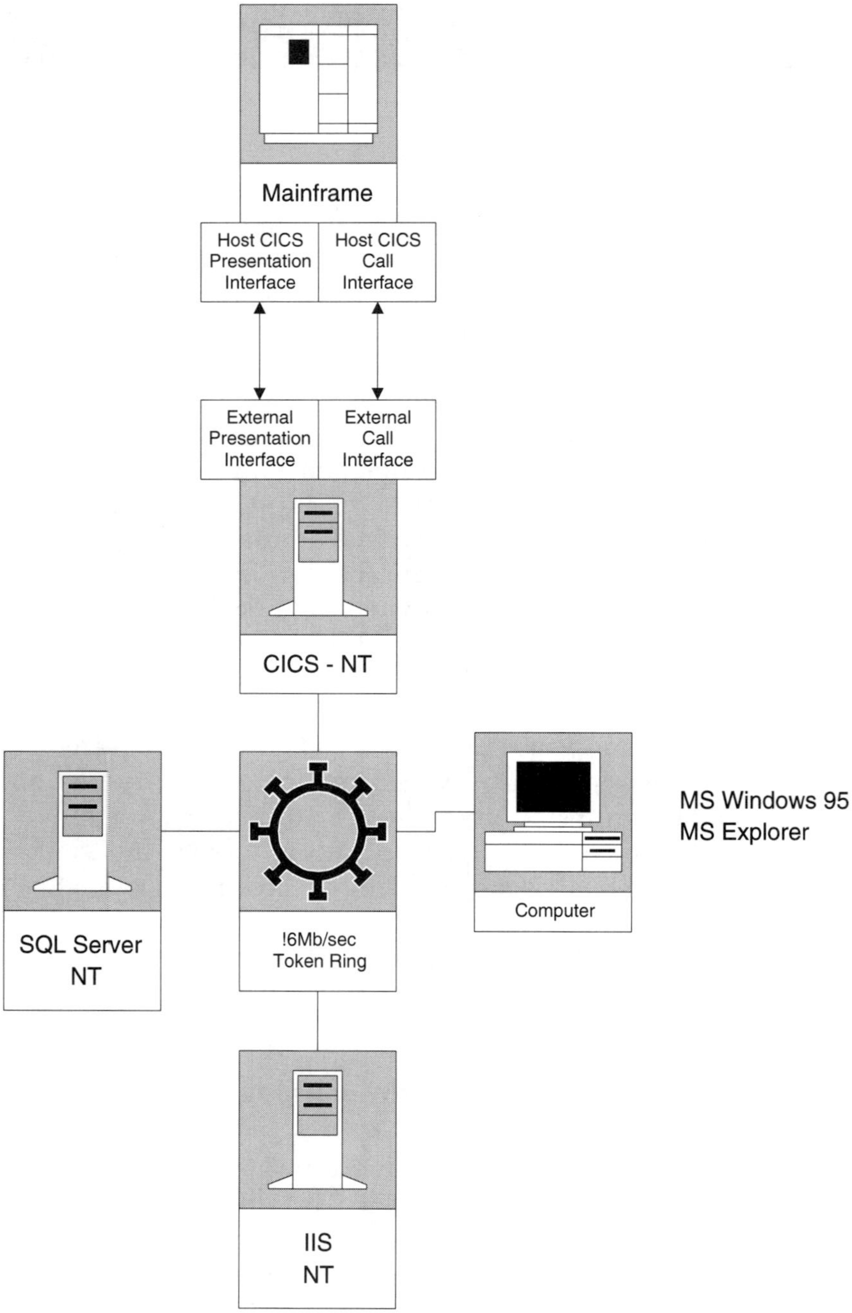

Figure 9.3 Web-3270 integration.

SOLUTION SCENARIO *Continued*

External Presentation Interface. Provides the ability to interact directly with the mainframe via LU6.2 calls. Using a precompiler, this tool maps the screen position information for a CICS screen and then generates C++ class libraries, which can be used to access the information on that screen.

In the analysis, we determined that the optimal integration approach was to hit the CICS business transactions via the External Call Interface. This would provide the highest performance and the lowest maintenance, since it broke the dependency on the legacy Presentation Service, which the screen-scraping approach had. Unfortunately, when we looked at the CICS transactions, we found some real nastiness in their design. It is an accepted design principle that CICS transactions are developed with the Presentation and Business logic separated out; however, this client had not opted for that design. As a result, the relatively simple CICS Business Service integration we had assumed was shot, and we had to drop back to the Presentation Service integration.

The major impacts of this change were several:

The External Call Interface was still used to handle session management, login, and file transfer to the local DBMS every three minutes.

The External Presentation Interface was used to hit the CICS transactions, and a screen-scraping approach pulled from the screens the required elements to feed the new Web Presentation Layer.

Performance on a transactional level decreased; the Presentation Interface is more highly abstracted than the Call Interface, and this resulted in slower throughput.

(*continued*)

SOLUTION SCENARIO *Continued*

> The system would run fewer users on the originally specified hardware, which changed the scalability assumptions. However, this was not seen as a major problem since another Intel server was about $10,000 and another copy of CICS for NT was $1,500.

For this project, there was a clear Microsoft predisposition. The basis for the application was to be Active Server Pages (ASP), working in concert with Visual Basic and some MS Visual C++. This combination worked well with the libraries generated from the IBM tools and made integrating the ASP environment very clean. The team also put no business logic in the ASP scripting, opting instead for inclusion in the VB objects themselves. While this complicated the initial build itself and added some effort to the process, it removed the problem of having Business Services spread throughout the ASP environment—something that we have found to be a maintenance and cost nightmare, and not particularly scalable from an operations model. The invocation mechanism was ISAPI. This was a performance issue, plain and simple. While we considered CGI briefly, the poor performance of CGI on NT was the determining factor. VB objects as in-process DLLs also provided the basis for scaling the Business Services to a DCOM environment in the future, should DCOM become robust enough to fill this role.

Performance of the final system was interesting, since the use of the External Presentation Interface became the system bottleneck. The Web server was a low-end Pentium, and even in stress testing with 50 users it was never more than 25 percent utilized. This is likely due to the large system memory cache, meaning that most of the ASP pages and other components were held in memory, which dramatically reduced the

(*continued*)

SOLUTION SCENARIO ***Continued***

amount of slower disk I/O and also improved the efficiency of the processor. The SQL Server was never fully utilized, although much of the conversion logic was implemented in stored procedures on the server to minimize network traffic resulting from the periodic load process.

Overall, the project took approximately 2,000 man hours, which included:

- Implementation of the development environment
- Implementation of the prototype environment
- Implementation of the production environment
- Installation of several servers' operating systems
- Installation of the CICS-NT product, which required updating some elements of the mainframe to current revisions and permanent temporary fix (PTF) status.
- Installation of MS IIS, MS SQL Server
- Development of two prototype applications
- Refinement and enhancement to production
- Training of three client COBOL programmers in the project technologies including VB, ActiveX, C++, and the use of the IBM CICS tools

Using Stored Procedures

What is the appropriate use for the stored procedures (SP) and triggers in a distributed architecture? In many two-tiered designs, stored procedures have become major system components, often running for pages and pages through circuitous logic. For many programmers, the SP is a significant simplifying component, since it allows the use of a single programmatic interface (DB-RPC) and

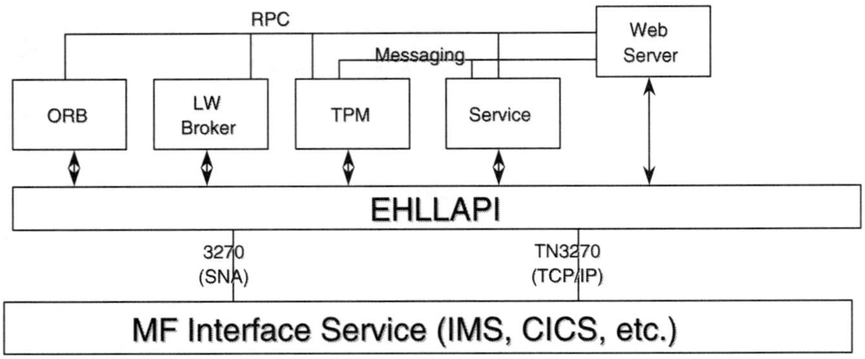

Figure 9.4 Legacy integration scenario.

can be readily hit using ODBC and similar tools. It is this ease of use that has led to ill-informed abuse.

When it comes to these facilities in an architecture, we apply the following guideline: *The purpose of stored procedures and triggers is to protect the integrity of the DBMS.*

Stored procedures were originally developed by Sybase as a way of providing a distributed data environment in which the complexity of distribution, including the development of two-phase commit logic, was hidden from the average developer. Likewise, triggers were developed as a way of ensuring that referential integrity was preserved. The purpose of both of these facilities was to "invert out" this complexity from the programmer's code, a common process in complex development environments. It was to ensure that the DBMS protection schemes were implemented once and correctly, and to remove the ability for a programmer to circumvent these protections for purposes of fraud. In short, it had nothing to do with Business Processing logic.

Cut to the surge of two-tier client server several years ago. As early client/server environments began to grind to a halt, one of the reasons for the poor performance was implementation of Business Processing in the Presentation client. This resulted in tremendous network traffic, often making these systems wholly unsuitable for deployment in corporate WAN environments. The stored procedure was recast as a way to save these efforts from failure. They moved the processing closer to the data, did not require additional software or training, kept it simple for the programmer, and hid the poor design from the boss—all valid imperatives! However, it was soon discovered that the SP was unwieldly, had limited debugging tools, and encouraged the development of more procedural spaghetti.

These facilities should never be used to implement business logic. Why? Don't they simply provide an abstraction of the DBMS from the Presentation Layer and a single repository for Business logic, which improves time to market, and provides a single location for Business logic? Aren't all of these good and desirable things? Yes, they are, but SP is the wrong way to achieve these ends.

The guiding principle for distributed architectures is that system components should be logically distributed and physically distributable. Several agendas are bound up in this statement, including:

Scalability. Systems scale by moving functionality to a more appropriate platform or conceivably creating several instances of the service concurrently.

Atomicity of development. Breaking the system into a number of smaller pieces minimizes construction interdependence and the impact of change.

Ease of maintenance. The use of large procedural code blocks is not conducive to achieving this goal, since finding the appropriate point to do maintenance is difficult, and performing adequate regression testing is very time-consuming.

Performance tuning. Anyone who has tuned a system knows it is easy to optimize a platform for one type of work, such as DBMS or Business Processing, but running the two together makes for suboptimization of both. The use of stored procedures for Business Processing results in just this situation.

So do not give in to the temptation of apparent simplicity. What do we recommend instead? If you need the performance offered by a precompiled procedure, use compiled code like C++. In addition, improve your network connections between the database server and the Business Processing server so that they do not become an obstacle. If you are using 10Mb/sec Ethernet or 16Mb/sec Token Ring, you are going to see a major difference in performance over the performance inside a single box. If you have to stay with these technologies, explore the use of switching implementations to ensure full bandwidth between the processes when they are interacting. Tune your code. Most decent development environments come with a profiling tool of some sort, which allows you to focus on the elements that are most time-consuming. Finally, understand what you are doing. In many cases folks develop applications with no understanding of the trade-offs of distributed designs. This is a recipe for failure.

Business Services Layer Integration

Integration at this level is the most desired point in terms of reconciling the issues of current leverage, future flexibility, and time to market. There are a number of technologies that can be used to fill this role, and we will be discussing several of them in this section. It is important that you look at each of these technologies closely when you are debating how to apply them in your specific situation, since they are expensive, can be very complex, and often require tremendous coordination between legacy and "new system" groups that may not be part of your corporate culture.

How do you integrate to the Business Services Layer? (See Figure 9.5.) The alternatives are bounded only by your innovation and budget, but we will discuss several of the common alternatives here. These are:

- Remote Procedure Call (RPC)
- Messaging (Message Queing)
- Object Request Broker (ORB)

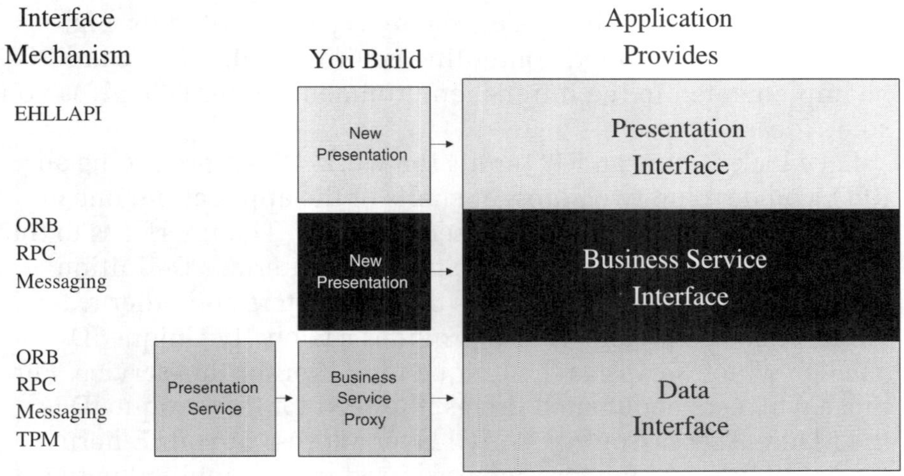

Figure 9.5 Application integration—Business Services Layer.

RPC and messaging can be used in two modes, either to wrap and supplement an existing Business Services layer as discussed in this section or to implement one of their own.

Remote Procedure Calls (RPCs)

All of us are familiar with the programming construct for calling a procedure or a piece of code with a specific purpose. We never question where these functions execute since normal programming assumes they take place in the same process as the program being executed. However, distributed computing allows processes to be located across the network, and that network component adds a lot of additional work. If every programmer had to write all that code, the task would be onerous and probably frequently wrong! RPCs allow the programmer to continue to interact with a familiar calling syntax, while hiding the complexity of network programming from them. RPCs are inherently synchronous; that is, they require the call to the process to respond to the client before the client can continue processing. Finally, RPCs are process-process; that is, both processes need to be available for the RPC to execute. This makes them very well suited for high-performance distributed computing environments. How can RPCs be implemented in the intranet environment? Figure 9.6 gives you some ideas.

Let's look at how an RPC splits the work. When producing an RPC, you develop two *stubs,* or shells of the application, one of which is the client and one the service itself. The interfaces to the service are described in the specific RPC's Interface Definition Language (IDL), which describes the parameters and other external interface behaviors. It also provides a Globally Unique ID (GUID), which serves as the unique identifier for this service. For those who care about such things, the seed for this unique ID is the Media Access Control (MAC) layer address of your Ethernet card, which is unique for each card produced, combined with a highly granular date/time stamp. Any instance of the service will register its location using this ID when started, assuming it is so instructed in the start-up or service initialization code. When the stubs are generated, you fill in the blanks on the service itself, actually adding the specific functionality that the RPC will perform. This gets compiled and linked and placed on the server. When the service is started, it registers itself with some location

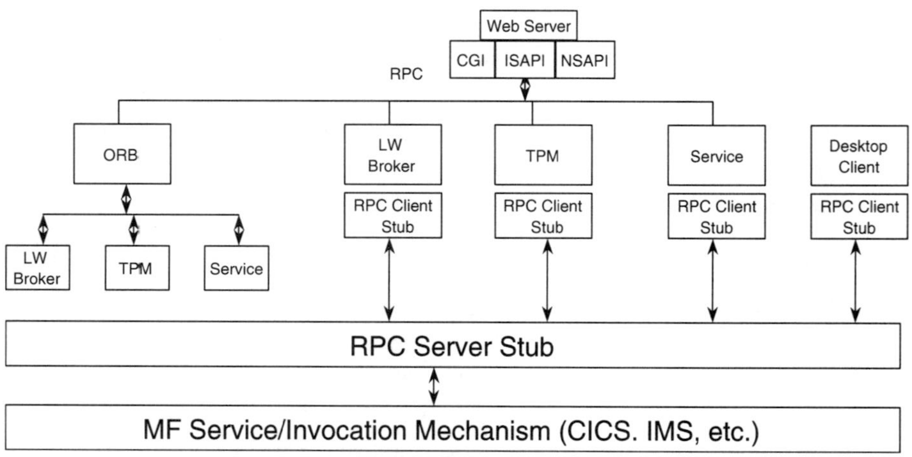

Figure 9.6 Remote Procedure Call (RPC) alternatives.

service, or *broker,* which can then direct users to it when requested. Thus, the complexity of the service's implementation is hidden from the client-side programmer.

On the client side, the programmer gets a library that has a call like any local call in its invocation, but much more complex in its implementation. This is because the stub is responsible for all the network programming. This includes the concept of *marshalling* the data being passed—putting it into a format which the server can understand on the receiving side. This is necessary since some processors are *big-endian* and some are *little-endian.* This is simply a statement of which bit processors see as most significant, but it is the equivalent of reading something backward. "Audit" read backward means something very different from what it means when read forward! For example, when RPC communication comes from a big-endian computer like a VAX, Windows NT must convert the information to little-endian format on a Pentium or other x86 computer. For example, a unicode string has the length passed. A DWORD length of 9 is passed as 0x09000000 on a little-endian computer, but as 0x00000009 on a big-endian computer. As you can see, marshalling is important.

The stub is also responsible for the network programming, submitting it to the lower layers of the network stack and making sure that any errors are handled correctly. As you can tell, this vastly uncomplicates the programmer's job. In many cases, use of RPC generators also dramatically improves code quality and consistency—not insignificant benefits!

The following is an example of a DCE RPC client module. This is the piece that application programmers would develop themselves and from which they would call the RPC. In this case, the RPC call is to getalias(), which allows a client to request an RPC without manually locating a server first:

```
/*
   This is a DCE RPC client module which invokes the GetAlias RPC.

   The client accepts a name as input and requests the alias from
   the service provider.
*/
#include <stdio.h>
#include <stdlib.h>
```

```
#include <string.h>
#include "getalias.h"

void main(int argc, char** argv)
{
   char szAlias[80];
   char *szName = "Steve Papermaster" ; /* = default name */

   if (argc > 1) {
      szName = argv[1] ; /* use input name */
   }
   szAlias[0] = '\0' ;
   /*
      Invoke the Business Logic tier to process this request.
   */
   GetAlias(szName, szAlias) ;
   printf("The alias for %s is %s\n", szName, szAlias);
   exit(0);
}
```

The following code is the client stub that is generated for the programmer. Note the value of generating RPC code.

```
/* Generated by IDL compiler version DCE 1.0.0-1 */
#define IDL_GENERATED
#define IDL_CSTUB
#include <getalias.h>
#include <dce/stubbase.h>

static rpc_syntax_id_t NIDL_ndr_id = {
{0x8a885d04, 0x1ceb, 0x11c9, 0x9f, 0xe8, {0x8, 0x0, 0x2b, 0x10, 0x48,
0x60}},
2};

static rpc_if_rep_t NIDL_ifspec = {
  1, /* ifspec rep version */
  1, /* op count */
  1, /* if version */
  {0x0074f794, 0x8b46, 0x1b96, 0x81, 0x01, {0x8, 0x0, 0x38, 0x42, 0x12,
0xf4}},
  2, /* stub/rt if version */
  {0, NULL}, /* endpoint vector */
  {1, &NIDL_ndr_id} /* syntax vector */
};
/* global */ rpc_if_handle_t Alias_v1_0_c_ifspec =
(rpc_if_handle_t)&NIDL_ifspec;
static RPC_SS_THREADS_ONCE_T NIDL_interface_client_once =
RPC_SS_THREADS_ONCE_INIT;
static RPC_SS_THREADS_MUTEX_T NIDL_auto_handle_mutex;
static rpc_ns_handle_t NIDL_import_cursor;
```

```
static rpc_binding_handle_t NIDL_interface_binding = NULL;
static idl_boolean NIDL_error_using_binding = idl_false;
static error_status_t NIDL_auto_handle_status=rpc_s_ss_no_import_
cursor;
static void NIDL_auto_handle_init()
{
RPC_SS_THREADS_MUTEX_CREATE( &NIDL_auto_handle_mutex );
}
void GetAlias
#ifdef IDL_PROTOTYPES
(
   /* [in] */ idl_char *szName_,
   /* [in, out] */ idl_char szAlias_[80]
)
#else
(szName_, szAlias_)
#endif

#ifndef IDL_PROTOTYPES
idl_char *szName_;
idl_char szAlias_[80];
#endif
{
rpc_op_t op;
rpc_mp_t mp;
ndr_format_t drep;
rpc_ss_mem_handle mem_handle;
volatile rpc_call_handle_t call_h = NULL;
rpc_transfer_syntax_t transfer_syntax;
volatile error_status_t st;
rpc_iovector_elt_t outs, *elt = NULL;
ndr_boolean buffer_changed;
volatile ndr_ulong_int NIDL_fault_code=error_status_ok;
volatile RPC_SS_THREADS_CANCEL_STATE_T NIDL_async_cancel_state;
unsigned long space_in_buffer;
IoVec_t(1) sp_iovec;
rpc_ss_marsh_state_t unmar_params;
rpc_ss_marsh_state_t *NIDL_msp= &unmar_params;
error_status_t NIDL_st2;
volatile handle_t assoc_handle;
volatile idl_boolean NIDL_restartable=idl_true;
idl_boolean NIDL_timeout_was_set_low=idl_false;
IoVec_t(4) iovec;
ndr_byte packet[44];
rpc_mp_t pmp = (rpc_mp_t)&packet[0];

/* local variables */
idl_ulong_int IDL_B_1;
idl_ulong_int IDL_A_1;
idl_ulong_int IDL_count_1;
```

```
idl_ulong_int IDL_index_1;
idl_char *IDL_element_1;
idl_ulong_int IDL_B_0;
idl_ulong_int IDL_A_0;
idl_ulong_int IDL_Z_0;
idl_ulong_int IDL_size_0;
idl_ulong_int NIDL_block;
idl_ulong_int IDL_count_0;
idl_ulong_int NIDL_frag;
idl_ulong_int IDL_index_0;
idl_char *IDL_element_0;

RPC_SS_INIT_CLIENT
mem_handle.memory=(rpc_void_p_t)NULL;
mem_handle.node_table=(rpc_ss_node_table_t)NULL;
RPC_SS_THREADS_DISABLE_ASYNC(NIDL_async_cancel_state);
RPC_SS_THREADS_ONCE(&NIDL_interface_client_once,NIDL_auto_handle_init);
TRY
st = error_status_ok;
sp_iovec.num_elt = 1;
NIDL_msp->p_iovec = (rpc_iovector_t*)&sp_iovec;
NIDL_msp->p_st = (error_status_t*)&st;
NIDL_msp->version = 0;
assoc_handle = NULL;
rpc_ss_make_import_cursor_valid(&NIDL_auto_handle_mutex,
&NIDL_import_cursor,
   (rpc_if_handle_t)&NIDL_ifspec,&NIDL_auto_handle_status);
if(NIDL_auto_handle_status!=error_status_ok)
{
st=NIDL_auto_handle_status;
goto IDL_auto_binding_failure;
}
find_server:
TRY
rpc_ss_import_cursor_advance(&NIDL_auto_handle_mutex,
&NIDL_timeout_was_set_low,&NIDL_import_cursor,
(rpc_if_handle_t)&NIDL_ifspec,&NIDL_error_using_binding,
&NIDL_interface_binding,(rpc_binding_handle_t*)&assoc_handle,
(error_status_t*)&NIDL_auto_handle_status,(error_status_t*)&st);
if(st!=error_status_ok)
{
NIDL_restartable=idl_false;
goto closedown;
}
rpc_call_start((rpc_binding_handle_t) assoc_handle, 0,

(rpc_if_handle_t)&NIDL_ifspec,0,(rpc_call_handle_t*)&call_h,&transfer_
syntax,(unsigned32*)&st);
if (st != error_status_ok) goto closedown;
```

```
NIDL_msp->p_mem_h = &mem_handle;
NIDL_msp->call_h = (rpc_call_handle_t)call_h;
rpc_init_op(op);
/* Start of marshalling block */
iovec.num_elt = 4;
rpc_align_mp(pmp, 8);
iovec.elt[0].data_addr = (byte_p_t)pmp;
iovec.elt[0].flags = 0;
iovec.elt[0].buff_dealloc = NULL_FREE_RTN;
IDL_Z_0 = rpc_ss_strsiz((idl_char *)szName_,1);
rpc_marshall_ulong_int(pmp, IDL_Z_0);
rpc_advance_mop(pmp, op, 4);
IDL_size_0 = IDL_Z_0;
IDL_A_0 = 0;
IDL_B_0 = IDL_Z_0;
rpc_marshall_ulong_int(pmp, IDL_A_0);
rpc_advance_mop(pmp, op, 4);
rpc_marshall_ulong_int(pmp, IDL_B_0);
rpc_advance_mop(pmp, op, 4);
IDL_count_0 = IDL_B_0;
if (IDL_count_0 > IDL_size_0) RAISE(rpc_x_invalid_bound);
iovec.elt[0].data_len = (byte_p_t)pmp-iovec.elt[0].data_addr;

#ifdef PACKED_CHAR_ARRAYS
iovec.elt[1].data_addr = (byte_p_t)&szName_[IDL_A_0];
iovec.elt[1].flags = 0;
iovec.elt[1].data_len = IDL_B_0*1;
iovec.elt[1].buff_dealloc = NULL_FREE_RTN;
rpc_advance_op(op, iovec.elt[1].data_len);
#else
mp = (rpc_mp_t)malloc(7+IDL_B_0*1);
if(!mp)RAISE(rpc_x_no_memory);
iovec.elt[1].buff_addr = (byte_p_t)mp;
rpc_synchronize_mp(mp, op, 8);
iovec.elt[1].data_addr = (byte_p_t)mp;
iovec.elt[1].flags = 0;
iovec.elt[1].buff_dealloc = (rpc_ss_dealloc_t)rpc_ss_call_free;
IDL_element_0 = &szName_[IDL_A_0];
for (IDL_index_0 = IDL_count_0; IDL_index_0; IDL_index_0--)
{
rpc_marshall_char(mp, (*IDL_element_0));
rpc_advance_mop(mp, op, 1);
IDL_element_0++;
}
iovec.elt[1].data_len = (byte_p_t)mp - iovec.elt[1].data_addr;
#endif
rpc_synchronize_mp(pmp, op, 8);
iovec.elt[2].data_addr = (byte_p_t)pmp;
iovec.elt[2].flags = 0;
```

```
iovec.elt[2].buff_dealloc = NULL_FREE_RTN;
rpc_align_mop(pmp, op, 4);
IDL_A_1 = 0;
IDL_B_1 = rpc_ss_strsiz((idl_char *)szAlias_,1);
rpc_marshall_ulong_int(pmp, IDL_A_1);
rpc_advance_mop(pmp, op, 4);
rpc_marshall_ulong_int(pmp, IDL_B_1);
rpc_advance_mop(pmp, op, 4);
IDL_count_1 = IDL_B_1;
if (IDL_count_1 > (79-0+1)) RAISE(rpc_x_invalid_bound);
iovec.elt[2].data_len = (byte_p_t)pmp-iovec.elt[2].data_addr;

#ifdef PACKED_CHAR_ARRAYS
iovec.elt[3].data_addr = (byte_p_t)&szAlias_[IDL_A_1];
iovec.elt[3].flags = 0;
iovec.elt[3].data_len = IDL_B_1*1;
iovec.elt[3].buff_dealloc = NULL_FREE_RTN;
rpc_advance_op(op, iovec.elt[3].data_len);
#else
mp = (rpc_mp_t)malloc(7+IDL_B_1*1);
if(!mp)RAISE(rpc_x_no_memory);
iovec.elt[3].buff_addr = (byte_p_t)mp;
rpc_synchronize_mp(mp, op, 8);
iovec.elt[3].data_addr = (byte_p_t)mp;
iovec.elt[3].flags = 0;
iovec.elt[3].buff_dealloc = (rpc_ss_dealloc_t)rpc_ss_call_free;
IDL_element_1 = &szAlias_[IDL_A_1];
for (IDL_index_1 = IDL_count_1; IDL_index_1; IDL_index_1--)
{
rpc_marshall_char(mp, (*IDL_element_1));
rpc_advance_mop(mp, op, 1);
IDL_element_1++;
}
iovec.elt[3].data_len = (byte_p_t)mp - iovec.elt[3].data_addr;
#endif
elt = &outs;
rpc_call_transceive((rpc_call_handle_t)call_h,
(rpc_iovector_p_t)&iovec,
elt, &drep, (unsigned32*)&st);
if (st != error_status_ok)
{
NIDL_restartable=NIDL_restartable&&(!(rpc_call_did_mgr_execute((rpc_
call_handle_t)call_h,&NIDL_st2)));
goto closedown;
}
/* End of marshalling block */
rpc_init_mp(mp, elt->data_addr);
NIDL_msp->p_rcvd_data = elt;
NIDL_msp->src_drep = drep;
```

```
rpc_init_op(op);
if((drep.int_rep==ndr_g_local_drep.int_rep))
{
rpc_align_mop(mp, op, 4);
rpc_unmarshall_ulong_int(mp, IDL_A_1);
rpc_advance_mop(mp, op, 4);
rpc_unmarshall_ulong_int(mp, IDL_B_1);
rpc_advance_mop(mp, op, 4);
IDL_count_1 = IDL_B_1;
if (IDL_count_1 > (79-0+1)) RAISE(rpc_x_invalid_bound);
}
else
{
rpc_align_mop(mp, op, 4);
rpc_convert_ulong_int(drep, ndr_g_local_drep, mp, IDL_A_1);
rpc_advance_mop(mp, op, 4);
rpc_convert_ulong_int(drep, ndr_g_local_drep, mp, IDL_B_1);
rpc_advance_mop(mp, op, 4);
IDL_count_1 = IDL_B_1;
if (IDL_count_1 > (79-0+1)) RAISE(rpc_x_invalid_bound);
}
if((drep.char_rep==ndr_g_local_drep.char_rep))
{
IDL_element_1 = &szAlias_[IDL_A_1];
while (IDL_count_1)
{
/* compute a lower bound on the number of elts in this buffer */
NIDL_frag = (elt->data_len - ((byte_p_t)mp - elt->data_addr))/1;
if (NIDL_frag > IDL_count_1) NIDL_frag = IDL_count_1;
#ifdef PACKED_CHAR_ARRAYS
NIDL_block = NIDL_frag*1;
memcpy((char *)IDL_element_1, (char *)mp, NIDL_block);
rpc_advance_mop(mp, op, NIDL_block);
IDL_element_1 += NIDL_frag;
IDL_count_1 -= NIDL_frag;
#else
{
while (NIDL_frag--)
{
rpc_unmarshall_char(mp, (*IDL_element_1));
rpc_advance_mop(mp, op, 1);
IDL_element_1++;
IDL_count_1—;
}
}
#endif
if (IDL_count_1)
{
if ((byte_p_t)mp - elt->data_addr >= elt->data_len)
```

```
{
rpc_ss_new_recv_buff(elt, (rpc_call_handle_t)call_h, &(mp), &st);
}
}
}
}
else
{
IDL_element_1 = &szAlias_[IDL_A_1];
while (IDL_count_1)
{
/* compute a lower bound on the number of elts in this buffer */
NIDL_frag = (elt->data_len - ((byte_p_t)mp - elt->data_addr))/1;
if (NIDL_frag > IDL_count_1) NIDL_frag = IDL_count_1;
{
while (NIDL_frag--)
{
rpc_convert_char(drep, ndr_g_local_drep, mp, (*IDL_element_1));
rpc_advance_mop(mp, op, 1);
IDL_element_1++;
IDL_count_1--;
}
}
if (IDL_count_1)
{
if ((byte_p_t)mp - elt->data_addr >= elt->data_len)
{
rpc_ss_new_recv_buff(elt, (rpc_call_handle_t)call_h, &(mp), &st);
}
}
}
}
if (elt->buff_dealloc) (*elt->buff_dealloc) (elt->buff_addr);

closedown: elt = NULL;
CATCH(rpc_x_ss_pipe_comm_error)
ENDTRY
if ((st != error_status_ok) && (st != rpc_s_no_more_bindings))
{
if (NIDL_restartable)
{
if (call_h!=NULL)
rpc_call_end((rpc_call_handle_t*)&call_h,(unsigned32*)&st);
call_h=NULL;
if( elt != NULL )
{
if (elt->buff_dealloc) (*elt->buff_dealloc) (elt->buff_addr);
elt=NULL;
}
```

```
pmp= (rpc_mp_t) &packet[0];
goto find_server;
}
else rpc_ss_flag_error_on_binding(&NIDL_auto_handle_mutex,
   &NIDL_error_using_binding,
   &NIDL_interface_binding,(rpc_binding_handle_t*)&assoc_handle);
}
IDL_auto_binding_failure:;
FINALLY
if((st==error_status_ok) && (elt!=NULL))
{
   if (elt->buff_dealloc) (*elt->buff_dealloc) (elt->buff_addr);
}
if(call_h!=NULL)rpc_ss_call_end(&call_h,&NIDL_fault_code,&st);
if(assoc_handle!=NULL)rpc_binding_free((rpc_binding_handle_t*)&assoc_
handle,&NIDL_st2);
if (mem_handle.memory) rpc_ss_mem_free(&mem_handle);
rpc_ss_report_error(NIDL_fault_code,st,NIDL_async_cancel_state,
 NULL,
 NULL);
RPC_SS_THREADS_RESTORE_ASYNC(NIDL_async_cancel_state);
ENDTRY
}
```

So how do RPCs fit in the integration model? You are most likely already using a specialized RPC today. If you are using Microsoft's SQL Server and running DBLIB.DLL, you are running an RPC environment. When you call "SP_EXEC(myprocedure-name)," you are really passing the name of a stored procedure to the server. The server-side process will invoke it on your behalf and return the results to you. Of course, you have read our previous diatribe against the use of stored procedures, so we know this won't be happening that frequently in your future. Similarly, if you are using Tuxedo or Encina, you are using T-RPC (Transactional RPC) or the Distributed Computing Environment RPC (DCE-RPC), respectively, to communicate with those services.

Any major UNIX vendor will provide support for some flavor of RPC, but the most popular seems to be the DCE-RPC mentioned above. DCE is much more than an RPC environment; rather, it has a number of services that make distributed computing easier and, being supported by multiple vendors, multiplatform. With services like the Distributed File Server, the Distributed Time Service, and the Distributed Security Service, as well as the RPC Service, DCE is a major player. Microsoft uses a variant of the DCE-RPC to support RPC in the NT environment; all the major UNIX vendors provide DCE support on their platforms. With the release of OS-390, IBM now provides DCE support on all of its platforms, providing tremendous scalability, since a service can be deployed on an NT box, and then recompiled and moved to the mainframe.

However, RPC is but one way of integrating your intranet to the legacy environment. It requires both sides of the connection to be up at once, but what about when you may not need that type of service? For example, what if you need to check someone's credit rating to allow the person to submit a credit card application, but do not need to process that application in real time? You will want to *queue* the transaction for later processing, and messaging architectures provide an excellent mechanism for doing so.

Messaging-Oriented Middleware (MOM)

When you want to send E-mail to a friend, the recipient doesn't have to be online to get it. Rather, there is a queue, or holding area, in which your message sits until your friend gets it. If you both had to be online, the whole process would not work. Message-Oriented Middleware (MOM) fills a similar role when integrating systems. Unlike the process-process integration of RPC, MOM is *queue-queue,* which means the application that is the destination of the message does not need to be online or actively processing its queue when the message is submitted. When it does come back online and the MOM environment is started, it will automatically synchronize its queues with other systems, and messages will be passed on. This guaranteed-delivery model is a powerful one in a number of situations, including the following:

The process-process interaction need not be synchronous.

The communications between the processes are unreliable or have scheduled transcience.

There is a need for persistence and auditability of messages, so they must be written to a persistent medium before processing.

Of course, MOM has its own issues, including:

Lack of standardization of services. Some MOM products support applications such as the Publish/Subscribe model (which we discuss later), while others do not.

Lack of interoperability. Each MOM product has its own set of interfaces, and they do not interoperate. Contrast this to the work done with DCE or with CORBA for multivendor integration and you realize that MOM is a single product in an enterprise—unless you want to create more problems than you solve.

Lack of platform consistency. Many of the vendors do not support all the necessary platforms, MVS support being a key omission among several and a solid, multithreaded NT implementation being required.

Lack of implementation expertise. While one of the major advantages of RPC is the consistency of the calling syntax from the programmer's standpoint, MOM is not so cut-and-dried. Some products require extensive programmer knowledge of underlying queues and queue management functions. In addition, understanding how to develop messages and prevent the MOM environment from being turned into an expensive and overly elaborate file transfer mechanism is another issue. MOM should not be implemented without experienced help through requirements definition, product evaluation, design, and implementation.

TIP *While a number of vendors produce Message-Oriented Middleware, one of the more significant players is IBM. Recently, IBM announced the next release of MQ Series, and there are some changes which make it worth looking at. Traditionally Message Queuing required the use of a transaction manager like CICS to insure that database updates were applied with the ability to "commit" or "rollback" a transaction.*

With release 5.0, IBM introduces Database Message Resource Coordination (DMRC). This provides:

- *The ability to define a unit of work which supports commits and rollbacks*
- *Restart synchronization between MQ Series and supported DBMS*
- *Support for DB2 and Oracle*
- *Support for coordination with any XA-compliant resource manager including various TP Monitors and DBMS engines such as Tuxedo, Encina, and CICS.*

Figure 9.7 shows how MOM can be used as part of your enterprise intranet integration strategy. Figure 9.8 makes the operation of MOM more apparent.

Looking at Figure 9.8, let's assume that Process1 is part of an intranet application that collects information required to process a request for a loan from your 401(k) plan. The approval is not done in real time; rather, the information is collected and then the application is processed in the back end. The applicant will be notified by phone if he or she has been accepted. This does not

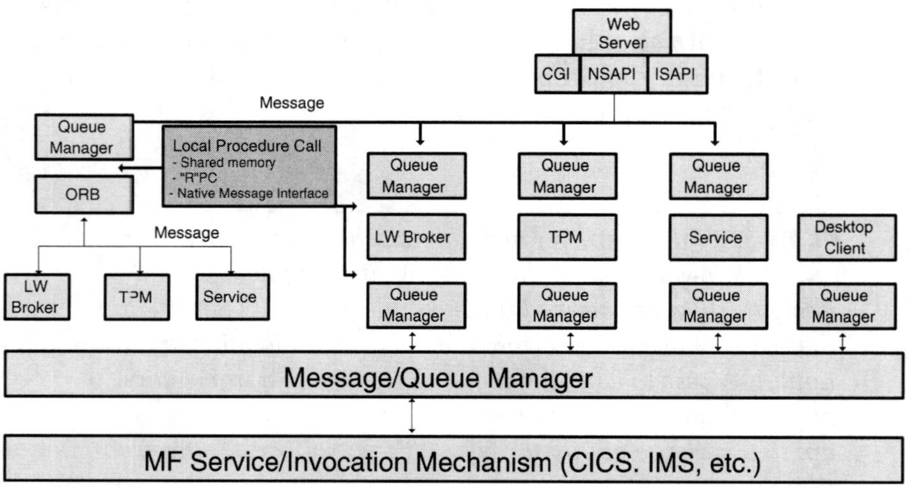

Figure 9.7 Message-Oriented Middleware (MOM) alternatives.

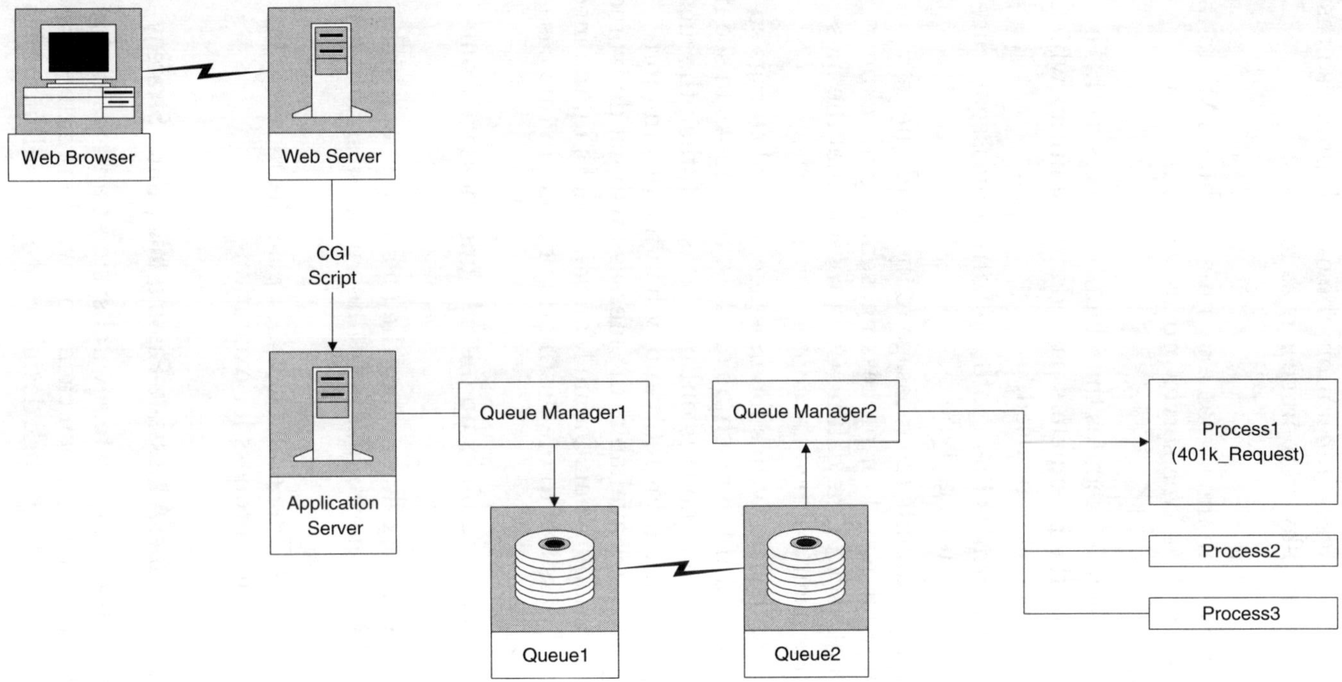

Figure 9.8 Queueing for service.

require process-process integration; the overall process is asynchronous. The step-by-step process is as follows:

1. The user fills in the screen and submits the HTML to the Web server. The Web server processes the inbound HTML.
2. The Web server executes the identified CGI script. This script takes the parameters passed and identifies which message type is to be used.
3. The script formats them into the correct message structure for that message type.
4. The script submits the message to the local queue (Queue Manager1) for processing, sending an acknowledgment back to the calling CGI program that the message has been/not been accepted for delivery.
5. Queue Manager1 writes the message to local storage so it won't be lost if the machine crashes, then looks to see if the destination queue is online. If it is not, then the message gets marked for retry and, when the destination queue becomes available, the message will get delivered. If it is available, then Queue Manager1 picks up the message and passes it to the destination queue, in this case Queue2.
6. Queue Manager2 picks up the inbound message from Queue2.
7. Queue Manager2 determines the message type, which allows him or her to identify which process should get the message.
8. Step 7 allows Queue Manager2 to pass the message to the destination process for execution.

Publish and Subscribe: A Message-Passing Integration Strategy

If you were to try to integrate several systems and wanted to build at least one interface between each, you would rapidly evolve an interface model that network designers would call *full mesh*. In

TABLE 9.1 The Tangled Web We Weave

Number of Systems	Number of Interfaces
2	2
4	12
6	30
8	56
10	90

this model, everyone talks to everyone else. In most organizations this seems to be the case, where a myriad of interfaces ship data between systems, often creating problems of redundancy and accuracy. Of course, there is the maintenance issue. To any one area, the maintenance issue may be a nuisance, but when you look at all the interfaces, you have a nightmare. Table 9.1 illustrates the point, showing the number of interfaces required to support connectivity between systems in a full-mesh model using the algorithm $C=N(N-1)$, where C is the count of interfaces and N the number of systems.

Of course, this gets even scarier when you realize that a table of increases in your staff and budget looks nothing like this one. With the seemingly endless promulgation of new systems, the need for a quick and effective way to broadcast or *publish* information between systems is apparent. Such an approach allows systems to *subscribe* to data already being published in the environment without mandating the development of a point-point interface between the involved systems. See Figure 9.9 for the publish-and-subscribe (P&S) model.

Object Request Brokers (ORBs)

What is an object? It depends whom you listen to. However, for purposes of this book an object does *not* use Microsoft's Component Object Model (COM) or Distributed Component Object Model (DCOM). Today, the most common, legitimate objects are built using the Common Object Request Broker Architecture (CORBA). The good news is that this section does not care about the difference between the two, except to point out a few things:

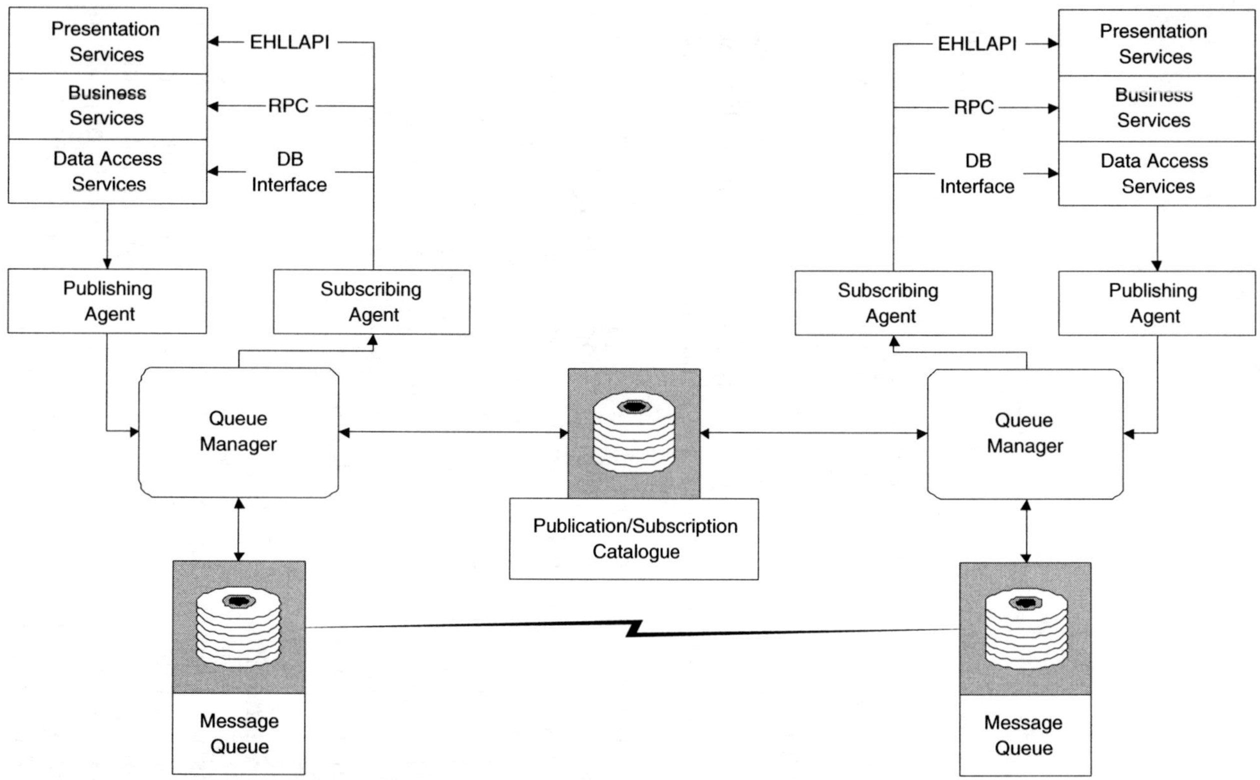

Figure 9.9 Publish and subscribe.

Solution Scenario

Publish and Subscribe

In the P&S model, the subscribing system is responsible for imposing context upon the received data that is appropriate for the receiving system. For example, a point-of-sale (POS) register in an arena is responsible for booking sales, depleting inventory, and logging the time of the stand personnel. However, each of these functions has a specific server that contains a purchased application for processing the data in the transactions. Our challenge is to integrate the packages and preserve the value of the purchased system.

In this design, inventory management, the food management decision support system (DSS), and the labor management system all need transactions that originate at the POS client, while the POS needs the menu management information that originates in menus. Rather than building interfaces between all these systems, a P&S architecture is implemented in which the POS publishes each transaction. For the sake of simplicity, let us assume that there are four messages defined:

- Sell_Something(Stand_ID, Time_Date, Item_ID, Quantity)
- Clock_In(Stand_ID, User_ID, Time_Date)
- Clock_Out(Stand_ID, User_ID, Time_Date)
- Add_Menu_Item(Menu_Id, Item_ID)

The system design might resemble Figure 9.10.

When a stand opens up before an event, the first thing that happens is the staff have to log in. In this case, the Clock_In message is valuable only to the labor management system, so

(*continued*)

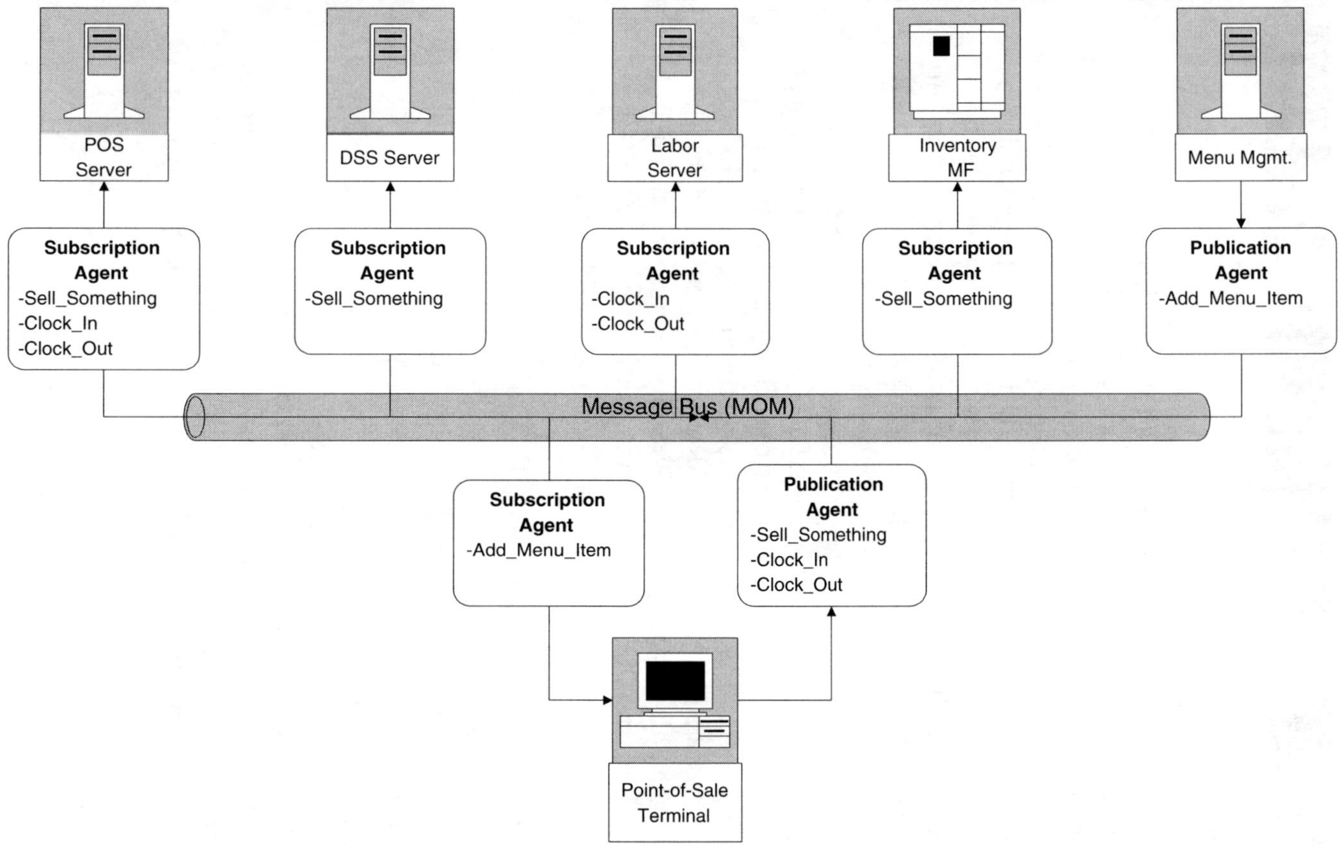

Figure 9.10 Publish and subscribe in action.

SOLUTION SCENARIO *Continued*

only this system subscribes to that message. The terminals in this case use a POS application built in an intranet model, except for some legacy terminals that run on PCs. The first thing the staff person does is make sure the POS has the right information for the event menu, so the POS subscribes to any menu updates. If one is received, it is up to the POS to figure out how the information affects the local presentation. The event begins, and the $6 hot dogs and $8 beers are soon in great demand. The POS systems begin to generate sales transactions, and the data is flowing fast and furious into the inventory, POS, and DSS systems as the venue tries to maximize revenue and make sure that none of the stands run out of inventory. The advantage of the P&S architecture here is obvious: The systems can leverage a single data output to drive multiple data inputs.

In the case of this system, the effort was fairly massive to implement. However, the total cost is based on a design that was generalized enough to be put into a number of venues of different types throughout the country. In addition, it required some fairly extensive work on the part of the team to integrate these packages up front, since the various vendors provided only data-level integration and there was a need to build Business Service proxies, which took longer than expected.

In this case, the decision to use the P&S design had several drivers:

The need for the systems to operate independently. Not every site would have all the services described, so the architecture had to be very loosely coupled.

The need for the systems to queue transactions if another system was lost. After all, not having the DSS

(*continued*)

SOLUTION SCENARIO *Continued*

system available was not a reason to stop selling hot dogs.

The need to integrate off-the-shelf back ends and wrap front ends in custom Presentation Layers.

The need to rapidly extend the architecture to support multiple types of back-office, POS, and ancillary service systems with minimal rewrite.

COM/DCOM is less mature than CORBA, but with MS behind it, the momentum is there.

COM/DCOM is not as scalable, given the restrictions of NT today, as the CORBA implementations.

COM/DCOM is suited for the desktop and small workgroup; it is not currently suited to provide the basis of an enterprise architecture.

CORBA is a nice idea that is not fully implemented.

You can bridge the two (CORBA/COM).

Users don't care.

ORBs fill an interesting role in legacy integration, abstracting the location of a thing and the nature of its implementation using well-defined interfaces. ORB concepts are similar to those of RPCs. For example, both provide a *location broker* function that allows a client to request a service or object of some type (remember the GUID?) and will pass back to the client a location. Both describe themselves using an IDL to describe their interfaces.

How do objects play with your intranet? Perhaps the most important innovation is the inclusion of an ORB in your browser. If you are a user of Microsoft's Internet Explorer, then you have a DCOM ORB; if you use the Netscape browser you have a CORBA

ORB. Inclusion is an important step, since it begins to make the components that are shipped to the client part of a run-time distributed processing architecture, a step up from the plain browser and a giant leap beyond the sophistication of first-generation client/server systems.

TIP *In the beginning, there was the Transaction Processing Monitor (TPM), and DP managers looked upon it and saw it was good. Then came objects, young, immature and lacking in transaction services. So some of the TPM folks sat and composed the basis for CORBA's Object Transaction Service (OTS). Much of the work came from Transarc, the developer of the Encina DCE-based TP monitor.*

With the introduction of the CORBA 2.0 specification came the OTS service. It is a complex implementation, and this complexity is forcing many to have looked to the TP Monitors as a transition technology. The bet is that vendors like BEA Systems (Tuxedo, Object Broker) and Transarc/IBM (Encina, SOM/DSOM) will provide the migration between these various technologies with investment protection and skills protection. So, when looking at vendors in the TP Monitor space, question closely how they are going to get you to objects. The major work in the Intranet seems to be heading the object route, and you don't want to be left behind.

Finally, objects are a wonderful way to implement a producer-consumer model. This is a highly leveraged or factory model of development in which the nature of something's implementation is entirely hidden from the consumer of the thing. The interface-centric model of component and object development is highly enabling of this model. The model allows the abstraction of things like network programming, object location, data location, data structure, and algorithms from the component consumer. If implemented in the ActiveX world, it can also refresh the component with a more recent copy every time it is updated.

What is the advantage of this model? It ultimately reflects the reality of the marketplace in several ways:

The complexity and pace of technology are forcing more producers and fewer consumers, and the cost of a competent producer is increasing.

Applications become assembled collections of discrete business functionality to solve the needs of a particular moment, rather than a monolithic or vertical cut at business functionality. This provides greater corporate process integration and flexibility for change.

The goal is to drive the P:C ratio as low as possible, reflecting increased usability, improved time to market, and shorter training time for consumers.

COM: MICROSOFT'S OBJECT SOLUTION

Microsoft's Component Object Model (COM) and its distributed cousin, DCOM, are the logical outgrowth of Microsoft's efforts to increase support for application-application interaction, compete in a rapidly distributing universe, and provide a differentiation between producers and consumers in the development world. ActiveX is the most recent step in this journey to application integration maturity. However, the road has been a long one (see Figure 9.11).

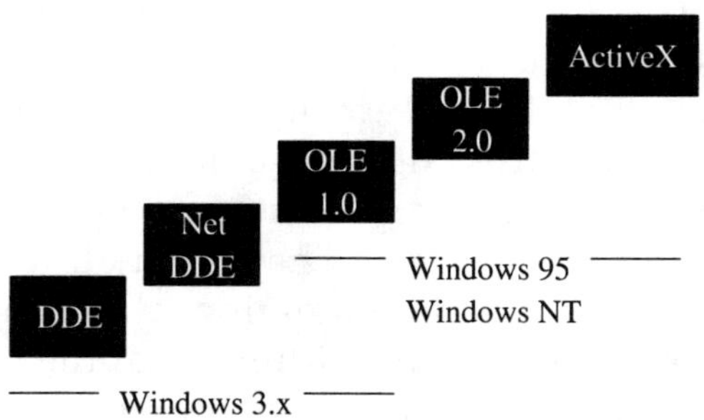

Figure 9.11 Evolution of COM/DCOM.

Microsoft's object efforts are interesting in that they rely on *aggregation* to provide a high degree of flexibility in construction, but they still support inheritance between classes during construction. When integrating COM into your intranet, the tool of choice is Microsoft's IIS since it uses ActiveX to support this aggregation of functionality. Microsoft has implemented the COM facilities using Active Server, a mechanism that allows ActiveX components to be placed on a Web page and then loaded at run time. The advantage of this approach is that it facilitates the division of producers and consumers discussed above, allowing consumers to simply combine components on the page and then use a scripting language to interact with them.

CORBA: A STANDARD FOR OBJECT COMPUTING

CORBA is a reference implementation for object services promulgated by a consortium of major vendors, which includes everyone in the industry except Microsoft. For more information on CORBA, please see www.omg.org. This multivendor flavor has given rise to accusations that CORBA is like a mule—a horse developed by a committee. In fact, CORBA is a robust and mature concept, but even the most mature implementations of it are still far from complete. To give you an idea of CORBA's scope, the following list includes the specified CORBA services:

- Naming
- Persistence
- Life cycle
- Properties
- Concurrency
- Collections
- Security
- Trader
- Externalization
- Events
- Transactions
- Query

- Relationship
- Time
- Licensing
- Change management

None of the available ORBs implements all of these services fully today, although more are closing the gap quickly. The relative maturity of these services compared to their Microsoft alternatives is amazing, but CORBA is still not winning the war at the desktop.

Some key CORBA terms include the following:

General Inter-Orb Protocol (GIOP). GIOP specifies a set of message formats and data representations for communication between ORBs. It is designed for connection-oriented transports like TCP/IP, so MOM interfaces have been a bit tough to fit into the CORBA world. Seven messages are defined for all ORB request/reply semantics. For marshalling of data, GIOP relies on the Common Data Representation (CDR), which handles interplatform byte ordering and interplatform memory alignments.

Environment-Specific Inter-Orb Protocol (ESIOP). ESIOP supports alternative protocols for integrating with CORBA ORBs, the first of which is our old friend DCE. In addition, ESIOP provides support for the DCE Kerberos security environment, DCE's cell services, and DCE's Time Service. These provide rich integration and migration for a company currently in a DCE environment and looking to move to an ORB. Ultimately, it is the entry point for additional protocols to play in the CORBA space, and guesses as to what those might be are welcome.

Internet Inter-Orb Protocol (IIOP). IIOP provides the basis for communication between heterogeneous ORBs. By specifying how GIOP messages are exchanged over TCP/IP networks, the backbone of the Internet, IIOP provides the mechanism necessary for transmitting context data associated with transactions and security services in a heterogeneous environment. This is the basis for distributed object computing.

Dynamic Skeleton Interface (DSI). DSI is the CORBA 2.0 run-time binding mechanism for servers to handle incoming method calls for components lacking IDL-based compiled skeletons. In addition, DSI reads the parameters of inbound messages to identify the destination object and method. It is used to build generic bridges between ORBS.

Figure 9.12 shows how this is put together in the CORBA stack.

BRINGING THEM TOGETHER: CORBA-COM INTEROPERABILITY

Whether object purists like it or not, COM is here to stay and will likely control the desktop, where its aggregation or composition ability is most welcome. However, there are solutions for integration. It is critical to remember that if you make the decision to use both of these object approaches in supporting your integration, you will be adding a performance burden to your environment, with obvious impacts on scalability and performance. As Figures 9.13 and 9.14 show, the integration of the two alternatives is based on IIOP, with proxies representing to one ORB the services provided by the other.

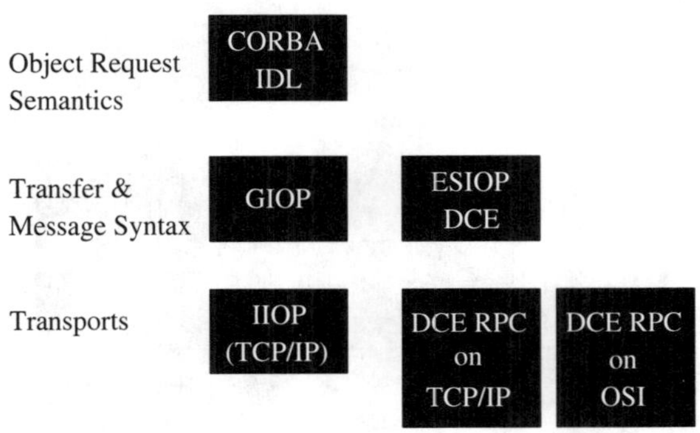

Figure 9.12 The CORBA stack.

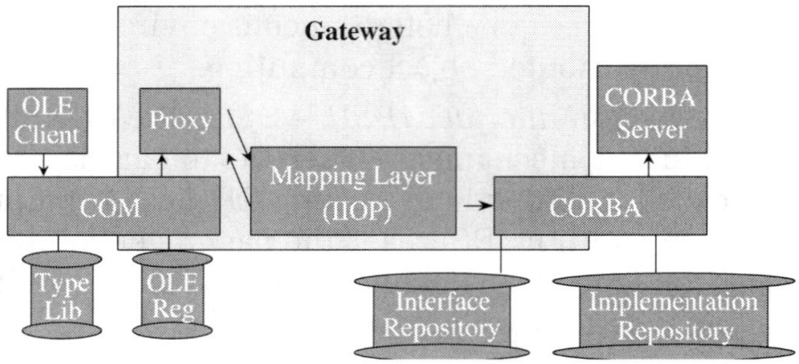

Figure 9.13 COM-CORBA integration.

Data Access Layer Integration

We are at the bottom of the stack, and this section is blessedly brief, since most of the tools and techniques discussed previously can be used at this level. (See Figure 9.15.) Here, we have only a database interface, something like ODBC, which can provide integration. In most cases, you will not find this level of integration to legacy mainframe environments, since most access there is regulated by CICS, IMS, or a similar mechanism. However, two-tier client/server systems were all about direct resource access, or tight binding to the data layer, and as such most of those applications will provide only a data layer integration point. This means rebuilding all the business logic in the system. Again.

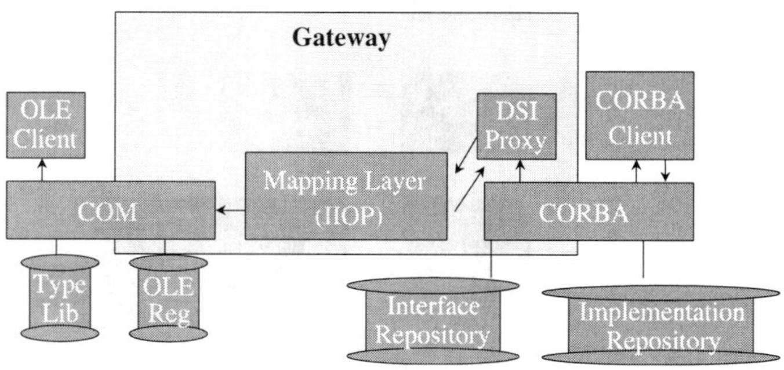

Figure 9.14 CORBA-DCOM integration.

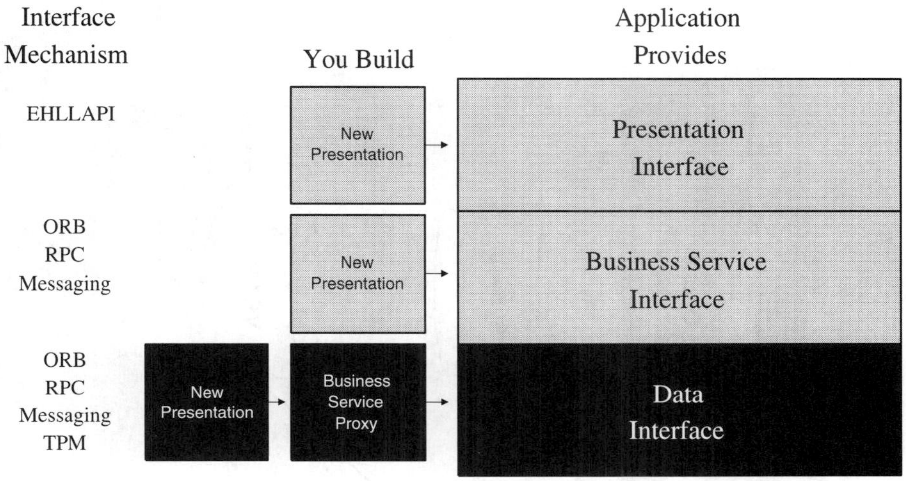

Figure 9.15 Application integration—Data Access Services Layer.

In this section, we will look at the last of the major middleware solutions: the transaction processing monitor. The reason for its inclusion here is that it provides services at the data layer that none of the others really do—namely, transactional semantics on nontransactional data structures.

Transaction Processing Monitors (TPMs)

Similar to the RPC in that they are synchronous, the TPM is enjoying a resurgence in popularity as two-tier client/server systems collapse under their own weight and intranets find the power of integration.

Transaction monitors are by no means new, finding their roots in the mainframe environment of CICS and IMS/DC. They serve several critical functions:

They provide a procedural language in which business transactions can be developed and stored in a single place.

They provide transactional semantics in distributed transaction systems, allowing logical records to be saved across repositories with full commit and rollback security.

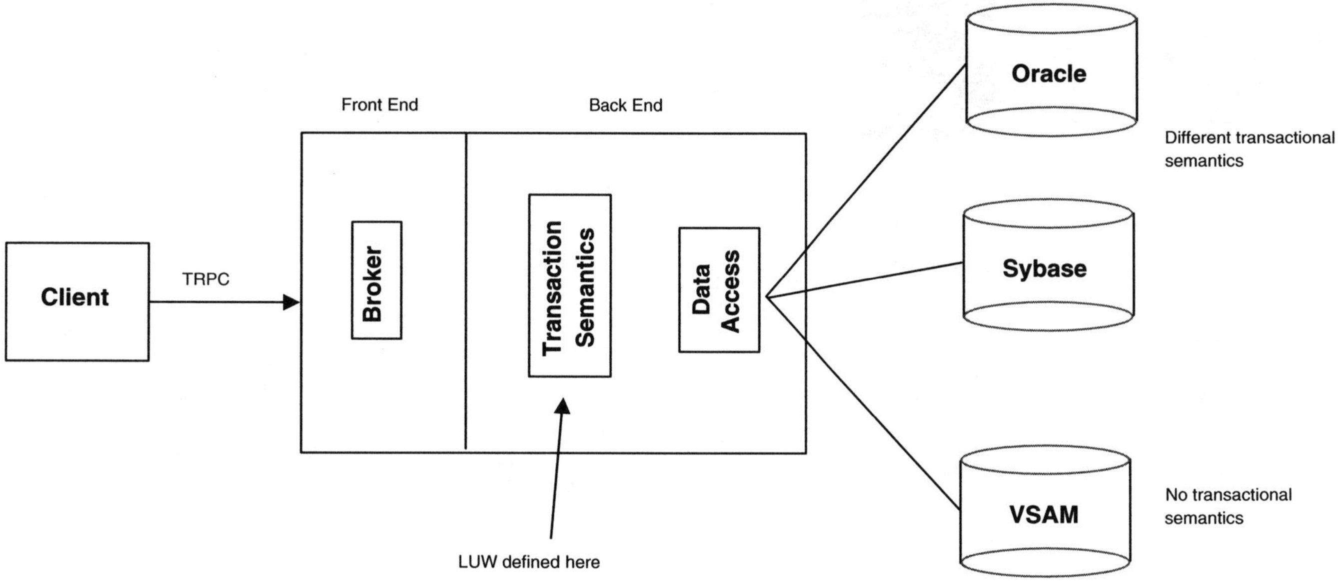

Figure 9.16 Transaction processing monitor dissected.

They provide transactional semantics to nontransactional data structures like VSAM, allowing transactions to enjoy full commit and rollback security.

They provide a mechanism for pooling database connections so the ratio of hardware to client is reduced.

They provide high reliability by providing automatic failover protection, whereby the loss of a TPM will result in redirection of a request for service to another TPM providing that same service, without user intervention or knowledge.

TPMs contain a number of things that we have previously discussed to perform these services, as you can see in Figure 9.16.

Most of the major players in this area now provide integration tools for your intranet, including IBM for their CICS products and BEA Systems for Tuxedo.

Summary

As we have seen in this chapter, there are many different approaches to legacy systems integration that can help leverage your current IT resources on your intranet. The trick to doing it well is to look for the optimal integration point and use efficient techniques so that reliable data delivery does not suffer at the hands of performance.

APPENDIX A

Web Administrator's Checklist

If you are a Web administrator (sometimes called a *Webmaster*), you may have a wide variety of responsibilities, ranging from HTML page edits to security audits. Consequently, although it is difficult to formulate a checklist that is applicable to everyone, we have included the following as a sample. We have also included a few sample project plans for various intranet activities that may be useful to you in your planning.

Completed	Task	Notes
	End-user policies and procedures	Annual, as necessary.
	Create and file base policy	Store in accessible repository for employee reference.
	File updates to policy	
	Notify users of policy changes	
	Internet access form/approval	As necessary.
	User profile input or maintenance	Receive request forms and update user lists.
	Log and report number of requests	Report via status report.
	Style guide	Annual, as necessary.
	Create and maintain style guide	Store in accessible repository for developer reference.
	Templates	Store standard templates.
	Wizards	Store wizards.

Completed	Task	Notes
	New administrator guide	Create and maintain instructions for being a Web administrator. Store in accessible repository.
	Application development standards	Create and maintain development standards for application developers.
	File updates	
	Notify users and developers of changes	
	Application documentation	Monthly, weekly, as necessary.
	Scope documents	For projects.
	Interface design	For each application.
	System design documents	For each application.
	Functional maps	For each application.
	Other design documents	Relevant data modeling and database design, middleware if applicable.
	Site map update	Monthly.
	Add/delete sites/pages	Maintain central files for reference.
	File	Check that other Web administrators regularly update their site maps.
	Storyboards	Weekly, monthly.
	Storyboard plans	Keep storyboards in a common repository for administrator access. Make sure key design changes are added to the plans.
	Editorial calendar	Weekly/monthly.
	Create and maintain editorial calendar	Keep all editorial calendars in common repository for reference. Track content requirements from contributors for sites. Report difficulties in accessing content to owner for issue resolution. Keep old editorial calendars for reference.

Completed	Task	Notes
	Source control	Weekly.
	Source control	Look for file conflicts that require resolution (e.g., simultaneously save conflicts if your package does resolve them internally).
	Link maintenance	Weekly (at minimum).
	Link maintenance	Ensuring that all links are accurate is critical to the operability of your application. If you have a site that changes little, you should use your site management software to check your links at least weekly. If you are subject to frequent updates or prone to changes outside of your control, you should check one or more times a day as seems appropriate.
	File migration	Daily, weekly.
	File migration	Change and update content on live site. Ensure that old files are properly cataloged and filed. Make sure all links are still functional. Make sure the update information in the file is accurate (if your software does not do this automatically).
	Security maintenance	Daily, weekly (as necessary).
	Security maintenance	Common threats to be aware of include: Network sniffers that have captured passwords and other sensitive pieces of information passing through the network as they are transmitted. IP spoofing attacks that have been used by attackers to break into hosts on the Internet.

Completed	Task	Notes
		Connection hijacking that has been used by attackers to seize control of existing interactive sessions (i.e., Telnet). Data spoofing that has been used by attackers of a rogue computer on a network to insert data into an ongoing communication between two other hosts. Data spoofing has been demonstrated as an effective means of compromising the integrity of programs executed over the network-form NFS servers. Remember to look for things out of the ordinary: Users logging in at strange hours Unexplained reboots Unexplained changes to the system clock Unusual error messages from the mailer FTP or other network servers Failed login attempts with bad passwords Unauthorized or suspicious use of commands Users logging in from unfamiliar sites on the network If you discover a log file deleted or containing corrupted information, there is a possibility that the computer has been successfully broken into. (*Note:* A break-in is not the only possible conclusion in this case; missing or corrupted logs might mean that one of your system administrators was careless or there is an automatic program in your system that erases the log files at periodic intervals.)

Completed	Task	Notes
		You may also discover that your system has been attacked if you notice unauthorized changes in system programs or in an individual user's files. A tool like Tripware is a good way to help monitor files for these types of changes.
	Setting up internal firewalls	A firewall that is designed for use within an organization is very similar to one that is used to protect an organization against external threats. However, there is a great temptation to share information or services via an internal firewall when such information services should in fact be blocked. Follow these basic guidelines when setting up independent internal networks: Make sure that each local area network has its own server. Make sure that each server and its clients have their own netgroup domain. Don't let any server or workstation on one network trust hosts on any other network or any gateway machine. Make certain that users who have accounts on more than one local network have different passwords for each subnet. If possible, use a one-time password scheme or a token-based system. Enable the highest level of logging for the gateways and the most restrictive security possible. Do not allow user accounts on the gateway machines. Do not NFS-mount file systems from one LAN to another LAN.

Completed	Task	Notes
	Check firewall audit trails	Check for the following in your audit trails: Time and date of session start Time and date of session end Source host address Destination host address Protocol used Destination port (or service request) Action taken (connection accepted or denied) Username if authentication was used Number of packets passed within the session
	Perform and review security audit	Review the audit information to look for suspicious activities such as: Repeated failed accesses from a host going to different services A flood of allowed connection requests going to the same host Connections made at odd hours of the night Multiple failed authentication attempts The firewall should also provide a method for reviewing the audit or log file for the previous 24 hours and up to a week. Archives of the audit files should be kept on removable storage such as tapes or floppy disks. The firewall should be configured to constantly scan the audit trail looking for events defined by the administrator and take the defined action.

Completed	Task	Notes
		1. Recording the action in a log or alarm file 2. Sending E-mail to an administrator 3. Displaying a message on the firewall console 4. Sending an alarm to a window or Xwindows terminal 5. Sending an SNMP alarm to a network manager system 6. Activating and sending a message to an administrator's beeper 7. Running a special application or script file on the firewall.
	Inappropriate site visits	Check logs for contact of inappropriate sites as defined by corporate policy. Report to management as necessary for violation. (*Note:* Ordinarily a warning procedure is in place with escalating severity of consequences for repeat violation.)
	Performance monitoring	Weekly.
	Performance monitoring	Coordinate with network administrators to optimize load balancing and network performance. If performance begins to degrade, it is important to find where the bottleneck is located in the system. Likely bottlenecks and potential solutions include: Network bandwidth on a remote segment—especially a T1 or ISDN link. Because it may be very costly to upgrade these circuits to a higher bandwidth, you may want to consider locating an additional server on the other end of the connection to help reduce the traffic.

Completed	Task	Notes
		Router throughput on the local router. Upgrading the router and collapsing the backbone into the router may be an effective remedy. Network bandwidth on the local segment. Upgrading from Ethernet to 10base100 or FDDI may resolve this type of bottleneck. Network interface card (NIC) throughput on the server. You may want to consider adding network interface cards; most servers allow multiples. Processing speed or memory capacity. These characteristics are often complementary—adding more memory is usually almost as effective as speeding up the processor. Adding additional processors may also be beneficial, but first be sure the application can take advantage of multiple processors. System I/O capacity. Exceeding this limit may leave you with no recourse but to increase the number of computers in the system. Disk capacity. Adding disk capacity is a fairly straightforward procedure.
	Usage monitoring	Daily or weekly.
	Analyze usage volume	Record and review number of hits per site and per page.
	Analyze usage paths	How are users traversing the site? Is it usable?
	User location/profile	Review user data to analyze trends and needs of various workgroups.
	Other statistics	Review other statistics as necessary including:

Completed	Task	Notes
		Duration Forms submitted Times of activity (especially relevant to performance tuning)
	Bulletin board	Daily.
	Respond to questions/issues	Post answers or route questions to users not on BBS as necessary.
	Delete inappropriate postings	Remove inappropriate material as determined by policy and report in status report.
	Intranet services	Daily.
	Mail server	Ensure operability. Check logs for errors or security breaches. Update user profiles as necessary.
	News server	Ensure operability. Check logs.
	Push server	Ensure operability. Check logs. Update content as necessary. Review user access and usage to analyze trends.
	Project plan update	
	Project plans	Create, maintain, update project plans. Store in accessible repository. Archive with other project documentation (e.g., scope and design documents) for public reference and reuse.
	Status reporting	Weekly.
	Status reports	Prepare and file weekly status report with issues and action items to coordinate intranet team members and accomplish goals.

Completed	Task	Notes
		Store in a referenceable location for future access.
	Virus scan	Weekly or monthly (as necessary).
	Environment virus scan	Perform periodic virus scan of all servers and workstations for contamination. Notify users of problems and track on status report.
	Report	Send report to PC Services for virus software install as necessary.
	Backup	Daily/weekly/monthly as deemed appropriate.
	Backup	*Day-zero backup.* A copy of the original system. When the system is first installed, before it is used, back up every file and program on the system. Such backups can be invaluable if there is a break-in. *Full backup.* A copy of every file on the system to the backup device. This method is similar to a day-zero backup, except that it is done on a regular basis (recommend monthly for most systems). *Incremental backup.* A copy to the backup device of only those items in a file system that have been modified after a particular event or date (recommend daily for most systems).
	Backup	Once a month, or after a major software package is installed, back up the entire system. At the beginning of each year, make two complete backups and store them in different locations. Make an incremental backup every evening of everything that has been modified since the last full backup. Full backups should be stored for 2 years.

Completed	Task	Notes
		Full annual backups are for indefinite storage.
	Backup	Store backup media in a secure, limited-access, off-site area; do not store them in the same room as your computer system. Additionally, you may wish to invest in a fireproof safe to protect your backups; however, it should still be placed off-site. After removing a backup tape from a drive, make sure to flip the write-protect switch so that it cannot be accidentally erased. If you are using the tape for incremental backups, you can flip the write-protect switch when you remove the tape, and then flip it again when you reinsert the tape later. If you accidentally leave the write-protection on, your software will probably give you an error and let you try again. On the other hand, write-protection will save your data if you accidentally put the wrong tape in the tape drive or run a program on the wrong tape. Backup media should be moved off-site on a daily basis and a sign-off procedure should be defined to facilitate the recall from archive.
	Recovery	Yearly.
	Recovery procedure	The full set of recovery mechanisms should be tested periodically as if they were actually being used. This should be performed annually at minimum with all involved personnel.
	Application maintenance	Daily—as necessary.
	Application maintenance	If using ActiveX controls, is the codebase correct? If using ActiveX controls, is the run-time license (LPK) file referenced correctly?

Completed	Task	Notes
		If using ASP, are there any nested virtual roots that could cause global.asa conflicts? If using COM servers, are they registered? If using CGI, is enough memory available to launch your CGI program? If using CGI, does your program attempt to make UI calls? If using any server-side add-ins, are all required DLLs available?
	Client management	All browsers: If using proxy, is proxy information correct? If not using DNS, is hosts table complete? If using DNS, are DNS tables complete? If using VPI or PPTP, are both ends of tunnel configured correctly? If using custom content types, are the appropriate readers (Acrobat, etc.) installed? Netscape Navigator: If using ActiveX controls, is Netscape plug-in installed? Are you falling prey to the refresh bug? Internet Explorer: If using scripting, are the latest scripting engines installed? If using ActiveX controls, are required run-time license files available?

Completed	Task	Notes
		News readers and mail readers: Is the server's address entered correctly? Does your workstation's IP number have access to the server? Are your POP3/NNTP usernames and passwords correct?
	Server maintenance	Daily, weekly.
	Server software	Netscape servers: Is the server listening on the correct port? Are virtual roots defined correctly? Are virtual servers defined correctly? If you are using NSAPI extensions, are they referenced correctly in obj.conf? If you are using CGI programs, are they in directories marked as executable or do they have extensions marked as executable? Do the permissions on all files needed by your server allow the account under which the server is running to access/execute the files? If you are running multiple NS servers, does your machine have enough RAM for all of them? Microsoft IIS: Are virtual roots defined correctly? Are virtual servers defined correctly? If you are using ISAPI extensions, are they installed correctly?

Completed	Task	Notes
		If you are using CGI programs, are they in directories marked as executable? Do the permissions on all files needed by your server allow the account under which the server is running to access/execute the files? Mail and news servers: Have you opened access to your servers to all possible IP numbers on your intranet?

Workplan 1 is a sample from a project in which several applications were added to an existing intranet.

Workplan 2 was to build an application for an existing intranet that involved 11 business components in an Active Server Page model.

Workplan 3 includes the implementation of a large amount of content management through SourceSafe and approval procedures described in Chapter 6.

ID	Task Name	Duration	Start Date
1	**HQ Intranet**	**115.25d**	**Tue 5/20/97**
2	**Project Initiation**	**1d**	**Tue 5/20/97**
4	**Understand**	**17d**	**Wed 5/21/97**
5	**JRP I - Design & Integration**	**6d**	**Wed 5/21/97**
6	JRP I - Planning	2d	Wed 5/21/97
7	JRP I	1d	Fri 5/23/97
8	JRP I - Analyze Results	3d	Mon 5/26/97
9	**JRP II - Application 1**	**3.5d**	**Thu 5/29/97**
10	JRP II - Planning	0.5d	Thu 5/29/97
11	JRP II	0.25d	Fri 5/30/97
12	JRP II - Analyze Results	0.75d	Mon 6/2/97
13	**JRP III - Application 2**	**6.5d**	**Fri 5/30/97**
14	JRP III - Planning	0.5d	Fri 5/30/97
15	JRP III	0.25d	Thu 6/5/97
16	JRP III - Analyze Results	0.75d	Mon 6/9/97
17	**JRP IV - Application 3**	**5.25d**	**Fri 5/30/97**
18	JRP IV - Planning	0.5d	Fri 5/30/97
19	JRP IV	0.25d	Wed 6/4/97
20	JRP IV - Analyze Results	0.75d	Thu 6/5/97
21	**JRP V - Application 4**	**6.75d**	**Mon 6/2/97**
22	JRP V - Planning	0.5d	Mon 6/2/97
23	JRP V	0.25d	Mon 6/9/97
24	JRP V - Analyze Results	0.75d	Tue 6/10/97

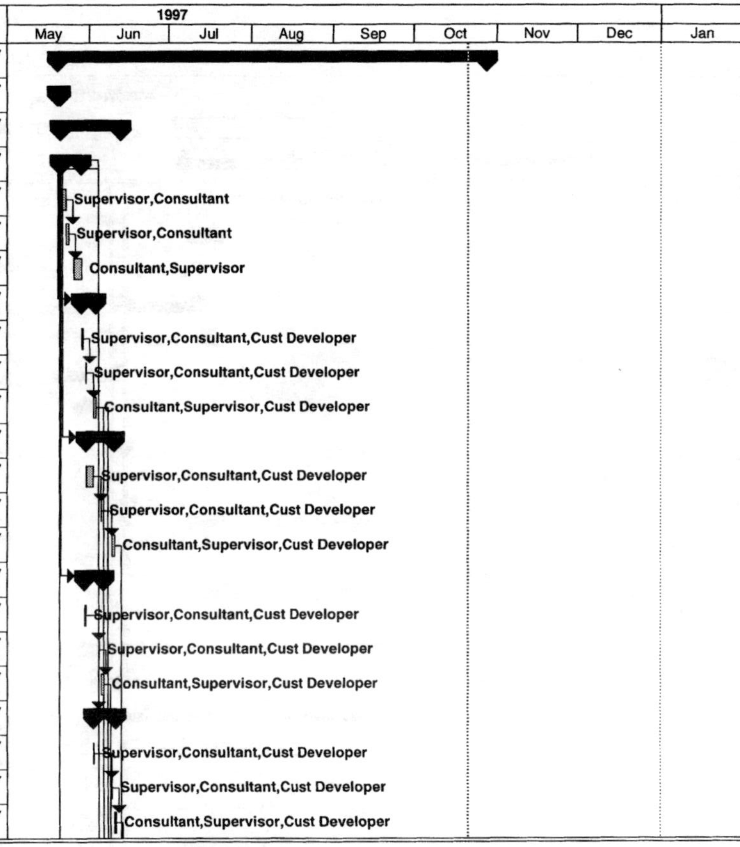

Project: Workplan 1

Task · Progress · Milestone · Summary · Rolled Up Task · Rolled Up Milestone · Rolled Up Progress

Page 1

Figure A.1.1 Workplan 1

ID	Task Name	Duration	Start Date
25	**JRP VI - Application 5**	**5.25d**	**Wed 6/4/97**
26	JRP VI - Planning	0.5d	Wed 6/4/97
27	JRP VI	0.25d	Wed 6/11/97
28	JRP VI - Analyze Results	0.75d	Wed 6/11/97
29	**JRP VII - Application 6**	**4d**	**Thu 5/29/97**
30	JRP VII - Planning	0.5d	Thu 5/29/97
31	JRP VII	0.25d	Tue 6/3/97
32	JRP VII - Analyze Results	0.75d	Tue 6/3/97
33	**Prototype Corporate Applications**	**5.75d**	**Wed 6/4/97**
34	Application 1	1d	Fri 6/6/97
35	Application 2	0.5d	Tue 6/10/97
36	Application 3	0.75d	Fri 6/6/97
37	Application 4	0.5d	Wed 6/11/97
38	Application 5	0.25d	Thu 6/12/97
39	Application 6	1d	Wed 6/4/97
40	**Write Scope Document**	**1d**	**Thu 6/12/97**
42	**Write Style Guide and Application [**	**1d**	**Thu 5/29/97**
44	**Write Accpetance Test Plan**	**15d**	**Wed 5/21/97**
46	**Blueprint**	**24d**	**Fri 6/13/97**
47	**GUI Design and Site Layout Design**	**20d**	**Fri 6/13/97**
49	**Application Architecture**	**20d**	**Fri 6/13/97**
51	**Design Corporate Applications**	**4d**	**Fri 7/11/97**
52	Application 1	3d	Fri 7/11/97

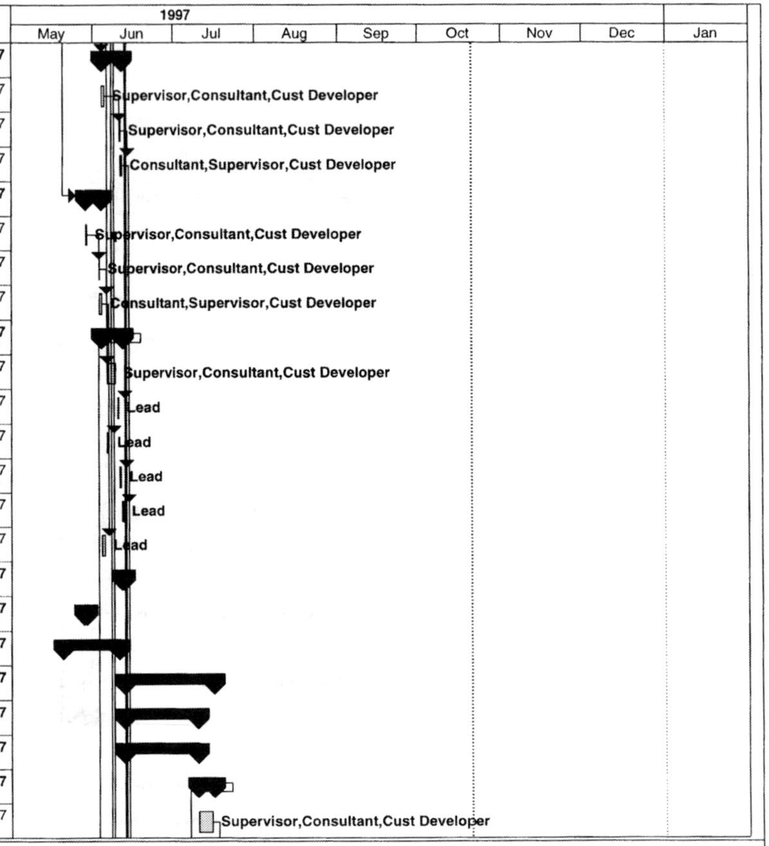

Project: Workplan 1

Task | Progress | Milestone | Summary | Rolled Up Task | Rolled Up Milestone | Rolled Up Progress

Figure A.1.2 Workplan 1, continued

ID	Task Name	Duration	Start Date
53	Applicaiton 2	2d	Fri 7/11/97
54	Application 3	3d	Fri 7/11/97
55	Application 4	3d	Fri 7/11/97
56	Application 5	1d	Wed 7/16/97
57	Application 6	1d	Wed 7/16/97
58	**Implement**	**65d**	**Tue 7/15/97**
59	**Implement Corporate Applications**	**25d**	**Tue 7/15/97**
60	Application 1	**24d**	**Wed 7/16/97**
62	Applicaiton 2	**14d**	**Tue 7/15/97**
64	Application 3	**20d**	**Wed 7/16/97**
66	Application 4	**24d**	**Wed 7/16/97**
68	Application 5	**8.5d**	**Thu 7/17/97**
70	Application 6	**8.5d**	**Thu 7/17/97**
72	**Integrate Department Homepages**	**40d**	**Tue 8/19/97**
73	**Finance**	**26d**	**Tue 8/19/97**
74	Customize Corporate Applic	16d	Tue 8/19/97
75	Flash Report / Top Manager	10d	Wed 9/10/97
76	**Information Technology**	**8d**	**Mon 9/22/97**
77	Customize Corporate Applic	8d	Mon 9/22/97
78	**Benefits**	**8d**	**Mon 9/22/97**
79	Customize Corporate Applic	8d	Mon 9/22/97
80	**Public Relations**	**19d**	**Wed 9/10/97**
81	Customize Corporate Applic	8d	Wed 9/10/97

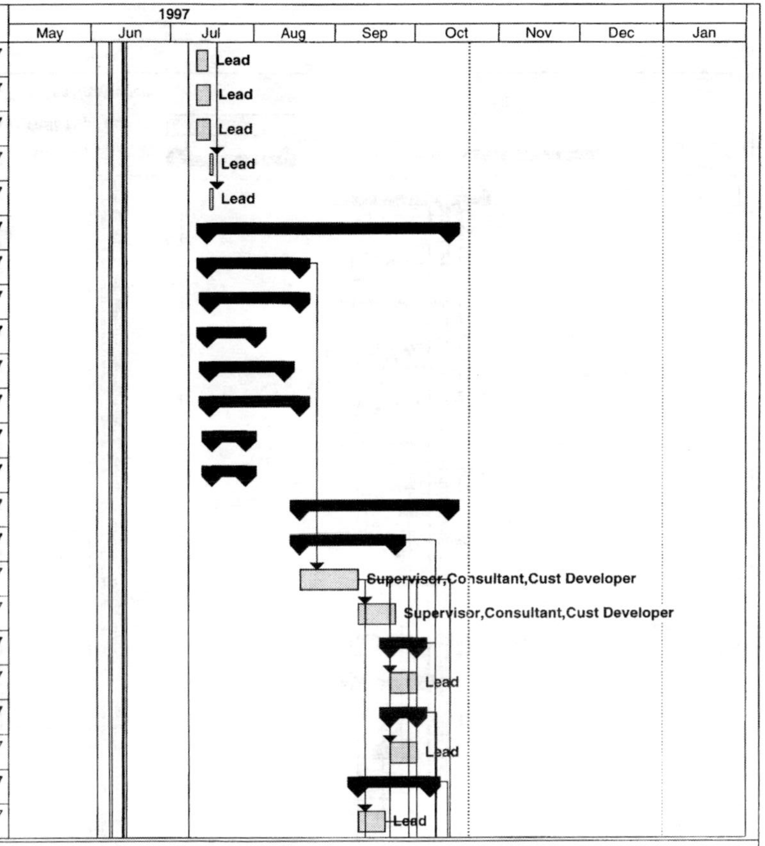

Project: Workplan 1

Task		Summary		Rolled Up Progress	
Progress		Rolled Up Task			
Milestone	◆	Rolled Up Milestone	◇		

Page 3

Figure A.1.3 Workplan 1, continued

ID	Task Name	Duration	Start Date
82	Volunteer Feedback Form	3d	Thu 10/2/97
83	**Purchasing**	**21.25d**	**Wed 9/10/97**
84	Customize Corporate Applic	8d	Wed 9/10/97
85	Add customized link	0.25d	Thu 10/9/97
86	**AR**	**8d**	**Mon 9/22/97**
87	Customize Corporate Applic	8d	Mon 9/22/97
88	**Risk management**	**8d**	**Mon 9/22/97**
89	Customize Corporate Applic	8d	Mon 9/22/97
90	**Human Resources**	**21d**	**Wed 9/10/97**
91	Customize Corporate Applic	8d	Wed 9/10/97
92	Job Postings	5d	Thu 10/2/97
93	**Corporate Communications**	**8d**	**Mon 9/29/97**
94	Customize Corporate Applic	8d	Mon 9/29/97
95	**Audit**	**8d**	**Thu 10/2/97**
96	Customize Corporate Applic	8d	Thu 10/2/97
97	**Facilities**	**21d**	**Wed 9/10/97**
98	Customize Corporate Applic	8d	Wed 9/10/97
99	Matching Grant Form	5d	Mon 9/22/97
100	Academic Awards Form	5d	Thu 10/2/97
101	**Legal**	**22d**	**Wed 9/10/97**
102	Customize Corporate Applic	8d	Wed 9/10/97
103	Legal Form	3d	Tue 10/7/97
104	**Sustain**	**45.25d**	**Tue 8/26/97**

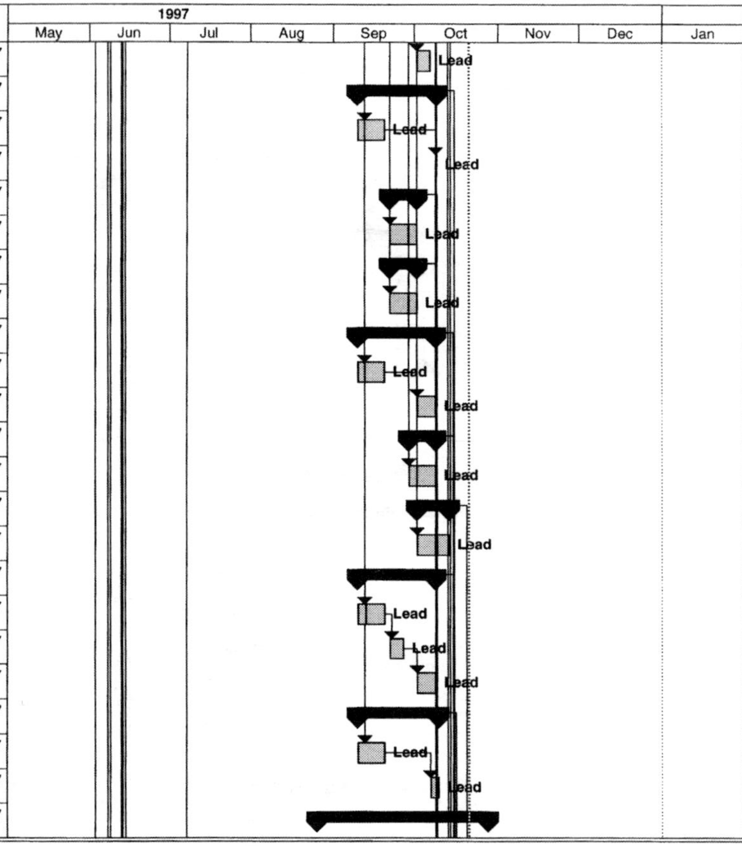

Project: Workplan 1

Task
Progress
Milestone
Summary
Rolled Up Task
Rolled Up Milestone
Rolled Up Progress

Page 4

Figure A.1.4 Workplan 1, continued

ID	Task Name	Duration	Start Date
105	**Install Corporate Applications**	**5d**	**Tue 8/26/97**
107	**Install Department Applications**	**3.25d**	**Thu 10/9/97**
108	Finance	0.25d	Thu 10/9/97
109	Information Technology	0.25d	Thu 10/9/97
110	Benefits	0.25d	Thu 10/9/97
111	Public Relations	0.25d	Thu 10/9/97
112	Purchasing	0.25d	Thu 10/9/97
113	AR	0.25d	Thu 10/9/97
114	Risk management	0.25d	Thu 10/9/97
115	Human Resources	0.25d	Thu 10/9/97
116	Corporate Communications	0.25d	Thu 10/9/97
117	Audit	0.25d	Tue 10/14/97
118	Facilities	0.25d	Thu 10/9/97
119	Legal	0.25d	Fri 10/10/97
120	**Produce Training Guides**	**5d**	**Tue 10/14/97**
121	Produce Training Guides	5d	Tue 10/14/97
122	**Train Department Personnel**	**5d**	**Tue 10/21/97**
123	Train Department Personnel	5d	Tue 10/21/97
124	**Milestones**	**34d**	**Thu 5/29/97**
125	Scope Document Complete	0d	Thu 6/12/97
126	Style Guides and Application Developme	0d	Thu 5/29/97
127	Functional Requirements Complete	0d	Wed 6/11/97
128	High-level Site Map Complete	0d	Wed 6/11/97

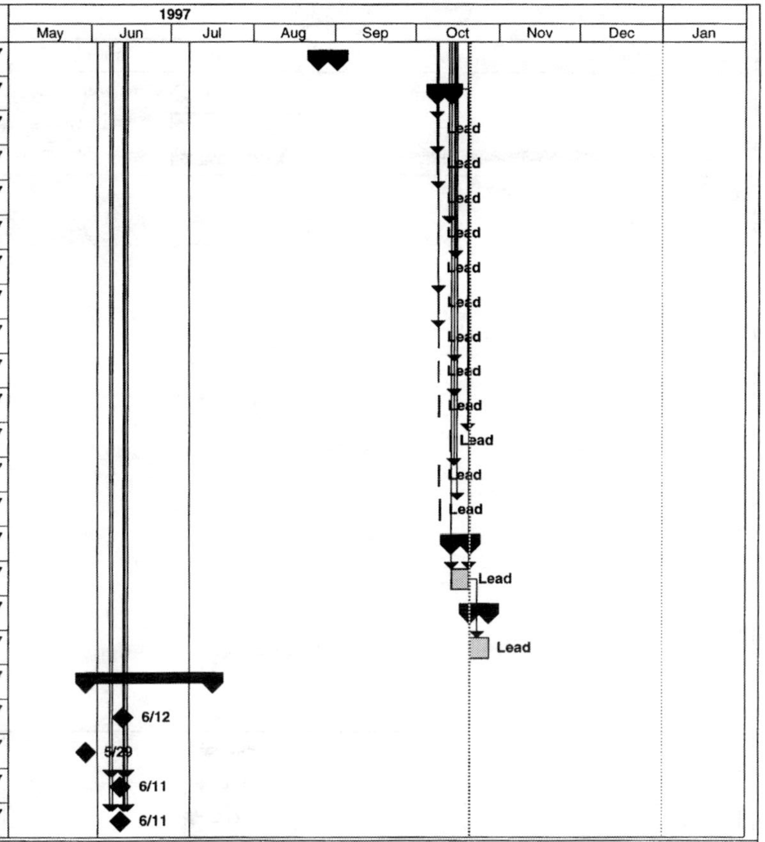

Project: Workplan 1

Task | Progress | Milestone | Summary | Rolled Up Task | Rolled Up Milestone | Rolled Up Progress

Page 5

Figure A.1.5 Workplan 1, continued

ID	Task Name	Duration	Start Date
129	Project Plan Complete	0d	Thu 6/12/97
130	Prototype Complete	0d	Thu 6/12/97
131	Acceptance Test Plan Complete	0d	Thu 6/12/97
132	Sample Art Work and Site Layout Design (	0d	Thu 7/10/97
133	Storyboards Complete	0d	Thu 7/10/97
134	Content Complete	0d	Tue 7/15/97
135	Data Model Complete	0d	Wed 7/16/97

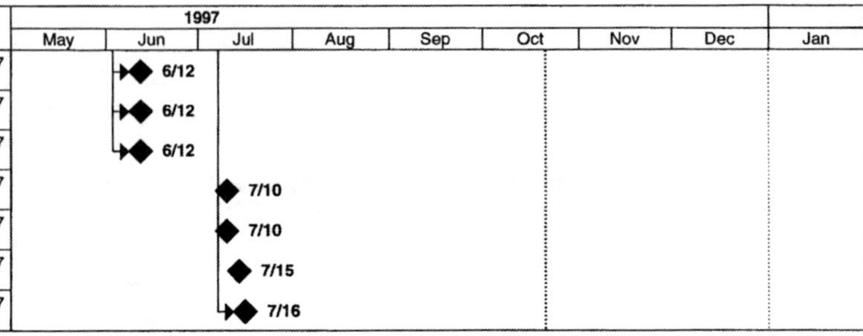

Project: Workplan 1

Task | Progress | Milestone | Summary | Rolled Up Task | Rolled Up Milestone | Rolled Up Progress

Page 6

Figure A.1.6 Workplan 1, continued

ID	Task Name	Work	Start	Finish
1	**Management System**	**1176h**	**Mon 2/3/97**	**Wed 5/28/97**
2	**Understand**	**132h**	**Mon 2/3/97**	**Tue 2/18/97**
3	**Project Initiation**	**52h**	**Mon 2/3/97**	**Thu 2/6/97**
4	Project Kickoff	8h	Mon 2/3/97	Mon 2/3/97
5	Confirm Scope and Deliverables	4h	Mon 2/3/97	Mon 2/3/97
6	Document Scope	8h	Tue 2/4/97	Tue 2/4/97
7	JRP Prep	32h	Wed 2/5/97	Thu 2/6/97
8	**Requirements Definition**	**64h**	**Fri 2/7/97**	**Fri 2/14/97**
9	Process/Functional Requirements	32h	Fri 2/7/97	Mon 2/10/97
10	Build Process Model	16h	Tue 2/11/97	Wed 2/12/97
11	Document Functional Requirements	8h	Thu 2/13/97	Thu 2/13/97
12	Document Site Map	8h	Fri 2/14/97	Fri 2/14/97
13	**Phase Completion**	**16h**	**Mon 2/17/97**	**Tue 2/18/97**
14	Revise Project Plan	8h	Mon 2/17/97	Mon 2/17/97
15	Phase End Mtg	8h	Tue 2/18/97	Tue 2/18/97
16	MS: Phase End & Delivery	0h	Mon 2/17/97	Mon 2/17/97
17	**Blueprint - Plan Application**	**420h**	**Tue 2/18/97**	**Thu 3/27/97**
18	**Data Design**	**40h**	**Tue 2/18/97**	**Tue 2/25/97**
19	Build Datamodel	40h	Tue 2/18/97	Tue 2/25/97
20	**Design Framework**	**72h**	**Tue 2/18/97**	**Thu 2/27/97**
21	**UI Design**	**56h**	**Tue 2/18/97**	**Thu 2/27/97**
22	User Meetings	32h	Tue 2/25/97	Thu 2/27/97
23	Design Layout	24h	Tue 2/18/97	Fri 2/21/97

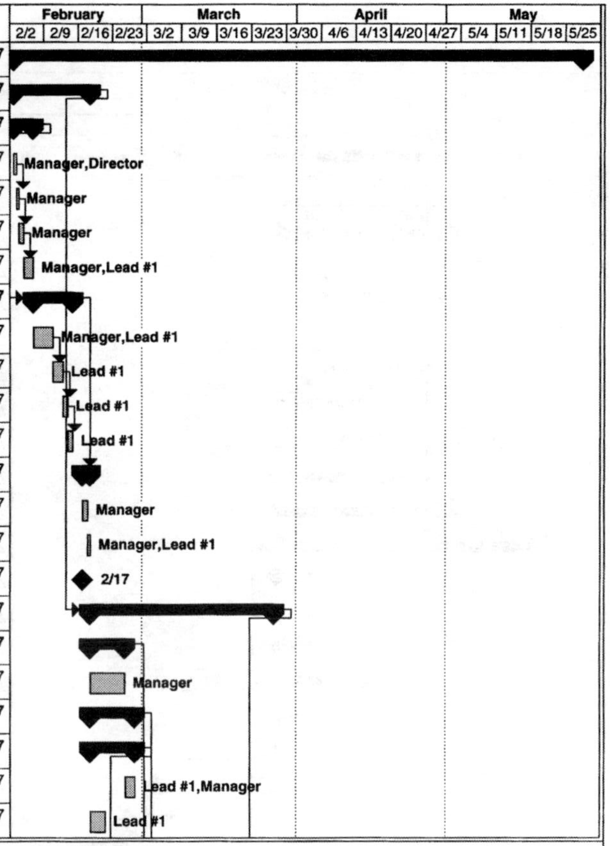

Workplan 2

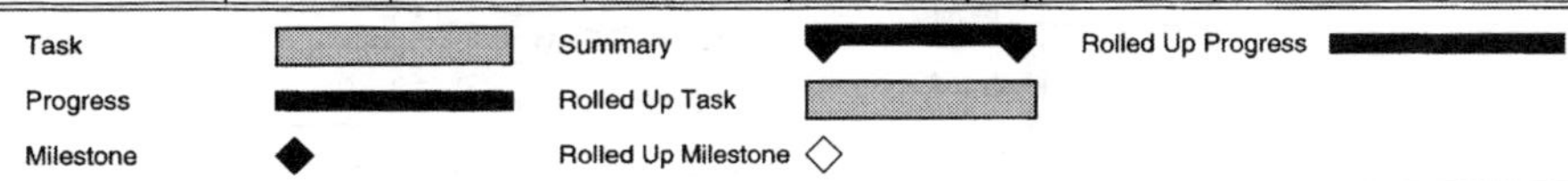

Page 1

Figure A.2.1 Workplan 2

ID	Task Name	Work	Start	Finish
24	Business Layer Design	16h	Fri 2/21/97	Tue 2/25/97
25	MS: Design Sign Off	0h	Thu 2/27/97	Thu 2/27/97
26	**Acceptance Test Plan**	**40h**	**Tue 2/18/97**	**Tue 2/25/97**
27	Write Acceptance Test Plan	40h	Tue 2/18/97	Tue 2/25/97
28	MS: Sign Acceptance Test Plan	0h	Tue 2/25/97	Tue 2/25/97
29	**Detailed Design**	**268h**	**Mon 3/3/97**	**Tue 3/25/97**
30	11 Business Component Design	128h	Mon 3/3/97	Tue 3/25/97
31	Business Component Des QA	10h	Mon 3/24/97	Tue 3/25/97
32	ASP Design	120h	Mon 3/3/97	Mon 3/24/97
33	ASP Design QA	10h	Fri 3/21/97	Mon 3/24/97
34	**Phase Completion**	**0h**	**Thu 3/27/97**	**Thu 3/27/97**
35	MS: Phase End & Delivery	0h	Thu 3/27/97	Thu 3/27/97
36	**Implement**	**560h**	**Thu 3/27/97**	**Fri 5/16/97**
37	**Code + Unit Test**	**400h**	**Thu 3/27/97**	**Thu 5/1/97**
38	**ASP Development**	**200h**	**Thu 3/27/97**	**Fri 4/25/97**
39	Artwork	24h	Thu 3/27/97	Tue 4/1/97
40	Develop Site Prototype	24h	Thu 3/27/97	Tue 4/1/97
41	Prototype Review - 1	12h	Tue 4/1/97	Wed 4/2/97
42	Protoype Revisions	8h	Wed 4/2/97	Thu 4/3/97
43	Prototype Review - 2	12h	Thu 4/3/97	Fri 4/4/97
44	15 Pages	120h	Fri 4/4/97	Fri 4/25/97
45	**Business Component Developmen**	**200h**	**Thu 3/27/97**	**Thu 5/1/97**
46	Devel & Unit Test	200h	Thu 3/27/97	Thu 5/1/97

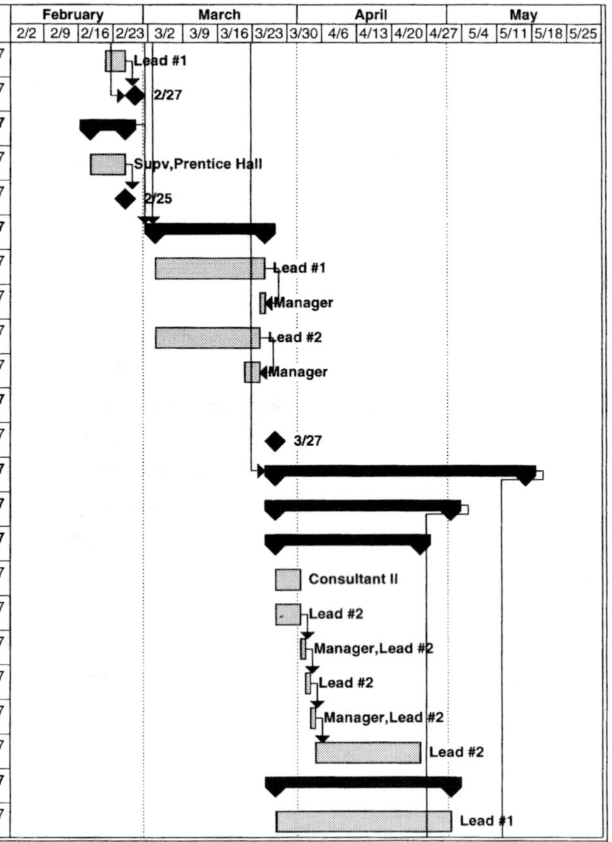

Workplan 2

Task | Progress | Milestone | Summary | Rolled Up Task | Rolled Up Milestone | Rolled Up Progress

Page 2

Figure A.2.2 Workplan 2, continued

ID	Task Name	Work	Start	Finish
47	**Integration & Acceptance Test**	**144h**	**Thu 5/1/97**	**Thu 5/15/97**
48	Integration Testing	80h	Thu 5/1/97	Thu 5/15/97
49	Acceptance Test	24h	Thu 5/1/97	Tue 5/6/97
50	Quality Assurance	40h	Thu 5/1/97	Thu 5/8/97
51	**Phase Completion**	**16h**	**Thu 5/15/97**	**Fri 5/16/97**
52	Phase End & Delivery	16h	Thu 5/15/97	Fri 5/16/97
53	MS: Implementation Phase Complet	0h	Fri 5/16/97	Fri 5/16/97
54	**Sustain**	**64h**	**Fri 5/16/97**	**Wed 5/28/97**
55	Technical Documentation	40h	Fri 5/16/97	Fri 5/23/97
56	Transfer to Support	24h	Fri 5/23/97	Wed 5/28/97
57	MS: Sustain Phase Complete	0h	Wed 5/28/97	Wed 5/28/97

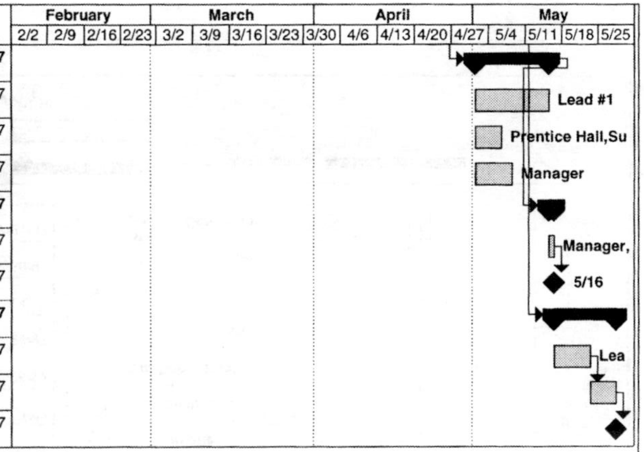

Workplan 2				
	Task	Summary	Rolled Up Progress	
	Progress	Rolled Up Task		
	Milestone	Rolled Up Milestone		

Page 3

Figure A.2.3 Workplan 2, continued

ID	Task Name	Duration	Start	Finish
1	**Intranet Site**	**91d**	**Mon 7/14/97**	**Mon 11/17/97**
2	**Phase 1**	**60d**	**Mon 7/14/97**	**Fri 10/3/97**
3	**Project Initiation**	**3d**	**Mon 7/14/97**	**Wed 7/16/97**
4	Review/refine Workplan	2d	Mon 7/14/97	Tue 7/15/97
5	Review/Refine Estimates	1d	Wed 7/16/97	Wed 7/16/97
6	Develop Baseline Web Infrastructre Design	5d	Mon 7/14/97	Fri 7/18/97
7	Implement Development Environment	5d	Mon 7/21/97	Fri 7/25/97
8	**Install Web Service and Software Components**	**14d**	**Thu 7/17/97**	**Tue 8/5/97**
9	Review NT Guildelines	1d	Thu 7/17/97	Thu 7/17/97
10	Install NT Server Software (8)	4d	Fri 7/18/97	Wed 7/23/97
11	**Source Management Server**	**5d**	**Mon 7/21/97**	**Fri 7/25/97**
12	Implement SW	1d	Mon 7/21/97	Mon 7/21/97
13	Develop staging plan	2d	Tue 7/22/97	Wed 7/23/97
14	Develop security / access mgmt. plan	1d	Thu 7/24/97	Thu 7/24/97
15	Implement staging plan	1d	Fri 7/25/97	Fri 7/25/97
16	**Site Server**	**5d**	**Tue 7/22/97**	**Mon 7/28/97**
17	Implement SW	1d	Tue 7/22/97	Tue 7/22/97
18	Develop staging plan	2d	Wed 7/23/97	Thu 7/24/97
19	Develop security / access mgmt. plan	1d	Fri 7/25/97	Fri 7/25/97
20	Implement staging plan	1d	Mon 7/28/97	Mon 7/28/97
21	Web Authoring Server	2d	Wed 7/23/97	Thu 7/24/97
22	Staging Server	2d	Tue 7/29/97	Wed 7/30/97
23	Production Internet Web server	1d	Thu 7/31/97	Thu 7/31/97

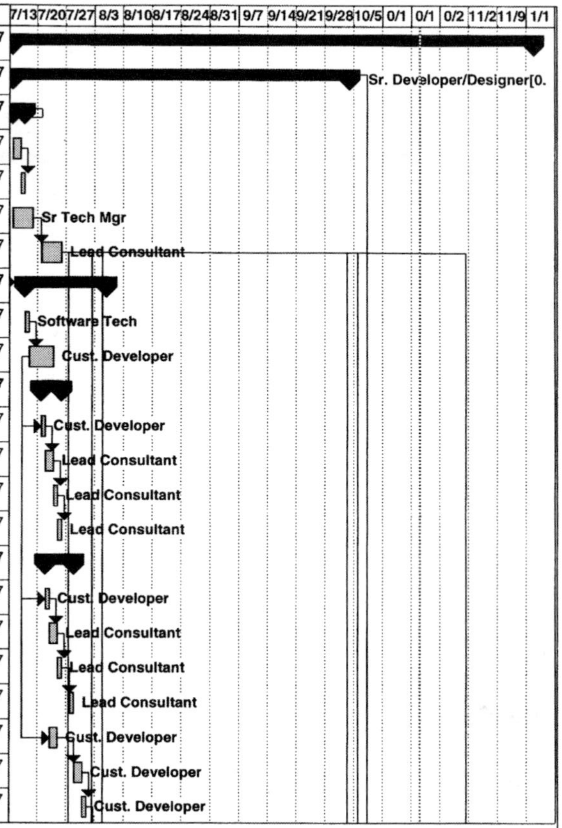

Project: Workplan 3.MPP

Task — Progress — Milestone — Summary — Rolled Up Task — Rolled Up Milestone — Rolled Up Progress

Page 1

Figure A.3.1 Workplan 3

ID	Task Name	Duration	Start	Finish
24	Production Intranet Web Server	1d	Fri 8/1/97	Fri 8/1/97
25	Production Internet DB Server	1d	Mon 8/4/97	Mon 8/4/97
26	Production Intranet DB Server	1d	Tue 8/5/97	Tue 8/5/97
27	**Application Development**	**18d**	**Mon 7/28/97**	**Wed 8/20/97**
28	**Base Application**	**18d**	**Mon 7/28/97**	**Wed 8/20/97**
29	**Design Application Standard model**	**11d**	**Mon 7/28/97**	**Mon 8/11/97**
30	App framework Dev.	5d	Tue 8/5/97	Mon 8/11/97
31	**Security**	**6d**	**Mon 7/28/97**	**Mon 8/4/97**
32	Specify security/access contol ı	2d	Mon 7/28/97	Tue 7/29/97
33	Design access control mechani	2d	Wed 7/30/97	Thu 7/31/97
34	Implement security/access mec	2d	Fri 8/1/97	Mon 8/4/97
35	**Develop DB Facilities**	**6d**	**Mon 7/28/97**	**Mon 8/4/97**
36	Develop data storage approach	2d	Mon 7/28/97	Tue 7/29/97
37	Develop data model	2d	Wed 7/30/97	Thu 7/31/97
38	Implement data model	2d	Fri 8/1/97	Mon 8/4/97
39	**Application**	**7d**	**Tue 8/12/97**	**Wed 8/20/97**
40	Build App	3d	Tue 8/12/97	Thu 8/14/97
41	Design/Build Review App	4d	Fri 8/15/97	Wed 8/20/97
42	**Design/Build GuestBook**	**7d**	**Tue 8/12/97**	**Wed 8/20/97**
43	Build Feedback App	3d	Tue 8/12/97	Thu 8/14/97
44	Desing/Build Feedback Review App	4d	Fri 8/15/97	Wed 8/20/97
45	**Web Request Form**	**7d**	**Tue 8/12/97**	**Wed 8/20/97**
46	Build Web Request App	3d	Tue 8/12/97	Thu 8/14/97

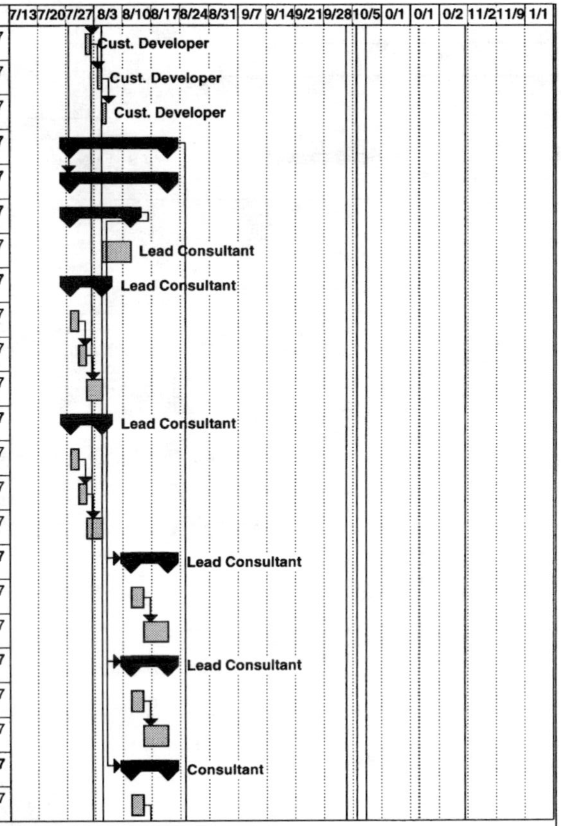

Project: Workplan 3.MPP

Task | Progress | Milestone | Summary | Rolled Up Task | Rolled Up Milestone | Rolled Up Progress

Page 2

Figure A.3.2 Workplan 3, continued

ID	Task Name	Duration	Start	Finish
47	Desing/Build Web request Review A	4d	Fri 8/15/97	Wed 8/20/97
48	**Employee Home Page Wizard**	**10d**	**Tue 8/5/97**	**Mon 8/18/97**
49	Build Employee Home Page Wizard v 1.(	10d	Tue 8/5/97	Mon 8/18/97
50	**Testing**	**34d**	**Mon 7/14/97**	**Thu 8/28/97**
51	Develop Integration Test Plan	3d	Mon 7/14/97	Wed 7/16/97
52	Develp Acceptance Test Plan and Acceptanc	3d	Thu 7/17/97	Mon 7/21/97
53	Integration Test	3d	Thu 8/21/97	Mon 8/25/97
54	User Acceptance Test	3d	Tue 8/26/97	Thu 8/28/97
55	Sign-Off	0d	Thu 8/28/97	Thu 8/28/97
56	**Train the Trainer Training**	**36d**	**Tue 7/22/97**	**Tue 9/9/97**
57	Develop Coursewear	10d	Tue 7/22/97	Mon 8/4/97
58	Conduct Class	2d	Mon 9/8/97	Tue 9/9/97
59	**Production Implementation**	**11d**	**Fri 8/22/97**	**Fri 9/5/97**
60	Deliver Web Procedures	0d	Fri 8/22/97	Fri 8/22/97
61	Deliver Appropriate Use Policies and Commu	0d	Fri 8/22/97	Fri 8/22/97
62	Deliver Web Standards	0d	Fri 8/22/97	Fri 8/22/97
63	User Setup	3d	Fri 8/22/97	Tue 8/26/97
64	Data Conversion/loading	5d	Fri 8/22/97	Thu 8/28/97
65	System Load	3d	Fri 8/29/97	Tue 9/2/97
66	System Cutover	3d	Wed 9/3/97	Fri 9/5/97
67	**Post Implementation Support/Knowledge Trans**	**20d**	**Mon 9/8/97**	**Fri 10/3/97**
68	Helpdesk Support	20d	Mon 9/8/97	Fri 10/3/97
69	Knowledge Transfer	20d	Mon 9/8/97	Fri 10/3/97

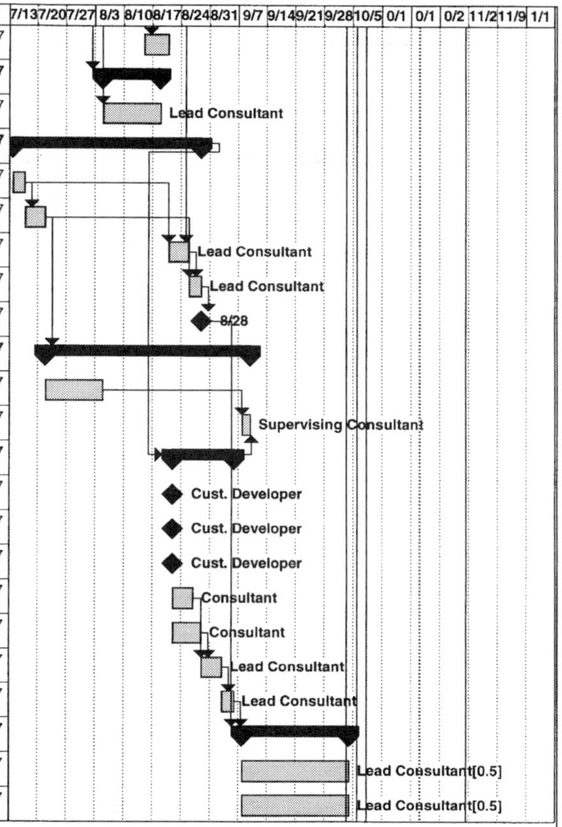

Project: Workplan 3.MPP

Task | Progress | Milestone | Summary | Rolled Up Task | Rolled Up Milestone | Rolled Up Progress

Page 3

Figure A.3.3 Workplan 3, continued

ID	Task Name	Duration	Start	Finish
70	**Phase II Development**	**31d**	**Mon 10/6/97**	**Mon 11/17/97**
71	**Content Approval Process**	**21d**	**Mon 10/6/97**	**Mon 11/3/97**
72	Design Content approval process	8d	Mon 10/6/97	Wed 10/15/97
73	Prepare process alternatives	2d	Thu 10/16/97	Fri 10/17/97
74	Select process	0d	Fri 10/17/97	Fri 10/17/97
75	Review/revise Content Approval Process estir	1d	Mon 10/20/97	Mon 10/20/97
76	Implement Content Approval Process	10d	Tue 10/21/97	Mon 11/3/97
77	**Product Services**	**23d**	**Mon 10/6/97**	**Wed 11/5/97**
78	**Security**	**6d**	**Mon 10/6/97**	**Mon 10/13/97**
79	Specify security/access contol requireme	2d	Mon 10/6/97	Tue 10/7/97
80	Design access control mechanisms	2d	Wed 10/8/97	Thu 10/9/97
81	Implement security/access mechansims	2d	Fri 10/10/97	Mon 10/13/97
82	**Develop DB Facilities**	**6d**	**Tue 10/14/97**	**Tue 10/21/97**
83	Develop data storage approach for subs)	2d	Tue 10/14/97	Wed 10/15/97
84	Develop data model	2d	Thu 10/16/97	Fri 10/17/97
85	Implement data model	2d	Mon 10/20/97	Tue 10/21/97
86	**Develop Product Promotion Apps**	**11d**	**Wed 10/22/97**	**Wed 11/5/97**
87	Product Calendar	5d	Wed 10/22/97	Tue 10/28/97
88	Product Registration	3d	Wed 10/29/97	Fri 10/31/97
89	Product	3d	Mon 11/3/97	Wed 11/5/97
90	Design/Build Product Data Maintenance	8d	Wed 10/22/97	Fri 10/31/97
91	**Department Home Page**	**10d**	**Tue 11/4/97**	**Mon 11/17/97**
92	Build Department Page Wizard	10d	Tue 11/4/97	Mon 11/17/97

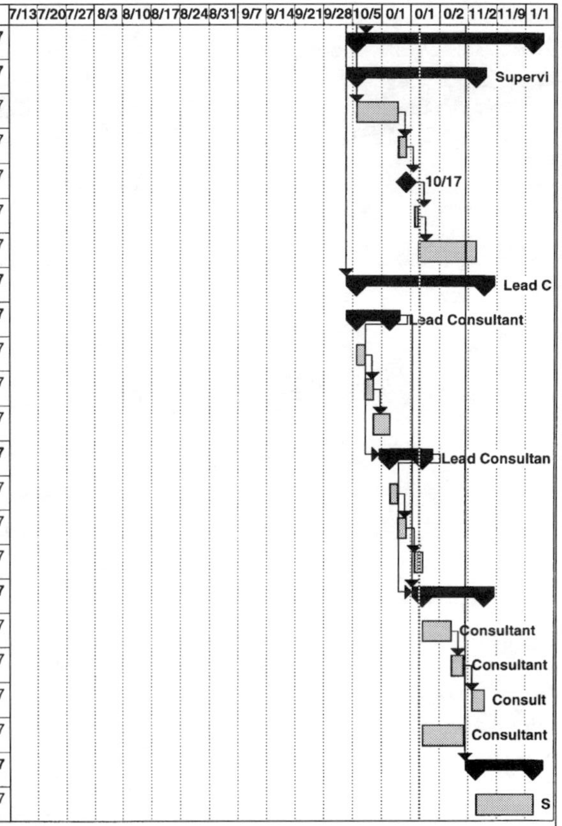

Project: Workplan 3.MPP

Task		Summary		Rolled Up Progress	
Progress		Rolled Up Task			
Milestone	◆	Rolled Up Milestone	◇		

Page 4

Figure A.3.4 Workplan 3, continued

APPENDIX B

The 12 Steps to Building an Intranet

By now, you've probably recognized that building a corporate intranet is a more complex task than just adding a Web server to your network environment. However, like any large, complex issue, building an intranet is only as complex as its component parts. If you can break up the building process into digestible pieces, then the intranet can be built in a very logical manner.

The 12-Step Program that we introduced in *Building the Corporate Intranet* is designed to accomplish that goal. It is most definitely a play on words, as we decided that any good system's "recovery" strategy must involve 12 steps! However, it is also meant to provide a comprehensive framework for thinking about and building an intranet from beginning to support. It is *not* intended to oversimplify the technology or replace expert advice.

As mentioned in Chapter 1 of this book, many times when we help a company restructure or enhance its intranet systems, we find that the company did not go through a comprehensive planning phase prior to execution. Thus, its infrastructure is often insufficient for the company's new needs, its management policies are nonexistent (this is more common than you would imagine), or it still has not chosen a core set of tools and technologies to build with (the company may choose many tools in an ad hoc manner and have trouble integrating them at production time). Consequently, a recap of the 12 steps can be a useful way to kick off our efforts. We hope that by including them here it will help you in the process as well.

Before beginning, we ask that you keep the following guiding principles in mind as you use our process:

Take I-Net systems as seriously as any other mission-critical platform.

Use existing systems methodologies that *work* as a starting point.

Use common sense.

Common sense is important, because we have noticed a tendency for some people to accept our advice without understanding the context of their own decision making. For instance, although we discuss certain tools and techniques more than others, we do *not* claim to have researched and listed them all. We simply can state that in working for a variety of different kinds of companies around the Fortune 1000, there are certain technologies that seem to work well and others that do not. We hope that you will rely as much on your own experience and good judgment as ours.

The following text is an excerpt (with minor modifications) from the overview of *Building the Corporate Intranet* (Guengerich, Graham, Miller, and McDonald, Wiley, 1996).

The Major Steps Decision Tree

Figure B.1 illustrates the overall process of planning, implementing, and managing an intranet. As you can see, the process is broken down into a series of discrete, interrelated steps. To be sure, each of the steps involves several (sometimes many) activities and decisions, but taken one by one, they add up to an implementation plan that you can address in a logical, linear fashion.

Now that you know a little more about the implementation process and the tools that we'll be using, let's summarize each of the steps in the 12-Step Program.

Step 1: Should We Implement?

This really is the fundamental question that you must deal with before moving on to the planning process. Take nothing for

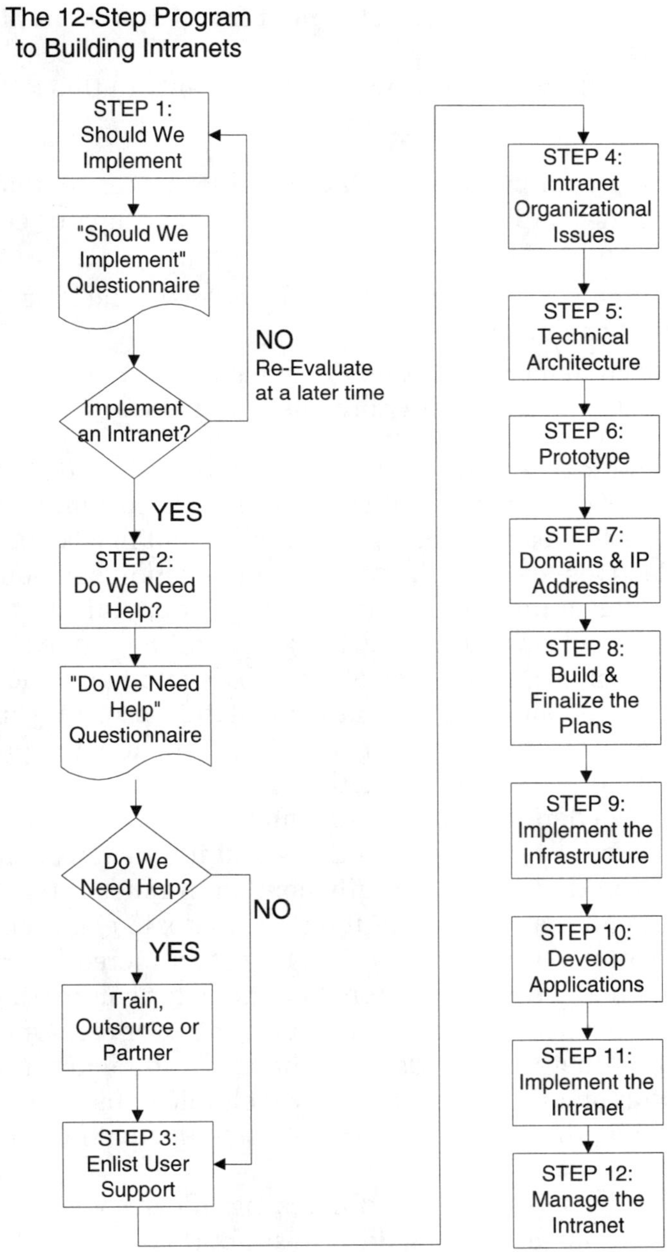

Figure B.1 Major steps decision tree.

granted; your company may not benefit from intranet implementation at this time.

Essentially, there are three major components in this decision step:

1. Defining your business goals and values to ensure that an intranet implementation is consistent with your corporate and/or IT objectives
2. Assessing your information needs to determine if an intranet can meet those needs
3. Identifying the business-enabling technology environments that support your core business values

Any technology effort, intranet or otherwise, should meet your organization's goals for the future as well as its current needs. You must be able to clearly identify both the current needs and the future objectives to determine if your organization can benefit by implementing an intranet at this time. If your organization doesn't already have a clearly defined set of goals and objectives (e.g., a mission statement), this is a good time to develop one. Ideally, at any point during a technology implementation project, you should be able to clearly identify and illustrate how the project contributes value to the organization.

After you've defined (and documented) your organization's objectives, you're ready to begin the actual intranet evaluation process. If you decide *not* to implement an intranet at this time, we recommend that you revisit the issue in six to eight months. Communications technology is changing at an incredibly rapid pace, as are many of the traditional methods for conducting business in our increasingly global economy. In six or eight months, you may find that your needs have changed sufficiently to warrant an intranet, or that the necessary technology has decreased in price to a level that makes an intranet cost-effective for your organization.

You should also keep in mind that a significant portion of technology development is being done to support and expand intranet development. Although it is doubtful that other major systems topologies are heading for extinction, this is definitely where cutting-edge solutions will be found. Can your business afford not to participate? Maybe. Some companies in slowly moving industries really can afford to wait. Take a hard look at your competitors. Are you keeping ahead of them or moving with the pack? This is why knowing your organization's objectives and strategies will so strongly influence your efforts.

If you decide that your organization can benefit from an intranet implementation at this time, you can start to assess your specific information needs and begin planning the type of intranet you want to implement.

Information needs assessment is, by definition, a complex process and one that is likely to require considerable time and energy. For this reason, many organizations choose to hire an outside consultancy to assist them in the needs assessment phase of an implementation project. But whether you decide to perform your needs assessment with in-house personnel or hire outside help, you're going to need a base set of information about your organization, users, and existing information systems.

The actual process of determining how business and technology values translate into tangible technology sets can be confusing. You'll need to evaluate a range of factors including (but not limited to) data access requirements—speed and frequency of retrievals, the integrity of your information base, and the age of your existing information system and database. Also, consider how your data should be structured or organized for consumption.

Fortunately, there are some good sources to help you with your information needs assessment and to ensure that your technology goals are consistent with your business goals. Our Technology Infrastructure Planning Service (TIPS) is an intensive, facilitated process that guides you through a complete analysis of your business and IT structure, then helps you to formulate a technology strategy for the future. There are other methods that will help you derive this information as well. The important thing is to correctly define your information needs and match them to a feasible technology strategy as part of your intranet foundation.

Step 2: Do We Need Help?

If you've decided to proceed with your intranet implementation project, your next step is finding the people power to get the job done. You've probably heard how easy the HTML authoring language is to work with (and it is!), but implementing an intranet involves numerous tasks in addition to HTML authoring—many of which are quite complex. The overall process, from these early planning stages through implementation, requires a variety of skills and experience levels. Few organizations initially have all of the resources they need to complete the process.

Of course, your existing staff is the first place to look for the resources that you'll need for your intranet implementation team. Begin by reviewing their capabilities and experience with respect to your implementation project requirements. Then, determine what additional resources you're likely to need and make plans to acquire those resources. Essentially, you have a choice of providing additional training for your in-house staff, hiring new staff members that already have experience in Inter/intranet computing, outsourcing the project to a vendor, or partnering with an expert. Each option has its merits—and drawbacks—and may represent a viable solution for your organization. The "Do We Need Help" questionnaire on our Web site (www.per-se.com) is intended to help you identify some of the key issues to consider in deciding if you do need outside help.

USING AN OUTSIDE RESOURCE

If you do decide to look outside of your organization for the skill sets you need, you still must decide what kind of help you need and to what degree. Your options range from using an independent contractor for a single facet of the project (e.g., to implement the security system) to outsourcing the entire project to a consulting firm that specializes in Inter/intranet technology. Partnering, an arrangement that combines some of the advantages of outsourcing with the advantages of in-house development, is another alternative you can consider.

The beauty of outsourcing is that it allows you to pass off the burden—all those complex considerations and decisions—to others and let them figure out how to satisfy your organization's needs. The arrangement is not without its drawbacks, however. Outsourcing is typically the most expensive type of outside help, it does little to increase you internal staff's knowledge and experience, and the success of your intranet relies almost entirely on an outside organization. Thus, your choice of an outsourcing firm is crucial to the success of your project. Our Web site (at the URL listed previously) includes a checklist to help you select an outsourcing firm—never an easy decision.

Partnering offers an excellent compromise for organizations that are wary of outsourcing (and many are) and do not have sufficient in-house experience to successfully implement an intranet. In a partnering arrangement, you share the responsibilities and benefits of an IT project with an expert provider.

If you decide to try a partnering arrangement for your intranet project, find a company with experience in intranet implementation and have it work *with* (rather than for) your organization. This type of arrangement has two distinct advantages: The partnering company brings the skills and experience that you need for the project and it works closely with your staff to build their skill level and ensure that your organization's needs are adequately addressed.

CONTINUE BUILDING YOUR PLAN

Incorporate the results of Step 2 into your intranet plan. By this time, you should be able to document your goals for the intranet and your strategy for implementing it (Step 1), as well as your plans for acquiring the necessary experience and skills to build it (Step 2). Now that you have a firm understanding of what you want to do, it's time to enlist assistance from outside of IT.

Step 3: Enlist User Support

Don't ever underestimate the value of your user community's support. Your project may be doomed from the start if the users don't support it. While this may sound overly dramatic, anyone who has been through technology migration can tell you how true it is. And the need for user support is ongoing through all phases of your intranet implementation plan and through all segments of the organization.

First, you'll need to get executive-level support for the project. This support is important for two reasons: The executives are "steering the ship" and it is your responsibility, as one of the main "engines," to let them know if there is sufficient power to reach the corporate goals. And, because the executives are ultimately responsible for paying the bills, they need to clearly understand that the intranet is a high-value decision.

After you've enlisted the backing of the executives, try to identify the grassroots decision makers in your organization and gain their support as well. These grassroots leaders exist in all organizations—and they're not necessarily the individuals with titles. They are, however, usually individuals with considerable experience and responsibility, and their support for your intranet project can be nearly as valuable as that of the executives. Making a conscious investment to win this type of support and make sure these key individuals are advocates for your project will yield significant benefits as you move toward implementation and enhancements.

When your intranet plan is complete, be sure to communicate it to the rest of the organization or, at a minimum, share it with your user base. Use whatever information distribution resources are available within your organization (i.e., electronic discussion forums, newsletters, or bulletin boards) to let people know about the intranet project—the benefits it offers to the organization as a whole and how it may affect them as individuals.

Depending on the magnitude of change that the intranet represents in your organization, you may want to consider using more sophisticated methods to communicate the who/what/why/when/how of the intranet project. Remember, change is frightening to many people and your project is much more likely to be successful if you address those fears at the beginning, rather than at the end, of the project.

COMMUNICATE VALUE

A demonstration of intranet capabilities is, unquestionably, the best way to convince users of the value of the technology. While nearly everyone knows about the existence of the Internet, surprisingly few have actually seen or used it (although this is changing rapidly!). Even individuals who are familiar with cyberspace don't fully comprehend how the medium translates to *real* business.

Above all, be honest and realistic with your future users (and everyone else in the organization, of course). You definitely don't want to encourage unrealistic expectations. If anything, let the users be pleasantly surprised that the intranet is everything they expected and a little more.

Because you'll need to maintain user support throughout the intranet project (and beyond), we recommend that you include in the intranet plan specific mechanisms for communicating with users and soliciting feedback. Typically, you'll want to devote from 5 to 10 percent of your intranet management effort to this type of ongoing communication.

Step 4: Address Organizational Issues

The intranet is a new breed of information technology. Much like the IT culture that conceived it, the intranet is a fast-paced, evolving medium that changes with ever increasing speed. So how do you reconcile this type of technology with the existing corporate IT structure—especially an IT structure that is rigidly defined or resistant to change?

NEW TIMES, NEW ORGANIZATION

The answer—and it isn't always easy—is based on making corresponding changes in the IT structure. Where there were rules and rigidity, now there must be openness and agility. Just-in-time implementations of best-of-breed technologies are requisite to the new, dynamic IT organization. In today's fast-paced IT environment, it is no longer possible to spend months or years making plans and decisions; now, there are only weeks or months to debate issues, reach decisions, and implement changes. Fortunately, the entire industry seems to be moving in the same direction; users, vendors, programmers, and support people are all adjusting to the new pace of technology—albeit at different rates and with varying levels of resistance.

MANAGING THE INTRANET CULTURE

Effectively managing the new IT organization is a challenging task. The opportunities are great, but there are also lots of opportunities for chaos—and few organizations can survive chaos, let alone remain profitable through it. Some of the potential affects of the intranet culture on organizations include increased openness, diversity, and collaboration across workgroups. Although these can be very positive changes for most organizations, they should be introduced slowly so that the company is not overwhelmed (look at the mountains of E-mail many companies endure when they first open this powerful new communications channel; now think how much more powerful intranet technology can be).

With some planning and organization, intranets do tend to be very manageable. But, as we discuss in both of our books, you'll need to consider manageability in your intranet design, and there are some trade-offs with the other major design criteria.

Step 5: Determine Technical Architecture

One of the most fundamental decisions that you'll make with regard to your intranet is the technical architecture. There are essentially five basic intranet architectures, each of which satisfies a specific set of needs. To choose the one that is right for your company, you will need to understand how the various components function together. We typically use the 10-Layer Model (described briefly in Chapter 1 of this book) to illustrate the basic components of intranet architecture and explain how they fit into the intranet infrastructure, layer by layer.

The architectural components are the heart and soul of your intranet. Be sure to thoroughly research all of the available options, then seek information and bids from as many providers as you reasonably can. And don't forget to document your decisions in the intranet implementation plan at each step along the way.

Finally, your selection of an appropriate communications technology is key to your intranet's performance. You should talk to your peers and find a good, solid Internet service provider (ISP) and telecommunications company (such as MCI, Sprint, or AT&T) to service your needs. If you already have a WAN, much of this infrastructure may be in place, but you will need to review your long-term needs. Installing an intranet can mean pushing and pulling tremendous amounts of data over your network—documents, graphics, audio clips, video clips, executable files, and who knows what else. Be sure to spend some time doing volume predictions and then leave yourself a good size buffer for growth.

Step 6: Decide on Applications and Prototype

The next step in building your intranet is to decide which applications you're going to implement in the short (3 to 6 months), medium (6 to 12 months), and long term (12 to 18 months). Obviously, you can't implement all of the selected applications at the same time, but prioritizing the information needs of the various departments and constituencies (customers, vendors, executives, etc.) will help you determine the appropriate implementation sequence.

Be warned that this process can be rather intensive, depending on the size and complexity of the applications that you're considering moving to the intranet. On the other hand, try not to let your team get bogged down in details; this is not the design phase for the applications—merely the research and prioritization.

CHOOSE A PROTOTYPE

If you have not already done so, now is the time to pick a high-value, quick-turnaround prototype that you can show to all levels of your support base. We discuss three basic types of prototypes: the "Strawman," the "Trojan Horse," and the "Glitz," all of which are intended to serve a specific purpose.

After you've prioritized your applications and determined their implementation sequence, be sure to document those decisions and the corresponding implementation schedule in your intranet plan. If possible, begin developing your prototype application immediately—even while you're still hammering out details of your plan. If you choose an appropriate prototype and have a talented staff to implement it, the prototype may well be finished before your final plan.

Step 7: Complete Registration and IP Addressing

As soon as you decide to implement an intranet, be sure to register your Internet domain name and IP address with the InterNIC—domain names are disappearing rapidly! Even if your intranet is going to be completely isolated from the outside world and you don't anticipate any need for Internet connectivity, you may well change your mind in the future. (Remember, the Internet is going to be a multibillion-dollar transaction medium for consumers and businesses alike.)

Some companies are opting to reserve domain names now—even if they don't need them yet. Registering a domain name is still remarkably inexpensive and having a good, easily identifiable name can be extremely valuable to your organization in the future. Depending on the outcome of your technical evaluation (in Step 1), you may want to reserve several domain names at once to accommodate your future needs.

Step 8: Finalize the Plan

At this stage, your intranet plan should really be taking shape and now is a good time to consider some longer-range issues for the intranet project. While you won't be dealing with the issues of migration, maintenance, and support for weeks or months yet, you should begin planning for them now and include your decisions in your intranet plan. Of course, as you get closer to the actual production environment, you may change some of your decisions, but at least you will have a structure for the entire planning and implementation process.

As you wrap up the plan, don't forget to build in management time for ongoing user interaction and communication. A relatively minimal investment in time at this stage can really pay off later in a satisfied user community. Also, put the finishing touches on the skills procurement plan you began in Step 2—adding whatever resources you think you may need. Remember, in some cases it's more expedient to hire an experienced consultant than to add to your permanent staff.

ESTIMATE TIME AND COSTS

Now is also the time to assemble all of your plan details and generate time and cost estimates. It is, unfortunately, nearly impossible to accurately estimate the cost of the hardware and software that you'll need for your intranet since prices fluctuate so wildly and vendors are bundling more and more items in their intranet-specific products. Do, however, try to list all of the various components that you know you'll need. You should be able to generate some type of ballpark cost estimate from this list; then, when you're quite close to beginning the actual implementation, obtain bids from as many suppliers as is feasible.

PLAN APPROVAL/SIGN-OFF

Depending on your organization's internal procedures, you may need to have your intranet plan reviewed and approved by multiple departments and/or levels of management. It is advisable to begin this approval/sign-off procedure as soon as possible after you finalize your plan, since it is often a lengthy process and you don't want to delay the intranet implementation.

The deliverable from this step is a working *intranet implementation plan.* Use this plan as a living document, modifying it as necessary throughout the build process. You—and your successors—will need the valuable information that you've collected during the planning stages to complete the implementation effort.

Step 9: Implement the Architecture

Now you're executing the plan! Your top priority now is to get the ball rolling on your communications infrastructure. Communications providers are notoriously slow and bureaucratic, so be sure to give yourself plenty of lead time. In fact, if you identify your communications requirements before you finish your implementation plan (and if you don't need prior approval of the entire plan), begin soliciting bids from the communications companies as early in the planning process as possible.

Building your intranet architectural infrastructure is relatively straightforward—if you chose well during the planning phases. Now is the time to solicit bids from suppliers to acquire the hardware and software you're going to need. Remember to consider essential factors like ongoing support and upgradability, along with price, when you select the necessary vendors and components. Finally, you—or the suppliers—will need to configure the various components to fit your particular intranet infrastructure.

Step 10: Develop the Applications

After you've successfully implemented your architecture, you can begin to design your intranet applications—using the implementation priority plan that you developed in Step 6. Of course, because intranet implementation is a dynamic process, you may have already started to design your applications, beginning, of course with your prototype. And, by this stage, your prototype may be up and running, having (hopefully) gained an enthusiastic user base—all of whom are clamoring for additional intranet applications.

The functional design process for an intranet is much like that for any other system. Once you understand the business processes (which, of course, you should before you lock yourself into a toolset), you can apply the appropriate technology to solve the issue at hand. Designing for the intranet does, however, differ from traditional development efforts in a number of ways. The development time frame, for example, is typically much shorter than that of traditional applications, and users are much more involved in the entire development effort—from defining application requirements through testing. And intranet applications must be designed to function within the Web environment—taking advantage of the versatility and graphics capabilities of Inter/intranet computing while maintaining compatibility with an ever increasing number of specialized tools and interfaces, as well as the numerous legacy systems that maintain huge bases of information. Finally, testing is also somewhat different in an intranet environment. Rather than a set amount of time at the end of a development project, testing in an intranet environment is an ongoing (almost constant) process in which the users and developers share responsibility for the applications. The frequent iterations of an intranet application necessarily involve regular communication between the users and the developers. In fact, it's not rare for the users in an intranet environment to do much of their own HTML coding (the current Web authoring tools are that easy to use!).

Management of the development process can be a bit different, however. By planning in advance you can use it to your advantage. Be sure to take advantage of such (now) commonalities as:

- Rapid, incremental iterations and early prototyping
- User involvement
- Location-independent development

Rapid, iterative development (i.e., the "spiral" method) is a common practice for rapid application development tools and environments like client/server and the Web. Using them means more participation and interaction with your users that hopefully will translate into a final product that meets or exceeds expectations.

Telecommuting is becoming the norm in many development shops—sometimes to places as remote as India and Ireland. The wide availability of phones, electronic mail, teleconferencing (with or without video), and Internet relay chat (a real-time chatting facility also known as IRC) are only the beginning of the collaborative tools that will make low-cost virtual workplaces a reality.

Step 11: Implement the Intranet

Once your intranet infrastructure is in place and you are implementing applications, you'll need to establish some type of information dissemination policy. Whether your IT department maintains centralized control of the information that is published on the intranet or the users have authoring tools at their disposal, you must be able to control the information that goes onto the intranet. If you don't establish policies to deal with who can (and can't) publish and to determine how information is to be linked and indexed, as well as updated and/or deleted, your intranet is likely to become a totally unorganized tangle of largely unusable information. And don't fail to consider the liability issues involved in publishing information on your intranet—especially if your intranet is available to external users (i.e., linked to the Internet).

Remember, you're likely to be swamped with requests for additional applications as soon as your intranet goes into production—especially if you've garnered user support throughout the planning process and your prototype is an unmitigated success. You can make your life a bit simpler at this stage if you plan ahead and establish some mechanisms (even if it's only your

E-mail box) for receiving suggestions, then categorizing and prioritizing them in your working intranet plan.

CONVERSION AND IMPLEMENTATION ISSUES

As with any production environment, you'll need to address conversion and implementation issues for your intranet project. Since you are most likely an IT professional, our assumption here is that you've taken a product live before, so your focus should be on intranet-specific issues that are likely to come into play as you implement the system.

It is important to track your progress throughout the intranet implementation process (as it is with any development effort), both for reporting purposes and for future reference. When you embark on your next intranet development cycle, the time and effort that you've expended in this, your initial implementation effort, will be invaluable—so don't rely on memory alone! Be sure to document each step of the way, focusing especially on your initial expectations and decisions.

Step 12: Managing the Intranet

What we've learned is that managing an intranet is a more daunting task to many than it may initially sound. Building the intranet is only the beginning, just as having a baby is only the beginning of being a parent. There is much that will need to be done to help your toddler intranet grow and mature into a productive member of society.

Many of these tasks are the usual from traditional systems management—performance monitoring, network management and administration, backup, and recovery. We have touched on those that are somewhat different in the intranet environment, but some—such as system backup—are really the same in this implementation of technology as in any other. The important thing is to remember to still do them! The elaboration on this subject from the original 12-Step Program is really what the book you are holding is all about.

APPENDIX C

Sample Policies and Procedures

As discussed in Chapters 1 and 6, the effective use of policy can help you manage your intranet and set expectations among your constituencies (users, staff, executives). The following sample baseline policies and procedures have been used as drafts for corporate policy by Per-Se consultants both internally and with clients. However, they are provided for reference only; you should work with your corporate legal counsel to develop appropriate policies for your needs.

Security Policy

Corporate security is provided in order to:

- Prevent intruders from gaining access to the organization and its information.
- Ensure the integrity of data and computer systems.
- Create a level of privacy.
- Protect against current and former employees.
- Develop a sound security policy that encompasses the entire organization.

Corporate Authentication Standard

Every user account on each multiuser machine shall have only one person authorized to use it. That user will be required to authenticate his or her identity to the system using some positive proof of identity. This proof of identity can be through the use of an approved authentication token or smart card, an approved one-time password mechanism, or an approved biometric unit. Reusable passwords will not be used for primary authentication on any machine that is ever connected to a network or modem, that is portable and carried off company property, or that is used outside of a private office.

Computer Documentation

Guideline details:

1. Introduction

   This guideline specifies the minimal documentation requirements and additional considerations for the *Company Name* network.

2. Minimum documentation requirements

   a. The following documentation is required:

      File server hardware configuration

      Network cable diagrams

      NIC listing by workstation

      Hardware/software service contracts

      Inventory of hardware/software

      Operating system configuration information

      Specific organizational policies and procedures

      A listing of all mission-critical systems and their related files

      A listing of applications that support daily operations

      A daily, weekly, and monthly schedule of when specific applications must be run

      A priority list of applications and data that must be restored in the event of a disaster

   b. There should be processes and guidelines in place for establishing LAN connectivity and eventually WAN and network management. This should include documentation of routers, bridges, and gateways.

c. Processes and guidelines should address the storage of vital company records including magnetic media, manuals, and a copy of the Business Resumption Plan off-site.

d. Processes and guidelines should be in effect for day-to-day system administrator activities such as:

   Setup of new users

   Directory structures

   Purchasing procedures for LAN hardware/software

3. Additional considerations

   a. The communication links should also be clearly identified.

   b. A comprehensive Disaster Recovery/Business Resumption Plan must be in effect. It should be maintained and tested on a regular basis. It should include all departments that provide a support function to the organization.

   c. There should be a method of tracking incident calls and guidelines for escalating issues to higher levels in the support chain when appropriate.

   d. Standardization of applications should be done to reduce conversion activity among users and not require a larger knowledge base at the help desk.

   e. A systems plan should be in place for future LAN installation, growth, and corporate direction, to ensure consistency in implementation and future WAN connectivity.

   f. Network components that concentrate cabling should be secured. All cabling should be identified and recorded on a network diagram. Procedures for troubleshooting the LAN should be established to minimize disruption and erroneous disconnection.

Computer Viruses

Guideline details:

1. Introduction

   This guideline outlines the procedures that protect company network facilities from becoming contaminated by computer viruses. The IT Department *requires* all employees to adhere to these guidelines.

2. Software scanning

   All software will be scanned for viruses and found uncontaminated before it can be loaded.

   a. (*Company Name*) personnel should scan all software media before use.

   b. All employees must report virus detections to the LAN Administrator immediately.

3. Unlicensed software

   In the event that your job requires the loading of unlicensed "test" or "evaluation" software—including any "free" diskettes or programs and data obtained from public or private bulletin boards—please follow the following guidelines.

   a. The downloading of software or data to a company workstation is permitted only under strictly controlled conditions, to isolated local workstations only, *not to a server.* Anything that is downloaded must be scanned before it is allowed on the LAN.

   b. Download software only to a nonnetwork drive.

   c. A known uncontaminated backup of the system must be available before any new software is loaded, in case a step-back is required.

4. LAN maintenance

   a. The LAN Administrator will scan all vendor maintenance (diagnostic) diskettes before they are allowed to be loaded.

b. (*Company Name*) personnel will supervise vendor maintenance personnel at all times.

5. Network and stand-alone scanning
   a. LAN Administrators will perform regular scans of network and local drives using Intel's LANDesk VirusProtect. An NLM module will run on the server at all times to scan incoming files and the most current image file.
   b. Intel's VSCAND DOS-based product will scan all (*Company Name*) workstations on a weekly basis. (*Company Name*) employees can also run this DOS-based scanner (VSCAND.EXE or run SCAN.BAT) or the Windows-based utility, Intel Virus Protect. This icon will be located on the network under Network Utilities (or Windows Utilities in some offices).
   c. (*Company Name*) employees must scan their portable computers (including laptops and notebooks) periodically (at least once a week). Intel's licensing permits users to download the software to disk for home use, as long as they are a (*Company Name*) employee; and (*Company Name*) is officially licensed. The icon is located on the network under Intel Virus Protect.

LICENSED SOFTWARE

Guideline details:

1. Introduction

   This guideline outlines the procedures that protect the company from legal liability and assure compliance with software licensing arrangements. The IS Department *requires* all employees to adhere to these guidelines.
2. License agreements
   a. (*Company Name*) policy prohibits unauthorized copying.
   b. Only software licensed by (*Company Name*) or developed by (*Company Name*) personnel will be allowed on our systems.

3. (*Company Name*) will provide sufficient software and software licenses for use on (*Company Name*) PCs used by its personnel. This process will include all desktop PCs in (*Company Name*) offices, portable PCs, and PCs located at company sites.

   (*Company Name*) will acquire the licenses necessary to remain within software licensing guidelines for each software package that the company uses. (*Company Name*) IS will monitor the actual legal usage of these licenses.

   (*Company Name*) will not purchase software for PCs owned by employees.
4. Installation

   The user must virus scan licensed software and evaluation copies of licensed software before it is installed. If the software proves suspect, the user may not load it. Notify the LAN Administrator immediately.
5. Signature authority

   Only an appropriate company officer (CFO, CEO) can sign a licensing agreement that obligates the company in any manner and that requires a signature.
6. Students

   It is (*Company Name*) policy that software residing on (*Company Name*) systems is not to be copied to media except when being backed up. All customers who attend a (*Company Name*) training course will be informed about this policy and will be instructed *not* to bring diskettes to our training facilities.

PASSWORD SECURITY

Guideline details:

1. Introduction

   This guideline outlines the steps for the proper use of workstation and LAN passwords. Passwords are a first line of defense; they represent one of the most effective means of protecting company data from unauthorized exposures. The IT Department *requires* all employees to adhere to these guidelines.

2. Password security procedure
   a. Each user must enter a user ID and password in order to gain access to company data and software (LAN or workstations).
   b. Set passwords at a length of at least five characters.
   c. Create unique passwords and change them at least every 30 days. Do not choose a password that can be easily guessed (common names). It is recommended that the system password generator be used. Software will be run periodically to detect inappropriate passwords.
   d. Keep passwords confidential and never reveal them to anyone. Sharing passwords is a violation of company policy. If more than one person requires access to a file, they should each be granted access by the LAN administrator.
   e. Do not change passwords to previously used passwords (the LAN Operating System will keep track of the last ten passwords used and will not let them be repeated).
   f. Protect mail server and workstation keyboards and screens (e.g., PC/DACS) with screen blinker and keyboard lock software that require a password to gain access. All employees will use time-out features and will set them for a no more than ten-minute inactivity level.

Software Purchases

Guideline details:

Company Name's goals are to (1) *stay legal,* (2) get the best price we can, and (3) make the acquisition process for the user as simple and painless as possible.

Purchase and expense:

If the software to be purchased is for a development or special office function *and*

If the software is not something that is part of (*Company Name*)'s standard product set (such as MS Office) *and*

If the purchase price is less than $1,000

The employee should purchase directly from his/her preferred source and expense the purchase via credit card. Upon receipt, send the registration and license information to IT Records (for tracking purposes). Keep original warranty/proof of purchase with software to use for upgrades.

SOFTWARE REQUEST FORM

If your software purchase does not meet the criteria above, create a request via the Software Request form in your mail file.

Conduct—Standards of Professional Conduct

Guideline details:

It is especially important that employees maintain the highest degree of professionalism. Excessive personal phone calls or attending to personal business are examples of unacceptable conduct. Dating company personnel is discouraged and could result, depending on the circumstances, in being transferred from the project or being subject to disciplinary action. It is highly recommended that you discuss any such situation with your supervisor.

In addition, because of the position of responsibility that some employees assume, it is likely that you will gain knowledge of sensitive or confidential information about the company, our vendors, and our customers. Employees must recognize this position and honor it by not discussing company-related matters in public or leaving company-related documents in a place subject to company exposure. Violating this company trust is an example of misconduct.

Equipment

Process details:

Introduction

The purpose of this process is to guide those (*Company Name*) personnel who are responsible for ordering and receiving hardware and software. It also contains general information regarding software use that is applicable to all employees.

1. Equipment requests
2. Liability for lost or stolen equipment
3. Equipment chargebacks
4. Delivery policy
5. Equipment returns and transfers
6. Purchase of hardware/software needed to complete project work
7. Getting hardware/software prices for proposals

E-Mail and Other Document Privacy

Process details:

Messages on (*Company Name*)'s E-mail systems should not be considered private.

While (*Company Name*) does not routinely monitor E-mail systems, legitimate needs may exist for us to do so in specific cases, including but not limited to the following:

1. Discovery in lawsuits: E-mail records have been subpoenaed in various civil lawsuits.
2. Harassment lawsuits: Employers have faced claims of harassment when the harasser uses the E-mail system as a tool.

All employees should be aware that

1. Our E-mail system and (*Company Name*)'s computer systems are (*Company Name*) property and should be used for company purposes only.

2. Any document in a (*Company Name*)'s computer system is the property of (*Company Name*).
3. Employees should disclose documents from (*Company Name*) E-mail and other computer systems only to other authorized employees.
4. (*Company Name*) reserves the right to monitor E-mail and any document in its systems to ensure that (*Company Name*) property is used for (*Company Name*) purposes only.
5. Employees do not have a personal privacy right in any matter created, received, or sent using (*Company Name*) E-mail systems or (*Company Name*) computer systems in general.
6. No E-mail messages should be created or sent that might violate any (*Company Name*) policies, including intimidating, hostile, or offensive material on the basis of sex, race, color, religion, national origin, sexual orientation, or disability.
7. (*Company Name*) will take corrective and/or disciplinary action if we become aware of misuse of any part of our technology platform.

Computer Backup

Process details:

1. Introduction

   In the event of a loss of system resources (e.g., because of a disaster), the company's survival may depend upon being able to restore data and software within a reasonable amount of time. To ensure that we have that capability, it is (*Company Name*) policy that these resources must be protected through regular backups.
2. Performing backups

   All company data and software will be backed up on a regular basis to ensure that normal operations can be restored in a minimal amount of time. Backups will be done at least daily (partial) and weekly (full). Partial backups will involve saving all changes made to software and data since the most recent backup was completed. Certain critical systems may require more frequent (even continuous) backups. It is a manager's responsibility to determine frequency requirements. The LAN Administrators will perform LAN backups.

All (*Company Name*) mail servers will be backed up on a daily basis. If possible, a tape backup system will be attached to it. Tapes will be secured per the (Company Name) *Backup Tape Rotation Guideline* (double-click here to access this guideline).

3. Off-site storage

   At least one backup copy and its father will be kept off-site, in a physically protected, climate-controlled area. This policy includes backup tapes, diskettes, CD-ROM, and so on, and their logs.

4. Restoration

   There should be a regular test of the restoration function of the tape management system. This test should be done on a monthly basis, if not more frequently.

5. Backup system

   The tape system should be certified by the operating system vendor and should include such features as:

   a. A standard backup system/vendor for each operating system environment
   b. Unattended backup
   c. An error log (to be reviewed daily)
   d. A prearranged agreement for replacement within 24 hours

6. Security

   a. Backup tapes should be secured when not being used for backup.

Company Intranet Team

The (*Company Name*) intranet is a company resource designed to facilitate and expedite the sharing of information. The guiding vision is a knowledge capture and sharing system that will give our employees the information to work efficiently and productively. Our goals are to

- Encourage departments to develop information sharing through Web technology.
- Serve as the umbrella for net-based information management.
- Provide an infrastructure for net-based systems that ensures that it meets mission-critical standards.

Guidance and feedback is provided by the Inter/Intranet *Steering Committee* that has representatives from around the company. This group, which meets monthly, makes the visionary decisions for the (*Company Name*) intranet and is the ultimate policymaking body for the effort.

The (*Company Name*) Intranet *Management Team* is a core group of Steering Committee members that dedicate a larger amount of their time to responding to Inter/intranet issues and concerns. This group convenes whenever operations decisions need to be made (usually semimonthly).

The day-to-day operations of the (*Company Name*) intranet are the responsibility of the IT Inter/Intranet Team, supporting the needs of all (*Company Name*) intranet users. This group actively works with Systems Engineering and Security to ensure that the (*Company Name*) intranet is a harmonious contributor to the full (*Company Name*) IT environment.

Questions, concerns, and general information about the (*Company Name*) intranet—its vision, purpose, operation, and participants—may be obtained by contacting the Inter/Intranet Team office.

Internet/Intranet Usage Policy

Guideline details:

Introduction

With technology comes both opportunity and responsibility. Use of the (*Company Name*) intranet, including the software, hardware, and information that compose it, constitutes your agreement to adhere to the following.

The intranet is solely for (*Company Name*) information dissemination and use.

Intranet components including browser software and modems are for (*Company Name*) business use only. They are not to be used for Internet/World Wide Web access, online service providers (e.g., CompuServe, America Online), or access to noncompany entities.

If you require external access, contact IT for information and follow the External Access Policy.

If you do access external entities of any kind, you are responsible for performing virus scans as appropriate and taking other reasonable precautions to protect (*Company Name*) from external agents and security breaches. Refer to the External Access Policy for more information.

Viewing, distributing, and/or downloading of material of any kind and in any medium that is in conflict with (*Company Name*) values is strictly prohibited. This includes anything that can be construed as libelous or offensive. Refer to other (*Company Name*) policies on equal opportunity, nondiscrimination, sexual harassment, conduct, and gaming/gambling for more information.

Failure to adhere to this policy constitutes grounds for disciplinary action up to and including termination.

INDEX

A

access, controlling news servers
  by address, 158
  by user, 159
ActiveX controls, client management
  advantages in using, 48
  described, 48
  disadvantages, 49–50
  tip for finding, 49
  vs. Java, 50
ADC (Advanced Data Connector), 231
Adobe Acrobat, software distribution, 54
address, intranet building, 395
addressing
  logical, 94
  physical, 94
administrator/developer, roles and responsibilities, 12. *See also* Web administrator's checklist
AltaVista, search engines, 219
analysis tools, performance tuning, 169
anonymous user log in, 151
application
  10-layer model, 35–37
  development subprocesses roles, 20
  flow development, 19
application conflict, client management, 43, 44
application instrumentation, 132
applications, intranet, 223. *See also* 12 steps to building an intranet; intranet
  categories of, 224
  change, impact of, 225
  daily management, 225
    auditing, 227
    backups, 228
    data protection layers, 225
    performance monitoring, 228
    program access, controlling, 226
    security combinations, 227
    security concerns, 225
    security integration, 226
  development, intranet building, 398
  development time line, 225
  expansion of, 229
    reasons for, 231
    security implications, 229–230
  extension of, 230
    caveat, layering, 231
    functionality, 230
    options in, 230
  functionality, increasing, 223–224
  satisfying business need, 224
  summary, 257
  technology change, 232
    choosing initial set, 233
    ground rules, 235
    limiting change, 236
    planning for change, 234
    reacting to change, 236
approval and sign off, intranet building, 397
approval processes, content management, 203
  extending the environment, 209
approver, content management, 13, 14
architecture implementation, intranet building, 397
Argus, security tool, 310

ARP (Address Resolution Protocol) spoofing, 275
access, managing, 277
accidental, 275
intentional, 276
list example, 276
process of, 275
ASP (Active Server Pages), 164
development of, 239
migrating from CGI, 249
workplan projects outlines
application development, 377–379
asymmetric key, encryption, 286
attacks, emulating, 297
auditing, 227
authoritative reply, DNS, 282

B

backplane, 102
backups, 228
policy guidelines, 410
BackWeb, push technology, 217
bandwidth management, network communications, 78
basic network infrastructure, 80
elastic applications, 81
traffic, routing with network segments, 79
big-endian processors, 327
bootp, IP addressing, 108
relay agents, DHCP and, 109
breaches, security, 260
broadcast technology, 217
recommendations for, 217
browser
10-layer application model, 35
impact, performance tuning, 171
software distribution, 51
building intranets. *See* 12 steps to building and intranet; intranet
business process layer entry point, 314
business services layer integration, 324
MOM, 336
ORBs, 341, 346
publish and subscribe, 340, 343
RPCs, 325

C

capacity planning, network communications, 92–93
Castanet, push technology, 217
CC-NUMA (cache coherent NUMA), 127–129
CERT (U.S. Computer Emergency Response Team), 291
CGI (Common Gateway Interface), 36
intranet application server software, 161
migrating to ASP, 2491
effort, 255
planning, 249
results, 256
time, 253
change, addressing in intranet building, 393
CIAC (Computer Incident Advisory Capability Group), 290
client browser, 10-layer model, 35
client management, 43. *See also* management
10-layer model analysis, 38
application conflict, 43
classic client/server, 43–44
thin-client intranet, 43–44
configuration management, 60–61
DMI (Desktop Management Interface), 62–64
hardware issues, 61, 62
operating system, 62
SMS (Systems Management Server), 66–69, 76
SNMP (Simple Network Management Protocol), 64–66
software distribution, 51
Adobe Acrobat, 54
browsers, 52, 53
conferencing software, 54
custom install scripts, 51–52
mail and news readers, 53–54
security, 55
systems management server (SMS), 52
specialized viewers, 54–55
summary, 76

client management *(Continued)*
technology options, 44–45
ActiveX controls, 48–50
client-side scripting, 46–48
DHTML, 45–46
HTML, 45
Java, 50–51
Netscape plug-ins, 50
client-side scripting, client management, 46
code management caveat, 48
compatibility concerns, 46, 47
cluster. *See also* clustering
DB environment, 136
clustering
architecture, 122, 123
vs. SMP model, 123, 124
cluster
architecture, 126
characteristics, 123
loss of one node, 124
near term vendor solutions, 127
NT clustering, 125
scalability and high availability, 124, 125
COAST (Computer Operations, Audit, and Security Technology), 292
COB (continuity of business), 138
considerations in, 138–140
coherency, clustering, 123
COM (Component Object Model), 134, 348
ORBs, 341
CORBA-COM interoperability, 351
Common Gateway Interface. *See* CGI
communications technology, intranet building, 394
competitive advantage, via security, 261
computer documentation, policy guidelines, 402
computer viruses, policy guidelines, 404
conduct, professional, policy guidelines, 408
conferencing software, software distribution, 54
custom install scripts, software distribution, 51, 52
content, organization and management, 177. *See also* 12 steps to building an intranet; Web administrator's checklist
10-layer model analysis, 39, 40
archiving old content, 185
approval processes, 203
extending the environment, 209
approver, roles and responsibilities, 13, 14
distribution, push technology, 214
broadcast technology, 216
challenges for intranet, 216
tools for, 217
using, 220, 221
effectiveness of, 213
quantifying, 214
tools for, 213
link management, 211
organizing, 177, 178
editorial calendar, 185–188
functional maps, 180–183, 184
interface design documentation, 183–185
site maps, 178–180
search engines, 218
recommendations for, 219
standards, 188, 190–194
development and administration, 190
single accountability, importance of, 188
templates, creating, 192
summary, 219
version management, 201
software feature recommendations, 202
workplan projects outlines
content management expansion, 380–383
COPS, security tool, 309
CORBA (Common Object Request Broker Architecture)
objects, network capacity and, 102
ORBs and, 350
CORBA-COM interoperability, 351
key terms in, 350
stack, 351
TPM and, 134–135

corporate authentication standard, policy guidelines, 401
cost
  estimation, intranet building, 396
  of not developing, intranet building, 388
Courtney, security tool, 309
CPM, security tool, 309
custom software installation set, preparing. *See also* client management
  effort, 58–60
  planning, 56–58
  results, 60
  time, 58

D

daemon, RIP, 280
daily management. *See* management; Web administrator's checklist
DASDs (direct access storage devices), 102
data access layer integration, 352
  TPMs (Transaction Process Monitors), 353
Data Communications magazine, 6
data protection layers, 225
Database Management System. *See* DBMS
database servers, 160
  security, levels of, 161
DBMS (Database Management System), 37
DCOM (Distributed Component Object Model), 341
DDA (Demand Deposit Accounting), 266
decision tree, intranet building, 386
DES (data encryption standard), 285
Desktop Management Interface. *See* DMI
development process management, intranet building, 398
DHCP (Dynamic Host Control Protocol), 109–111
  vs. DNS, 97
DHTML, client management, 45, 46
disaster, security threat, 302
disk usage, performance tuning, 175, 176
DLL (dynamic link libraries), 162
DMI (Desktop Management Interface), 38
  configuration management, 62–66
DNS (domain naming service), 95, 96
  copyrights and branding, 99, 100
  future of, 100, 101
  how to name, 96, 97
  mail servers, 155
  naming hierarchy, 98
  spoofing, 281
  system redundancy and, 97
  unresolved names, 99
  vs. DHCP use, 97
DOD security classifications, 291
domain names, 96. *See also* DNS
  reservation, 396
downstream servers, 158

E

e-mail, policy guidelines, 409
editorial calendar, organizing content, 185
  example, 189
  generic calendar, 187, 188
  importance of using, 187
  location of, 187
EHLLAPI (Extended High Level Language Application Programming Interface), 315
elastic traffic, 80
  conditions affecting, 81–83
electronic signals, as threat, 303
encryption, 285
  asymmetric key, 286
  legal issues and, 286
  private key, 285
  public key, 285
  solutions, 287–289
equipment, policy guidelines, 409
Excite!, search engines, 219
executive-level support, importance of, 391
expansion, application 229
  workplan projects outlines
    intranet application expansion, 371–376
extension, application, 230
external connections, as threat, 304
extranet, vs. Internet, intranet, VPN, 20, 21

F

failover, 103
firewall
  NAT-capable, 107
  usage, 292
FPUs (floating-point units), 68
FTP (File Transport Protocol), 79
  server software, 151–152
full mesh interface model, 340
functional design process, intranet building, 398
functional maps, 180
  functional information flow, 183, 184

G

Gabriel, security tool, 309
GIFs (graphic interface formats), 13
graphic interface formats. *See* GIFs
GUID (Globally Unique ID), RPC, 326

H

hardware, 10-layer application model, 37
hardware, evolution of, 113, 114
  architectures, 116, 117
    clustering, 122–127
    comparisons in, 118, 119
    MPP (massively parallel processing), 129, 130
    NUMA (non uniform memory access), 127–129
    SMP (symmetric multiprocessing), 117, 118, 119, 121, 122
  COB (continuity of business), 138
    considerations in, 139, 140
  IBM mainframes, 115
    legacy platforms, 116
  network design, 137, 138
  server platform, 114, 115
  Web server software, 130, 131
    application type, 131–137
hardware issues, configuration management, 61, 62
hop count, RIP, 280
host names, 97
HLLAPI (High Level Language Application Programming Interface), 315
HTML, client management, 45
HW. *See* hardware

I

IBM mainframes, hardware evolution, 115
  legacy platforms, reasons for using, 116
IDL (Interface Definition Language), RPC, 326
IETF (Internet Engineering Task Force), 85, 86
ifstatus, security tool, 309
IIS (Internet Information Server), Microsoft, 130
  access privileges, 150
  as a true server, 148
  configuration options for, 148, 149
  content directory mappings, 149, 150
  first-pass access control, 150
  managing applications with InterDev, 239–250
  starting and stopping caveat, 149
  user interfaces, management functions, 149
  virtual servers, specifying, 150
inelastic traffic, 80
information needs assessment, intranet building, 389
Information Superhighway, 2
information systems, 20, 21
information technology. *See* IT
integration, systems. *See* legacy systems integration
InterDev, managing IIS applications with, 237
  effort, 244
    SourceSafe, procedures for using, 245
    tracking files status, 244
  planning, 237
    ASP development, 239
    assigning server roles, 243
    development servers, using, 238
    file progression, 240

importance of, 237
Internet application layers, importance of, 241
server specific trees, 242
testing changes and new apps, 237
results, 248
time, 243
interface design documentation, organizing content, 183
internal resources, intranet building, 390
Internet
access, increases in, 2
as security threat, 292
protocol. *See* IP
vs. intranet, extranet, VPN, 20, 21
intranet. *See also* 10-Layer Model; 12 steps to building an intranet; applications
ad hoc, clarity issues and, 21
as mission-critical technology, 3
culture, intranet building, 393
development, guidelines for developing, 195–197
functionality, increasing, 223
implementation, examining, 7–10
12-step plan in, 8, 9
increasing importance of, 1, 2
management, 4
10-layer model, 28, 35–40
people, 5
process, 5
summary of, 41
technology, 5, 6
misconceptions in, 7
planning phase, examining, 7–9
process, 10
roadblocks to development of, 2
roles and responsibilities, 12
server application software, 161. *See also* performance tuning; Web server software
ASP (Active Server Pages), 164
CGI, 161–162
distribution, 167
ISAPI, 163–164
LiveWire, 164
NSAPI, 162–163
performance tuning, 169–176
version control, 164–167
servers, 143, 144
strategy, importance of, 7
team, policy guidelines, 412
technologies involved in, 3
technology change, handling, 232
10-Layer Model, 4
vs. Internet, extranet, VPN, 20, 21
WWW resources, 5
Intranet Design Webzone, 6
IP (Internet protocol), 1
addressing, 101
determining class address, 105
dynamic addressing, 108
IPv6, tips for migrating to, 105, 106
setting up IP environment, 107
technology alternatives, 108–111
IP traffic management challenges, 83, 85
PacketShaper, 88
RSVP (Resource Reservation Protocol), 86–88
solutions, 85, 86
ISA (Integrated Services Architecture), purpose of, 80, 81
ISAPI, 163, 164
ISS, security tool, 309
IT (information technology), 1
changing role of, 10, 11
infrastructure support, 14, 15
iterative
reply, DNS, 282
request, DNS, 283

J

Java, client management, 50
classes and libraries, viewing, 51
vs. ActiveX controls, 50

L

LAN (local area network), 47
latency, performance management, 91

legacy systems integration, 311
architecting for, 311
implications of, 312
point of entry, 312
business process layer entry point, 314
business services layer integration, 324
MOM, 336
ORBs, 341
publish and subscribe, 340
RPCs, 325
data access layer integration, 352
TPMs (Transaction Process Monitors), 353
presentation layer integration, 314
advantages, 315
drawbacks, 316
stored procedures, using, 321
summary, 355
Web legacy integration, example, 317
legal approver, roles and responsibilities, 14
legal issues, encryption, and, 286
licensed software, policy guidelines, 405
link management, content management, 211
little-endian processors, 327
LOBs (lines of business), 77
logical addressing, 94
logs
managing, 167
performance tuning, 176
LiveWire, 164
LUW (logical unit of work), 183
Lycos, search engines, 219

M

MAC (Media Access Control), 326
layer address, 108
mail
news readers and, software distribution, 53, 54
servers, 153
client access to mail, 155, 156
connectivity for, 154
DNS, handling mail, 155
POP3 (Post Office Protocol), 156
mailbox configurations, 156
server-server configuration, 155
tasks of, 153, 154
transferring mail between servers, 154, 155
transferring between servers, 154, 155
mailbox configurations, mail servers, 156
management, 4, 225–229. *See also* client management
10-Layer Model, 28, 35–40
intranet, 400
people, 5
process, 5
summary of, 41
technology, 5, 6
marshalling data, 327
mechanical failure, as threat, 302
Microsoft Internet Information Server. *See* IIS
middleware, Microsoft products
MSMQ (Microsoft Message Queue Server), 313
MTS (Microsoft Transaction Server), 313
MOM (Message-Oriented Middleware), 336. *See also* legacy systems integration
advantages, 336
asynchronous process of, 340
drawbacks, 337
intranet integration strategy, as part of, 338
queue-queue, 336
MPP (massively parallel processing), 129, 130
MS COM/DCOM, network capacity, 103
MSMQ (Microsoft Message Queue Server), 313
MTS (Microsoft Transaction Server), 313
MTTR (mean-time-to-recover) constraints, database implementation, 136
classification categories, 140, 141

N

naming standards, 93
Internet connections and, 93
IP addresses, use of, 93, 94

NAT-capable (Network Address Translation) firewall, 107, 108
Netlog, security tool, 310
Netscape Application Programming Interface. *See* NSAPI
Netscape Enterprise Server, 145. *See also* Web server software
  access to server, 146, 147
  configuration file information, 145, 146
  content, controlling, 14
  functionality, adding to, 145
  improving response time, 146
  physical path mappings, URL to, 148
  popularity of, 145
  script files, designating, 147, 148
  server configuration, 156
Netscape plug-ins, client management, 50
network communications, 77, 78
  addressing, issues in, 93–95
  bandwidth management, 79
    basic network infrastructure, 80
    elastic applications, 80–81
    ISA, purpose of, 80, 81
    traffic, routing with network segments, 79
  capacity planning, 92, 93
  DNS (domain naming service), 95, 96
    copyrights and branding, 99, 100
    future of, 100, 101
    how to name, 96, 97
    naming hierarchy, 98
    system redundancy and, 97
    unresolved names, 99
    vs. DHCP use, 97
    what to name, 97
  expanding network capacity, dealing with, 102
    design flexibility, 103
  fault isolation, 92
  infrastructure management, importance of, 77, 78
  IP addressing, 101
    determining class address, 105
    dynamic addressing, 108
    IPv6, tips for migrating to, 105, 106
    setting up IP environment, 107
    technology alternatives, 108–111
  IP traffic management challenges, 83, 85
    PacketShaper, 88
    RSVP (Resource Reservation Protocol), 86–88
    solutions, 85, 86
  naming standards, 93
    Internet connections and, 93
    IP addresses, use of, 93, 94
  network management solutions, 78
  performance management, 91
    latency, 91
    queue length, 91
    throughput, 91
  summary, 111, 112
  umbrella managers, 88
    best-of-breed, 88–90
    integrated, 90, 91
network communications services, 10-layer application model, 35, 36
network computer, 62
network design, hardware evolution, 137, 138
network level, performance tuning, 172
network management, 10-layer model analysis, 38, 39
  solutions, 78
network PC, 62
Network Solutions, domain naming, 100
news access, providing, 159, 160
news servers, 156
  configuring, 157, 158
  controlling access, 158–159
  downstream servers, dealing with, 158
  news access, providing, 159, 160
  NNTP (Network News Transfer Protocol), 157
  NT security integration, importance of, 159
  operating news server, 160
  protocol usage, 157
  typical configuration, 157
NIC (Network Interface Card), 108
  spoofing, 274

NID (Network Intrusion Detector), security tool, 309
NNTP (Network News Transfer Protocol), 157
NOCOL, security tool, 310
nonauthoritative reply, 282
NSAPI (Netscape Application Programming Interface), 36, 162
  limitations of, 163
NT security integration, importance of, 159
NUMA (non uniform memory access), 127
  CC-NUMA, 128, 129
  physical implementation of, 128
  RMC, 127, 128
  SMC, 127

O

Object Management Group, 85
.OCX, file extension, 48
ODBC (Open Database Connectivity), log management, 168
OLTP, Web server software, 134
  application platform design, 135
operating news server, 160
operating system
  configuration management, 62
  services, 10-layer application model, 37
OPS (Oracle's Parallel Server), 124
ORBs (Object Request Brokers), 341. *See also* legacy systems integration
  COM, 348
    CORBA-COM interoperability, 351
  CORBA, 349
    key terms in, 350
    stack, 351
  legacy integration role, 346
  objects
    intranet environment, 346
    producer-consumer model, implementing, 348
organizational
  goal, intranet building, 388
  issues, intranet building, 393
outside resources, intranet building, 390
owner, roles and responsibilities, 11, 12

P

packet sniffer, performance tuning, 172, 173
password
  security, policy guidelines, 406
  strategies, 297
people and process, 10
  intranet management, 5
  methodology, 24
    goals and objectives, 24–26
    policies and procedures, 26–28
  roles and responsibility, 10, 11
    administrator/developer, 12, 13
    assigning, 16–18
    changing IT roles, 10, 11
    content approver, 13, 14
    intranet roles and responsibilities, 12
    IT infrastructure support, 14, 15
    legal approver, 14
    owner, 11, 12
    production/application manager, 16
    project/application sponsor, 16
    role relationships in intranet management, 20–24
    roles working together, 18–20
    users, 15
    Webmaster, 12
people, as threat, 305
performance monitoring, 228
performance tuning, intranet server, 169
  analysis tools, 169, 170
  browser impact, 171
  complications in, 169
  disk usage, 175, 176
  logs, importance of, 176
  network level, 172
  packet sniffer, using, 172, 173
  print services performance, 169
  software component issues, 174
  standard services functions, 171
  tools, 170
PGP (pretty good privacy), encryption, 285

physical addressing, 94, 95
physical threat, 301
PointCast I-Server, push technology, 217
policies and procedures
  importance of communicating, 28
  intranet building, 399
  sample guidelines, 401
    backup, computer, 410
    conduct, 408
    computer documentation, 402
    computer viruses, 404
    corporate authentication standard, 401–402
    e-mail, 409
    equipment, 409
    intranet team, 412
    licensed software, 405
    password security, 406
    privacy, 409
    security policy, 401
    software purchases, 407
    software request form, 408
    usage policy, Internet/intranet, 413
POP3 (Post Office Protocol), mail servers, 156
presentation, 10-layer model, 35
presentation layer integration, 314
  advantages, 315
  drawbacks, 316
  stored procedures, using, 321
print services performance, performance tuning, 169
privacy, policy guidelines, 409
private key, encryption, 285
procedures. *See* policies and procedures
process, intranet management, 5. *See also* people and process
production/application manager, roles and responsibilities, 16
program access, controlling, 226
programmed threats, 303
project/application sponsor, roles and responsibilities, 16
promiscuous mode, snooping, 266
prototype selection, intranet building, 395
proxy servers, 152
  features for intranet, 152, 153
  support for, 153
  working, 152
public key, encryption, 285
publish and subscribe, 340. *See also* legacy systems integration
  example, 343–346
  maintenance issues, 341
push technology, content distribution, 214
  broadcast technology, 217
  challenges for intranet, 216
  tools for, 217–219
  using, 220–221
  vs. pull technology, 216, 217
PVCS, content and version management, 210, 212

Q

queue length, performance management, 91
QuickServer, push technology, 218

R

RAOD (redundant array of independent disks), 102
RDS (Remote Data Services), 230
recursive reply, DNS, 282
redundant intranet design, 103, 104
registration and address, intranet building, 395
remote procedure call. *See* RPC
RIP (Routing Information Protocol), spoofing, 280
RMC (replicated memory cluster), 127, 128. *See also* clustering
routers, 79
role relationships in intranet management, roles and responsibilities, 20–24
roles and responsibility. *See also* people and process
  assigning, 16–18
  role relationships in intranet management, 20–23
  roles working together, 18–20

root-level vulnerabilities, strategy for, 299
root server, 67
routers and routing protocols, spoofing, 278
  ICMP (Internet Control Message Protocol), 279
    methods for, 279
    preventing ICMP attacks, 279
  RIP, spoofing, 280
RPC (remote procedure call), 37
  business services layer integration, 324. *See also* legacy systems integration
    alternatives, 326
    client side process, 327
    DCE RPC client module example, 327
    fitting into integration model, 335
    limitations of using, 336
    UNIX support for, 336
    work division, 326
RSVP (Resource Reservation Protocol), 86–88

S

search engines, content management, 218
  importance to intranets, 218
  recommendations for, 219
security, 259
  attacks, emulating, 297
  breaches, major cause of, 260
  checklist, security actions, 305
  combinations, 227
  competitive advantage via, 261
  concerns, 225
  encryption, 285
    asymmetric key, 286
    described, 285
    legal issues and, 286
    private key, 285
    public key, 285
    solutions, 287
  firewall usage, 292, 294
  goals for, 262
  implications, application expansion, 229
  information resources, 289
  integration, 226
  Internet threat, 292
  management, 10-layer model analysis, 40
  NT environment, 259
  organizations concerned with, 290
    CERT, 291
    CIAC, 290
    COAST, 290
    DOD security classifications, 291
  password strategies, 297
  physical design
    importance of, 264
    incorporating trust level and interaction, 272
    secured network design, 273
  policy guidelines, 401
  root-level vulnerabilities, strategy for, 299
  snooping, 266
    challenges in, 266
    need for, 267
    overcoming challenges, 268
    promiscuous mode, snooping, 266
  software distribution, 59
  spoofing, 274
    ARP (Address Resolution Protocol), 275
    DNS, 281
    hardware access, 274
    routers and routing protocols, 278
  sufficiency, 261
  threats
    categories of, 301
    evaluating, 294
  tools, 309
  trust issues, 264
    trust diagram, 269–270
  UNIX environment, 259
  VPIs, increasing use of, 260
server application interface, 10-layer model, 35, 36
server management, 10-layer model analysis, 39
server platform, hardware evolution, 114, 115
server-server configuration, mail servers, 155
server software, 143
  importance of, 143
  intranet server application software, 161
    ASP (Active Server Pages), 164
    CGI, 161, 162

distribution, 167
ISAPI, 163, 164
LiveWire, 164
NSAPI, 162, 163
performance tuning, 169–176
version control, 164–167
intranet servers, 143, 144
logs, managing, 167–168
minimum requirements, 143
related software, 150, 151
database servers, 160, 161
FTP servers, 151, 152
mail servers, 153–156
news servers, 156–160
proxy servers, 152, 153
summary, 168
Web server software, 144
IIS, 148–150
Netscape Enterprise Server, 145–148
role of, 144
security support, 143
service, 10-layer model, 35, 37
service function, 145
services interface, 10-layer model, 35, 37
Simple Network Management Protocol. *See* SNMP
Site Analyst, link management, 212
site maps, content, 177
depth, usability and, 177, 179
importance of, 177, 178
mapping packages, 180, 181, 182
posting of, 180
SMC (shared memory cluster), 127. *See also* clustering
SMP (symmetric multiprocessing), 117
architecture
comparisons, 118
graph, 122
boxes, 136
cross OS applicability, 121
model, vs. clustering, 123, 124
shared nature of, 119
processor efficiency, 121
value of, 120, 122
SMS (Systems Management Server), configuration management, 66
batch files, launching, 76
centralized workstation management, using SMS, 69
effort, 73–75
planning, 69–72
results, 75
time, 73
goal of, 66
information gathering, 68
installation hierarchy, 67
interoperatability, 76
logon server, 68
overview, 66, 67
planning, importance of, 66
primary SMS server, 67
programs, launching, 76
remote control, workstation, 76
root server, 67
secondary server, 67, 68
site servers, 67
software distribution, 52
SMTP (Simple Mail Transfer Protocol), 154
SNA (System Network Architecture), 79
SNMP (Simple Network Management Protocol), 38
configuration management, 64
agents, 64, 65
model, 65
monitor, 63
using with DMI, 66
vs. DMI, 65
snooping, 266
challenges in, 266
need for, 267
overcoming challenges, 268
promiscuous mode, 266
software. *See also* intranet server application software; Web server software
component issues, performance tuning, 174
distribution, 51–55
purchases, policy guidelines, 407
request form, policy guidelines, 408

SourceSafe, procedures for using, 245
SP (stored procedures), presentation layer integration, 321
  appropriate use for, 321
  origins of, 322
  precompiled procedures solution, 324
  system component agenda, 323
  two-tier client-server impact, 322
specialized viewers, software distribution, 54, 55
SPI, security tool, 310
spoofing, 274
  ARP (Address Resolution Protocol), 275
  DNS, 281
  hardware access, 274
  routers and routing protocols, 278
standards, organizing content, 188
  development and administration, 191
    application creation, 192, 193
    recommendations for, 191, 192
  records and documentation, 193
    recommendations for, 193, 197
    whom-to-call list, 194
  single accountability, importance of, 190
  strictness of, 190
  templates, creating, 193
static content, Web server, 2
store-and-forward service, 155
stubs, RPCs, 326
sufficiency, 261
  factors determining, 262
  operational issues, importance, 263
systems integration. *See* legacy systems integration

T

TCO (total cost of ownership), 60
TCP (Transmission Control Protocol), 79
TCP/IP, 4
technical architecture, intranet building, 394
technology
  change, handling, 232
    choosing initial set, 233
    ground rules, 235
    limiting, 236
    planning for, 234
    reacting to, 236
  intranet management, 5, 6
templates, organizing content, 193
10-layer application model, 35
  application, 36–37
  client browser, 35
  hardware, 37
  network communications services, 35–36
  operating system services, 37
  presentation, 35
  server application interface, 36
  service, 37
  service interface, 37
  Web server, 36
threats, security. *See also* security
  categories of, 301
  evaluating, 294
3270 streams, 37
throughput, performance management, 91
Tiger, security tool, 310
time estimation, intranet building, 396
time-to-live parameter, 283
TP (transaction program), 37
TPM (Transaction Processing Monitors), 134
Transaction Processing Council, 85
transaction program. *See* TP
traps, SNMP, 65
Tripwire, security tool, 310
trust issues, security, 264
  trust diagram, 271
tuning intranet servers. *See* performance tuning
12 steps to building an intranet, 385
  applications and prototype, deciding on, 395
  applications development, 398
  architecture implementation, 397
  decision tree, major steps, 386–387
  deciding what to implement, 386
  finalizing plans, 396
  help, determining need for, 389
  managing the intranet, 400
  organizational issues, 393

policies and procedures, implementing, 399
registration and address, completing, 395
technical architecture, determining, 394
user support, enlisting, 391

U

umbrella managers, 88
best-of-breed, 88–90
integrated, 90, 91
uniprocessor boxes, 136
WINS (Windows Internet Name Service), problems with, 108, 109
UNIX environment, security, 259
usage policy, Internet/intranet, policy guidelines, 413
user support, enlisting, 391
users, roles and responsibilities, 15
UUID (universally unique identifier), 49

V

value, communicating, 392
vector distance, RIP, 280
version control, intranet server software, 164
application, determining, 166
recommendations for handling, 211
strategies for
stand-alone, 165
Web-centric, 165
version management, organizing content, 201
need for, 201
software feature recommendations, 202
Virtual Private Internet. *See* VPI
viruses, as security threat, 404
Visual SourceSafe, content management, 207
VPI (Virtual Private Internet)
increasing use of, 260
vs. Internet, intranet, extranet, 20, 21

W

W3 Consortium, 6, 85
WAN (wide area network), 47
Web. *See* WWW
Web administrator's checklist, 357–370
workplan projects outlines
application development in ASP model, 377–379
content management expansion, 380–383
intranet application expansion, 371–376
Web Integrity, version management, 211
Webmaster, roles and responsibilities, 12. *See also* Web administrator's checklist
Web server
10-layer model, 35, 36
static content, 2
Web server software, 130, 131
application type, 131
collaborative computing, 132
content, 132–134
content distribution, 131
DBMS direct integration, 131
non-traditional integration, 131, 132
OLTP, 134–137
traditional process integration, 131
IIS, 148–150
Netscape Enterprise Server, 145–148
role of, 144
security support, 143
WebTrends, effectiveness analysis tool, 213
wizards, organizing content, 193, 194
DMZs, 198–200
effort, 201
planning, 200
results, 201
time, 200
World Wide Web. *See* WWW
WWW (World Wide Web), 1

What's on the Web Site

If you are interested in more information about intranet management or about Per-Se Technologies, please visit the Web site for this book at www.wiley.com/compbooks/miller. On this site we have included some of the tips and checklists from this text, available for you to download (so you don't have to do so much typing)! We also will have updates on the authors, where they are speaking, and their recent articles and publications.

Some of what is included at www.wiley.com/compbooks/miller:

- The Web Administrator's Checklist from Appendix A
- The Roles and Responsibilities guidelines outlined in Chapter 1
- A Sample Editorial Calendar (Chapter 6)
- A Brief Legacy Integration Presentation (Chapter 9)
- Links to the 12 Step Web site from *Building the Corporate Intranet,* by Guengerich, McDonald, Graham, Miller, 1996 (also by John Wiley & Sons), and some of the tools from that book
- Links to our favorite intranet research and news sites
- Ways to contact us

However, there are some rules and restrictions, of course:

1. The authors provide tips and tools for download to private users only; the material is copyrighted and resale or reuse for profit is strictly prohibited.
2. The tips and tools are provided without warranty or support of any kind, implied or explicit, and are provided for the user's reference only.

For direct access to Per-Se Technologies Web site, please point your browser at www.per-se.com.